THE 80386/387 ARCHITECTURE

Nov. 19/87

To Larry,

Thanks for your Help, Eh!

Kindest Regards,

Barry

THE 80386/387 ARCHITECTURE

Stephen P. Morse
Eric J. Isaacson
Douglas J. Albert

John Wiley & Sons, Inc.
New York • Chichester • Brisbane • Toronto • Singapore

Publisher: Stephen Kippur
Editor: Therese A. Zak
Managing Editor: Andrew B. Hoffer
Electronic Production Services: Publishers Network

This publication is designed to provide accurate and
authoritative information in regard to the subject matter
covered. It is sold with the understanding that the publisher is
not engaged in rendering legal, accounting, or other
professional service. If legal advice or other expert assistance is
required, the services of a competent professional person
should be sought. FROM A DECLARATION OF PRINCIPLES
JOINTLY ADOPTED BY A COMMITTEE OF THE AMERICAN
BAR ASSOCIATION AND A COMMITTEE OF PUBLISHERS.

The excerpt from *Through the Looking Glass* is reprinted
courtesy of Macmillan of London, Ltd., publishers.

The following figures are reprinted with permission of Hayden
Book Company from *The 8086/8088 Primer* by Stephen P.
Morse, copyright© 1982: Figures 3.5, 3.6, 3.7, and 3.10.

Library of Congress Cataloging-in-Publication Data

Morse, Stephen P.
  The 80386/387 architecture.

  Includes bibliographies.
  1. Intel 80386 (Microprocessor) 2. Intel 80387
(Microprocessor)   I. Albert, Douglas J.   II. Isaacson, Eric,
III. Title.
QA76.8.I2684M67   1987   004.165   87-13366
ISBN 0-471-85352-6

Printed in the United States of America

87 88 10 9 8 7 6 5 4 3 2 1

To Erica, Megan, Melanie, and Anita

CONTENTS

Acknowledgements

We would like to thank Richard Schell and John Oxaal for providing us with up-to-date reference information for the Intel and Weitek processors. We would also like to thank Joseph C. Krauskopf from Intel for reviewing the entire manuscript, and Chris Tice for reading the draft of the Weitek chapter, and correcting errors that we made.

CHAPTER
1

INTRODUCTION

The 80386 is the latest member in an ever-evolving family of microprocessors. To best appreciate the current generation of microprocessors, we must look back and see where it all started and how we got to where we are. This chapter presents such a historical perspective, along with a review of some fundamentals of computers, the representation of numbers within computers, and the use of stacks in computers.

The remaining chapters in this book are organized in the following manner. The basic architecture of the 386 is presented in Chapters 2 and 3. The 386's 32-bit architecture is a significant change from the 8086 and the 286; you'll want to read much of Chapters 2 and 3 even if you're familiar with those predecessors. Chapter 4 presents the 387 architecture. This, for the most part, is similar to both the 8087 and 287 architectures and can be skipped if you're familiar with the floating-point instruction set. Chapter 5 deals with 386 features that are retained for compatibility with the 8086 and 286. Chapter 6 describes the support that the 386 gives to operating systems; the 386 is similar to the 286 in these respects. You may skip Chapter 6 if you are familiar with the 286, or if you aren't interested in operating-system software. Finally, Chapter 7 describes an interface designed by Weitek Corporation to provide floating-point processing even faster than the 387.

The History of Microcomputers

The evolution that led to the modern-day microcomputer can be broken down into two periods: a period of shrinkage followed by a period of enhancement. During the shrinkage period (circa 1940 to 1970) computers became smaller as the technology for fabricating their components evolved. This period culminated with a computer (albeit primitive even by 1970 standards) no larger than a postage stamp. The enhancement period (circa 1970 to the present) saw the postage-stamp computers become as powerful as their larger counterparts.

The Period of Shrinkage   In the 1960s all electronic devices from radios and televisions to computers were built of bulky vacuum tubes. Computers of that vintage are sometimes referred to as first-generation computers, for example, IBM's 650 and 704. These computers were housed in large rooms containing several racks of electronic equipment. By the end of the decade, transistors and other solid-state devices began to replace vacuum tubes. Computers using this technology are called second-generation computers (the IBM 7090 and the Burroughs B5500, for example).

In the 1960s many discrete electronic components (transistors, resistors, etc.) were combined to form more complex electronic components called *integrated circuits*. An integrated circuit is fabricated on a wafer of silicon smaller than a postage stamp. It is mounted on a centipedelike structure that can be plugged into a system. This pluggable integrated circuit became known as a *chip*. Computers built from integrated circuits are the third generation computers (the IBM 360, the GE 635, and the Burroughs B6700). But integrated-circuit technology continued to advance, and by the early 1970s many of the components of a computer could be put together onto a single chip (Intel's 4004 and 8008). This led to the coining of the term *computer-on-a-chip*.

Computers-on-a-chip are called microcomputers or microprocessors. Although the terms are sometimes used interchangeably, there is a difference. A *microprocessor* is a single chip. It usually contains the control logic and arithmetic units of a computer but not the computer's memory or input/output devices. A *microcomputer* is an entire computer system consisting of a microprocessor chip, memory chips, and input/output devices. Sometimes the entire computer system is contained on one chip (Intel's 8048). This is called a *single-chip microcomputer*.

The Period of Enhancement   The microprocessor era started with the introduction of Intel's 4004 and 8008 processors in 1971. This was the first generation of microprocessors. Both of these chips were designed for specialized applications—the 4004 in a calculator and the 8008 in a computer terminal. These microprocessors were intended as replacements for complex, custom-designed circuits. Now there was an alternative to designing a complex electronic circuit; one could design instead a simple circuit involving a microprocessor chip and write a program for it that simulated the functions of the intended complex circuit. Some typical applications in this period were electronic cash registers, intelligent typewriters, traffic light controllers, and microwave ovens. These are called *embedded* applications because the microprocessor is embedded into something other than a computer.

In 1974, when the 8008 matured into the 8080 (the second-generation microprocessor), a revolution occurred in the microprocessor field. Instead of being used as electronic logic replacements, 8080s were now appearing in applications which would have been infeasible if designed without microprocessors. Applications such as word processing machines, aircraft inertial navigation systems, and cruise missiles required either the ability to be easily modified (reprogrammed) or to fit into a small space, or both. The microprocessor provided these abilities, and the 8080 became the "standard" microprocessor to use.

It was now only a small step to go from a special-purpose, reprogrammable circuit such as a word processing machine to a general-purpose computing system based on a microprocessor. One of the first such machines was the Intel Microprocessor Development System (MDS) introduced in 1974. Even though this was probably the first personal computer, Intel never wanted to call it that for several reasons. For one, they didn't want to attract the attention of the industry giants (IBM and DEC) who, coincidentally, were Intel customers; and for another, Intel knew the purchasing policies of most large corporations: an engineer could easily order a piece of laboratory equipment (such as a development system) but a request for a computer would have to go through the data processing department.

The microprocessor was now able to perform the computational tasks of the older and bulkier equipment and was inexpensive enough to find its way into the hands of the hobbyist. Many companies other than Intel began building 8080 chips, and some companies (notably Zilog) built enhanced versions of the 8080 (the Z80). Intel itself introduced an enhanced version in 1976 called the 8085. But the basic character of the 8080 wasn't to be significantly changed until 1978 when Intel came out with the 8086, the first member of the 86 family of microprocessors.

The 86 Family of Microprocessors   Up to this point, the development of the microprocessor had followed the historical development of the mainframe computers that came before. But now Intel wanted to make a giant step forward that would put microprocessors in the lead. To this end they embarked on an advanced processor development. This processor, initially known as the 8816, incorporated the most advanced operating system and programming language concepts then known. Unfortunately, the 8816 took much longer to develop than was initially forecast. Intel was under continuing pressure to come out quickly with a processor that was better than the Zilog Z80. This provided the impetus for the development of an 8080 successor, namely the 8086. The 8086 was intended to tide Intel over until the introduction of the 8816, which by then was being called the 8800.

In 1978 Intel produced the 8086. This was the first microprocessor capable of working with sixteen bits of data at a time (the 8080 worked with eight bits). Two other companies quickly announced plans for 16-bit processors, namely Zilog with its Z8000 and Motorola with its 68000 (big numbers were in fashion at that time). This was the start of the third generation of microprocessors.

The 8088, an 8-bit version of the 8086, appeared in 1979. Two years later IBM announced its entry into the personal computer field and revealed that the 8088 would be the processor in its first personal computer—the IBM PC. With that endorsement behind them, the 8086 and 8088 were on their way to becoming the most popular microprocessors ever.

With the advent of the IBM PC, the nature of the microprocessor industry began to change. Instead of being used in a wide variety of embedded applications (traffic lights, microwave ovens, etc.), the bulk of the 16-bit microprocessors produced were now used in personal computers.

In 1982 Intel brought out enhanced versions of the 8086 and 8088, namely the 186 and 188. These chips embodied the 8086/8088 along with some of the support chips needed in a microprocessor system. This did not add any new capabilities but rather reduced the number of chips (and hence the cost) needed for a complete system.

That same year, 1982, Intel came out with the 286. This represented Intel's first big leap beyond the 8086. Plans for the 286 had begun four years earlier, long before the widespread use of personal computers. The primary reason for developing the 286 was the 8086's lack of memory management, a feature which Intel's competitors (mainly Motorola) provided for their 16-bit line. Another reason for Intel's commencing on the 286 was the continued slippage of the 8800 back in the late 70s. In fact, the 8800 slipped all the way to 1982 when it finally arrived (again renamed) as the iAPX 432!

The personal computer industry was flourishing by this time. IBM had set the standard with its PC and PC/XT machines, and others were producing close copies of the IBM machines. In 1983 Apple came out with a competitor to the IBM PC called the MacIntosh, which uses a microprocessor from Motorola's 68000 family. The second generation IBM personal computer was the IBM PC/AT (AT standing for advanced technology) which came out in 1984 and incorporates the 286 processor. The AT too became a standard which was widely copied.

Parallel to the development of the 86 family at Intel, Motorola was developing its 68000 family of microprocessors. The first two members of this family, namely the 68000 and the 68010 had 32-bit registers but could accommodate only 24-bit addresses. Furthermore, contrary to Intel's fears, early members of the 68000 family had great difficulty in supporting memory management. The 68020, introduced in 1984, corrected both these deficiencies.

Finally, in 1985, Intel formally unveiled the 386, the most significant advance yet within the 86 family. Not only was this Intel's offering for the next generation of IBM-compatible personal computers, it was also Intel's answer to Motorola's 68020 32-bit microprocessor. The 386 introduces a 32-bit general register set, an enormously expanded memory space, a more complete set of memory indexing modes, memory paging, and an enhanced facility for 8086 emulation. In 1987 IBM introduced its Personal System/2 line of computers, choosing the 386 for its high-end models and the earlier 86 family microprocessors for its low-end models. Some speculate that the 386 is the ultimate microcomputer architecture, since there is no pressing reason to have register sizes and memory addresses greater than 32 bits. We feel that it is dangerous to call anything ultimate in the world of computers: you may be assured that even as this book is being written, Intel is working on successors to the 386.

During the evolution in the microprocessor area, a parallel evolution was occurring in the area of microcoprocessors. A *coprocessor* is a subordinate processor that performs a specialized function for a general-purpose processor. The first popular coprocessor was the 8087, which performed floating-point computations for the 8086 and 8088. Concurrent with the development of the 8087, the Institute of Electrical and Electronic Engineers (IEEE) was developing a standard for microprocessor floating-point arithmetic. The 8087 was the first math processor to implement the standard being proposed at that time.

Besides being a coprocessor for the 8086, the 8087 served as a coprocessor for the 186 and 188 when those processors came along. But due to a different coprocessor interface incorporated in the 286, a modified version of the 8087 was needed to function with that processor: the 287. Finally, the 32-bit bus supported by the 386 dictated yet another coprocessor interface. By this time the proposed IEEE standard had been modified and formally adopted as a standard. Since a new coprocessor would be needed for the 386 anyway, the coprocessor was designed to implement the newly adopted standard. This new coprocessor, the 387, is therefore slightly incompatible with the 287 and 8087.

A word about nomenclature is in order here. Once upon a time the nomenclature was clear: everybody called the 8080 "the 8080," for example. When the 8086 was introduced, everybody called it "the 8086." Then Intel, in an attempt to make their products sound more impressive, replaced the prefix "80" with "iAPX" (please don't ask what APX means). They retroactively declared the 8086 to be the iAPX86, and referred to the successors as the iAPX186, iAPX188, and iAPX286. But outside of Intel the iAPX prefix never caught on. People were too entrenched in their habits of referring to the part numbers: 80186, 80188, 80286, 80287. Intel has finally surrendered; no mention of the iAPX386 appears in Intel literature, and 80386 and 80387 are the official names. We refer to the 8086 and 8087 as such, using the full part number, but for simplicity, we follow the common practice of omitting the "80" prefix on the names of successors: 186, 188, 286, 287, 386, 387. We refer to the entire family of processors as the "86 family."

Fundamentals of Computers

It is assumed that you are already familiar with the basic concepts of computers so we will just review them quickly here. A computer obtains data from an *input device*, processes the data, and delivers the final results to an *output device*. The particular processing to be done is specified by a list of instructions called a *program*. The program is stored in the computer's *memory*.

The operations of the computer are controlled by the *central processing unit*, or *processor* for short. The processor fetches instructions from the memory, decodes the instructions to determine what operations are to be performed, and executes the instructions by performing the operations. In order to perform the operations, the processor must sometimes send control signals to other devices within the computer. The operations that are performed during instruction execution consist of moving data and performing computations on data. The computer memory is used to supply inputs for the computations and to hold the results of the computations.

To see how all this ties together, let's analyze the execution of an *add* instruction. The processor sends a signal to the memory requesting the next instruction. The memory responds by sending an instruction to the processor. The processor then decodes the instruction and discovers that it's an *add* instruction. It then (1) sends out signals to the memory telling it to move two values to the processor, (2) adds the two values it received, and (3) sends out signals to the memory telling it to receive the result of the addition.

A *memory* is a collection of sequential *locations*, each having a unique *address*. Each location contains a sequence of *bits* (short for *binary digits*). These bits are the *contents* of the location. Each bit is either a 0 or a 1.

Registers, like memory, are also used to hold intermediate results. The registers are inside the processor, and therefore it's easier and faster to access values in registers than in memory. *Flags* inside the processor are used to keep track of what's going on. There are two kinds of flags—those that record information about the effects of previously executed instructions (status flags) and those that control the operations of the computer (control flags). An example of a status flag is a flag that indicates if a result is too big for the computer to handle. An example of a control flag is a flag that tells the computer to execute instructions at a slower rate, such as one per hour. It's also possible to have a flag that is both a status flag and a control flag. An example is the 386's NT flag (described later).

Representation of Numbers

We are accustomed to representing integers as a sequence of decimal digits, such as 365. This is interpreted as 3 hundreds, 6 tens, and 5 ones. It is sometimes called a base-ten representation. Integers in computers are usually represented as a sequence of binary digits (bits) such as 11010. This is the base-two representation of twenty-six: 1 sixteen, 1 eight, 0 fours, 1 two, and 0 ones. Binary numbers can be added, subtracted, multiplied, and divided directly (no need to convert them to decimal numbers first) as long as we remember that 1 plus 1 is 10 (1 two and 0 ones) and not 2. For example:

1001	binary representation of nine
+ 0101	binary representation of five
1110	binary representation of fourteen

We tend to get confused with long sequences of binary digits, although computers aren't perturbed the least bit. For example, 10110101 is the binary representation for one hundred eighty-one. To make things simpler, we have devised a scheme of compressing long sequences of binary digits by grouping the bits four at a time. Each group of four bits (sometimes called a *nibble*) is represented by a single character as shown in Table 1.1. Thus 10110101 is abbreviated to B5. This is called a *hexadecimal* number and is exactly the number system we would have used if we had been born with sixteen fingers.

The binary notation is perfect for describing positive numbers and zero. But when we want to allow for negative numbers, we need an additional mechanism to indicate the sign of the number. The simplest way to do this is to use the most significant (leftmost) bit of the number to indicate the sign. For example:

0000	0100	would be +4
1000	0100	would be −4
0111	1111	would be +127
1111	1111	would be −127

Table 1.1 Hexadecimal Representation

Group of Four Bits	Hexadecimal Digit	Value
0000	0	zero
0001	1	one
0010	2	two
0011	3	three
0100	4	four
0101	5	five
0110	6	six
0111	7	seven
1000	8	eight
1001	9	nine
1010	A	ten
1011	B	eleven
1100	C	twelve
1101	D	thirteen
1110	E	fourteen
1111	F	fifteen

Such a representation is called *sign-magnitude* representation and has one serious drawback: it requires a new set of arithmetic rules. This becomes obvious when we try to use binary arithmetic to subtract $+1$ from 0 and expect to get -1.

$$
\begin{array}{ll}
\ 0000\ \ 0000 & \text{0 in sign-magnitude} \\
-\ 0000\ \ 0001 & \text{+1 in sign-magnitude} \\
\hline
\ 1111\ \ 1111 & \text{-127 in sign-magnitude}
\end{array}
$$

If we want to use the same binary arithmetic on signed numbers that we used on unsigned numbers, we need a signed-number representation in which 1111 1111 represents -1, not -127. Furthermore, subtracting $+1$ from -1 should give -2. Let's perform this subtraction to see what -2 should look like.

$$
\begin{array}{ll}
\ 1111\ \ 1111 & \text{here's -1} \\
-\ 0000\ \ 0001 & \text{subtract $+1$} \\
\hline
\ 1111\ \ 1110 & \text{and call this -2}
\end{array}
$$

This is called a *two's complement* representation; it has the property that binary additions and subtractions will give the correct two's complement result. For example:

$$
\begin{array}{ll}
\ 0000\ \ 0011 & \text{+3 in two's complement} \\
+\ 1111\ \ 1110 & \text{-2 in two's complement} \\
\hline
\ 0000\ \ 0001 & \text{+1 in two's complement}
\end{array}
$$

It also has the property that the most significant bit of every nonnegative (positive or zero) number is 0 and of every negative number is 1. Thus, just as in sign-magnitude representation, this bit serves as a sign bit.

The sign of a two's complement number can be changed by changing the value of each bit and adding $+1$. For example, we can obtain the two's complement representation of -5 from the two's complement representation of $+5$ as follows:

```
    0000   0101     +5 in two's complement
    1111   1010     +5 with each bit changed
+   0000   0001     +1 in two's complement
    ─────────────
    1111   1011     −5 in two's complement
```

We must be careful when lengthening two's complement numbers. If an 8-bit two's complement number is to be extended to 16 bits (so that it can be added to a 16-bit two's complement number, for example), some thought must be given as to what goes into the additional eight bits.

Suppose we want to add 0000 0001 ($+1$ in two's complement) to 0000 0000 0000 0011 ($+3$ in two's complement). In this case, there's no doubt that we would simply append eight 0's on the left side of the $+1$ and then add:

```
    0000   0000   0000   0011     +3 in two's complement
+   0000   0000   0000   0001     +1 in two's complement
    ──────────────────────────
    0000   0000   0000   0100     +4 in two's complement
```

However, if we want to add 1111 1111 (-1 in two's complement) to 0000 0000 0000 0011 ($+3$ in two's complement), we must append eight 1's to the left side of -1 (appending 0's would make it a positive number). The addition is then:

```
    0000   0000   0000   0011     +3 in two's complement
+   1111   1111   1111   1111     −1 in two's complement
    ──────────────────────────
    0000   0000   0000   0010     +2 in two's complement
```

Thus the extension of an 8-bit number to a 16-bit number looks like this:

Value	8-bit Representation		16-bit Representation			
+1	0000	0001	0000	0000	0000	0001
−1	1111	1111	1111	1111	1111	1111

The rule for extending a two's complement number is to append additional bits on the left side of the number with each appended bit having the same value as the original sign bit. This process is called *sign extending*.

Stacks

A stack is a concept that is frequently found in microprocessors as well as in larger machines. Other names for stacks are "pushdown lists" or "last-in-first-out queues." These names are intended to convey the image of a device for stacking cafeteria trays. When a new tray is placed on top of the stack of trays, it pushes all trays beneath it down one level. When the top tray is removed from the stack, all trays pop up one level. The last tray placed on the stack will be the first tray to be removed.

To understand what all this has to do with computers, we have to look at subroutines. *Subroutines* (sometimes called *procedures*) are parts of a program that are called upon (*called*) to perform specific tasks. This provides a means of subdividing the total problem to be solved into smaller and simpler parts. A subroutine itself might call upon other subroutines to further subdivide the work. After a subroutine finishes its task, it returns control back to the routine that called upon it. The result is a sequence of subroutines, each calling other subroutines, until the last subroutine called upon decides to return. In other words, the last subroutine called will be the first subroutine to return.

When a subroutine is called, there is a certain amount of information that must be saved. This might include the current contents of some of the registers and the current settings of the flags. It certainly includes the address in the calling routine to which the subroutine will eventually return control. When the subroutine completes its task, it will retrieve this saved information so that it can restore the contents of the affected registers, set the flags to their original settings, and use the "return address" to return control to the appropriate instruction. But since the last subroutine called is the first subroutine to return, the last piece of information saved must be the first to be retrieved. Thus the information must be stacked like cafeteria trays.

So far we have described how a stack behaves and why a stack would be a useful thing in a computer. Now let's see how a computer stack can be implemented. Since the stack has to hold information, it must be some kind of memory. Actually, any portion of the available memory (so long as it can be written to as well as read) can be used as a stack. All that is needed is a pointer to the last piece of information that was placed in the stack portion of memory. This pointer is often called the *stack pointer*, and the information it points to is usually called the *top of the stack*. When a new piece of information is placed on the stack (a process referred to as *pushing*), the stack pointer is updated so that it points to the next memory location, and the information is placed in that location. When a piece of memory is retrieved from the stack (a process known as *popping*), the information is retrieved from the memory location that the stack pointer is pointing at, and the stack pointer is again updated—but this time in the opposite direction.

On to the 386

Now that we've been introduced to computers and a couple of associated general concepts, we are ready to learn about a particular processor, namely the 386. The next chapter presents the machine organization of this device.

References

An informative discussion of the evolution of the Intel family of microprocessors is found in reference 1.

1.   S.P. Morse, B.W. Ravenel, S. Mazor, W.B. Pohlman, "Intel Microprocessors—8008 to 8086," *Computer*, October 1980; also *Computer Structures: Principles and Examples*. McGraw-Hill, New York, 1982.

CHAPTER
2

MACHINE
ORGANIZATION

Overview

One way to describe a computer is to describe the functional components that make up that computer. A description of these components and the interaction between them is sometimes referred to as the *architecture* of the computer. The description includes such things as how many registers are in the computer, what functions the registers serve, how much memory can be connected, how the memory is addressed, and what sort of input/output facilities are available.

The 386 is a single integrated-circuit chip containing most of the components that make up a computer. The circuitry that controls all the functions of the computer is contained on that chip. Also contained on the chip are all of the registers and flags. The memory and input/output devices are not contained on the chip but can be easily connected to the chip to form a computer. The collection of all those things on the chip is sometimes referred to as the *processor*.

A functioning 386 chip will be mounted on a circuit board, which is usually housed inside a box. (A nonfunctioning 386 chip will be encased in plexiglass and presented to an Intel employee as a memento.) The box is the *computer*. It will also contain a power supply, disk drives, and connectors for cables leading to display screens, keyboards, printers, and other computers. When power is applied to the computer, the 386 starts executing a program that manages all the major functions of the computer. This program, the *operating system*, usually remains in some part of the computer's memory at all times, ready to assist any other programs in the management of the computer.

Before proceeding, let's mentally draw a line through the 386 processor, dividing it roughly in half. On the near half of the line are the control functions, registers, and flags visible to all programs running on the 386. On the far half of the line are the control functions, registers, and flags visible only to the operating system. If the operating system is well designed, you'll never have to think about the far half of the 386 processor, unless you are the unfortunate soul who must revise the operating system. We'll discuss the far half of the processor in Chapters 5 and 6. Until then, we'll pretend that the near half of the 386 processor is the whole processor.

We can summarize the architecture of the 386 as follows: The 386 has a set of eight general-purpose registers, each 32 bits long. These registers can be used to hold intermediate results, or they can be used as pointer and index registers to locate information within a specified portion of memory. Embedded within parts of the 32-bit general registers are eight 16-bit registers and eight 8-bit registers. There is also a 32-bit instruction pointer, and ten flags on the 386. The flags are used to record the state of the processor and to control its operation. The 386 can access approximately 34 billion bits of memory and 65,000 input or output ports. The first half of this chapter elaborates on these features.

Typical computer instructions involve locating designated *operands* (data to be processed), performing an operation on the values of these operands, and storing the result back into a designated *result* location. The locations of the operands and of the result can be either in memory or in a register as designated by the instruction. The facilities available for designating these locations are referred to as the *operand-addressing modes* of the computer. The operand-addressing modes of the 386 are described in the second half of this chapter. The actual instructions that operate on the designated operands are described in the following chapters.

Memory Structure

The memory in a 386 system is a sequence of up to 2^{32} (approximately 4.3 billion) 8-bit quantities called *bytes*. Each byte is assigned a unique address (unsigned number) ranging from 0 to $2^{32} - 1$ (00000000 to FFFFFFFF in hexadecimal). This is illustrated in Figure 2.1.

Any two consecutive bytes in memory are defined as a *word*. Each byte in a word has a byte address, and the smaller of these two addresses is used as the address of the word. Examples of words are shown in Figure 2.2.

A word contains 16 bits. The byte with the higher memory address contains the eight most significant bits of the word, and the byte with the lower memory address contains the eight least significant bits. On first reading, this seems very natural. Of course the most significant byte should have the higher memory address. But when you consider that memory is a sequence of bytes starting at the lowest address and going toward the highest address, it becomes apparent that the 386 stores its words backwards. (Perhaps they should be called *backwords*.)

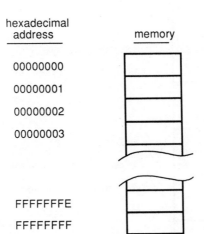

Figure 2.1 Memory addresses.

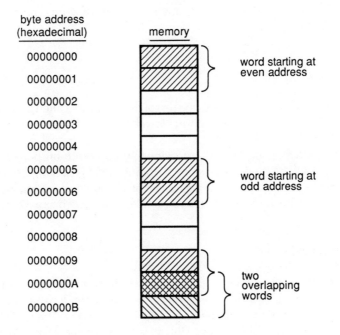

Figure 2.2 Examples of words in memory.

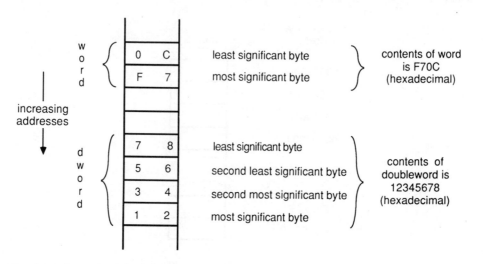

Figure 2.3 Example of "backwords" storage in memory.

Finally, any four consecutive bytes in memory are defined as a *doubleword*. A doubleword contains 32 bits. Again, the bytes are "backwords": the byte with the highest address contains the most significant bits, and the byte with the lowest address contains the least significant bits. The backwords storage of words and doublewords is illustrated in Figure 2.3.

Input/Output Structure

The things connecting a 386 system to the rest of the world are called *ports*. It is through these ports that the 386 can receive information about external events and can send out signals that control other events.

The 386 can access up to 2^{16} (approximately 65,000) 8-bit ports analogous to memory bytes. Each 8-bit port is assigned a unique address ranging from 0 to $2^{16}-1$. Any two consecutive 8-bit ports can be treated as a 16-bit port analogous to memory words. Any four consecutive 8-bit ports can similarly be treated as a 32-bit port.

Register Structure

The 386 processor contains nine 32-bit registers and ten one-bit flags. Eight of the nine registers are general-purpose registers. They can be used interchangeably for most of the 386's arithmetic, logical, and memory indexing functions. The ninth register, the instruction pointer, is not directly accessible to the programmer. The 386 registers and flags are shown in Figure 2.4.

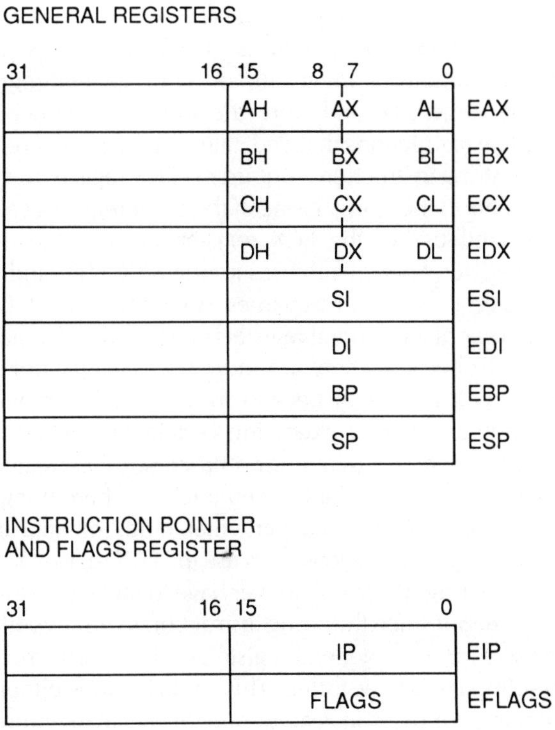

GENERAL REGISTERS

31	16	15	8	7	0	
		AH	AX		AL	EAX
		BH	BX		BL	EBX
		CH	CX		CL	ECX
		DH	DX		DL	EDX
			SI			ESI
			DI			EDI
			BP			EBP
			SP			ESP

INSTRUCTION POINTER
AND FLAGS REGISTER

31	16	15	0	
		IP		EIP
		FLAGS		EFLAGS

Figure 2.4 80386 basic registers and flags.

Registers and Arithmetic   In a processor without general registers, each instruction would fetch its operands from memory and return its result to memory. But memory accesses take time. This time can be reduced by temporarily keeping frequently used operands and results in a quickly accessible place. The set of general registers in the 386 processor is such a place.

The general registers of the 386 are the 32-bit registers EAX, EBX, ECX, EDX, ESI, EDI, ESP, and EBP. The *E* at the beginning of each register name stands for *Extended* because each of these registers is the extension of a 16-bit register which is its lower half (least significant 16 bits). The 16-bit registers are called AX, BX, CX, DX, SI, DI, SP, and BP, respectively. Note that these 16-bit registers are the registers in the 386's predecessors, the 86 and 286. The first four 16-bit registers are further divided into 8-bit registers. This time, both the upper and lower halves are used. The least significant (low) halves are named AL, BL, CL, and DL; the most significant (high) halves are named AH, BH, CH, and DH. The ability of the 386 to address 8-bit and 16-bit subsets of its 32-bit general registers permits the 386 to handle byte, word, and doubleword quantities with equal ease.

For the most part, the contents of the general registers can participate interchangeably in the arithmetic and logical operations of the 386. For example, the ADD instruction can add the contents of any 8-, 16-, or 32-bit general register to any other general register of the same size and store the result into either of the registers. However, there are a few instructions that dedicate certain general registers to specific uses. For example, the string instructions require the ECX register to contain the count of the number of elements in the string. None of the other registers can be used for this purpose. This specialized use of the ECX register suggests the descriptive name COUNT for the ECX register. Specialized uses for the EAX, EBX, and EDX registers (to be described later) suggest the descriptive names ACCUMULATOR, BASE, and DATA.

These specialized uses of the general registers have the disadvantage of making the processor harder to learn because there are more special rules to memorize. And it appears that programs will be longer because of the need to move data from one general register to another prior to executing certain instructions. However, let's consider how we would write a program for a processor that treated all the general registers as equals all the time. In order to keep track of where things are, we would probably organize the program so that particular kinds of data always reside in particular registers. We might choose to always use the ECX register to keep track of the number of elements in a string. We would never have to move the string size into ECX; it would always be there. But since the string instruction in our hypothetical processor can obtain the string size from any general register, each string instruction would have to specify where its string size is to be found. This could be done either by making each string instruction longer (two bytes instead of one) or by having more one-byte string instructions. The first solution has a direct impact on making programs longer. The second also makes programs longer because there are only a small number of one-byte instructions (256 to be exact), and having more one-byte string instructions means that some other one-byte instruction must be increased to two bytes. So, because it has dedicated registers for certain instructions, the 386 architecture has actually resulted in a decrease in program size.

Registers and Memory Addressing   An instruction that accesses a location in memory could specify the address of that location directly. This address takes up space in the instruction, thereby increasing the size of the code. If addresses of frequently used locations could be stored in registers, instructions that access these locations would no longer need to contain the address but could instead specify the register that contained the address.

This use of registers is not unlike abbreviated telephone dialing. You can call anyone in your town by dialing his or her seven-digit phone number. Or, if your telephone company provides this service, you can enter some frequently called phone numbers into a set of "registers." Then you can call these selected people by dialing only the one or two digits that specify the register.

The use of registers to address memory serves another (and perhaps more important) function in addition to reducing the size of instructions: it permits instructions to access locations whose addresses are the result of previous computations performed while the program is running. It is often necessary to perform such computations in order to establish the locations of variables, especially in high-level language programs. The 386 facilitates this by providing the same general register set for memory indexing, as well as for arithmetic. It is not necessary to move a calculated address from an arithmetic register to an indexing register, because all general registers have a well-rounded set of both arithmetic and indexing capabilities.

The last four general registers, ESI, EDI, EBP, and ESP, are intended to be used primarily for memory addressing. There are some differences among the registers that result in dividing this set of registers into the pointer registers, ESP and EBP, and the index registers, ESI and EDI. The pointer registers are intended to provide convenient access to data on the stack, as opposed to the general data area. This use of the stack as an auxiliary data area has certain advantages (which will be discussed at the end of this chapter) for the implementation of high-level languages.

There are instructions that make further distinctions between the two pointer registers, ESP and EBP. The PUSH and POP instructions obtain the address of the top-of-stack location from the ESP register, thereby suggesting the descriptive name STACK POINTER for this register. The ENTER and LEAVE instructions set up EBP as the "base" of a data area on the stack, thereby suggesting the descriptive name BASE POINTER.

Finally, the string instructions make a distinction between the two index registers, ESI and EDI. Those string instructions requiring a source operand obtain the address of the source operand from ESI; similarly, EDI contains the address of the destination operand. This suggests the descriptive names SOURCE INDEX and DESTINATION INDEX. For those string instructions, the roles of ESI and EDI may not be interchanged. As an example, the string-move instruction will move the string pointed to by ESI to the location pointed to by EDI; the ESI and EDI registers are not explicitly mentioned by the string-move instruction.

Flags   The 386 contains ten flags that are used to record processor status information (*status flags*) or to control processor operations (*control flags*). The status flags are generally set after the execution of arithmetic or logical instructions to reflect certain properties of the results of such operations. These flags are the carry flag (CF), indicating whether the instruction generated a carry out of the most significant bit; the auxiliary carry flag (AF), indicating whether the instruction generated a carry out of the four least significant bits; the overflow flag (OF), indicating whether the instruction generated a signed result that is out of range; the zero flag (ZF), indicating whether the instruction generated a zero result; the sign flag (SF), indicating whether the instruction generated a negative result; and the parity flag (PF), indicating whether the instruction generated a result having an even number of 1-bits.

The control flags are the direction flag (DF), which controls the direction of the string manipulation instructions; the interrupt-enable flag (IF), which enables or disables external interrupts; the trap flag (TF), which puts the processor into a single-step mode for program debugging; and the resume flag (RF) which suppresses the processor's built-in debugger breakpoints for the next single instruction.

More details will be given on each of these flags throughout Chapter 3, and the final section of Chapter 3 summarizes the behavior of the flags.

Instruction Operands and Operand-Addressing Modes

Instructions in the 386 usually perform operations on one or two operands. For example, the ADD instruction adds the value contained in one operand to the value contained in a second operand and stores the result back into one of these operands. The INCrement instruction adds 1 to the value contained in the operand and stores this result back into the operand. The 386 allows a wide variety of operand-types to be used by its instructions. The time has come to spell out how an instruction specifies its operands and what types of operands it can specify. This is more formally referred to as the processor's *operand-addressing modes*.

Before we plunge into the following discussion, let's realize that there are two points of view towards the instruction set of any given processor. The first point of view is that of the person writing assembly-language programs for the processor, the *programmer*. The second point of view is that of the processor itself, the *machine*. The programmer thinks of the instruction set as a group of distinct assembler-source lines. The machine "thinks" of the instruction set as a group of distinct bit-encodings (*opcodes*). For many processors, the two points of view are almost the same: every opcode has a different assembly-language mnemonic, and every operand-addressing mode has a straightforward encoding into an operand bit field. For the 386, the points of view are very different. First, the 386 assembly language can use the same instruction mnemonic for different opcodes. For example, the MOV mnemonic has at least seventeen opcodes. Second, the 386's bit-encodings for operands are much more convoluted than the assembler's rules for specifying those operands.

In this and the following chapters, we'll concentrate on the programmer's point of view, because it makes the 386 look simpler. We'll discuss opcodes only to consider how many program bytes are occupied by each instruction. The bit encodings themselves will be considered in Appendices A and B.

Table 2.1 shows the operand-addressing modes of the 386. Before discussing these modes in detail, we must first examine the effects of operand size.

Table 2.1 Operand-Addressing Modes

IMMEDIATE
REGISTER
DIRECT MEMORY ADDRESSING
INDIRECT MEMORY ADDRESSING
    base
    (scaled) index
    base + (scaled) index
    base + displacement
    (scaled) index + displacement
    base + (scaled) index + displacement

Operand Sizes   Operands come in three sizes: byte, word, and doubleword. It's easy to see how the programmer specifies the operand size if the operand is a register: the 8-, 16-, or 32-bit general register name is used. For memory operands, the distinction is more subtle. The assembler must often act like a detective, and search for clues from which the operand size can be deduced. The possible clues are:

1.   There is another operand in the instruction, usually a register. The size of this operand must be the same as the size of the other operand.

2.   The operand has a name, which was previously defined using one of the following assembly-language directives: DB, DW, or DD. A DB directive defines bytes, DW words, and DD doublewords. So the size of the operand is deduced from the particular assembly-language directive used when the operand's name was defined.

3.   The programmer gives the size explicitly. This is necessary when there are no other clues; the memory reference is *anonymous*. Intel tried to discourage anonymous memory references by making the explicit size-specifier painfully verbose: the operand is preceded by BYTE PTR, WORD PTR, and DWORD PTR. For example:

        INC BYTE PTR [EBX]   ; [EBX] means "operand whose address is in EBX"
        INC WORD PTR [EBX]
        INC DWORD PTR [EBX]

You can get around this verbosity by including the following declarations at the top of your program:

        B EQU BYTE PTR 0
        W EQU WORD PTR 0
        D EQU DWORD PTR 0

Then you can use the appropriate one-letter abbreviation in place of the verbose form as follows:

        INC B[EBX]
        INC W[EBX]
        INC D[EBX]

Let's switch now from the assembler's point of view to the machine's point of view. To the machine, the size specification is always explicit. In fact, it's separate from the rest of the operand specification. A byte operand is distinguished from a word/doubleword operand by bits within the opcode. You can see in Appendix A that instructions with byte operands have different opcodes than instructions with word/doubleword operands.

Now let's see how the machine distinguishes words from doublewords. This is accomplished by using a special *operand size prefix* preceding the instruction opcode. The meaning of the prefix depends on the state of the 386:

1. If the 386 is emulating one of its predecessors, the 8086 or the 286, then the default size for non-byte operands is the 16-bit word. The absence of the operand size prefix means that a non-byte operand is a word; the presence of a prefix means the operand is a doubleword.

2. If the 386 is not emulating a predecessor, then the default size for non-byte operands is the 32-bit doubleword. The absence of the operand size prefix means the non-byte operand is a doubleword; the presence of a prefix means the operand is a word.

We'll discuss when and how the 386 enters its emulation modes in Chapter 5. For now, we need to know only that we can tell the assembler in which mode the program will be running and which size operand we want; the assembler will automatically generate the operand size prefixes for us, as necessary. We mention the prefix byte here in case we are concerned about the size of our programs. All instructions with operands of the non-default size take up an extra byte of program space.

Now that we've examined the concept of operand size, we proceed to the various operand-addressing modes.

Register Operands   If an operand is a register, it is specified simply by giving its name. For example, the instruction MOV EAX,EDX copies the contents of the EDX register into the EAX register.

Memory Operands   If an operand is in memory, then things are more complicated. The location of the memory operand is computed by adding together up to three values: a *base*, an *index*, and a *displacement*. First let's look at each of the three possible component values in turn and then we'll discuss the reasons for adding them together.

Base   The base, if present, is the value in one of the eight 32-bit general registers at the time that the instruction is executed. The programmer specifies a base by giving the name of the register, enclosed in square brackets. Any 32-bit general register can be used. For example, suppose that we want to load the doubleword from the memory location pointed to by the EDX register into the EAX register. The instruction that does this is MOV EAX,[EDX].

Note the effect that the square brackets have on the instruction. The instruction without the brackets, MOV EAX,EDX, simply moves data from one register to another. The brackets tell the assembler that the register does not contain the data to be moved; the register instead contains a *pointer* to the location in memory of the data to be moved.

Index   The index, like the base, is a value that is determined when the instruction is executed and added into the address calculation. Like the base, the index value comes from one of the 32-bit general registers. Any 32-bit general register *other than ESP* can be used. But before being added into the other components of the address, the index is first multiplied by a *scale factor* of 1, 2, 4, or 8. The programmer specifies an index by using an obvious multiplication notation for the scaling, and enclosing the scaled register in square brackets, just like the base. A scale factor of 1 may be omitted. For example, suppose we wish to load a byte from memory into the AL register, using EBP as a base, and using EDX as an index with a scale factor of 2. We can code this as:

MOV AL,[EBP][EDX*2]

Instead of concatenating the square brackets, we could instead use an addition notation. Thus, the following is exactly the same instruction:

MOV AL,[EBP+EDX*2]

Let's plug in some actual values to see the address calculation work. Suppose the above instruction is executed with EBP set to 10000 and EDX set to 3. The processor will fetch the 3 from EDX, multiply it by the scale factor, 2, to get 6, and then add the scaled index to the base, 10000, to get 10006. Finally, the processor will fetch the byte at memory location 10006 and copy it to the AL register.

Before leaving this section, let's return to the prohibition of using ESP as an index. The reason is simply that there are not enough bit encodings in the machine's instruction formats to allow for all possible registers. Since ESP is used as the stack pointer, it is unlikely that anybody would have reason to use it as a scaled index. Hence ESP was selected as the register to be dropped. For further information on instruction formats, see Appendix A.

Displacement   The third and final component added into a memory address calculation is the displacement, which is a constant (up to 32 bits long) supplied as part of the instruction. The displacement appears in the program as either an explicit constant or a variable name whose location in memory is the displacement, or both. Examples:

MOV AX,[EBP+8]   ; constant displacement is 8
MOV AX,TABLE[ECX*2]   ; displacement is the address of TABLE in memory
MOV AX,TABLE[EBX+8]   ; both constant and name: displacement is
                           ; TABLE + 8
MOV AX,TABLE[EBX+ECX*2+8] ; all components present!

Let's do another calculation with actual values. Suppose the last instruction above is executed with EBX containing the value 1000 and ECX containing the value 20. Suppose further that TABLE is located at address 30000 in memory. The processor multiplies ECX by its scale factor of 2 to get 40. It adds in EBX to get 1040. Finally, it adds the constant displacement, which was calculated by the assembler to be TABLE + 8 = 30008. Thus, the memory address is 31048. The processor fetches the 16-bit word at location 31048 in memory and copies it to the AX register.

Note the special case in which there is a displacement but no base or index. This is simply the access of a memory variable whose location is completely determined by the assembler. The displacement is the address of the variable. This mode is distinct from the other modes on many machines, and is sometimes known as *direct memory addressing*. All modes involving a base and/or an index are known as *indirect memory addressing* modes.

Immediate Operands   The remaining operand-addressing mode, *immediate*, refers to a constant operand, supplied as part of the instruction. The programmer specifies immediate mode by giving an operand whose type is constant. Such operands are most often either simple numbers, or pointers into memory that have been specified as constants via the assembler's OFFSET operator. (The OFFSET operator yields the address of its argument.) Examples:

```
MOV CL,100              ; an immediate numeric constant is loaded into CL
MOV ESI,OFFSET ARRAY    ; point to an array whose location is constant
```

The machine identifies immediate operands via special opcodes for the immediate forms of instructions. Because immediate MOVes into general registers occur extremely frequently in both assembly language programming and high-level language code generation, a lavish portion of the opcode space is devoted to them. You can see this in the opcode chart given in Appendix C.

Some Uses of Operand-Addressing Modes

After reading about all the operand-addressing modes just described, you might be wondering why there are so many? To understand the answer, you must recall that the 86 family of processors was designed so that a program written in a high-level language could be translated into efficient code. Typical high-level language features were examined to determine what kinds of operand-addressing modes would best support them. Some of these features will now be discussed.

Most programming languages have the concept of simple variables and arrays. A *simple variable* is a variable that represents a single value; an *array* is a variable that represents a sequence of values. Consider an assignment statement typical of the kind found in many high-level languages:

A(I) = X

This statement is read "Ith element of A becomes X." Let's assume that X is byte-sized and A is an array of bytes. Then the statement could be translated into code that first moves the contents of the memory location corresponding to the simple variable X into a register, say BL, and then moves the contents of BL into the memory location corresponding to the Ith element in the array A. The 386 MOV instruction allows any operand to be moved to or from any general register of the same size. A simple variable is a special case of a memory operand; it has a fixed displacement, but no base or index is used. Thus the compiler for the high-level language will first generate a MOV instruction of the form MOV BL,X.

For the second move, from BL to the array, let's assume that the array index I already exists in a register ESI. Then the destination is yet another form of memory operand: an index ESI plus a displacement (the location of the array A). Thus the compiler will generate an instruction of the form MOV A[ESI],BL. Such array accesses point out the need for the indirect memory-addressing mode "index + displacement." Accesses to array elements such as A(I + 2) present no additional complication; the displacement is merely the location of A(2) instead of A(0). For example, MOV A[ESI + 2],BL moves the contents of BL into the I + 2 element of the array A.

So far, we have translated the statement "A(I) = X" assuming that X is a byte and A is an array of bytes. What if X is a word or doubleword, and A is a corresponding array of words or doublewords? In general, we obtain the address of the Ith array element by adding I times the length of a single element (in bytes) to the starting address of the array. Since words are two bytes long, and doublewords are four bytes long, we can use scale factors to perform the necessary calculations in both cases. For words:

```
MOV BX,X
MOV A[ESI*2],BX
```

and for doublewords:

```
MOV EBX,X
MOV A[ESI*4],EBX
```

Thus the scale factors 1, 2, and 4 can be used for arrays of bytes, words, and doublewords, respectively. We shall see a use for the scale factor 8 when we discuss double-precision floating-point operands in Chapter 4.

Certain high-level languages have the concept of a pointer. A *pointer* is a variable containing the memory address of some other variable which we shall call the *pointee*. (If you didn't like backwords, you certainly won't like this.) If the value of the pointer changes, the pointee will correspond to a different memory location. A convenient way to access the pointee is to place the value of the pointer in a register, say EBX, and then use the operand-addressing modes involving EBX. Specifically, the mode [EBX] would be used to access a simple pointee (a simple variable pointed at by a pointer) and [EBX + ESI] or [EBX + ESI*2], for example, would be used to access an element in a pointee array (an array pointed at by a pointer).

Some high-level languages employ the concept of a record. A *record* (sometimes called a *structure*) is a collection of named data items, possibly of differing types. This is in contrast to an array, which is a sequence of (unnamed) data items, all of the same type. A payroll program, for example, might have a record corresponding to each employee. Each record might contain the employee's name, social security number, year-of-hire, and salary. A particular record item, such as year-of-hire, is in the same position in every employee record. For example, if year-of-hire is contained in the fourth byte from the start of each employee record, and the employee record for John Doe starts at address 03B4 (hexadecimal), then John Doe's year-of-hire is contained in the memory location at address 03B7. Thus the location of any given item in a record is at a fixed location and can be accessed with direct addressing; it is in essence no different from a simple variable.

Consider now a pointee record and assume that the value of the pointer to the record is contained in the EBX register. The operand-addressing mode to access an item from such a record would be "EBX + displacement," where displacement would be the position in the record corresponding to the item. For example, displacement would be 3 if the item were year-of-hire in a pointee employee record. The operand-addressing mode would then be [EBX + 3].

Although the operand-addressing mode for accessing items in pointee records appears similar to the mode for accessing array elements (both are "register + displacement"), there is a big difference. In the case of array elements, the displacement corresponds to the start of the array, and the register corresponds to the distance into the array. In the case of pointee records, the register corresponds to the start of the record, and the displacement corresponds to the distance into the record. In assembly language we can distinguish these two cases by writing A[EBX] in the case of the array and [EBX + 3] in the case of the record.

Arrays and records can be combined. Consider an array in which each element of the array is an employee record. Furthermore, consider that this is a pointee array. Assume that the pointer is in EBX and an index corresponding to an array element is in ESI. The operand-addressing mode needed to access the year-of-hire item of the particular record being indexed is "EBX + ESI + displacement," where displacement would be a 3. But let's look at things more carefully. Suppose the record being accessed is the seventeenth record of the pointee array. It does not suffice to load the value 17 into the indexing register ESI; we must first multiply 17 by the length of a record. This must usually be performed by an explicit multiplication or shift instruction. We can use scale factors here only if the length of a record is 1, 2, 4, or 8 bytes long. For example, if the employee records were 8 bytes long, then we could load 17 into the ESI register and access the year-of-hire item via the mode [EBX + ESI*8 + 3]. This justifies the need for the 386's most complicated operand-addressing mode, namely "base + scaled index + displacement." So it appears as though the operand-addressing modes aren't overkill after all.

Finally let's discuss operand-addressing modes involving EBP as the base register and the corresponding use of the stack as an alternate data area. These modes allow an efficient implementation of block-structured languages and re-entrant procedures. A

Table 2.2 Use of Memory-Addressing Modes in High-Level Languages

	Not Pointee	Pointee	Stack Frame
SIMPLE VARS	disp	[base]	disp[EBP]
ARRAYS	disp[s*index]	[base][s*index]	disp[EBP][s*index]
RECORDS	disp	[base + disp]	[EBP + disp]
ARRAYS OF RECORDS	disp[index + disp]	[base][index + disp]	disp[EBP][index + disp]

re-entrant procedure is a procedure that may be invoked (called upon) while it is already in execution from a previous invocation. This could occur if (1) the procedure invoked itself, (2) the procedure invoked some other procedure that in turn invoked the original procedure, or (3) the execution of the procedure was suspended because an interrupt occurred, and during the processing of the interrupt, the procedure was invoked again.

All the data (local variables and parameters) utilized by a re-entrant procedure must have a unique memory location for each concurrent invocation of the procedure, otherwise the data being used by one invocation of the procedure might be corrupted by a subsequent invocation. This means that memory must be allocated for the procedure's data every time the procedure is invoked. Such a memory area is called a *stack frame*. (More will be said about stack frames in Chapter 3.) Although it's not essential, it would be highly desirable for the procedure to release this memory when the procedure is finished. Since the last procedure invoked is the first procedure to finish, the stack serves as a convenient place from which to allocate such memory. Each time a procedure is invoked, a block of memory on the top of the stack is reserved for the stack frame by simply changing the contents of register ESP, the STACK POINTER. During the execution of the procedure, it is necessary to maintain a pointer to the beginning of the stack frame; this is the reason for having EBP, the BASE POINTER. Accesses to items within the stack frame can be performed with the operand-addressing modes involving EBP. Specifically, a simple variable within the stack frame can be accessed by the mode "EBP + displacement," and an array element within the stack frame can be accessed with "EBP + index + displacement."

The uses of the memory-addressing modes in high-level languages are summarized in Table 2.2.

Still to Come

In this chapter we have presented the underlying structure of the 386 and the format of its instructions. It's now time to describe the actual 386 instructions. They are the topic of the next chapter.

References

Just as the 386 is based on the 8086 and 286, this chapter is based on references 1 and 2. The 386 machine organization is described in Intel literature as well (reference 3).

1.   S.P. Morse, *The 8086/8088 Primer*, Hayden Book Company, Rochelle Park, N.J., 1982.

2.   S.P. Morse, D.J. Albert, *The 80286 Architecture*, Wiley Press, New York, 1986.

3.   *ASM386 Assembly Language Reference Manual*, Intel Corporation, 1986.

3

BASIC INSTRUCTION SET

The previous chapter described the source and destination operands of an instruction, and this chapter describes the operation an instruction performs on these operands. The instructions are described in an informal manner. A more formal description can be found in the Intel manual (reference 1).

We remind you once again of the division of the 386 processor into a near half and a far half. In this chapter we describe the instructions in the near half only; the instructions in the far half are described in Chapters 5 and 6. Most of the basic (near-half) instructions appear in the entire family, starting with the 8086. A few basic instructions were added when the 186 was introduced, and a few more have been added for the 386. We identify the new instructions as we describe them.

For convenience, the basic instructions are grouped into the following categories: data-transfer instructions, arithmetic instructions, logical instructions, string instructions, transfer-of-control instructions, interrupt instructions, flag instructions, synchronization instructions, bit-array instructions, and high-level language support instructions. Each of these categories is described in detail in this chapter.

Assembly Language Notation

The 386 instructions will be described using the notation of Intel's 386 assembly language, ASM386. The intent of this chapter is not to teach ASM386 assembly language programming but rather to use the assembly language as a tool for describing the processor. A detailed description of the assembly language can be found in reference 2.

As with most assembly languages, an instruction is specified by a mnemonic, followed as necessary by one or more operands. The instruction may be followed by a comment, which is identified by a leading semicolon. If there are two operands following the mnemonic, the first is the destination operand, and the second is the source operand. Hence:

MOV BX,CX

is the move instruction that moves into BX (the destination operand) the contents of CX (the source operand).

In Chapter 2 we discuss the kinds of operands that can appear in ASM386 instructions: immediate, register, and memory. Let's review some of those forms by listing some examples:

```
ADD CX,35              ; immediate source, register destination
INC  EDX               ; register
INC  MEMLOC            ; direct memory
INC  [ESI]             ; indirect memory
INC  [EDI + 4]         ; indirect memory
INC  [EBX][ESI*2]      ; indirect memory
INC  MEMBYTE [EDI]     ; indirect memory
INC  VALUE [EDI + EBP] ; indirect memory
```

For simplicity, all examples of memory operands in this chapter are shown as direct memory addressing; any of the indirect memory addressing forms can be used wherever a direct memory address is used.

A unique feature of assembly languages for the 86 family is that they are *typed assembly languages*. Specifically, each operand has an associated type (byte, word, etc.) and this type is used by the assembler to determine which opcode (bit encoding) to generate for a given instruction. In contrast, the opcode in a *nontyped language* is determined entirely by the mnemonic in the instruction field. For example, in a nontyped language we might write:

```
INCD  LOC   ; increment doubleword at address LOC
INCW  LOC   ; increment word at address LOC
INCB  LOC   ; increment byte at address LOC
```

to designate doubleword, word, and byte increments, respectively. In a typed language, LOC would be specified as being a doubleword, word, or byte (by the statement that allocates space for LOC) and the statement:

INC LOC

would represent the type of increment that corresponds to the size of variable LOC. Similarly, each register has a type (e.g., EAX is a doubleword, BX is a word, CL is a byte), so in ASM386 we write doubleword, word, and byte register increments as:

```
INC EAX      ; increment doubleword register
INC BX       ; increment word register
INC CL       ; increment byte register
```

Data Transfer Instructions

The 386 has three classes of data transfer instructions: general-purpose transfers, accumulator-specific transfers, and flag transfers. These are summarized in Table 3.1.

General-Purpose Transfers The general-purpose transfers are MOV (move), MOVZX (Move with Zero extend), MOVSX (Move with Sign Extend), XCHG (exchange), PUSH, POP, PUSHA/PUSHAD (push all), and POPA/POPAD (pop all).

The MOV instruction performs a byte, word, or doubleword transfer from the source operand to the destination operand. One of the operands can be in a register or in memory. The other operand can be in a register or in the instruction itself (immediate operand). Examples of the various MOV instructions are shown in Table 3.2.

Table 3.1 Data Transfer Instructions

General Purpose		
MOV (move)	SOURCE	→ DEST
MOVZX (move zero ext)	SOURCE	→ zero-extended DEST
MOVSX (move sign ext)	SOURCE	→ sign-extended DEST
XCHG (exchange)	SOURCE	⟷ DEST
PUSH (push)	SOURCE	→ stack
POP (pop)	stack	→ DEST
PUSHAD (push all)	registers	→ stack
PUSHA (push all)	16-bit regs	→ stack
POPAD (pop all)	stack	→ registers
POPA (pop all)	stack	→ 16-bit registers
Accumulator Specific		
IN (input)	port	→ accumulator (AL, AX, or EAX)
OUT (output)	accumulator	→ port
XLATB (translate)	table(AL)	→ AL
Flag Transfers		
LAHF (load AH with flags)		SF,ZF,0,AF,0,PF,1,CF → AH
SAHF (store AH into flags)		AH → SF,ZF,x,AF,x,PF,x,CF
PUSHFD (push flags)		flags → stack
PUSHF (push flags)		low 16 flags → stack
POPFD (pop flags)		stack → flags
POPF (pop flags)		stack → low 16 flags

Table 3.2 Examples of MOV Instructions

register to register	MOV AH,BH
	MOV BX,DX
	MOV EAX,ESI
immediate to register	MOV BL,35
	MOV CX,850
	MOV ESI,OFFSET SIGN_ON_MSG
memory to register	MOV CL,MEM_BYTE
	MOV DX,MEM_WORD
	MOV EAX,MEM_DWORD
register to memory	MOV MEM_BYTE,DL
	MOV MEM_WORD,CX
	MOV MEM_DWORD,EBX

All MOV operations are between operands of the same size. The 386 has two special instructions, not available on the 386's predecessors, that allow moves from smaller (register or memory) operands to larger (register) ones. Thus, we can move data from a byte to a word, from a byte to a doubleword, or from a word to a doubleword. The two instructions differ in the method for filling out the high-order bits of the destination. MOVZX always fills the high-order bits with 0's; MOVSX fills the high-order bits with the high bit of the source operand. Recall from our discussion of numbers that this action, called *sign extension*, is what we want if we are interpreting the operands as signed integers using two's complement notation. For example, suppose that the BL register contains the value 80 hexadecimal. The MOVZX AX,BL instruction zero-extends the value 80 to 0080 and loads AX with that value. The MOVSX AX,BL instruction sign-extends 80 to FF80 and loads AX with FF80. Note that in the signed two's complement notation, both byte 80 and word FF80 stand for the decimal value minus 128. Examples of MOVZX and MOVSX instructions are shown in Table 3.3.

The MOVSX sign-extension instruction is supplemented by some special-purpose sign-extension operations: CBW, CWD, CDQ, and CWDE. These operations are discussed in the section on multiplication and division.

The XCHG instruction performs a byte, word, or doubleword interchange between two operands. One of the operands can be in a register or memory and the other in a register. There is no distinction between source and destination operand. Table 3.4 gives examples of XCHG instructions.

The PUSH instruction transfers a word or doubleword from the source operand to the stack. The POP instruction does just the opposite: it transfers a word or doubleword from the stack to the destination operand. The ESP register points to the last quantity (word or doubleword) entered onto the stack. This quantity is called the *top of the stack*. As successive data is pushed onto the stack, it is placed in consecutively lower memory addresses. (The stack grows toward lower memory and shrinks toward higher memory.) The PUSH instruction *starts* by *decrementing* the contents of ESP, thereby locating the next free stack word or doubleword. The POP instruction *finishes* by

Table 3.3 Examples of MOVZX and MOVSX Instructions

byte register to word register	MOVSX AX,BL	MOVZX BX,CL
byte memory to word register	MOVSX BX,BYTE_MEM	MOVZX SI,BYTE_MEM
byte register to dword register	MOVSX EDX,AL	MOVZX EAX,DH
byte memory to dword register	MOVSX EAX,BYTE_MEM	MOVZX EBX,BYTE_MEM
word register to dword register	MOVSX ECX,CX	MOVZX EAX,BX
word memory to dword register	MOVSX EBP,WORD_MEM	MOVSX ECX,WORD_MEM

Table 3.4 Examples of XCHG Instructions

register with register	XCHG AL,AH
	XCHG CX,DX
	XCHG EAX,ESI
register with memory	XCHG BL,MEM_BYTE
	XCHG CX,MEM_WORD
	XCHG EDX,MEM_DWORD

incrementing the contents of ESP, thereby removing the word or doubleword just accessed from the stack. Figure 3.1 illustrates the effect of a PUSH instruction and a POP instruction.

The operand of a PUSH or POP instruction can be any word or doubleword general register or memory operand. Furthermore, the PUSH instruction can also take as its operand a value contained in the instruction, that is, an immediate operand (this was not possible with the 8086 PUSH instructions). Since it makes no sense to pop a value into an instruction, the POP instruction never takes an immediate operand. Examples of the PUSH and POP instructions are shown in Table 3.5.

Because it is very common for a portion of a program (for example, a subroutine or procedure) to save and restore the values of 386 registers, the 386 provides single-byte opcode forms for register pushes and pops. Those forms refer to either word or doubleword registers, depending on the 386's emulation mode. Recall from Chapter 2 that the 386 provides an operand size prefix to switch from the word or doubleword default size to the other, nondefault size. Thus, when the 386 is not emulating one of its predecessors, it takes a single opcode byte to push or pop a doubleword; it takes two opcode bytes to push or pop a 16-bit word.

Two other push and pop instructions are provided, namely PUSHA/PUSHAD (push all 16/32-bit registers) and POPA/POPAD (pop all 16/32-bit registers). These instructions were originally intended for the 8086 but, in order to simplify the chip, they were not implemented in that processor. PUSHA and POPA first appeared in the 186, and the 32-bit versions PUSHAD and POPAD were introduced with the 386.

The PUSHAD and POPAD instructions provide an efficient means of allowing a procedure to save all general registers as the first thing it does when it starts executing and later restore them as the last thing it does. Once it does so, the procedure is free to modify the contents of any register with the assurance that any important values that were left in the registers by the procedure's caller will still be there when the caller resumes execution.

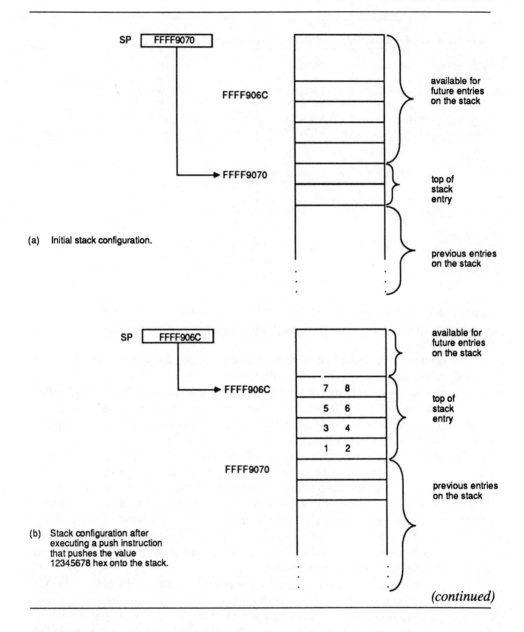

(a)   Initial stack configuration.

(b)   Stack configuration after
      executing a push instruction
      that pushes the value
      12345678 hex onto the stack.

(continued)

PUSHAD pushes the registers on the stack in the following order: EAX, ECX, EDX, EBX, ESP, EBP, ESI, EDI. The value of ESP pushed by PUSHAD is the value it had prior to executing the PUSHAD instruction. The execution of PUSHAD will cause ESP to be decremented to account for the registers that are pushed on the stack. Similarly, the popping performed by POPAD will cause ESP to be incremented by the same amount, and hence POPAD has no need for the value of ESP that was saved on the stack (it merely discards that saved value).

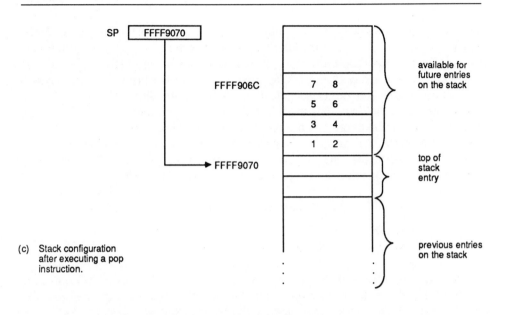

(c) Stack configuration
     after executing a pop
     instruction.

Figure 3.1 Example of pushing and popping entries on stack.

Table 3.5 Examples of PUSH and POP Instructions

	push	pop
word register	PUSH AX	POP BX
dword register	PUSH ECX	POP EBP
word memory	PUSH MEM_WORD	POP MEM_WORD
dword memory	PUSH MEM_DWORD	POP MEM_DWORD
immediate	PUSH 895	
all	PUSHAD	POPAD
all 16-bit	PUSHA	POPA

The instructions PUSHA and POPA perform the equivalent set of pushes and pops on the 16-bit registers derived from 386's predecessors in the 86 family. They are provided mainly for compatibility with the predecessor's instruction set.

Accumulator-Specific Transfers   The accumulator-specific transfers are IN (input), OUT (output), and XLATB (translate byte). Unlike the previous transfers, which treated all general registers as equals, these transfers discriminate by permitting only the ACCUMULATOR to serve as the operand. The reason they were made accumulator specific was to reduce the number of bytes per instruction.

The IN instruction transfers data (byte, word, or doubleword) from an input port to the ACCUMULATOR (AL, AX, or EAX). Similarly, the OUT instruction transfers data from the ACCUMULATOR to an output port. The port number can be specified either directly by a byte in the instruction or indirectly by the contents of the DX register. Note that this is a specialized use of the DX register; none of the other general registers can be used for this function. Only the first 256 ports can be specified directly in the instruction, whereas any of the 2^{16} (approximately 65,000) ports can be specified indirectly via DX. The direct specification, although requiring the instruction to contain an additional byte, has the advantage of not requiring the execution of an additional instruction to preload the port number into a register. The indirect access has the advantage that program loops can be used to access consecutive ports. Examples of the IN and OUT instruction are shown in Table 3.6. The difference between the direct and the indirect port specification is shown below.

```
IN AL, 5        ; direct port specification

MOV DX,5
IN AL,DX        ; indirect port specification
```

The XLATB instruction "translates" the value of AL. It does this by replacing the value of AL with a byte from a table pointed to by EBX (another specialized use of a general register). The index into the table is the original contents of AL.

The XLATB instruction is useful for translating an encoded value into the same value under a different encoding. For example, consider the following encoding of the decimal digits 0 through 9:

Digit	Encoding
0	11000
1	00011
2	00101
3	00110
4	01001
5	01010
6	01100
7	10001
8	10010
9	10100

Table 3.6 Examples of IN and OUT Instructions

	byte	word	doubleword
IN (direct)	IN AL, 1	IN AX,10	IN EAX,8
OUT (direct)	OUT 50,AL	OUT 30,AX	OUT 25,EAX
IN (indirect)	IN AL,DX	IN AX,DX	IN EAX,DX
OUT (indirect)	OUT DX,AL	OUT DX,AX	OUT DX,EAX

This encoding is of practical interest because each encoded value contains exactly two 1-bits (sometimes referred to as a 2-out-of-5 code) and is actually used in telephone signaling applications. Suppose we want to translate the binary digit 7 into a 2-out-of-5 code. The program to perform this translation is as follows:

```
MOV AL,7                ; place binary 7 (0000 0111) into AL
MOV EBX,OFFSET TABLE    ; place address of table containing encodings into EBX
XLATB                   ; fetch seventh entry from table ...
                        ; ... (0001 0001) and place it in AL.
```

This translation is illustrated in Figure 3.2.

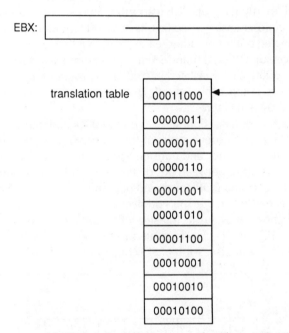

(a) Translation table for converting binary to 2-out-of-5 code.

(b) Contents of register AL before executing XLATB instruction.

AL: 00010001

(c) Contents of register AL after executing XLATB instruction.

Figure 3.2 Example of using XLATB instruction to translate the digit 7 from binary encoding to a 2-out-of-5 encoding.

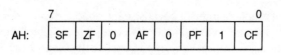

Figure 3.3 Correspondence between flags and bits of AH.

Flag Transfers The flag transfer instructions provide access to the set of processor flags. The instructions are LAHF (load AH with flags), SAHF (store AH into flags), PUSHF/PUSHFD (push flags), POPF/POPFD (pop flags), and SETcond (set byte according to condition).

The LAHF instruction transfers the five flags SF (sign flag), ZF (zero flag), AF (auxiliary carry flag), PF (parity flag), and CF (carry flag) into specific bits of the AH register. The SAHF instruction transfers specific bits of the AH register into these flags. These five flags were singled out for no other reason than that they were the five flags present in the 8080 processor. (The LAHF and SAHF instructions exist mainly to permit programs written for the 8080 to be translated into efficient programs for the 86 family of processors—isn't upward compatibility great!) The correspondence between bits in AH and the five flags is shown in Figure 3.3.

The PUSHFD instruction enters a doubleword on the stack and transfers *all* of the flags (not just the above five) into specific bits of this word. The POPFD instruction removes a doubleword from the stack and transfers specific bits of this word into the flag registers. The correspondence between bits of the stack doubleword and the flags is shown in Figure 3.4. PUSHF and POPF push and pop only the bottom 16 bits of the flags register, the part that existed on the 386's predecessors.

The SETcond instructions allow us to transfer a flag setting to a byte register or memory operand. Since SETcond is closely related to the set of conditional transfer instructions (Jcond), we defer our discussion of SETcond until after we discuss Jcond.

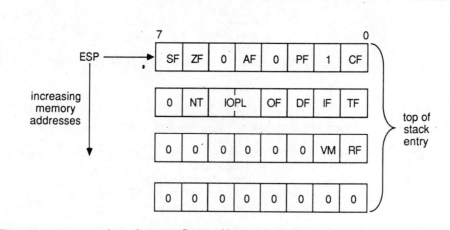

Figure 3.4 Correspondence between flags and bits on the stack.

Arithmetic Instructions

The 386 provides the four basic arithmetical operations in several different forms. The arithmetic instructions of the 386 are shown in Table 3.7. Both signed and unsigned arithmetic operations are provided, for each size of operand (byte, word, and doubleword). Furthermore, correction operations are provided to allow arithmetic to be performed directly on decimal rather than on binary digits.

The difference between signed and unsigned numbers is in the interpretation of the bit patterns. Unsigned numbers are interpreted in binary notation, and signed numbers are interpreted in two's complement notation. Figure 3.5 shows the range and representation of 8- and 16-bit signed and unsigned numbers. (32-bit numbers work analogously but are a little cumbersome to illustrate!) Addition and subtraction operations are the same on all types of numbers. Thus the ordinary binary addition and subtraction instructions designed for unsigned numbers will also give the correct results when applied to signed numbers. The only difference between signed and unsigned addition and subtraction is the mechanism for detecting out-of-range results. The add and subtract instructions set the CF flag if the result, when interpreted as an unsigned number, is out of range; and they set the OF flag if the result, when interpreted as a signed number, is out of range. It is possible for either the signed or unsigned result to be out of range with the other result being in range. Figure 3.6 illustrates this.

Table 3.7 Arithmetic Instructions

Addition
ADD (add)   DEST + SOURCE → DEST
ADC (add with carry)   DEST + SOURCE + CF → DEST
INC (increment)   DEST + 1 → DEST

Subtraction
SUB (subtract)   DEST − SOURCE → DEST
SBB (subtract with borrow)   DEST − SOURCE − CF → DEST
DEC (decrement)   DEST − 1 → DEST
NEG (negate)   0 − DEST → DEST
CMP (compare)   DEST − SOURCE is discarded; flags set

Multiplication
MUL (multiply) $AL * SOURCE_8 → AX$
                              or $AX * SOURCE_{16} → DXAX$
                              or $EAX * SOURCE_{32} → EDXEAX$

IMUL (integer multiply)   Same as above but signed multiply

Division
DIV (divide) $AX / SOURCE_8 → AL$; remainder → AH
                              or $DXAX / SOURCE_{16} → AX$; remainder → DX
                              or $EDXEAX / SOURCE_{32} → EAX$; remainder → EDX

IDIV (integer divide)   Same as above but signed divide

	unsigned		signed	

number	representation	number	representation
0	0000 0000	- 128	1000 0000
1	0000 0001	- 127	1000 0001
2	0000 0010	- 126	1000 0010
.	.	.	.
126	0111 1110	- 1	1111 1111
127	0111 1111	0	0000 0000
128	1000 0000	+ 1	0000 0001
.	.	.	.
253	1111 1101	+ 125	0111 1101
254	1111 1110	+ 126	0111 1110
255	1111 1111	+ 127	0111 1111

(a) unsigned 8-bit numbers   (b) signed 8-bit numbers

(8-bit)

number	representation	number	representation
0	0000 0000 0000 0000	- 32,768	1000 0000 0000 0000
1	0000 0000 0000 0001	- 32,767	1000 0000 0000 0001
2	0000 0000 0000 0010	- 32,766	1000 0000 0000 0010
.	.	.	.
32,766	0111 1111 1111 1110	- 1	1111 1111 1111 1111
32,767	0111 1111 1111 1111	0	0000 0000 0000 0000
32,768	1000 0000 0000 0000	+ 1	0000 0000 0000 0001
.	.	.	.
65,533	1111 1111 1111 1101	32,765	0111 1111 1111 1101
65,534	1111 1111 1111 1110	32,766	0111 1111 1111 1110
65,535	1111 1111 1111 1111	32,767	0111 1111 1111 1111

(c) unsigned 16-bit numbers   (d) signed 16-bit numbers

(16-bit)

Figure 3.5 Range of 8- and 16-bit signed and unsigned numbers.

Six status flags are set or cleared by most arithmetic operations to reflect certain properties of the result of the operations. We have just discussed two of these flags, CF and OF. In general, the six flags are set to recognize the following conditions:

1. CF is set if the operation resulted in an unsigned result being out of range.

2. OF is set if the operation resulted in a signed result being out of range (called *signed overflow*).

3. ZF is set if the result of the operation is zero (signed or unsigned).

4. SF is set if the most significant bit of the result of the operation is a 1, thereby indicating a negative result.

5. PF is set if the the low eight bits of the result contain an even number of 1 bits (called *even parity*).

6. AF is set if a correction is needed for decimal operations (discussed in detail later).

	representation	interpretation as unsigned numbers	interpretation as signed numbers
(a) both signed and unsigned results in range	0000 0100 + 0000 1011 ——— 0000 1111	4 11 —— 15 CF = 0	· 4 · 11 —— · 15 OF = 0
(b) unsigned result out of range	0000 0111 + 1111 1011 ——— 0000 0010	7 251 —— 2 CF = 1 ···out of range···	· 7 – 5 —— · 2 OF = 0
(c) signed result out of range	0000 1001 + 0111 1100 ——— 1000 0101	9 124 —— 133 CF = 0	·· 9 · 124 —— – 123 OF = 1 ···out of range···
(d) both signed and unsigned result out of range	1000 0111 + 1111 0101 ——— 0111 1100	135 245 —— 124 CF = 1 ···out of range···	– 121 – 11 —— · 124 OF = 1 ···out of range···

Figure 3.6 Examples of out-of-range results in unsigned and signed additions.

A summary of the behavior of these flags appears at the end of this chapter.

Notice the curious restriction on the PF parity flag, which checks only the bottom byte of a word or a doubleword result. PF was originally introduced in the 8008 (predecessor to the 8080) so that 8-bit serial input data could be efficiently checked for parity errors. The intended use of the 8008 was to control a terminal and so parity checking was obviously important there. For compatibility, PF was incorporated into the 8080, then the 8086, then the 286, and now the 386. But now everyone uses a serial controller peripheral chip to check for input parity so PF has become an orphan that nobody uses. Thus it doesn't even matter whether PF checks parity on one byte or four bytes (just as long as it's compatible with the 8008!)

Multiple-precision arithmetic is a means of dealing with unsigned numbers larger than 32 bits by breaking the numbers into 8-, 16-, or 32-bit fields and performing repeated operations on successive fields starting with the least significant. If any of these operations yields an out-of-range result, the result is still valid, but a 1 is carried into (addition) or borrowed from (subtraction) the operation on the next field. As an example, consider adding the 24-bit number 0011 1010 0000 0111 1011 0010 to the 24-bit number 0010 0000 1100 0010 0101 0011. This can be done in three successive additions of 8-bit numbers, as shown on the next page.

1. The least significant eight bits are added together:

```
        1011  0010
    +   0101  0011
    _____
        0000  0101      with CF = 1
```

2. The middle eight bits are added together along with any carry generated by the previous addition:

```
                1       (last CF)
    +   0000  0111
    +   1100  0010
    _____
        1100  1010      with CF = 0
```

3. The most significant eight bits are added together along with any carry generated by the previous addition:

```
                0       (last CF)
    +   0011  1010
    +   0010  0000
    _____
        0101  1010
```

Thus the result is 0101 1010 1100 1010 0000 0101. This example points out the need to have an instruction (add-with-carry) that adds the values of the two operands and the value in CF all together. A similar instruction, subtract-with-borrow, is useful for multiple-precision subtraction.

An unsigned addition or subtraction result going out of range can be planned for performing tasks such as multiple-precision arithmetic. It is a normal event and does not indicate an error condition. A signed result going out of range, on the other hand, is usually unanticipated. It indicates that a fault has occurred and that the results must be corrected before computations can proceed.

Addition Instructions   The addition instructions are ADD (add), ADC (add-with-carry), and INC (increment). These instructions may, in general, be applied to any operands.

The ADD instruction (Table 3.8) performs a byte, word, or doubleword addition of the contents of the source and destination operands and stores the result back in the destination operand. One of the operands can be in a register or in memory; the other operand can be in a register or in the instruction itself (immediate operand).

Table 3.8 Examples of Two-Operand Arithmetic and Logical Instructions

reg1 = reg1 op reg2	opcode BL,CL opcode AX,BX opcode EBP,EAX
reg = reg op mem	opcode DL,MEM_BYTE opcode CX,MEM_WORD opcode EAX,MEM_DWORD
mem = mem op reg	opcode MEM_BYTE,AH opcode MEM_WORD,CX opcode MEM_DWORD,EDX
reg = reg op immediate	opcode BL,50 opcode DX,490 opcode ESI,OFFSET MEM_LOC
mem = mem op immediate	opcode MEM_BYTE,17 opcode MEM_WORD,600 opcode MEM_DWORD,100000

where opcode is any of the following: ADD ADC SUB SBB CMP AND OR XOR TEST

**Table 3.9 Examples of One-Operand Arithmetic and
Logical Instructions**

register	opcode DL opcode BX opcode EBP
memory	opcode MEM_BYTE opcode MEM_WORD opcode MEM_DWORD

where opcode is any of the following: INC DEC NEG NOT

The ADC instruction is similar to the ADD instruction except it includes the initial value of CF in the addition. This facilitates the multiple-precision arithmetic we just discussed. The forms of the ADC instruction are the same as the forms of the ADD instruction (Table 3.8).

The INC instruction has only one operand. The instruction adds 1 to the contents of the operand and stores the result back in that operand. Examples of the INC instruction are shown in Table 3.9.

The INC instruction is identical to the ADD instruction with an immediate operand of 1; except (1) it requires fewer bytes, and (2) it does not alter the Carry flag (we discuss why later in this chapter). INC was included in the instruction set because adding (and subtracting) 1 is a very frequent operation and should therefore be done in as few bytes as possible.

Subtraction Instructions The subtraction instructions are SUB (subtract), SBB (subtract with borrow), DEC (decrement), NEG (negate), and CMP (compare). The first three are analogous to the three addition instructions. Examples of SUB, SBB, and CMP are shown in Table 3.8, DEC and NEG in Table 3.9.

The NEG instruction changes the sign of its operand. For example, if the operand contained the representation of −1 (1111 1111), the NEG instruction would change it to +1 (0000 0001).

The CMP instruction is similar to the subtract instruction except the result is not stored back into the destination operand. In fact, the result is not stored anywhere; it is just lost inside the processor. No doubt you're wondering, "Of what use is an instruction that loses its result?" It turns out that the flag settings that reflect certain properties of the result are often more important than the result itself. From these flag settings, we can deduce the relationship between the value of the two operands that entered into the subtraction. For example, if the ZF flag is set to one, then the result is zero and the value of the two operands must have been identical. The flag settings for each of the various possible relationships are shown in Table 3.10. A CMP instruction is typically followed by a conditional jump instruction (discussed later) that tests the flag settings to see if a particular relationship was satisfied.

Multiplication and Division Instructions Multiplication of two 8-bit numbers has the potential for yielding a product up to 16 bits long. Consider, for example, the multiplication of the unsigned numbers shown in Figure 3.7.

Similarly, the multiplication of two 16-bit numbers can give a 32-bit product, and multiplication of two 32-bit numbers can give a 64-bit product. The 386 multiplication instructions permit multiplying an 8-, 16-, or 32-bit quantity contained in AL, AX, or EAX by an operand of the same size specified in the instruction itself. The bottom half of the double-length product is placed back into the accumulator AL, AX, or EAX. The top half is placed in different places, depending on the operand size. For the 8-by-8 case, the obvious destination for the top 8 bits is AH, and this is indeed the case. For the 16-by-16 case, the obvious destination for the top 16 bits is the upper part of EAX; but this

Table 3.10 Flag Setting After a CMP Instruction Is Executed

Relationship of Destination Operand to Source Operand		CF	ZF	SF	OF
	EQUAL	0	1	0	0
Signed Operands	LESS THAN	—	0	1	0
	LESS THAN	—	0	0	1
	GREATER THAN	—	0	0	0
	GREATER THAN	—	0	1	1
Unsigned Operands	BELOW	1	0	—	—
	ABOVE	0	0	—	—

Unspecified entries in above table can be either "0" or "1" depending on the actual values of the operands.

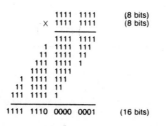

Figure 3.7 Example illustrating that a product can be up to twice as long as the operands.

is *not* the case! This is because 16-by-16 multiplication is available on the 386's predecessors, but EAX is not. Hence, DX was chosen to receive the high 16 bits on the predecessors. For compatibility, the 386 must also place the result in DX. For the 32-by-32 case, the analogous destination EDX is the choice for the high result bits. This quirky set of choices is summarized in Figure 3.8.

The division instructions of the 386 are designed to undo what the multiplication instructions did. Specifically, the division instructions divide the 16-, 32-, or 64-bit numbers in AX, DXAX, or EDXEAX by an operand of half the size, specified in the instruction. The quotient is placed in the lower half of the original number, and the remainder is placed in the upper half. This is illustrated in Figure 3.9.

There is a pitfall in the division instruction. Suppose we load the AX register with decimal 600, the BL register with 2, and we execute a DIV BL instruction. The quotient, 300, is supposed to go to the AL register, and the remainder, 0, goes to the AH register. But 300 is too big to fit in the byte register AL. Here we have a *divide overflow*. Unlike overflows for addition and subtraction, there is no way to interpret the operands or the answer so that the operation makes any sense. For this reason, the 386 generates an interrupt of type 0 whenever it encounters a divide overflow. (We discuss interrupts and interrupt handlers later in this chapter and in Chapter 6.) Note that division by zero is an instance (but, as we just saw, not the only instance) of divide overflow.

Unlike addition and subtraction, the ordinary binary multiplication and division instructions that work for unsigned numbers do not give the correct results when

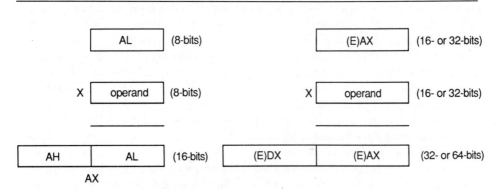

Figure 3.8 Source and destination operands for multiplication.

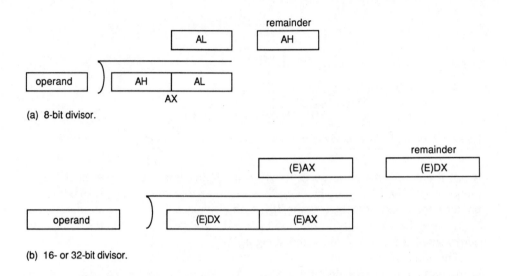

(a) 8-bit divisor.

(b) 16- or 32-bit divisor.

Figure 3.9 Source and destination operands for division.

applied to signed numbers. This is illustrated in Figure 3.10. Thus special multiplication and division instructions must be provided for signed numbers. The 386 multiplication and division instructions are MUL (unsigned multiply), IMUL (signed
multiply, sometimes called integer multiply), DIV (unsigned divide), and IDIV (signed
divide, sometimes called integer divide). Examples of the multiply and divide instructions are shown in Table 3.11.

   The IMUL instruction has a variety of general forms (not available with MUL, DIV,
or IDIV) that facilitate computing the addresses of odd-sized array elements. One form
provides for multiplying any word register or memory operand by an immediate
constant, with the destination being any word register. (This form was first introduced
in the 186.) In the 386, of course, this form was extended to allow doubleword register
or memory operands. Another form, which is not found in any of the 386 predecessors,
allows any word or doubleword register or memory to be multiplied into any register of
the same size. Note that all of the new forms for IMUL have a destination of the same
size as the operands. It is therefore possible for one of these new IMULs to overflow. In
this case, the upper bits are discarded, and the overflow flag is set. A summary of all the
forms of the IMUL instruction, with examples, is presented in Table 3.12.

   A word about signed division is in order. If we divide − 26 by + 7, we could get a
quotient of − 4 and a remainder of + 2. Or we could get a quotient of − 3 and a
remainder of − 5. Either pair of results would be correct. In one case the remainder is
positive, and in the other case it is negative. The 386 signed division instruction was
designed so that the remainder will have the same sign as the dividend. For the above

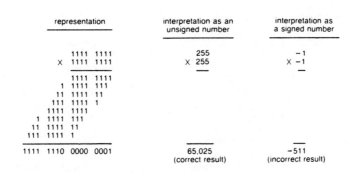

representation	interpretation as an unsigned number	interpretation as a signed number
1111 1111 X 1111 1111	255 X 255	−1 X −1
1111 1111 1 1111 111 11 1111 11 111 1111 1 1111 1111 1 1111 111 11 1111 11 111 1111 1		
1111 1110 0000 0001	65,025 (correct result)	−511 (incorrect result)

Figure 3.10 Example demonstrating that ordinary binary multiplication does not give correct result for unsigned numbers.

Table 3.11 Examples of Multiply and Divide Instructions

accum = accum op register	opcode CL opcode BX opcode EBX
accum = accum op memory	opcode MEM_BYTE opcode MEM_WORD opcode MEM_DWORD

where opcode is any of the following: MUL DIV IMUL IDIV

division, the 386 will produce a quotient of − 3 and a remainder of − 5. Division, defined in this manner, will give quotients (and remainders) with the same absolute value for − 26 divided by + 7, − 26 divided by − 7, + 26 divided by + 7, and + 26 divided by − 7.

Table 3.13 summarizes the number of bits in the operands and the results of various arithmetic instructions. The instructions were designed so that the double-length result of a multiplication could be used in a future division. What if we want to use the result of a multiplication for something other than division? For instance, how would we multiply 17 (0001 1001) by 10 (0000 1010) and add 20 (0001 0100) to the product? That's simple; we just ignore the 8 most significant bits of the product. But now comes the problem of performing a division on a number that was not generated by a previous multiplication. For example, let's try to divide a plain old 8-bit version of 35 (0010 0011) by 7 (0000 0111). The division instruction expects a 16-bit dividend to be in AX. Simply putting an 8-bit dividend into AL won't work because the division will use whatever garbage it finds in AH as the 8 most significant bits of the dividend. Well, that's no problem. We just make sure to zero out AH before doing an 8-bit division or zero out DX before doing a 16-bit division.

Table 3.12 Examples of IMUL Instructions

accumulator with register	IMUL BL	; AL * BL → AX
	IMUL CX	; AX * CX → DXAX
	IMUL EBX	; EAX * EBX → EDXEAX
accumulator with memory	IMUL MEM_BYTE	; AL * MEM_BYTE → AX
	IMUL MEM_WORD	; AX * MEM_WORD → DXAX
	IMUL MEM_DWORD	; EAX * MEM_DWORD → EDXEAX
register with immediate	IMUL DX,BX,300	; BX * 300 → DX
	IMUL CX,3	; CX * 3 → CX
	IMUL EAX,EDX,100000	; EDX * 100000 → EAX
	IMUL EBP,500	; EBP * 500 → EBP
memory with immediate	IMUL BX,MEM_WORD,400	; MEM_WORD * 400 → BX
	IMUL ECX,MEM_DWORD,13	; MEM_DWORD 13 → ECX
register with register	IMUL BX,CX	; BX * CX → BX
	IMUL EDX,EBP	; EDX * EBP → EDX
register with memory	IMUL DI,MEM_WORD	; DI * MEM_WORD → DI
	IMUL EBX,MEM_DWORD	; EBX * MEM_DWORD → EBX

Table 3.13 Size of Operands and Results

	First Operand	Second Operand	Result
ADD	8 (addend)	8 (augend)	8 (sum)
	16 (addend)	16 (augend)	16 (sum)
	32 (addend)	32 (augend)	32 (sum)
SUBTRACT	8 (minuend)	8 (subtrahend)	8 (difference)
	16 (minuend)	16 (subtrahend)	16 (difference)
	32 (minuend)	32 (subtrahend)	32 (difference)
MULTIPLY	8 (multiplicand)	8 (multiplier)	16 (product)
	16 (multiplicand)	16 (multiplier)	32 (product)
	32 (multiplicand)	32 (multiplier)	64 (product)
DIVIDE	16 (dividend)	8 (divisor)	8 (quotient)
			8 (remainder)
	32 (dividend)	16 (divisor)	16 (quotient)
			16(remainder)
	64 (dividend)	32 divisor)	32 (quotient)
			32 (remainder)

Zeroing out the most significant half of the double-length dividend works fine for unsigned division, but how does it work for signed division? Converting the 8-bit version of −2 (1111 1110) to the 16-bit version (1111 1111 1111 1110) involves setting the 8 most significant bits to all 1's, whereas converting the 8-bit version of +3 (0000 0011) to the 16-bit version (0000 0000 0000 0011) involves setting the 8 most

	SIGNED	UNSIGNED

8-bit by 8-bit	MOV AL, divisor
	
	CBW
	
	IDIV dividend
		MOV AL, divisor
		
		MOV AH, 0
		
		DIV dividend

16-bit by 16-bit	MOV AX, divisor
	
	CWD
	
	IDIV dividend
		MOV AX, divisor
		
		MOV DX, 0
		
		DIV dividend

32-bit by 32-bit	MOV EAX, divisor
	
	CDQ
	
	IDIV dividend
		MOV EAX, divisor
		
		MOV EDX, 0
		
		DIV dividend

Figure 3.11 Performing equal-length divisions.

significant bits to all 0's. The rule is simple: just extend the leftmost bit (sometimes called the sign bit) of the 8-bit version into every bit position in the most significant half of the 16-bit version. We've already seen that the MOVSX (Move with Sign-extend) instruction does this operation, but it won't work for the exotic destinations DXAX and EDXEAX. The 386 provides special-purpose instructions to handle these cases. These instructions, when initially incorporated into the 8086, were named SEX (sign extend) but were renamed (prior to ever appearing in Intel literature) to the more conservative CBW (convert *byte* to *word*) and CWD (convert *word* to *doubleword*). The CBW is a single-byte opcode instruction that performs the equivalent of MOVSX AX,AL; the CWD instruction extends the sign bit of AX into all bits of DX. Figure 3.11 summarizes the steps for performing divisions by equal-length operands. The advent of the 32-bit 386 processor caused two new sign extension instructions to be added: CWDE extends the top bit of AX into upper 16 bits of EAX; CDQ extends the top bit of EAX into all bits of EDX.

Effective Address Arithmetic Instruction (LEA) All the arithmetic instructions we have discussed so far have a simple building-block quality to them: they operate on at most two operands, and perform only one operation on those operands. This makes perfect sense—it would be silly to expect the hardware of a processor to do the job of a high-level compiler, interpreting and evaluating expressions of arbitrary complexity. But the 386 processor does do some complicated arithmetic in one context: when it calculates memory addresses involving base and/or indexing registers. We have seen in Chapter 2 that in a single memory address there can be an addition of as many as three terms, plus a multiplication for scaling. Since the hardware for such complicated arithmetic is already there, wouldn't it be nice if we could access it? The LEA (load effective address) instruction lets us do so.

The LEA instruction looks just like a MOV instruction with a doubleword destination (first) operand and a memory address source (second) operand. The difference is that LEA does not fetch any data from memory; instead, it loads the calculated address of the memory into the destination register. Because the result is a memory address, the destination is a doubleword register. The source is a memory operand of any size: byte, word, or doubleword.

For an example of LEA usage, let's recall the employee records example from Chapter 2. Suppose EBX points to an array of employee records, EDI is an index into that array pointing to a particular record, and the name of an employee is always found at the tenth byte within that employee's record. Since the name is a string of characters, it can be scanned using the string instructions that we discuss later in this chapter. The string instructions require the string pointer to be in the ESI register, so we'll want to load ESI with the pointer EBX + EDI + 10. Without the LEA instruction, we would be forced to use a sequence of instructions, such as:

```
MOV  ESI,10
ADD  ESI,EBX
ADD  ESI,EDI
```

LEA lets us replace the above sequence of arithmetic instructions with the single instruction:

```
LEA ESI,[EBX + EDI + 10]
```

Another noteworthy property of the LEA instruction is that it does not change the value of any flags. We can sometimes exploit this. For example, suppose we have made a test of memory pointed to by EBX, and we wish to advance the EBX pointer by four bytes before acting on the test we have made. We could code the instruction:

```
ADD EBX,4
```

but the ADD instruction will destroy the flag settings from our test. Even the INC instruction will destroy all the arithmetic flags except Carry. Without the LEA instruction, we would have to place a PUSHF above the ADD and a POPF below it. With LEA, we solve the problem by coding:

```
LEA EBX,[EBX + 4]
```

Finally, we note that LEA is often used by assembly language programmers to load a pointer to a fixed location in memory. For example, if ARRAY is a sequence of bytes at a fixed memory location, many programmers will load the pointer to ARRAY using the instruction:

    LEA ESI,ARRAY

Note that this consumes one more byte of program space than the equivalent instruction:

    MOV ESI,OFFSET ARRAY

Perhaps the programmer has deliberately sacrificed terseness in the object code for terseness in the source code. We suspect, however, that most programmers are unaware that they are sacrificing a byte of program space by using LEA to load a fixed address. The assembler could be instructed to silently substitute the more efficient MOV whenever it sees a fixed-address LEA (but most 86 family assemblers don't).

Decimal Arithmetic   Many business applications involve inputting numbers as character strings, performing a small amount of arithmetic, and then outputting the results as specially formatted character strings. For example, the input may be an amount of money to be withdrawn, the arithmetic may be subtraction against a balance, and the output may be a carefully printed check for the desired amount. In order to perform the arithmetic, we can first convert the numbers from characters into binary integers, then use the 386's integer arithmetic instructions to do the computation, and finally convert the results back into characters. If the amount of arithmetic is small, more time may be spent performing the conversions than performing the arithmetic. In such cases it may be more efficient to omit the conversions and perform the arithmetic directly on the decimal representation of the input numbers. Indeed, the business programming language COBOL provides just such facilities.

The 386 offers limited support for decimal arithmetic. We will briefly describe the relevant instructions. A more detailed description of decimal arithmetic, with algorithms, is given in reference 4.

The most popular decimal encoding is *binary coded decimal* or BCD. In this encoding, each nibble of the encoding is interpreted as a decimal digit. Table 3.14 lists the encoding of each decimal digit. Note that the BCD value of a number is obtained by simply "misinterpreting" the hexadecimal value of a number as a decimal value. The six hex digits A,B,C,D,E, and F are unused (wasted) in the BCD notation. Thus, binary notation is more compact than BCD. For example, the number 125 can be represented in 8 bits in binary notation (0111 1101) but requires 12 bits in BCD (0001 0010 0101).

How about arithmetic on numbers represented in BCD notation? Can BCD numbers be added, subtracted, multiplied, and divided? One way to do this is to have BCD addition, BCD subtraction, BCD multiplication, and BCD division included in

Table 3.14 BCD Encoding of Decimal Digits

Digit:	0	1	2	3	4
Encoding:	0000	0001	0010	0011	0100
Digit:	5	6	7	8	9
Encoding:	0101	0110	0111	1000	1001

the instruction set of the computer in place of (or in addition to) the conventional binary addition, binary subtraction, binary multiplication, and binary division instructions. Another solution is to use the binary arithmetic instructions on the BCD numbers, knowing full well that the wrong BCD answer will be obtained and then executing a special *adjustment* instruction that will convert the answer to the correct answer in BCD notation. The latter solution is used by the 386.

Consider, for example, adding the BCD representation of 23 to the BCD representation of 14 by using the (8-bit) binary addition instruction. Lo and behold, the binary addition gives 37, the correct BCD result! So in this example, no adjustment is necessary. Let's push our luck further and try to add 29 in BCD to 14 in BCD. The answer, 3D hexadecimal, is not correct because the hex digit D does not represent a decimal digit. Our calculation has carried the lower nibble into a gap of 6 unused codes. We must add 6 to the result to obtain the correct answer 43. A more subtle case occurs when we try adding 29 and 18. In this addition, we pass all the way though the gap and obtain the plausible but incorrect result of 41. We must still add 6 to obtain the correct result 47.

The DAA (decimal adjust after addition) instruction assumes that the result of a binary addition has just been placed in the AL register. DAA determines if an adjustment is necessary; if so, it makes the adjustment. In the last example given, the 386 must know that a carry was generated from the addition of the low-order nibbles 9 and 8. The 386 records this information in its *auxiliary carry* flag, which exists solely for the benefit of the adjustment instructions of this section.

The DAS (decimal adjust after subtraction) instruction makes similar adjustments after a binary subtraction from AL to transform AL into the correct BCD result.

In addition to adjusting AL to a BCD answer, both DAA and DAS set the carry flag to indicate if the BCD arithmetic yielded a carry. Thus, we can perform multiple-precision BCD arithmetic just like binary arithmetic: by using ADC (SBB) on the subsequent, high-order operand bytes. What about BCD multiplication and division? Alas, it is not possible to apply an adjustment for multiplication because the BCD result is buried under and indistinguishable from the cross terms generated. Similarly, a divide adjustment is not possible. So, if we need to perform multiplication or division on decimal numbers, we'll need to use the following decimal representation.

The BCD representation discussed so far is more accurately referred to as *packed BCD* because two digits are packed into a byte. Another representation, called *unpacked BCD*, contains only one digit per byte. The digit is contained in the four least significant bits; the most significant bits have no bearing on the value of the represented number. One example of unpacked BCD is the ASCII representation of digits. ASCII is a

Table 3.15 ASCII Representation of Digits

Digit	ASCII
0	011 0000
1	011 0001
2	011 0010
3	011 0011
4	011 0100
5	011 0101
6	011 0110
7	011 0111
8	011 1000
9	011 1001

seven-bit representation of a set of characters. The ASCII representation of digits are shown in Table 3.15. The three most significant bits contain 011, which is not relevant to the digit value.

Addition and subtraction of unpacked BCD representations can be adjusted in a manner similar to the packed BCD adjustments, except the least significant digit is the only one affected. Unlike packed BCD, multiplication and division adjustments are possible for unpacked BCD. The instructions that perform these four adjustments are called ASCII adjustment instructions (because ASCII is the most common example of unpacked BCD), and they are AAA (ASCII adjust after addition), AAS (ASCII adjust after subtraction), AAM (ASCII adjust after multiplication), and AAD (ASCII adjust before division).

As an example of unpacked BCD multiplication, consider multiplying 9 by 4. Assume unpacked 9 (0000 1001) is in the BL register and unpacked 4 (0000 0100) is in the AL register. Applying the (unsigned) binary multiplication instruction, specifying BL as the multiplier (IMUL AL, BL) will put the 16-bit binary product, namely 36 (0000 0000 0010 0100), in AX. The multiplication adjustment (AAM) must decompose the binary 36 in AX into 3 (0000 0011) in AH and 6 (0000 0110) in AL. This is nothing more than dividing the contents of AL by ten and placing the quotient in AH and the remainder in AL. In fact, it's no coincidence that the AAM instruction is two bytes long (it appears as though one byte would have sufficed) with the second byte being nothing more than the binary representation of ten (0000 1010). In reality, the AAM instruction is a kind of division instruction (although it doesn't put the remainder and quotient in the same places that DIV and IDIV do) with the divisor operand contained in the second byte of the instruction. Don't be surprised if changing the second byte from ten (0000 1010) to seven (0000 0111) results in a divide-by-seven instruction (although Intel makes no such promise). It follows that putting sixteen (0001 0000) in the second byte should result in converting a packed BCD number in AL into an unpacked BCD number in AH and AL.

Next consider an unpacked BCD division, such as 42 divided by 6. Assume unpacked 42 is in AX (0000 0100 in AH, 0000 0010 in AL) and unpacked 6 (0000 0110) is in BL. The unpacked representation of a single-digit number, such as 6, is nothing more than its binary representation. So let's put the dividend, 42, into binary. This can be done by multiplying the contents of AH by ten and adding it to the contents of AL. A binary division of AL (binary 42) by BL (6) would then give the binary representation of 7 in AL. But binary 7 is nothing more than unpacked 7, so the unpacked division is complete.

There are a couple of points to note from the preceding example. First, division adjustment (AAD) consists of multiplying AH by ten, adding in AL, and leaving the result in AL. (Again, it's no coincidence that the second byte of the AAD instruction is a ten.) Second, division adjustment *precedes* the division operations, whereas addition, subtraction, and multiplication adjustments *follow* the corresponding arithmetic operation. In other words, the addition, subtraction, and multiplication adjustments correct a bad (that is, non-BCD) result, whereas the division adjustment prevents a bad result from occurring.

Logical Instructions

The 386 logical instructions consist of Boolean instructions and shift/rotate instructions as summarized in Table 3.16.

Boolean Instructions   The Boolean instructions are NOT, AND, OR (inclusive or), XOR (exclusive or), and TEST. Examples of NOT are shown in Table 3.9; examples of the others, in Table 3.8.

The AND, OR, and XOR instructions perform a logical function between each bit of a source operand and the corresponding bit of a destination operand and place the result back in the bit of the destination operand. The NOT instruction has only one operand; it performs its function on each bit of that operand and places the result back in that same bit. The logical functions performed by these instructions are defined in Table 3.17.

Table 3.16   Logical Instructions

AND:	DEST and SOURCE → DEST
TEST:	DEST and SOURCE → ?
OR:	DEST or SOURCE → DEST
XOR:	DEST xor SOURCE → DEST
NOT:	not DEST → DEST

SHL (shift logical left):	CF ← DEST ← 0
SHR (shift logical right):	0 → DEST → CF
SAL (shift arithmetic left):	same as SHL
SAR (shift arithmetic right):	sign → DEST → CF

ROL (rotate left):	⟲ DEST ⟳
ROR (rotate right):	⟳ DEST ⟳
RCL (rotate left through carry):	⟲ CF ← DEST ⟳
RCR (rotate right through carry):	⟳ CF → DEST ⟳

The *and* function is useful for clearing (sometimes called *masking*) specified bit positions in a number; one operand specifies the bit positions and the other specifies the number. For example, we can clear the most significant four bits in an 8-bit number by *anding* that number with 0000 1111. (Recall that it was necessary to clear the most significant four bits of an unpacked decimal number prior to performing a decimal multiplication or division.)

In a similar manner, the *or* function and *exclusive-or* function are useful for setting and complementing specified bit positions in a number. For example, we can set the most significant bit in an 8-bit number by *oring* the number with 1000 0000, and we can complement the middle four bits in an 8-bit number by *exclusive-oring* that number with 0011 1100. The XOR instruction provides an efficient way to set a register to zero (simply *xor* the register with itself). The *not* function is useful for complementing every bit in a number; it is equivalent to *exclusive-oring* that number with all 1's.

The TEST instruction combines the features of the AND and CMP instructions. Like the AND instruction, TEST performs an *and* function between corresponding bits of two operands. Like CMP, TEST retains only the flag settings and not the result. Such an instruction is useful for examining specified bit positions in a number to determine if any of them are 1. Again, one operand specifies the bit positions and the other specifies the number. If the (discarded) result is nonzero, as indicated by the ZF flag (ZF = 0 means result is not zero), then at least one of the specified bits is a 1. For example, to determine if any of the least significant four bits of BL are 1, execute a TEST instruction that designates BL and 0000 1111 as its operands, then execute a conditional jump instruction that jumps if ZF is 0. Note that the AND instruction could have been used in place of the TEST instruction, but this would have destroyed the initial value of one of the operands because the AND instruction doesn't discard its result.

Shift/Rotate Instructions   The shift instructions provide a very efficient mechanism for doubling or halving a number (fewer bytes and fewer cycles than doing a multiplication or division). To double an unsigned number, just shift all bits one

Table 3.17 Definition of Logical Functions

	One Operand	
	Source Bit	Not
	0	1
	1	0

	Two Operands			
Source Bit	Destination Bit	And	Or	Exclusive-Or
0	0	0	0	0
0	1	0	1	1
1	0	0	1	1
1	1	1	1	0

position to the left and fill in the vacated rightmost bit with a 0. If the bit that was shifted off the left end is placed into CF, an out-of-range result can be detected by testing CF for a 1. For example, doubling the number 65 (0100 0001) by shifting left results in 130 (1000 0010) with CF becoming 0 (in-range), whereas shifting left the number 130 (1000 0010) results in 4 (0000 0100) with CF becoming 1 (out-of- range). Similarly, halving an unsigned number is accomplished by shifting all bits one position to the right, filling in the vacated bit position with a 0, and placing into CF the bit that was shifted off the right end. In this case, CF = 1 indicates that the number was not even. For example, halving the number 9 (0000 1001) results in 4 (0000 0100) with CF becoming 1.

The instructions that perform the doubling and halving of unsigned numbers are SHL (shift left) and SHR (shift right). Two other shifts, SAL (shift arithmetic left) and SAR (shift arithmetic right), are useful for doubling and halving signed numbers.

The difference between halving a signed number, SAR, and halving an unsigned number, SHR, is that in the former the leftmost bit (sign bit) must remain unchanged. For example, halving $+6$ (0000 0110) should result in $+3$ (0000 0011) and halving -120 (1000 1000) should result in -60 (1100 0100). Thus SAR will shift all bits one position to the right but at the same time leave the sign bit unchanged. SHR, on the other hand, puts a 0 into the sign bit.

Observe that using the SAR instruction to halve the $+5$ (0000 0101) gives $+2$ (0000 0010), and using it to halve -5 (1111 1011) gives -3 (1111 1101). Right-shifting an odd number always gives a result that is smaller than half the number (-3 is smaller than $-2\ 1/2$). Unfortunately this is not the result obtained by the IDIV instruction; dividing -5 by 2 using IDIV gives -2.

There is no distinction between doubling a signed number and doubling an unsigned number. So, in fact, SHL and SAL are simply two different names for the same instructions.

The 386 offers two instructions, SHLD and SHRD, that perform double-length (64-bit) shifts. They are special-purpose instructions, designed to allow efficient movement of a block of bits. We'll discuss SHLD and SHRD in the section on bit-array instructions later in this chapter.

The rotate instructions provide the ability to rearrange the bits in a number. ROL (rotate left) and ROR (rotate right) permit left or right rotation of the bits; the bit that falls off one end is rotated around to fill in the vacated position on the other end. Two other rotate instructions, RCL (rotate with carry left) and RCR (rotate with carry right), permit the carry flag CF to participate in the rotation; the bit that falls off one end winds up in CF, and the bit that was in CF is rotated around into the vacated bit—sort of a computerized version of musical chairs.

The operand to be shifted or rotated can be in memory or in a register. Furthermore, the operand can be 8, 16, or 32 bits; and the shift or rotation can be for a predetermined number of bits (fixed) or any number of bits (variable). In the fixed case, the distance is specified in the instruction; in the variable case, the distance is specified in CL, the COUNT register (another example of a specialized use of one of the general registers). Examples of the shift/rotate instructions are shown in Table 3.18. (The fixed shifts and rotates in the 8086 are limited to moving a distance of one bit only.)

Table 3.18 Examples of Shift/Rotate Instructions

	fixed	variable
register	opcode DL,1	opcode DL,CL
	opcode BX,13	opcode AX,CL
	opcode ESI,2	opcode EBX,CL
memory	opcode MEM_BYTE,2	opcode MEM_BYTE,CL
	opcodeMEM_WORD,1	opcode MEM_WORD,CL
	opcode MEM_DWORD,20	opcode MEM_DWORD,CL

where opcode is any of the following: SHL SHR SAL SAR ROL ROR RCL RCR

String Instructions

A *string* is simply a sequence of bytes, words, or doublewords in memory. A string operation is an operation that is performed on each item in a string. An example is a string move, which moves an entire string from one area of memory to another. Since string operations usually involve repetitions, they could take a long time to execute. The 386 has a set of instructions that decreases the time required to perform string operations. This speed up is accomplished by (1) having a powerful set of primitive instructions so that the time taken to process each item in the string is reduced, and (2) eliminating bookkeeping and overhead that are usually performed between the processing of successive items. The string primitives are summarized in Table 3.19.

Elementary String Instructions   To illustrate how string instructions speed up the processing of strings, consider how a sequence of bytes would be moved. We'll need some way of denoting where the bytes are now and where we'd like them to be. Let's use ESI (SOURCE INDEX) and EDI (DESTINATION INDEX) for that purpose. We'll point ESI to the first byte in the sequence to be moved, and we'll point EDI to the place the sequence is going. A likely place to store the count of the number of bytes to be moved would be ECX, the count register. If ECX is initially zero, no bytes should be moved. The steps for performing the string move are as follows:

1.   If ECX contains zero, we're done.

2.   Fetch the byte pointed to by ESI.

3.   Store that byte into the location pointed to by EDI.

4.   Increment ESI by 1.

5.   Increment EDI by 1.

6.   Decrement ECX by 1.

7.   Go back to step 1 and repeat.

Table 3.19 String Primitives

MOVS	move	[EDI] → [ESI] update ESI,EDI
CMPS	compare	[ESI] − [EDI] is discarded, flags set update ESI,EDI
SCAS	scan	accumulator − [EDI] is discarded, flags set update EDI
INS	input	input port → [EDI] update EDI
OUTS	output	[ESI] → output port update ESI
LODS	load	[ESI] → accumulator update ESI
STOS	store	accumulator → [EDI] update EDI

where the accumulator is AL for byte operations, AX for word operations, EAX for doubleword operations

Steps 2 and 3 perform the actual move of each byte. Steps 4–6 are bookkeeping. Steps 1 and 7 are overhead. The actual move of each byte can be speeded up by having a one-byte primitive instruction that transfers the byte pointed to by ESI to the byte pointed to by EDI. Furthermore, if that primitive instruction also incremented ESI and EDI, part of the explicit bookkeeping would be eliminated. With such a primitive, the string move is simplified to the following:

1.   If ECX contains zero, we're done.

2.   Perform "move-primitive."

3.   Decrement ECX by 1.

4.   Go back to step 1 and repeat.

Steps 1, 3, and 4 could be eliminated if the move-primitive were "souped up" to incorporate a test-decrement-and-repeat based on ECX. The result is a single step that incorporates the move-primitive within it. The string move now becomes as follows:

1.   Soup up the accompanying primitive.

   1a. Move-primitive

The 386 has an instruction, MOVS (move string element), which is the move-primitive described above. Furthermore, any string primitive can be "souped up" by preceding it with a special one-byte prefix called a *repeat prefix*. The combination of the repeat prefix and the MOVS primitive forms a two-byte instruction and is written as REP MOVS.

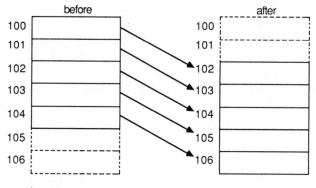

Figure 3.12 An overlapping move.

There can be a problem if the place that the sequence of bytes goes to overlaps the place that it came from. For example, consider moving the five bytes starting at location 100 into the five bytes starting at location 102 as shown in Figure 3.12. The bytes at 100 and 101 are copied successfully into 102 and 103. But when it comes time to copy the byte from 102 into 104, a problem occurs; the byte in 102 is not the byte that was there originally but rather the byte that came from 100. So the byte from 100 gets copied again, this time into 104. Eventually, it will also get into 106. Similarly, the byte from 101 will wind up in 103 and 105.

This problem would have been avoided completely if the bytes were moved in reverse order: the byte from 104 moved first, then the byte from 103, and so forth. However, if the overlap were in the opposite direction (100 through 104 into 98 through 102), the reverse move would have the problem, and the forward move would work properly.

Be aware that one man's curse might be another man's blessing. The "curse" of overlapped string moves becomes a useful feature when we need to repeat a pattern of bytes over a portion of memory (look carefully at the preceding example).

The 386 has a flag called DF (direction flag), which governs the direction in which strings are processed. If DF = 0, strings are considered as progressing in the forward direction (toward higher addresses) starting from the locations in ESI and EDI. If DF = 1, they progress in the reverse direction. This will tell the string primitives to decrement rather than increment ESI and EDI. Thus, if an overlapped move moves bytes to higher locations (thereby necessitating a reverse move), DF should be initialized to 1. Depending on the setting of DF, ESI and EDI will contain either the lowest locations (DF = 0) or the highest locations (DF = 1) in the strings. Instructions for setting and clearing DF (STD, CLD) will be discussed later under Flag Instructions.

Certain string operations are more efficiently performed on words or doublewords instead of bytes. A move, for example, would go much faster if the elements being moved were doublewords. To allow for word/doubleword strings, each string primitive instruction comes in two forms: one for the byte operation and one for the word/doubleword operation. The operand size prefix, discussed in Chapter 2, makes the distinction between the word and doubleword operations.

The move-primitive for words/doublewords is similar to the move-primitive for bytes except that ESI and EDI are incremented (decremented if DF = 1) by 2 or 4 instead of by 1. ECX, however, is always decremented by 1, and we must therefore initialize it to contain the number of words or doublewords (not bytes) if we are using word/doubleword primitives.

Let's now look at examples of repeated move-primitives. Repeated doubleword, word, and byte moves are written as:

```
MOV ESI,OFFSET MEM_DWORD1          ; source index points to
                                   ; MEM_DWORD1
MOV EDI,OFFSET MEM_DWORD2          ; destination index points to
                                   ; MEM_DWORD2
MOV ECX,DWORDS_COUNT               ; load the number of doublewords
REP   MOVS MEM_DWORD2,MEM_DWORD1   ; repeated doubleword move
MOV ESI,OFFSET MEM_WORD1           ; source index points to
                                   ; MEM_WORD1
MOV EDI,OFFSET MEM_WORD2           ; destination index points to
                                   ; MEM_WORD2
MOV ECX,WORDS_COUNT                ; load the number of words
REP   MOVS MEM_WORD2,MEM_WORD1     ; repeated word move
MOV ESI,OFFSET MEM_BYTE1           ; source index points to
                                   ; MEM_BYTE1
MOV EDI,OFFSET MEM_BYTE2           ; destination index points to
                                   ; MEM_BYTE2
MOV ECX,BYTES_COUNT                ; load the number of bytes
REP   MOVS MEM_BYTE2,MEM_BYTE1     ; repeated byte move
```

Note that the move-primitive moves the contents of the memory address pointed to by ESI into the memory address pointed to by EDI. Thus it appears that we should not need to specify any operands to the move-primitive since it has no choice as to which item to move and where. However, the assembler must decide whether to generate a byte, word, or doubleword move and it does this by observing whether the operands are bytes, words, or doublewords (they must both be of the same type).

An alternative method of specifying the operand size is to provide a separate mnemonic for each form of a string-move instruction. Thus, any of the three mnemonics—MOVSB, MOVSW, or MOVSD—may be used without operands for the string-move primitive. This method is preferred by many assembly language programmers because it is more concise and because it emphasizes the fact that the memory operands are predetermined. The multiple-mnemonic option is available for all of the string instructions we'll be discussing.

Now let's consider another string operation, namely scanning through a sequence of bytes looking for any byte other than a particular byte. An example would be finding the first nonzero entry in a table. Let's use EDI to point to the sequence and ECX to contain the number of bytes in the sequence. Place the byte being rejected into AL. The steps for performing the scan are as follows:

1.   If ECX contains zero, we're done.

2.   Compare AL to the byte pointed to by EDI. (Comparing means subtracting and setting flags, ZF in particular, while changing neither AL nor the memory byte.)

3.   Increment (decrement if DF = 1) EDI by 1.

4.   Decrement ECX by 1.

5.   If ZF = true, the two bytes were identical, so go back to step 1 and repeat.

Steps 2 and 3 are done by the 386 scan-primitive SCAS (scan string element). Steps 1, 4, and 5 are done if the scan-primitive is "souped up" with the repeat prefix. Word and doubleword scanning is similar to byte scanning except that AX is used in place of AL, and ESI is incremented (decremented) by 2 or 4 instead of by 1.

Note that the repeat prefix behaves slightly differently with the scan-primitive than it does with the move-primitive; with the scan it tests the ZF flag before deciding to repeat. In general, the repeat prefix will test the ZF flag whenever the accompanying primitive string instruction is one which may modify the ZF flag. (MOVS never affects the ZF flag; SCAS sets or clears ZF depending on whether the bytes match or not.)

Another string operation is scanning through a sequence of bytes to find a particular value. For example, if the bytes contain ASCII character codes, this operation finds the first occurrence of a specific character in a message. This is done by using a repeat prefix on the scan-primitive instruction as was done in the previous scanning operation, except that now the condition for repetition is ZF = 0. Since the testing of ZF is dictated by the repeat prefix, that prefix must indicate which value of ZF is to cause repetitions. This is specified by a bit in the prefix.

The assembly language mnemonics for these forms of repeat are REPZ (repeat while ZF set) and REPNZ (repeat while not ZF set). Alternate names for these are REPE (repeat while equal) and REPNE (repeat while not equal); these names more clearly indicate the underlying condition on which they are looping. In those cases where the repeat prefix does not test the ZF flag, the repeat prefix is written simply as REP, which is a synonym for REPZ.

The next string operation compares two sequences of bytes to see which one should come first. In particular, if the bytes contain ASCII character codes, this operation compares the sequence with respect to lexicographical order. (Lexicographical is simply a fancy term for alphabetical but takes nonalphabetic characters into account as well.) Again assume that the locations of the two sequences are in ESI and EDI, and the number of bytes to be compared (size of the shorter sequence) is contained in ECX. The steps for performing the string comparisons are as follows:

1.   If ECX contains zero, we're done.

2.   Fetch the byte pointed to by ESI.

3.   Compare it to the byte pointed to by EDI.

4.   Increment (decrement if DF = 1) ESI by 1.

5.   Increment (decrement if DF = 1) EDI by 1.

6.   Decrement ECX by 1.

7.   If ZF = true, the two bytes are identical, so go back to step 1 and repeat.

Steps 2, 3, 4, and 5 are done by the 386 compare-primitive CMPS (compare string elements), and the remaining steps are done if a repeat prefix (REPE) is appended to the CMPS instruction. Word/doubleword comparing is similar to byte comparing, except ESI and EDI are incremented or decremented by 2 or by 4 instead of by 1.

A word of explanation is in order here. As long as the bytes being compared in step 3 are identical, the zero flag (ZF) will be set to true and step 7 will keep looping back. The looping ends when either the two bytes are not identical (step 7 will no longer loop back) or the end of the shorter string is reached (step 1 will skip us out of the loop). After the looping ends, we can test ZF to see if we reached the end of the shorter string. (ZF will still be true in that case.) If we did not, we can test the carry flag (CF) to determine which string is greater. (CF = true means the string pointed at by EDI is greater.)

The next two string primitives permit reading data from an input device into consecutive memory locations and writing data from consecutive memory locations to an output device. This facilitates transfers of large blocks of data between memory and external devices; such block transfers occur frequently when performing disk input or output. The input-primitive (INS) transfers data from the input port specified by DX to the byte, word, or doubleword pointed to by EDI and increments (decrements if DF = 1) EDI by 1, 2, or 4. Similarly, the output-primitive (OUTS) transfers the byte, word, or doubleword pointed to by ESI to the output port specified by DX and increments (decrements if DF = 1) ESI by 1, 2, or 4. These two instructions, INS and OUTS, were added to the 86 family starting with the 186.

The final two string primitives are LODS (load string element) and STOS (store string element). The load-primitive loads the byte, word, or doubleword pointed to by ESI into AL, AX, or EAX and increments (decrements if DF = 1) ESI by 1, 2, or 4. The store-primitive stores the contents of AL, AX, or EAX into the memory operand pointed to by EDI and increments (decrements if DF = 1) EDI by 1, 2, or 4. Unlike the previous primitives, these two primitives were not intended to be used with the repeat prefix. They were included for use in building up more complicated string operations. However, the store primitive does perform a useful function when used in conjunction with the repeat prefix: it fills every byte or word of a sequence with the same value. (This could also be done with an overlapped string move but slightly less efficiently, requiring two strings instead of one.) A repeat prefix on the load-primitive repeatedly loads AL, AX, or EAX with successive memory operands in a sequence, each time destroying the previous value loaded. Such an operation is useful only to exercise the memory hardware.

Complex String Instructions   The five primitive string instructions provide the most common string operations. It would be a hopeless task to provide a primitive instruction for all conceivable operations. A strategy that makes more sense is to provide a means of building up efficient complicated string instructions, possibly using some of the primitives as building blocks. As an example, consider the operation of negating a sequence of bytes where each byte represents an 8-bit signed number. Let ESI point to the first byte of the sequence, and let EDI point to where the first byte of the negated sequence is to be placed. Let ECX contain the count of the number of bytes in the sequence. The steps for performing this operation are as follows:

1.   If ECX contains zero, we're done, so skip over the following steps.

2.   Fetch the byte pointed to by ESI.

3.   Increment ESI by 1.

4.   Negate the byte fetched.

5.   Store the result into the byte pointed to by EDI.

6.   Increment EDI by 1.

7.   Decrement ECX by 1.

8.   Go back to step 2 if ECX is not zero.

Analogous to the previous examples, we would like to have a primitive instruction that performs steps 2, 3, 4, 5, and 6. There is none! So the next best thing would be to build up these steps from 386 instructions. If some of the building blocks are string primitives, the incrementing of ESI and EDI can be done at no additional expense. Specifically, steps 2 and 3 can be done by the load-primitive, 4 by a negate instruction, and 5 and 6 by a store- primitive. This simplifies the task to:

1.   If ECX contains zero, we're done; so skip over the following steps.

2.   Perform "load-primitive."

3.   Negate byte in AL.

4.   Perform "store-primitive."

5.   Decrement ECX by 1.

6.   Go back to step 2 if ECX is not zero.

Steps 1, 5, and 6 were previously accomplished by souping up a string primitive with the repeat prefix. In this case, the body of the loop consists of more than just a string primitive, and thus the repeat prefix cannot be used. What is needed are a few efficient instructions that simulate the complex actions of the repeat prefix. Step 1 requires a conditional jump instruction that jumps if ECX contains zero. The destination of the jump should be specified in as few bits as possible. So naturally the 386 has an instruction, JECXZ, that will jump if ECX contains zero. The destination of the jump is specified in a single byte of the instruction; that byte contains the distance (as a signed number of bytes) from the JECXZ instruction to the destination. Our next wish would be for an instruction that decrements ECX and then jumps if ECX is not zero. That instruction also exists and is called LOOP; the destination of the jump in a LOOP instruction is specified in a single byte exactly as was done in JECXZ. The example now becomes the following:

1. JECXZ over the following steps.

2. Perform "load-primitive."

3. Negate the byte in AL.

4. Perform "store-primitive."

5. LOOP back to step 2.

Each step represents a single 386 instruction. The five instructions are:

```
        JECXZ L2
    L1:
        LODS MEMBYTE1
        NEG AL
        STOS MEMBYTE2
        LOOP L1
    L2:
```

The LOOP instruction introduced above does a jump based on the value of ECX. But we have already seen, for some string operations, that it is desirable to loop based on the setting of the ZF flag. The corresponding 386 instructions are LOOPZ (loop if ZF true) and LOOPNZ (loop if not ZF true). Of course, both LOOPZ and LOOPNZ decrement ECX and test it for zero before looping. Alternate names for these instructions are LOOPE (loop if equal) and LOOPNE (loop if not equal); these names more clearly indicate the underlying condition on which we are looping.

As an example of using the LOOPNZ instruction, consider the previous example of negating a sequence of bytes. However, this time the number of bytes is unspecified. It is known that none of the bytes in the sequence is zero. However, the sequence is followed by a zero byte. The steps now become as follows:

```
    L1:
        LODS MEMBYTE1
        NEG AL
        STOS MEMBYTE2
        LOOPNZ L1
```

Note that the initial JECXZ instruction is not necessary here. Why?

Let's wrap up the discussion on strings by considering an example that translates numbers between 0 and 15 into a *Gray code*. In a Gray code only one bit changes between adjacent values. An example of a Gray code for the numbers 0 through 15 is the following:

Binary	Gray
0000	0000
0001	0001
0010	0011
0011	0010
0100	0110
0101	0100
0110	0101
0111	0111
1000	1111
1001	1110
1010	1100
1011	1101
1100	1001
1101	1011
1110	1010
1111	1000

Assume that there is a sequence of bytes starting at MEMBYTE1 and containing binary numbers between 0 and 15. Also assume that ECX contains the number of bytes in the sequence. Further, assume that the sequence of sixteen bytes starting at GRAY is a Gray code translation table (the sixteen values given above). Notice that the conditions are ideal for using the XLATB instruction. Let's place the translated sequence into memory starting at MEMBYTE2. The steps for pulling this off are as shown:

```
        MOV ESI,OFFSET MEMBYTE1
        MOV EDI,OFFSET MEMBYTE2
        MOV EBX,GRAY
        JECXZ DONE
L1:
        LODS MEMBYTE1
        XLATB
        STOS MEMBYTE2
        LOOP L1
```

The XLATB instruction fits in perfectly with string loops as if it were designed for this purpose. It was!

Unconditional Transfer Instructions

The main types of unconditional transfer instructions in the 386 are jumps, calls, and returns. *Jumps* load a value into the instruction pointer, thereby breaking the sequential execution of instructions. *Calls* do the same thing, but first they save the current value of the instruction pointer on the stack so that, at some time in the future, execution can continue from where it left off. *Returns* occur at that time in the future: they remove an entry from the stack and place it back into the instruction pointer, thereby resuming the previous execution. Calls and returns are the mechanism used to invoke procedures.

The operands to jump instructions and call instructions come in two major flavors, *direct* and *indirect*. Most jumps and calls are direct—the operand tells us immediately where to go. Occasionally, an indirect transfer is used. An indirect transfer gives us the runaround: it tells us where to go to find out where to go. Indirect transfers are useful when we don't know where we want to go but must first compute it. For example, the indirect jump:

JMP TABLE[EBX*4]

fetches the destination from the memory array TABLE, indexed by the EBX register.

We do not need to provide an operand to the return instruction telling us where to return. The destination for the return is always found in the same place: on the top of the stack. Thus all returns are a form of indirect jump.

Let's consider for a moment the "nitty-gritty" mechanics of a jump or call instruction. Recall that the 386 maintains an instruction pointer that tells where in memory the next instruction is to come from. The CALL instruction manipulates the instruction pointer by performing the following steps:

1.   Increment the instruction pointer beyond the CALL instruction.

2.   Push the updated instruction pointer onto the stack.

3.   Fetch the destination of the CALL, and set the instruction pointer to that location.

Note that step 1 must be performed for all nontransfer instructions, simply to insure that the program follows its natural progression from one instruction to the next. For simplicity, then, the instruction pointer is incremented prior to executing *every* instruction, no matter what it is. In particular, the steps taken for a JMP instruction are as follows:

1.   Increment the instruction pointer beyond the JMP instruction.

2.   Fetch the destination of the JMP, and set the instruction pointer to that location.

Here it appears that step 1 is irrelevant, since the instruction pointer is about to be reset anyway. But let's consider how the destination operand of a direct jump is encoded. As an example, suppose the instruction pointer after step 1 has a value of 100008, and the destination of the jump is location 100000. Thus the instruction specifies that we jump back eight bytes from the end of the instruction. The value 100000 could have been contained in four bytes of the jump instruction and, indeed, in many processors it is. But this has two disadvantages. First, many jumps are to nearby places, and yet the instruction must dedicate four bytes to specifying the jump destination. Second, if for some reason the entire section of code from location 100000 to 100008 must be moved and placed at location 200000 to 200008, the jump instruction specifying location 100000 would no longer jump back by eight bytes. (Sections of code that can be moved and still execute properly are sometimes called *position-independent code*.) If the jump instruction did not specify 100000 but merely specified -8, then (1) the jump destination would fit in one byte and (2) the code would be position-independent. Thus direct jumps and calls specify not the destination, but rather the difference (as a signed number of bytes) from the point beyond the jump or call instruction to the destination. Furthermore, if that difference for a jump instruction can fit into eight bits (a very frequent occurrence), a short form of the direct jump instruction can be used, which is three bytes shorter than the regular direct jump. There is no short form of the call instruction because calls to nearby locations are not that frequent an occurrence.

Now we can see why it matters precisely when we increment the instruction pointer in a jump or call instruction. Each direct operand is encoded as a difference to be added to the instruction pointer to compute the destination. Since the instruction pointer is incremented *before* the jump or call is executed, the offset operand is added to the location *following* the jump or call instruction.

We've just seen two good reasons for using differences (relative offsets) rather than actual locations as jump destinations. Let's make sure there isn't a good reason for *not* using relative offsets. An actual location is a 32-bit unsigned number (from 0 to FFFFFFFF hex) and can designate any location in memory. Can a relative offset, which is a signed number, cover the same range? Clearly the answer is yes, since a four-byte relative offset has 2^{32} possible values. If we simply add the relative offset to the current instruction location without regard to sign, we'll get 2^{32} possible answers, one for every location in the memory space. It's just a question of interpreting the sign of the relative offset so that the addition makes sense. For example, suppose that a jump instruction ends at location 9000 hex. If we interpret the relative offset as having a range of -9000 to $+0$FFFF6FFF, then the values reached are precisely the locations 0 through 0FFFFFFFF.

Bear in mind that we do not have to calculate these differences. All we have to do is write the symbolic name of the destination in the JMP or CALL instruction and leave it to the assembler to do the subtraction and generate the correct instruction bytes.

The preceding discussion about using relative offsets rather than actual offsets does not apply to indirect jumps or calls. Indirect jumps and calls do not specify the destination; they specify where to find the destination. More than one indirect jump or call could specify the same place at which the destination is to be found. Thus the concept of relative offset has little meaning since we don't know which instruction it is to be relative to. For this reason, pointers in memory are encoded as absolute locations, never as relative offsets.

Before leaving the topic of unconditional transfers, one more thing needs to be said about the return instruction. There is a variation of the return instruction that, after restoring the instruction pointer by popping its value from the stack, adds a constant (contained in the instruction as an immediate operand) to the stack pointer. This has the effect of popping and discarding additional entries off the stack. (Recall that the stack grows downward, toward lower addresses.) Such entries could have been placed on the stack prior to issuing the call instruction so that a sequence of values (parameters) could be passed to the procedure being called. When the procedure completes its work and does a return, these values would no longer be needed. The form of the return instruction just described provides a convenient way for a procedure to discard its parameters. If such a return-and-discard instruction were not provided, the parameters would have to be discarded in the following manner:

1. Before using a return, the procedure removes the saved value of the instruction pointer from the stack and puts it somewhere else in memory for safekeeping. This uncovers the parameters that were sitting on the stack just below the saved instruction pointer.

2. The procedure then adds a constant to ESP. This has the effect of popping and discarding the parameters.

3. The procedure then replaces the saved instruction pointer (that was put somewhere for safekeeping) back onto the stack.

4. The procedure then executes a return instruction.

Certainly the return-and-discard instructions make this task much simpler.

Another way to discard parameters is by decrementing the stack pointer after the procedure executes the return instruction. At first, this seems almost as efficient as the return-and-discard instruction. But the decrementing of the stack pointer cannot be done by the procedure (it already returned), so it would have to be done at every place the procedure returns to. When you realize that the procedure could be called from a large number of different places, this solution starts looking less attractive.

The return-and-discard instructions use 16 bits to contain the number of bytes of parameters (value that must be added to ESP). In all but exceptional cases, 8 bits would have been sufficient, and the resulting instructions would have been one byte shorter. However, in those rare cases where 8 bits would be insufficient (a procedure has more than 256 bytes of parameters), the alternative method of parameter discarding as described above is too unpleasant to think about. So the extra byte was put onto the instruction. Note, however, that the 16-bit operand was not expanded to 32 bits when the 386 was introduced. It was decided that a procedure with more than 65536 bytes of parameters would be so rare that it need not be supported.

Examples of all the unconditional transfer instructions are shown in Table 3.20.

Table 3.20 Examples of Unconditional Transfer Instructions

	jump	call	return	return & pop
direct	JMP PROGLOC	CALL PROGLOC	RET	RET 14
register indirect	JMP EBX	CALL EDX		
memory indirect	JMP MEM_DWORD	CALL MEM_DWORD		

where PROGLOC is a location within the program, defined with a colon or PROC
   directive— e.g.   PROGLOC: or   PROGLOC PROC
            MOV AX,BX   MOV AX,BX

Conditional Transfer Instructions

The 386 provides *conditional jumps* that, along with the *compare instructions* (CMP), determine the relationship between two numbers. This is done in two steps. First the 386 executes the compare instruction that performs a subtraction of the two numbers, sets the flags based on the result, and discards the difference. It then executes a conditional jump instruction that tests the flags and performs a jump if the flags indicate the two numbers satisfy a particular relation. For example, suppose we wanted to execute certain instructions if the number in BH is equal to the number in BL. This is done as follows:

1. Compare BH to BL (flags become set).

2. Jump to step 5 if zero flag (ZF) is 0.

3. Special instructions to be . . .

4. . . . executed if BH = BL.

5. . . .

In this example, the compare instruction subtracted BL from BH and set the flags based on the result. If BH = BL, the result is zero and ZF would be set to true. Thus a test for equality is a test on ZF, and this is what was done by the conditional jump in step 2. Specifically, if BH = BL, ZF is false and steps 3 and 4 are skipped over.

    There is only one kind of operand for each conditional jump instruction: a direct memory operand. As with the unconditional jump instruction, the operand is encoded as a relative offset from the instruction following the jump. The predecessors to the 386 support only the short form of the conditional jump instruction, meaning that the destination must be within approximately 127 bytes of the instruction. The 386 supports a longer form, allowing the destination to any conditional jump (except JECXZ and its 16-bit predecessor JCXZ) to be anywhere in the 386 memory space. The longer form comes at a price, however: there is a 16-bit opcode, followed by the four-byte relative offset. The long form is thus a whopping four bytes longer than the short form!

The question arises, why bother adding the long form to conditional jumps? After all, most conditional jumps are to nearby locations; and, for example, the sequence:

```
        JNC L1        ; skip next instruction on the opposite condition
        JMP DEST      ; unconditional long jump
    L1:
```

occupies only one more byte of program code than the newer, long conditional jump JC DEST. The answer is that:

1. It was discovered that high-level language compilers were generating a lot of long conditional jumps, using the two-jump sequence just described. Many compilers are simply not clever enough to recognize when a short jump suffices. Also, compilers generate code less efficiently than expert human assembly language programmers. A 127-byte stretch of code is a lot less in a high-level language than it is in assembly language, so long conditional jumps occur far more frequently in high-level language.

2. The new, long-form conditional jump, although it is only one byte less efficient in terms of program space, is much better in terms of execution speed. The reason for this is the pipelined architecture of the 386. If no jump is taken, the 386 has prefetched the next instruction from the program stream. If there is a jump, then the 386 must take extra time to fetch instructions from the new location.

We have seen an example in which we make a conditional jump based on the equality of two numbers. We might also wish to jump if one number is bigger than the other. But this poses an interesting question: is the 8-bit number 1111 1111 bigger than 0000 0000? The answer is both yes and no. If these numbers were considered as unsigned binary numbers, the first number would have a value of 255, and this is indeed bigger than 0. But if the numbers were considered as signed binary numbers, the value of the first number would be −1, and this is smaller than 0. So we see that there are two ways of looking at "bigger" and "smaller," depending on whether the numbers are signed or unsigned. We therefore introduce some new terms to distinguish between the two cases. If we are comparing the numbers as signed numbers, we use the terms *less than* and *greater than*; if we are comparing them as unsigned numbers, we use *below* and *above*. So 1111 1111 is above 0000 0000 and, at the same time, it is less than 0000 0000. As another example, 0000 0000 is both below and less than 0000 0001.

To summarize, the various relationships that could exist between two numbers are equal, above, below, less than, and greater than. Each of these conditions can be determined by the flag settings after a compare instruction has been executed; these flag settings are shown in Table 3.10. The 386 provides conditional jump instructions that test the flags to determine if any particular relationship is or is not satisfied. The specific conditional jumps are as follows:

Name	Meaning
JE	jump on equal
JNE	jump on not equal
JL	jump on less than
JNL	jump on not less than
JG	jump on greater than
JNG	jump on not greater than
JB	jump on below
JNB	jump on not below
JA	jump on above
JNA	jump on not above

Some other relationships might come to mind, such as "less than or equal"; but this is the same as "not greater than." The following is a list of alternate names for the jump instructions just listed:

Name	Alternate Name	Meaning for Alternate Name
JE	JZ	jump on zero
JNE	JNZ	jump on not zero
JL	JNGE	jump on not greater than or equal
JNL	JGE	jump on greater than or equal
JG	JNLE	jump on not less than or equal
JNG	JLE	jump on less than or equal
JB	JNAE	jump on not above or equal
JNB	JAE	jump on above or equal
JA	JNBE	jump on not below or equal
JNA	JBE	jump on below or equal

For reference, the actual flag settings for the various conditional jumps are shown in the following list:

Name	Flag Settings
JE/JZ	ZF = 1
JNE/JNZ	ZF = 0
JL/JNGE	(SF xor OF) = 1
JNL/JGE	(SF xor OF) = 0
JG/JNLE	((SF xor OF) or ZF) = 0
JNG/JLE	((SF xor OF) or ZF) = 1
JB/JNAE	CF = 1
JNB/JAE	CF = 0
JA/JNBE	(CF or ZF) = 0
JNA/JBE	(CF or ZF) = 1

There are conditional jump instructions that are not concerned with the relationship between two numbers but rather with the settings of a particular flag. The JZ and JNZ instructions mentioned above are actually tests on the zero flag. Also, it turns out that the JB and JNB instructions are nothing more than tests on the carry flag. Other conditional jump instructions that test the setting of a particular flag are:

Name	Meaning	Flag Settings
JS	jump on sign	SF = 1
JNS	jump on not sign	SF = 0
JO	jump on overflow	OF = 1
JNO	jump on not overflow	OF = 0
JP	jump on parity	PF = 1
JNP	jump on not parity	PF = 0

Alternate names for the last two are:

Name	Alternate Name	Meaning for Alternate Name
JP	JPE	jump on parity even
JNP	JPO	jump on parity odd

Conditional Byte-Setting Instructions

Each of the Jcond instructions we just described has an analogous SETcond instruction. The SETcond instructions were introduced with the 386, to help high-level language compilers evaluate Boolean expressions. For example, suppose we have declared a Boolean variable WITHIN_LIMIT and an unsigned integer variable VAR in a high-level language program. Consider the compiler's problem in generating code for the statement:

$$\text{WITHIN\_LIMIT} = (\text{VAR} \leq 10000);$$

which should set WITHIN_LIMIT to true if VAR is less than or equal to 10000; to false otherwise. Without SETcond, the compiler must generate something like the following code:

```
   CMP   VAR,10000          ; "Below or Equal" is now set if VAR ≤ 10000
   MOV   WITHIN_LIMIT,1     ; set variable to one in case condition is true
   JBE   L1                 ; skip if the condition was indeed true
   DEC   WITHIN_LIMIT       ; condition was false: decrement to 0 instead
L1:
```

Such code is generated more often than you might think. For example, the clause:

IF (VAR ≤ 10000) OR (VAR ≥ 20000)

causes many compilers to generate an instruction sequence like the one shown for each of the clauses (VAR ≤ 10000) and (VAR ≥ 20000) before the results are combined with an OR instruction. (The results are usually stored in a register or on the stack, rather than in a memory variable.)

SETcond simplifies the instruction sequence by allowing us to store the result of any condition test directly in a byte register or memory variable. The condition is given as a part of the mnemonic, following the letters SET. The destination byte is given as the single operand. If the condition is true, the value 1 is stored; if the condition is false, 0 is stored. Thus, our instruction sequence becomes:

```
CMP VAR,10000          ; "Below or Equal" is now set if VAR ≤ 10000
SETBE WITHIN_LIMIT     ; store that result directly
```

Other examples of SETcond instructions are shown in Table 3.21.

Interrupts

Most modern processors provide facilities for being interrupted by external devices. This frees the processor from having to check on such devices periodically to see if they are in need of any attention. For instance, instead of having a processor frequently ask a keyboard if a key has been pressed and get back negative responses most of the time, it would be more efficient for the processor to ignore the keyboard but allow the keyboard to get the processor's attention when a key is pressed. The former method is referred to as *polling*, the latter as *interrupting*.

Interrupt Mechanism   The 386 has two "apron strings" that external devices can "tug on" to get attention. These "apron strings" are, in reality, two pins on the processor chip called the NMI (nonmaskable interrupt) pin and INTR ("plain old" interrupt) pin. Let's consider the NMI pin first. When an external device places a signal on the NMI

Table 3.21 Examples of Conditional Byte Setting Instructions

register	SETZ AL	; set AL to the value of the zero-flag
	SETGE CH	; set CH to 1 if greater or equal (SF = OF)
	SETO BL	; set BL to the value of the overflow flag
memory	SETNZ BVAR	; set BVAR to 1 if not equal
	SETC BVAR	; set BVAR to the value of the carry flag
	SETA BVAR	; set BVAR to 1 if above

pin, the processor will stop whatever it's doing (but not in the middle of an instruction) and take care of this interruption. However, the processor might have been in the middle of a very important task, so external devices should refrain from causing such interruptions except in real emergencies. An example of a real emergency is if an external device notices that the line voltage has just passed through 100 volts and is dropping. The technical term for this condition is *power failure*. In this case, the external device is justified in interrupting the processor to inform the processor that it hasn't long to live. In its few remaining milliseconds, the processor could then attempt to put its affairs in order (transfer important results to a safe place) before its little oscillator stops ticking. Barring such emergencies, if an external device wishes to interrupt the processor, it should use the INTR pin. The processor can choose to ignore this pin if it is not in the mood. The mood is set by the interrupt-enable flag (IF); when IF is 0, the processor will not respond to signals on the INTR pin. Interrupts are said to be *enabled* when IF = 1 and *disabled* when IF = 0. Instructions for setting and clearing IF (STI, CLI) will be discussed later under Flag Instructions.

In addition to placing a signal on the INTR pin, the external device must convey the reason for the interrupt to the processor. There may be any number of reasons (let's say 256) for an interrupt on the INTR pin, but there is only one reason (impending doom) for an NMI interrupt. The external device will, on request of the processor, supply a number between 0 and 255 representing the reason for the INTR interrupt. This number is often referred to as the *interrupt type*. For each different interrupt type, the processor has a program that it must execute before resuming its normal tasks. The addresses of these programs are contained in a 256-entry table. The location of this table is determined by the operating system, as we'll discuss in Chapter 6. The programs that are executed when interrupts occur are often referred to as *interrupt procedures*.

Now let's see what the processor does when it receives an interrupt on its INTR pin and interrupts are enabled (IF = 1). After completing the execution of the current instruction, the processor stops doing whatever it was doing and prepares to execute the piece of code corresponding to the type of the interrupt. First, the processor saves all relevant information about what it was doing, so when it finishes executing the interrupt procedure, it can resume what it was doing. A convenient place to save this information is on the stack. The values to be saved are the current values of all flags and the current value of the instruction pointer. Next, the processor gets the interrupt type from the external device and sets the instruction pointer according to the corresponding entry in the interrupt table. For example, suppose the external device supplied type 100. In this case, the instruction pointer comes from entry 100 of the interrupt table. Thus the next instruction to be executed is the first instruction in the interrupt procedure corresponding to interrupt type 100.

When the processor receives an interrupt on its NMI pin (regardless of the setting of the interrupt-enable flag IF), it will do everything that it did for INTR interrupts with one exception: it will not need to get the interrupt type from the external device since there is only one possible reason for an NMI interrupt. The type 2 entry in the interrupt table is reserved for locating the NMI interrupt procedure; hence the interrupt pointer comes from that entry.

Up to now we have discussed interrupts that are generated by external devices. These are called *external interrupts*. The processor itself will generate interrupts (called *internal interrupts*) when executing certain instructions if something unexpected happens. Such unexpected events are called *exceptions* and are usually indicative of serious errors. For example, divide instructions cause type 0 interrupts if the divisor is zero. Thus the type 0 entry in the table (another reserved interrupt type) should contain the location of a procedure that recovers from such a division.

The first 31 entries in the interrupt table are reserved for internal interrupts along with the NMI interrupt. The 386 reserved interrupts (along with any that might be generated by future processors in the 86 family) are shown in Table 3.22. The same 31 interrupts were reserved in the predecessors to the 386 but only the first five (0 through 4) were generated by the first predecessor (the 8086). None of the reserved interrupts depend on the value of the interrupt-enable flag (IF).

Signed overflow is another unexpected result. However, the processor does not generate an internal interrupt when signed overflow occurs. This is because the same ADD instruction is used for both signed and unsigned arithmetic, and the processor has no way of knowing if signed addition was actually intended (the same is true for subtraction). However, the processor does provide an efficient (one-byte) instruction that generates a type 4 interrupt if the overflow flag (OF) is set. This instruction, INTO (interrupt on overflow), should follow every arithmetic instruction applied to signed numbers whenever the potential for overflow exists.

An internal interrupt, type 6, is generated if an invalid instruction is encountered. The other internal interrupts shown in Table 3.22 will be discussed later as the appropriate topics are introduced.

Table 3.22 Reserved Interrupt Types

Type	Reserved for
0	Divide Overflow on DIV or IDIV Instruction
1	Debugger Trapping
2	External Non-Maskable Interrupt (NMI)
3	One-Byte Debugger Breakpoint Trap
4	Overflow Interrupt: INTO Executed with OF = 1
5	BOUND Instruction Fault
6	Illegal Instruction Fault
7	No Floating-Point Processor Available
8	Double Fault
9	Floating-Point Segment Overrun Fault
10	Invalid Task State Segment Fault
11	Segment Not Present Fault
12	Stack Fault
13	General Protection Fault
14	Page Fault
15	Reserved by Intel for Future Use
16	Floating-Point Processor Error
17–32	Reserved by Intel for Future Use

Now let's consider the interrupt procedure itself. The interrupt procedure does not have to feel guilty about altering values in flags because the initial values of the flags were already saved. However, if the interrupt procedure alters any other important item (items that the interrupted program could have been using—EAX, for instance), the interrupt procedure must first save the original value of that important item. Before the interrupt procedure terminates, it must restore any of these important items that it saved. Finally, the interrupt procedure terminates by executing an instruction called IRETD (interrupt return) that restores the values of the instruction pointer and the flags saved on the stack. Note that the IRETD instruction is necessary because the RET instruction does not pop the flags from the stack. If the 386 is emulating one of its predecessors in the 86 family, the instruction to use for interrupt returns is called IRET. IRET differs from IRETD in that it restores a 16-bit instruction pointer IP, instead of the 386's usual 32-bit instruction pointer EIP.

Another instruction usually associated with interrupts is the HLT (halt) instruction. HLT stops the processor and leaves the instruction pointer at the instruction following the HLT. When an interrupt comes along, this value of EIP is saved on the stack and the processor starts executing instructions: specifically, the instructions in the interrupt procedure. When the IRETD instruction is encountered, the saved value of EIP is restored. At this time the processor doesn't remember that it was resting prior to receiving the interrupt; it will proceed to execute the instruction that EIP is now pointing to—namely the instruction following the HLT. In effect, HLT provides the processor with a way to relax while waiting for an interrupt.

Now consider all those interrupt procedures, 256 of them, sitting at various places in memory, waiting for interrupts to occur so they can get called into execution. Some of them might be useful to invoke even when no interrupt occurs. Since the location of each procedure exists in a table, it appears as though we could invoke an interrupt procedure by simply executing an indirect call instruction that specifies the table entry. But beware! The interrupt procedure does not end with a normal return instruction; it ends with an IRETD, which will attempt to pop the saved flags off the stack. So the flags had better be on the stack if this return is to work properly. This could be accomplished by preceding the indirect call instruction with a push flag (PUSHF) instruction. But this is getting cumbersome. What would be nice is a single instruction that does everything the processor does when it recognizes an interrupt with one exception—the interrupt type is specified in the instruction rather than supplied by the external device. This instruction is INT (interrupt), and is written in programs as:

INT n

where n is an integer between 0 and 255. The value of the interrupt-enable flag (IF) has no effect on the execution of the INT instruction. This feature is so useful that most computers have interrupt procedures that are never invoked externally at all! In particular, many operating systems provide services to programs via one or more INT instruction types.

The interrupt instructions provided by the 386 are summarized in Table 3.23.

Table 3.23 Interrupt Instructions

INT n	; interrupt of type n (two bytes)
INT 3	; interrupt of type 3 (one byte)
INTO	; interrupt on overflow
IRET	; interrupt return
IRETD	; interrupt return (32-bit address)
HLT	; halt

Debugger Requirements

Large computer programs are so complicated that programmers will almost certainly make mistakes when designing and coding them. Such mistakes will cause any large program to function improperly the first time an attempt is made to execute the program. Remarkably, a universal terminology has emerged to describe such mistakes: they are called *bugs*. A program that assists us in finding and eliminating bugs is called a *debugger*.

A quintessential use of a debugger is to allow our "buggy" program to run until it reaches a point at which we suspect that bugs are having an effect. At that point, the debugger freezes the program and allows us to explore the state of the machine. The place in the program at which the debugger takes over is called a *breakpoint*. The 386 has a number of features that support the implementation of breakpoints for debuggers. These features assume that two interrupt slots, numbers 1 and 3, will be used for debugger breakpoint code.

Breakpoint Registers   The 386 has four special 32-bit registers, called DR0, DR1, DR2, and DR3, that can specify locations of debugger breakpoints. A special-purpose form of the MOV instruction allows us to transfer data between any breakpoint register and any of the 386's general-purpose doubleword registers. There are three types of breakpoints supported: *execution*, *write*, and *read/write*.

An execution breakpoint causes an interrupt of type 1 to occur if the 386 is about to execute the instruction located at the breakpoint. This is the most commonly used breakpoint type; indeed, it is the only type that can be supported by debuggers on the 386's predecessors, without special hardware.

A write breakpoint causes the interrupt to occur after data has been written to the breakpoint location. This type of breakpoint is extremely effective if our program is "clobbering" some memory location, and we have no idea where in the program this is taking place.

A read/write breakpoint causes the interrupt to occur after data has been either written to or read from memory. This type of breakpoint is the least commonly used of the three, but it can be handy at times. First, it can let us gather a run-time chronicle of the usage of a memory variable. Second, it can extricate us from the following thorny situation: suppose we have a program that sometimes works correctly and sometimes malfunctions (often called an *intermittent bug*). By experimentation, we find that the bug will occur if certain values happen to be in memory but not if other values are there. We finally isolate the phenomenon to a single memory location. By setting a read/write breakpoint at that location, we will find out where our program is reading that location, and thus where it is going wrong.

The write and read/write breakpoint types are further subdivided according to the size of the memory variable affected. This size can be specified as a byte, a word, or a doubleword. If a word is specified, then the bottom bit of the breakpoint address is assumed to be 0; that is, a 1 in the bottom bit will be ignored. The interrupt will occur if either byte of the memory word is written or read/written. Similarly, if a doubleword is chosen, the bottom two bits of the breakpoint address are assumed to be 0, and the interrupt occurs if any of the four bytes of the doubleword is written or read/written.

How does the debugger enable breakpoints and specify their types? A single doubleword register, called DR7, does it all. Like the breakpoint registers, the debugger can MOV data between DR7 and any of the general-purpose doubleword registers. Figure 3.13 shows the format of the DR7 register. The top four hex digits specify the types of breakpoints 3 to 0, respectively. The legal values for these hex digits are as follows:

0   execution breakpoint

1   byte write breakpoint

3   byte read/write breakpoint

5   word write breakpoint

7   word read/write breakpoint

D   doubleword write breakpoint

F   doubleword read/write breakpoint

Breakpoints are enabled by setting either bit Gn or Ln to 1, where n is the number of the breakpoint. The G-bits are the *Global* bits, and the L- bits are the *Local* bits. We'll discuss them in detail when we talk about multitasking in Chapter 6. For now, we'll just say that the L-bits are always used to enable breakpoints, except in one case: when we are debugging a multitasking operating system (not just debugging a program executing in a multitasking operating system, we must be the poor souls debugging the system itself). Whichever set of bits we do *not* use (usually Global) the debugger should set to 0.

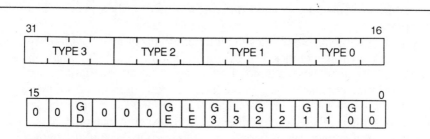

Figure 3.13 Format of the DR7 register.

1) set type
2) set Ln to 1
3) set Le for exact

set GD bit last, ret GD again
× also restart, ret GD again

× when multitasking is in place
G should be used

Manual - When using SLD, Fortran code can't access debug.
reg.

The two bits GE and LE exist to solve a problem encountered with write and read/write breakpoints. The 386's pipelined architecture makes it possible to start executing another instruction before the previous instruction has completed memory access. If this happens, the breakpoint interrupt will not occur immediately after the instruction causing the memory reference. In fact, there's no guarantee that the interrupt will occur at all! To solve this problem, the debugger must set an Exact Data Breakpoint control bit. This will cause the 386 to wait after every memory access until the access is complete before executing the next instruction. Because this slows down the entire processor, the bit should be set only by the debugger, and only when a write or read/write breakpoint is enabled. Like the enable breakpoint, the Exact Data Breakpoint bit comes in two flavors—Global and Local. Again, the debugger will use the Local bit, unless we are debugging a multitasking operating system.

The final bit of DR7 that we need to discuss is GD, the Global Debug Register access detect bit. This bit insures that the debugger has full control over the Debug Registers. If the GD bit is set to 1, then any attempt to access any of the Debug Registers will cause an interrupt of type 1 to be generated, causing control to pass back to the debugger. The GD bit is always cleared whenever a type-1 interrupt is invoked for any reason; the debugger itself is then free to access the Debug Registers. The debugger should always set GD to 1 as its last Debug Register access before restarting our program.

The Trap Flag   Another facility intended for the use of debugger programs is the trap flag (TF). Whenever this flag is set, the processor will execute a single instruction and then generate an interrupt of type 1 (see Figure 3.14). This permits the debugger to execute our program, one instruction at a time, and examine what was done after each instruction. Such a mode of execution is referred to as *single stepping*. (Don't worry about repeated string instructions; single stepping through them will cause an interrupt after each repetition instead of waiting for the end of the entire instruction.)

The debugger can cause our program to execute in single-step mode by modifying the set of flags saved on the stack by a previous interrupt so that the saved value of TF is 1, and then executing an interrupt return (IRETD) instruction. Since it is the debugger and not our program that decides when our program is to switch into single-step mode, there is no need for an instruction to set or clear TF. For example, suppose our program is stopped at a debugger breakpoint; and we would like to resume one instruction at a time. After each instruction we want to examine the contents of all the registers so we can determine if the program is behaving the way we expected. Recall that when invoking the breakpoint handler, the 386 pushed our program's flags onto the stack. If we instruct the debugger (supposedly through some interactive dialog) that we would like to single step the next instruction of our program, the debugger will set the value of TF saved on the stack to 1. It will then restart our program by executing an IRETD to restore the saved values of the instruction pointer and the flags. These are the values that existed when the breakpoint interrupt occurred, except that TF now contains a 1. As a result, our program will execute a single instruction, and then TF will cause the breakpoint (type 1) interrupt to be reinvoked. To prevent the processor from single stepping through the interrupt procedure, TF is automatically cleared after the flags are saved on the stack. The debugger will display the registers, and we can repeat the process by issuing another single-step command to the debugger.

The Debugger Status Register   So far, we've seen three reasons why the main debugger interrupt (INT 1) could be invoked: breakpoints, an attempt to access a debugger register when the GD bit is set, and single stepping (TF is set). An interrupt handler for interrupt number 1 might be perfectly justified in throwing up its hands and crying, "Just why was I invoked, anyway?" To remedy this situation, the 386 provides DR6, the debugger status register. The active bits of DR6 are shown in Figure 3.15. Each bit corresponds to a reason why INT 1 was invoked. When the 386 sees fit to invoke INT 1, it will set the corresponding reason bit to 1. The debugger's INT 1 handler will use a MOV instruction to load DR6 into one of the 386's general-purpose doubleword registers; the active bits with a 1 value will then tell the handler why it was called.

There is one bit in DR6 covering a reason we haven't discussed: a task-switch trap. We describe this trap in Chapter 6 when we talk about multitasking operating systems.

There are a couple of warnings concerning the DR6 register:

1.   It is possible for more than one reason bit to be set at one time. Furthermore, if the INT 1 occurs at a breakpoint location, the corresponding breakpoint reason bit will be set, even if the breakpoint was not enabled with its G or L bits. The debugger must check for this if it wants a totally accurate list of reasons.

2.   The reason bits in DR6 are *sticky*. This means that the hardware only sets them; the debugger must clear them by MOVing a zero value back into DR6 after the bits

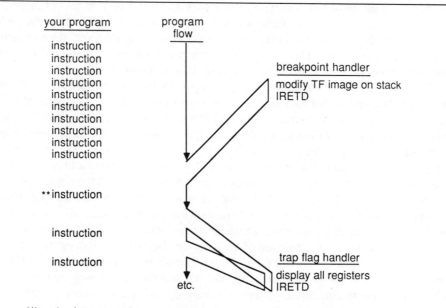

**breakpoint was set here

Figure 3.14 Executing a program in single-step mode.

have been read. Sticky bits help to insure that the information they convey is never lost: if the debugger chooses not to clear a reason bit, then that bit tells if the reason *ever* came into play.

The Resume Flag   Suppose that we have set an execution breakpoint in our program, and that the program has been interrupted at that breakpoint. Suppose further that we wish to retain the breakpoint, so that the debugger will again regain control when the breakpoint is reached a second time. We have a problem: if we restart the program, it will stop immediately, without executing anything, because we are already at a breakpoint. One way to get around this is for the debugger to disable the breakpoint, single step an instruction, reenable the breakpoint, and then restart the program normally. But then the debugger must record the fact that it is single stepping to get around the breakpoint, so that it should immediately restart the program instead of passing control back to us. This is getting messy. Wouldn't it be nice if the debugger could tell the 386 to ignore breakpoints when executing the first instruction? The Resume Flag (RF) is a feature, introduced with the 386, that lets the debugger do so. The debugger sets RF to 1 in the same way that it sets TF to 1 when single stepping: by altering the flags-image saved on the stack, and then restarting the program via the IRETD instruction. The 386 ignores all breakpoints when RF is set to 1. Furthermore, RF is cleared to zero after every instruction except instructions that explicitly restore the flags register (such as IRETD and POPFD). This is exactly what we want— the 386 will be guaranteed to execute at least one instruction in our program before the debugger regains control, but after that one instruction, all breakpoints will regain their effect.

INT 3 Breakpoints   Notice that there are two forms for the INT instruction. In the first form, the instruction is two bytes long, and the second byte specifies the interrupt type. In the second form, the instruction is one byte long, and the type is implicitly type 3 (see reserved types in Table 3.22). The fact that it is type 3 is irrelevant (it could have been any type), but the fact that it is one byte long is significant. A one-byte INT

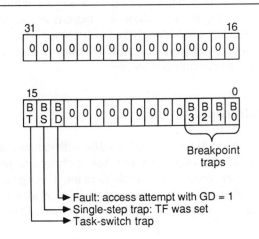

Figure 3.15 Format of the DR6 register.

instruction was essential for the implementation of breakpoints on the 386's predecessors; and it remains necessary on the 386 if we want more than the four breakpoints offered by the 386's debug registers.

To understand why, let's consider how breakpoints work when we don't have breakpoint registers. Suppose we want to set an execution breakpoint at address 100 within our program. We can do so by having the debugger plant an instruction at address 100 that will transfer control back to the debugger. The debugger can now let our program run, and when our program reaches address 100, it will transfer back to the debugger. Naturally the debugger would save the original contents of address 100 prior to setting the breakpoint and will restore the original contents after control returns to the debugger.

Now the question remains as to which 386 transfer instruction to plant at address 100. A jump instruction would work fine if there were only one breakpoint set at any given time. However, if more than one breakpoint is set, the debugger would need to know which breakpoint was actually reached. The INT instruction is ideal since it saves information (the instruction pointer) that locates the breakpoint. Using the two-byte INT instruction to set a breakpoint at address 100 would mean that the contents of both 100 and 101 would have to be overwritten. The debugger would save and eventually restore the original contents of both bytes. In most cases this would present no problems. However, sooner or later we'll write a program, such as the one in Figure 3.16, that jumps around and executes the instruction at 101 prior to executing the instruction at 100. But the instruction at 101 has been temporarily overwritten by the second byte of the INT instruction planted at 100. This is the reason the debugger must use a one-byte INT instruction.

Flag Instructions

The 386 has instructions for setting and clearing the carry flag (STC, CLC), the direction flag (STD, CLD), and the interrupt flag (STI, CLI). Furthermore, it has an instruction for complementing the carry flag (CMC). These instructions are summarized in Table 3.24. The uses of these flags have already been discussed—the carry flag (CF) for multiple-precision arithmetic, the direction flag (DF) for string processing, and interrupt flag (IF) for enabling and disabling interrupts.

Synchronization Instructions

Interrupts provide one means of synchronizing a 386 with external devices. There are two other forms of synchronization that the 386 architecture provides. The first involves using a subordinate processor to implement the floating-point instruction set for the 386. The second involves sharing resources (such as memory) with other processors in a multiple-processor system. Both of these cases will now be examined in detail.

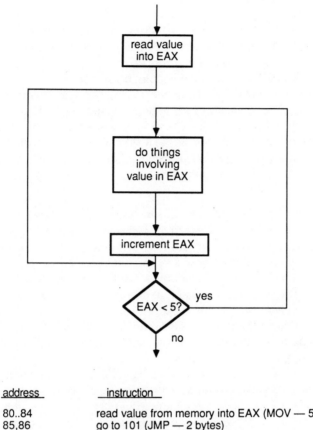

address	instruction
80..84	read value from memory into EAX (MOV — 5 bytes)
85,86	go to 101 (JMP — 2 bytes)
87..99	do things involving value in EAX
100	increment EAX (INC — 1 byte)
101..105	compare EAX to 5 (CMP — 5 bytes)
106,107	go to 87 if below (JB — 2 bytes)

Figure 3.16 Program that executes address 101 prior to executing address 100.

Table 3.24 Flag Instructions

CLC	(clear carry)	$0 \rightarrow CF$
CMC	(complement carry)	$1 - CF \rightarrow CF$
STC	(set carry)	$1 \rightarrow CF$
CLD	(clear direction)	$0 \rightarrow DF$
STD	(set direction)	$1 \rightarrow DF$
CLI	(clear interrupt-enable)	$0 \rightarrow IF$
STI	(set interrupt-enable)	$1 \rightarrow IF$

Floating-Point Instructions   Although the 386 has an impressive arsenal of capabilities built into the chip, this arsenal does not include the floating-point instruction set. Throughout the history of the 86 family, the execution of floating-point instructions has been assigned to a subordinate processor. The 386 accepts either the 287 or the 387 as its subordinate floating-point processor.

We'll go into more detail about how the floating-point processor works in Chapter 4. For now, we'll just describe the floating-point instruction set as viewed by the 386. The 386 interprets a floating-point instruction as a directive to synchronize with the subordinate processor, to communicate the instruction's identity to that processor, and to manage memory access for that processor. One of the 386's duties in that last category is to calculate the effective address of any memory operands.

Resource Sharing   Another form of synchronization is between two processors sharing a common resource. For example, consider an airline reservation system in which several computer processors are making entries into a common data base in some shared memory. As we'll now see, the data base could get corrupted if two processors tried to indiscriminately modify it simultaneously.

Suppose one of the processors wants to change the billing of Harry Jones on flight 351 from his VISA card to his American Express card. First, the processor will search the passenger list of flight 351 until it finds the entry for Harry Jones. It will then overwrite the credit-card portion of that entry with the new information. While this modification is taking place, suppose a second processor is busy verifying the credit-card numbers of each passenger. When that processor gets to Harry Jones, it might find part of the old number and part of the new one because the first processor hasn't finished making the update. Of course, the credit-card company would decline that invalid number.

We can avoid this problem by using something called a *semaphore*. A semaphore is nothing more than a memory location that tells one processor that another processor is currently using the shared memory and asks the second processor to please wait. Here's how it works: the record for Harry Jones would have its own semaphore byte. The processor that changes the billing would first examine the semaphore and find its value to be 0 (record is not in use). That processor would then change the value to 1 (record is in use), and make the modification. While the modification is being made, the credit-checking processor would examine the semaphore and find that its value is 1. The second processor would voluntarily wait until the first processor places a 0 in the semaphore. When that happens, the second processor sets the semaphore to 1 and makes its credit check, finding the complete updated card number in the entry.

We still have a problem, however, if events occur in the following sequence:

1.   The first processor reads the semaphore and finds it to be 0.

2.   The second processor reads the semaphore and also finds it to be 0.

3.   The first processor sets the semaphore to 1.

4.   The second processor sets the semaphore to 1.

Now our semaphore is defeated: both processors will attempt to use the shared memory simultaneously. We can try to prevent the problem by reading the semaphore value and setting it to 1 all in one instruction. The instruction we're talking about is exchange (XCHG), used as follows to fetch a value from the byte memory variable SEMA:

```
        MOV AL,1            ; the value that we want in the semaphore
    L1:
        XCHG AL,SEMA        ; SEMA → AL and 1 → SEMA
        CMP AL,0            ; was the semaphore 0?
        JNE L1              ; retest it if not
```

The idea is that the XCHG instruction performs steps 1 and 3 simultaneously, so that another processor cannot get in a step 2. Unfortunately, the hardware does not execute steps 1 and 3 simultaneously: there is a memory-read operation, followed a short time later by a distinct write operation. The problem is solved by providing a 386 output pin, called the LOCK pin, that sends a signal for the duration of the XCHG instruction. The hardware of the airline reservation system can now be designed to give exclusive memory access to any processor asserting the lock signal. If a second processor tries a step 2, it will be held in waiting by the hardware, until step 3 is completed by the first processor.

How often should the LOCK pin be asserted? If the 386 asserted LOCK during every instruction, it would degrade system performance so much that we would lose almost all the advantage of having more than one processor. So we allow program control over the LOCK pin by providing a LOCK prefix. An instruction preceded by LOCK will cause the LOCK pin to be asserted for the duration of the instruction. We'll see an example of the LOCK prefix when we discuss bit manipulation in the next section. The LOCK prefix is not necessary in the XCHG instruction, because the 386 automatically asserts the LOCK pin for all XCHG instructions involving a memory operand. This is done for historical reasons that are discussed in Chapter 5.

Bit-Array Instructions

In this section we'll talk about a set of instructions not available on any of the 386's predecessors. These instructions are designed to provide a complete facility for manipulating arrays of individual bits. You may be asking, "Isn't this contrary to the direction in which the 386 is moving?" After all, a 32-bit machine is designed for manipulating larger chunks of data, not smaller chunks. However, there are two major developments in the evolution of computers that have given bit-manipulation a high priority:

1. The plummeting cost and higher density of memory has made computer manipulation of visual and audio images possible. Unlike numeric and textual data, this

image data steadfastly refuses to organize itself into manageable chunks of multi-bit records. An ability to address individual bits is essential for unrestricted manipulation of image data.

2.   The increased power of high-level languages has made bit manipulation desirable for compiler-generated code. Most modern languages allow the user to declare arrays of Boolean variables. However, most compilers are forced to allocate a full byte for each element of a Boolean array, because there is no decent way to address individual bits of an array. Direct bit addressing would enable compilers to pack Boolean arrays with maximum efficiency.

To achieve a well-rounded set of bit-manipulation instructions, we'll need instructions for reading and writing individual bits, for searching within a bit array, and for performing block moves of bit arrays. Let's consider each group in turn.

For each of the instructions described below, the 386 observes the following convention for bit addressing: the bottommost bit of any memory operand is bit 0, and bit addresses run through the increasingly significant bits. Therefore, the highest bit of a byte is bit 7; of a word, bit 15; of a doubleword, bit 31.

Reading and Writing Individual Bits   At first glance, it would seem very simple to design instructions for reading and writing bits. We would have one instruction for loading a bit from memory to a register, and another instruction for storing a bit from a register to memory. After all, that is what we have for bytes, words, and doublewords, isn't it? But let's think about that a little. Computing with bytes, for example, typically consists of loading a byte into a register, manipulating it in some way, and storing the result back into memory. There is a plethora of arithmetic and logical manipulations we can perform on a byte, but individual bits are different. There are only four ways we can manipulate an individual bit:

• We can set it to 1.

• We can set it to 0.

• We can complement it.

• We can leave it unchanged.

This severe restriction of manipulations on a bit gives us an opportunity. Instead of making the programmer perform the sequence of instructions:

1.   Read a bit.

2.   Manipulate the bit.

3.   Write the resulting bit.

how about providing instructions that read, manipulate, and write all in one operation? This is what the 386 does with its Bit Test instructions BTS, BTR, BTC, and BT. Each instruction has two operands: the first is the word or doubleword containing the bit we are reading and manipulating; the second contains the address N of the bit within the word or doubleword. The address can be an immediate value, or it can be the contents of a register. The instruction manipulates bit N of the first operand in the way specified by the mnemonic: BTS Sets the bit to 1, BTR Resets the bit to 0, BTC complements the bit, and BT leaves the bit unchanged. In any case, the Carry flag is set to the value of the bit *before* it was manipulated.

For example, let's consider the instruction BTC AX,2, executed when the AX register has a value of decimal fifteen, which is binary 1111. The instruction loads bit 2 of AX into the Carry flag and then complements bit 2. According to the bit-addressing convention we described at the start of this section, bit 2 is the third-least-significant bit of the number. Hence the Carry flag is set, and the bit is complemented, leaving a binary value 1011, or decimal eleven.

Note that when the bit comes from a register, as in this example, then the bit address cannot go beyond the highest bit of that register, which is 15 for word registers and 31 for doubleword registers. This restriction should not apply when the bit comes from memory: in memory, we can simply advance though the number of bytes necessary to reach the Nth bit of a large array. For example, we should be able to address bit 100 of a memory array; we would do so by advancing 12 bytes (which is 12 * 8 = 96 bits, giving us bits 0 through 95 of the array), and then looking at bit 5 of the 13th byte. Indeed, the 386 lets us do this, but there is a catch: if the bit address is an immediate value, then the byte-advancement calculation is done by the assembler, not by the 386 itself. In the example just given, the assembler sees that the bit will be 12 bytes beyond the memory address specified; it will thus add 12 to the displacement field of the memory operand, and it will give 5 as the immediate operand. The 386 itself will ignore the top bits of the immediate bit-address operand. This little complication exists for two reasons:

1. A good assembler or compiler will make the complication invisible to the programmer.

2. The complication means that a single byte will always suffice as an immediate bit address. This saves code space.

A prime example of Bit Test usage involves arrays of semaphores. Recall from our discussion of the LOCK function that we can implement a semaphore by loading a value 1 into the AL register, and then exchanging AL with a byte-variable SEMA. The XCHG instruction simultaneously reads the old value of SEMA and replaces it with the value 1. Note that the BTS instruction does exactly the same thing, but with two additional advantages. First, the result is loaded directly into the Carry flag; we do not need a TEST or CMP instruction to set the flags according to the value of the semaphore. Second, the BTS instruction operates on just a single bit. If we have an array of semaphores, it can be a packed bit array, saving memory space. Because the Bit Test series is so effective for semaphores, it is among the instructions that accept a LOCK prefix.

Let's recode the semaphore loop presented in our discussion of the LOCK prefix. This time, SEMA will be a bit array, and our loop will test bit number EAX within the array:

```
L1:                            ; loop here until the semaphore bit turns 0
    LOCK BTS SEMA,EAX          ; read bit into Carry, also set it to 1
    JC L1                      ; loop if the bit was already 1
```

A word of warning is in order concerning the Bit Test instructions. Since these instructions manipulate a single bit of memory, you might expect the 386 to restrict its memory access to the single byte containing the affected bit. This is not the case! The (double)word form of the instructions can fetch and write the entire (double)word containing the affected bit. If what we are addressing really *is* memory, this will be of no concern to us. However, some 386 systems will have input/output devices mapped as though they were memory (this is called *memory-mapped I/O*). What appears to the 386 as a multi-byte memory access might appear to the I/O device as a sequence of individual control directives, causing the device to be misprogrammed. For this reason, you should not use the Bit Test instructions for memory-mapped I/O. You should instead MOV the data to and from a register and manipulate the register instead.

Searching within a Bit Array   Boolean arrays are frequently used for resource allocation. For example, a disk operating system might determine which of its disk sectors are free by maintaining a Boolean array. The Nth bit of the array would be 1 if sector number N were free; it would be 0 if the sector were in use. Thus, if the operating system wants to allocate a sector, it must find a 1-bit in the Boolean array. Note that there is already a string operation, REPZ SCASD, that will quickly find a doubleword in the array that contains a nonzero bit. We need only to polish off the job with an instruction that locates a 1-bit within a nonzero doubleword. The BSF (Bit Scan Forward) and BSR (Bit Scan Reverse) instructions do just that. Both instructions set the first (register) operand to the bit address of a nonzero bit within the second (register or memory) operand. BSF uses the least significant nonzero bit; BSR uses the most significant nonzero bit.

There is a slight problem. What if there aren't any 1-bits in the second operand? We can't return a result of zero; that result would mean that we did find a 1-bit in bit number zero. Instead, we use the zero flag to indicate this condition: if ZF is set, then the operand was zero (contained no 1-bits), and the value of the answer-register is undefined. If ZF is cleared, then a 1-bit was found, and the answer-register is valid.

Let us see how we would code the disk sector allocation routine that we mentioned. Suppose our bit array is called SECTORS_MAP, and the number of bits in the map is the immediate constant N_SECTORS. To make things simple, we'll assume that N_SECTORS is a constant multiple of 32, so that SECTORS_MAP occupies an integral number of doublewords. The following code will find the number of a free sector, return the value in the EAX register, and mark the sector busy:

```
MOV EDI,SECTORS_MAP        ; point to the sectors bit array
MOV ECX,N_SECTORS/32       ; load the number of doublewords in the sector
SUB EAX,EAX                ; we will match doublewords against zero value
REPZ SCASD                 ; find a nonzero doubleword in the array
JZ FAILURE                 ; failure if all words were zero
BSF EAX,[EDI-1]            ; get the bit-address within the nonzero dword
SUB EDI,SECTORS_MAP + 1    ; calculate the number of zero-dwords skipped over
SHL EDI,5                  ; convert it into the number of bits skipped
ADD EAX,EDI                ; add it into the bit address
BTR SECTORS_MAP,EAX        ; set the bit to 0
```

Observe that the JZ FAILURE instruction could appear either just before or just after the BSF instruction: both REPZ SCASD and BSF tell us if there is a nonzero bit in the array.

Moving a Block of Bits Now let's think about the problems associated with generating bit-mapped visual images. The problems are basically the same whether the images are going to a graphics video display or to a high-resolution graphics printer. In either case, we will want to copy a bit image from a source, such as a character font, to the display destination. To implement features such as proportional spacing, we must have the ability to shift the bit alignment as we copy. For example, the bottommost bit of a doubleword from the character font might be copied to bit number 10 of a doubleword in the destination buffer. Thus the data from the source stream needs to be shifted 10 bits before going to the destination.

At first glance it would seem that the 386's general-purpose shift instructions suffice for the graphics-copy operation just described. But let's look closely at the situation. In the example given, each doubleword of output (except the first and last) consists of 10 bits from a source doubleword and 22 bits from the following source doubleword. Thus the data is coming from a two-doubleword (64-bit) quantity. The general-purpose shift/rotate instructions take their source data from, at most, a 32-bit quantity. If we want to take advantage of the 32-bit bandwidth the 386 offers us, we will need a 64-bit shift instruction. The 386 gives us two such special-purpose instructions, SHLD (Shift Left Double Precision) and SHRD (Shift Right Double Precision).

Both instructions have three operands. The first and last operands are just like the two operands of the ordinary shift instructions SHL and SHR: they tell the register/ memory quantity being shifted and the number of bits being shifted, respectively. The difference is that while SHL and SHR shift 0-bits into the destination, SHLD and SHRD shift bits taken from the extra (middle) register operand. Thus, for example, the instruction:

SHRD EAX,EBX,10

shifts the EAX register right by 10 bits. The high 10 bits are shifted down from the bottom of EBX. EBX is unchanged by the operation.

As with the general shift/rotate instructions, the bit count can be either an immediate value or the contents of the CL register. There is no short form for an immediate shift count of 1; but this is, of course, a special case of the explicit-immediate instruction.

To illustrate usage of SHLD and SHRD, let's code a routine to perform the kind of shifted block-move required by a graphics operation. Our move will copy a single row from a character-font buffer onto a display buffer. The font source consists of EDX doublewords, pointed to by ESI. For simplicity, we'll assume that the source consists of an integral number of doublewords aligned to start at bit 0 in the source buffer. The destination starts at bit CH of the doubleword pointed to by EDI. We must preserve the contents of the bottom CH bits of the first destination doubleword and the top (32-CH) bits of the last destination doubleword. See Figure 3.17 for an illustration of the operation we want. Thus our code consists of three stages: first, special code to handle the first destination doubleword; second, a loop to handle the middle doublewords; finally, special code to handle the last destination doubleword. The code is as follows:

```
        MOV CL,32              ; we will compute (32-CH)
        SUB CL,CH              ; all shift counts will now be by 32-CH bits
        MOV EAX,[EDI]          ; fetch the existing first destination dword
        ROL EAX,CL             ; shift the bottom CH bits to the top—the
                               ; loop-code will shift them back to the bottom
L1:                            ; loop here to compute all but the last dword
        MOV EBX,[ESI]          ; fetch the next source dword
        ADD ESI,4              ; advance the source pointer
        SHRD EAX,EBX,CL        ; shift down CL bits from that next dword
        STOSD                  ; output the shifted result
        MOV EAX,EBX            ; the next source dword becomes this source-dword
        DEC EDX                ; count down the dwords
        JNZ L1                 ; loop for the next interior dword
        MOV CL,CH              ; we use CH shift count to construct the last dword
        SHR DWORD PTR [EDI],CL ; shift the top 32-CH bits to the bottom—they will
                               ; be shifted back up again by the next instruction
        SHLD [EDI],EAX,CL      ; shift in the bits from the final source dword
```

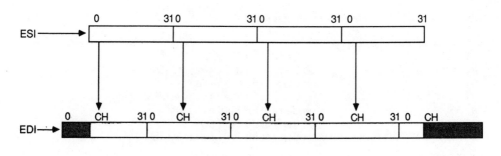

Figure 3.17 Block move of a bit array.

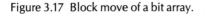

Note that we refrained from using the LODSD instruction to load from our source. We did so because we wanted the load to go to EBX, not EAX; and the instruction sequence we used executes more quickly than the equivalent sequence:

```
XCHG EAX,EBX
LODSD
XCHG EBX,EAX
```

which occupies less program space. There is a sneaky programming trick we can employ to further increase the execution speed of the middle loop. The trick is to insert a SUB ESI,EDI instruction before the loop and replace the first two instructions with the single instruction MOV EBX,[ESI + EDI]. There is at least one more way to adjust the code to milk a few more clock-counts out of the inner loop; we'll leave it as an exercise for you to find it.

As we already indicated, SHLD and SHRD were invented to provide a 64-bit shifting ability, and therefore will almost always be used with doubleword operands. Because of the symmetry between words and doublewords in the 386 architecture, however, SHLD and SHRD also accept pairs of 16-bit word operands, giving an exotic form of a 32-bit shift. (Such a 32-bit shift would, of course, have been welcome on the 16-bit 286 machine.) There was no need perceived for byte operands to SHLD and SHRD, so they are not allowed.

We conclude our discussion of SHLD and SHRD by observing, with some amusement, that the SHLD mnemonic conflicts with the Intel 8080 mnemonic for the Store HL Direct instruction. We are certain that if SHLD had been designed into the original 8086, then Intel would not have allowed the conflict to occur. It's remarkable how the 8080, once the king of microprocessors, has in just a few years faded from human memory!

Examples of all the bit-array instructions are shown in Table 3.25.

Table 3.25 Examples of Bit Array Instructions

Individual Bit Manipulation
BT AX,CX	; set Carry to bit CX of AX
BT MEM_VAR,BX	; set Carry to bit BX of array at MEM_VAR
BT EAX,EBX	; set Carry to bit EBX of EAX
BT MEM_VAR,ECX	; set Carry to bit ECX of array at MEM_VAR
BT AX,11	; set Carry to bit 11 of AX
BT EDX,20	; set Carry to bit 20 of EDX
BT MEM_VAR,100	; set Carry to bit 100 of array at MEM_VAR

BTS is identical to BT except set bit to 1 after reading it
BTR is identical to BT except reset bit to 0 after reading it
BTC is identical to BT except complement bit after reading it

Searching Within a Bit Array
BSF AX,BX	; set AX to position of lowest 1-bit in BX
BSF CX,MEM_WORD	; set CX to position of lowest 1-bit in MEM_WORD
BSF EBX,EAX	; set EBX to position of lowest 1-bit in EAX
BSF EDX,MEM_DWORD	; set EDX to position of lowest 1-bit in MEM_DWORD

BSR is identical to BSF except it returns the position of the highest 1-bit

Double-Length Shift Instructions
SHLD AX,BX,3	; high word of AXBX SHL 3 $\rightarrow$ AX
SHRD AX,BX,3	; low word of BXAX SHR 3 $\rightarrow$ AX
SHLD MEM_WORD,DX,9	; high word of (MEM_WORD,DX) SHL 9 $\rightarrow$ MEM_WORD
SHRD MEM_WORD,DX9	; low word of (DX,MEM_WORD) SHR 9 $\rightarrow$ MEM_WORD
SHLD ECX,EDX,23	; high dword of ECXEDX SHL 23 $\rightarrow$ ECX
SHRD ECX,EDX,23	; low dword of EDXECX SHR 23 $\rightarrow$ ECX
SHLD MEM_DWORD,EAX,2	; high dword of (MEM_DWORD,EAX) SHL 2 $\rightarrow$
	; MEM_DWORD
SHRD MEM_DWORD,EAX,2	; low dword of (EAX,MEM_DWORD) SHR 2 $\rightarrow$
	; MEM_DWORD

Indirect shift count CL may be substituted for the immediate count in any of the above instructions

High-Level Language Support

The 386 has three instructions (BOUND, ENTER, and LEAVE) that simplify the code needed to support certain features in high-level languages. In particular, BOUND efficiently performs some of the checking needed for arrays, and ENTER and LEAVE efficiently perform some of the bookkeeping functions involving procedures. A programmer writing in a high-level language is not aware that these functions are performed or are even necessary; all of the code to perform these functions is generated automatically by the compiler. None of these three instructions are in the 8086.

The BOUND instruction tests to see if the signed value in a word or doubleword register lies within specified limits. The limits are contained in two consecutive words or doublewords in memory. The value in the register must be greater than or equal to the first memory value and less than or equal to the second memory value, otherwise an interrupt (of type 5) is generated. An example of a BOUND instruction is:

BOUND EBX,DMEMLOCS

This instruction is useful for testing if an array index is within allowable limits; if not, a programming error has most likely occurred.

To understand what the bookkeeping functions involving procedures are, we must first learn something about the accessibility of variables in a block-structured high-level language. Consider the following portion of a Pascal program (you don't have to know Pascal to understand this program):

```
procedure A;                 {name of procedure}
    var a1,a2:integer;        {declarations of variables for procedure A}
    begin a1 := a2 + 1; end;  {body of procedure A}
```

A procedure has a declaration section and a body. The body contains the actions (executable statements) that will be performed by the procedure. Any variables declared in the declaration section of a procedure can be referenced by statements in the body of the procedure.

In addition to variables, other procedures can be declared in the declaration section of the procedure. For example:

```
procedure A;                 {name of procedure}

    var a1,a2:integer;        {declarations of variables for procedure A}

    procedure B;              {declaration of a procedure for procedure A}

        var b1,b2:integer;
        begin b2 := a1 + 2; end;

    procedure C;              {declaration of a procedure for procedure}
        var c1,c2:integer;
        begin c1 := a2 + 3; end;

    begin a1 := a2 + 1; end;  {body of procedure A}
```

Note that items (variables, procedures) declared in the declaration part of procedure A can be referenced by statements in the body of procedure B and C, as well as in the body of procedure A. However, items declared in the declaration part of procedure B can be referenced only by statements in the body of procedure B (not A or C) and similarly for procedure C.

It would be simple for the compiler to generate code that allocates all variables in memory when the program is loaded and never changes the location of any variable. Each variable could then be accessed by a direct memory reference. However, Pascal has the property that a procedure can call itself. Such procedures are known as *recursive* procedures. The use of recursion can greatly simplify some algorithms. For example, a sorting procedure might partition the array of elements to be sorted into two subarrays, then call itself twice to sort the subarrays. Each call of a recursive procedure must have its own unique storage for the variables declared within the procedure. Thus the variables must be allocated each time the procedure is called and deallocated each time the procedure returns. A convenient place to allocate such variables is on the stack.

To accommodate recursive procedures, Pascal compilers typically generate code that performs the following actions when a procedure is invoked: (1) allocate space on the stack (called a *stack frame*) for the variables declared in a procedure; (2) set EBP to point to the beginning (highest stack address) of the stack frame. Thus the actual memory location of a variable may be different each time the procedure is invoked (the stack frame doesn't necessarily start at the same place each time) and so direct memory addressing cannot be used. The only thing that stays constant is the distance of the variable from the start of the stack frame. The code the compiler generates to reference such variables must therefore be in terms of that distance. Such addressing is called *stack-frame-relative* addressing. For example, if variable a2 is eight bytes from the beginning of the stack frame and a1 is six bytes, the compiler could generate the following instructions for the body of procedure A.

```
MOV AL,[EBP-8]    ; move the value of a2 into register AL
INC AL            ; add 1 to the value of a2
MOV [EBP-6],AL    ; move the sum into a1
```

Now comes the problem of using stack-frame-relative addressing to access variables declared in one procedure from the body of another procedure. For example, a2 is used in procedure B but declared in procedure A. When procedure B is executing, the most recently allocated stack frame is the one for procedure B and does not contain a2. A picture of the stack frame at this time is shown in Figure 3.18a. Every variable that can be referenced from within a given procedure is contained either in the stack frame of the given procedure or in the stack frame of a procedure in which the given procedure is nested. Thus the stack frame for a given procedure must contain pointers to each of the stack frames just enumerated. Such a list of pointers is called a *display*. The stack frame, including the display, is shown in Figure 3.18b. The compiler can now generate code that utilizes the display to locate the appropriate stack frame and then adds the distance from the start of the stack frame to locate the variable.

When a given procedure is exited, the following actions must occur: (1) the stack frame must be deallocated; (2) the EBP register must be adjusted to point to the stack frame that was the current stack frame at the time the given procedure was invoked (this is called the *dynamic link*). Note that this is not necessarily the stack frame of the procedure in which the given procedure is nested (called the *static link*). For example, procedure B is nested within procedure A but it could have been invoked from either procedure A or procedure C. Deallocating the stack frame is accomplished by putting the current value of EBP into ESP (that is, making ESP point to the beginning of the

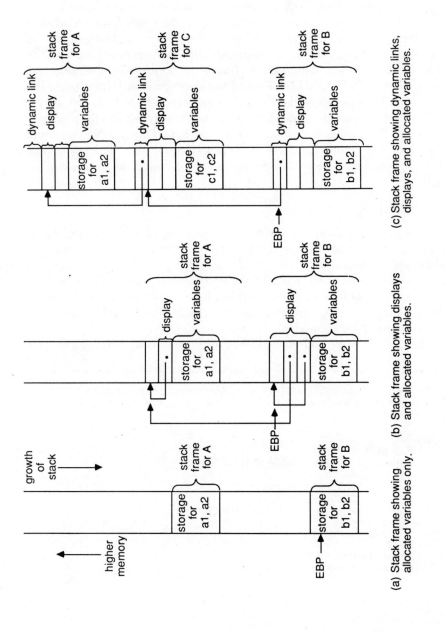

(a) Stack frame showing allocated variables only.

(b) Stack frame showing displays and allocated variables.

(c) Stack frame showing dynamic links, displays, and allocated variables.

Figure 3.18 Examples of stack frames.

current stack frame). Adjusting EBP is not possible unless we saved the value of EBP (the dynamic link) prior to invoking the given procedure. The dynamic link could be put in the stack frame just before the display. The stack frame, including the dynamic link, for the case of procedure B invoked from procedure C is shown in Figure 3.18c.

We now see that the compiler must generate code at the head of every procedure to allocate a stack frame, insert the dynamic link into the stack frame, and generate the display. Furthermore, prior to each return instruction, the compiler must generate code to deallocate the stack frame and restore EBP. This would normally involve numerous instructions. The 386's ENTER and LEAVE instructions perform exactly these tasks. The LEAVE instruction takes no operands, the ENTER instruction takes two. The second operand is the nesting level of the procedure (outermost level is 1). It tells the processor how many entries there are in the display. The first operand is the number of bytes of storage needed for the variables declared in the procedure. It tells the processor how many bytes to allocate for the stack frame exclusive of the dynamic link and the display. For example:

> ENTER 48,3

creates a stack frame consisting of a dynamic link, a display of three stack-frame pointers (one of which points to the stack frame being created), and 48 bytes for variables declared in the procedure.

If the second operand to ENTER is zero, the instruction does not include a display in the stack frame. This is useful for high-level languages which do not permit nested procedures and hence have no need for a display. A popular high-level language that does not permit nested procedures is C.

The exact behavior of the ENTER and LEAVE instructions is shown in Figure 3.19.

The formal definition of the ENTER and LEAVE instructions for all cases is given by the following listing. LEVEL denotes the value of the second operand.

```
ENTER:
    Push EBP
    Set a temporary value FRAME_PTR ← ESP
    If LEVEL>0 then
        Repeat (LEVEL-1) times:
            EBP ← EBP-2
            Push the word pointed to by EBP
        End repeat
        Push FRAME_PTR
    End if
    EBP ← FRAME_PTR
    ESP ← ESP- first operand


LEAVE:
    ESP ← EBP
    Pop EBP
```

Figure 3.19 Formal definition of ENTER and LEAVE (reprinted courtesy Intel Corp.).

Note that when the 386 is emulating one of its predecessors, then ENTER and LEAVE act upon the values of the 16-bit registers BP and SP, instead of the 32-bit registers EBP and ESP. This preserves object-code compatibility with the earlier processors.

A Postscript on Prefixes

We've now encountered three of the five types of instruction prefix bytes for the 386—repeat, lock, and operand size. (The other two prefixes, address length and segment override, are discussed in Chapter 5.) Three questions come to mind:

1. Can any prefix be used on any instruction?

2. Can more than one prefix be used on an instruction?

3. What happens when a prefixed instruction is interrupted?

Two of the five prefixes, repeat and lock, have restrictions on the instruction that follows; the other three prefixes can be used with any instruction (if the prefix is inapplicable, it is ignored). The REP prefix is valid only with string primitives. The LOCK prefix is valid only with instructions that read and write *the same* memory location in the same operation. These operations are listed in Table 3.26. If a REP or LOCK prefix is used with a disallowed instruction, then an invalid opcode exception (interrupt 6) will occur. These restrictions do not occur in the entire 86 family. The 8086 has no restrictions on prefix usage. The 286 has the same restrictions on REP that the 386 does, but usage of LOCK is related to a privilege level granted by the operating system, not by the identity of the following instruction. We say more about this evolution in Chapter 5.

Prefixes can appear in any combination and any order before an instruction, so long as the instruction is valid for every prefix. Observe that the sets of valid instructions for REP and LOCK are disjoint, so that REP and LOCK can never be used together. This prevents the 386 from locking up a multiple-processor system for the duration of a repeated string operation.

Table 3.26 Valid Instruction Forms for the LOCK Prefix

ADD mem,reg	ADD mem,imm	DEC mem
ADC mem,reg	ADC mem,imm	INC mem
AND mem,reg	AND mem,imm	NEG mem
OR mem,reg	OR mem,imm	NOT mem
SBB mem,reg	SBB mem,imm	
SUB mem,reg	SUB mem,imm	XCHG reg,mem
XOR mem,reg	XOR mem,imm	XCHG mem,reg
BT mem,reg	BT mem,imm	
BTR mem,reg	BTR mem,imm	
BTS mem,reg	BTS mem,imm	
BTC mem,reg	BTC mem,imm	

Finally, let's consider interrupts during prefixed instructions. For the most part, interrupts occur between instructions. However, if an interrupt is forced to wait until a repeated string instruction completes its execution, it might have to wait a (relatively) long time. So the processor was designed to permit interrupts to be serviced after any repetitions of a repeated string instruction. While the repetitions are occurring, the instruction pointer contains the address of the (first prefix byte of the) instruction. If the instruction is interrupted, this is the address that is saved, and this is the address at which execution resumes after the interrupt processing is complete. Thus, if the instruction contains any prefixes in addition to the repeat prefix, these prefixes will be part of the instruction when it is re-executed. This was not true for the 8086. (Note that the re-executed string instruction does not redo what was done during the initial execution; the count in ECX and string pointers in ESI and EDI were updated during each repetition prior to the interrupt, and the second execution starts with these updated values.)

Flag Settings

Throughout this chapter, references have been made to the flag settings following certain instructions. This section ties all that information together and completely describes the behavior of the flags.

Three flags (IOPL, NT, and VM) relate to the processor's protection mechanism and are described in Chapter 5. The remaining flags can be divided into two types: *status* flags and *control* flags. The former reflect properties of the results generated by certain instructions, and the latter control the operations of the processor. Table 3.27 shows the instructions whose results affect the status flags and the instructions that are used to establish the settings of the control flags. Let's attempt to explain the behavior of some of these flags.

Table 3.27 Flag Settings

A-Status Flags	OF	CF	AF	SF	ZF	PF
Addition & Subtract						
ADD ADC SUB SBB	+	+	+	+	+	+
CMP NEG CMPS SCAS	+	+	+	+	+	+
Increment & Decrement						
INC DEC	+	−	+	+	+	+
Multiplication & Division						
MUL IMUL	+	+	?	?	?	?
DIV IDIV	?	?	?	?	?	?
Decimal Arithmetic						
DAA DAS	?	+	+	+	+	+
AAA AAS	?	+	+	?	?	?
AAM AAD	?	?	?	+	+	+

Table 3.27 Flag Settings (continued)

A-Status Flags	OF	CF	AF	SF	ZF	PF
Boolean						
AND OR XOR TEST	0	0	?	+	+	+
Shift & Rotate						
SHL SHR (unit)	+	+	?	+	+	+
SHL SHR (variable)	?	+	?	+	+	+
SAR	0	+	?	+	+	+
ROL ROR RCL RCR (unit)	+	+	−	−	−	−
ROL ROR RCL RCR (variable)	?	+	−	−	−	−
Restore Flags						
POPF POPFD IRET IRETD	+	+	+	+	+	+
SAHF	−	+	+	+	+	+
Carry Flag Settings						
STC	−	1	−	−	−	−
CLC	−	0	−	−	−	−
CMC	−	*	−	−	−	−
Bit Array Instructions						
BT BTS BTR BTC	−	+	−	−	−	−
BSF BSR	−	−	−	−	+	−
SHLD SHRD	?	+	?	+	+	+

B-Control Flags	DF	IF	TF
Restore Flags			
POPF POPFD IRET IRETD	+	+	+
Interrupts			
INT INTO	−	0	0
Direct Flag Settings			
STD	1	−	−
CLD	0	−	−
Interrupt Flag Settings			
STI	−	1	−
CLI	−	0	−

Legend: + = affected   * = complemented
        1 = set to 1   ? = undefined
        0 = set to 0   − = unaffected

Addition and subtraction instructions affect all status flags in the following manner: the overflow flag (OF) and carry flag (CF) indicate if the instruction resulted in a signed or unsigned result out of range; the auxiliary carry flag (AF) indicates if a correction is needed for a decimal operation; and the sign flag (SF), zero flag (ZF), and parity flag (PF) indicate if the result is negative, zero, or contains an even number of 1's.

Grouped with the addition and subtraction instructions are the compare instructions (CMP, CMPS, SCAS) and the negation instruction (NEG). The compare instructions perform a subtraction, and the flags are set to reflect the result of this subtraction. The NEG instruction subtracts its operand from zero, and the flags are set to reflect the result of this subtraction. The only time NEG doesn't set the carry flag to 1 is when the value being "negated" is zero. The only time it does set the overflow flag to 1 is when the value being negated is the bottommost negative value: -128 for eight bits, -32768 for 16 bits, or -2147483648 for 32 bits.

The increment and decrement instructions affect the status flags in the same manner as addition and subtraction instructions, except they do not affect the carry flag. This gives us the ability to write the following loop, which performs multiple-precision arithmetic:

1. Point ESI to the least significant byte of first operand.

2. Point EDI to the least significant byte of second operand.

3. Clear carry (CLC).

4. Add-with-carry (ADC) byte pointed at by ESI to byte pointed at by EDI.

5. Increment (INC) ESI so it points at next higher byte of first operand.

6. Increment (INC) EDI so it points at next higher byte of second operand.

7. Jump back to step 4 if operands contain more bytes.

If the INC instructions in steps 5 and 6 affected the carry flag, the next executions of the ADC instruction in step 4 would not give the correct result.

Multiplication instructions (other than the special forms of IMUL) generate double-length results and would therefore have to base the status flags on as many as 64 bits. Since no other instruction bases its flag settings on more than 32 bits, the processor would need a special flag-setting mechanism just for this one instruction. It isn't clear what we would do with such flag settings anyway. To keep the processor simple, the values of most of the status flags are left *undefined* after a multiplication instruction. Undefined means the processor makes no attempt to set the flags in any particular manner; it just executes the instruction in the simplest way it can with total disregard for flag settings. Future versions of the processor might execute the instruction in a different manner and give different settings to the flags.

After a multiplication instruction is executed, it would be useful to know if the product can be considered as a single-length number without being out of range. (The product considered as a double-length number is never out of range.) This would enable us to do such things as multiply a byte by another byte and add the product to a third byte. For this reason, the overflow and carry flags are not left undefined; both are set if the product is not a single-length value.

For simplicity, all status flags are undefined after executing a division instruction.

The only status flag that is important after executing a decimal addition or subtraction adjustment is the carry flag (needed for multiple-precision arithmetic); all the other flags could have been left undefined. However, the 8080 has a DAA instruction (its only decimal instruction), and that instruction sets all five 8080 status flags. (The 8080 doesn't have an overflow flag.) So, for compatibility, the 386 DAA instruction does the same. DAS, AAA, and AAS should also affect these five flags just to be consistent; DAS does, but implementation difficulties caused the sign flag, zero flag, and parity flag to be undefined after an AAA or AAS. It's not clear what carry and auxiliary carry mean with respect to the AAM and AAD instructions, so these were left undefined.

Since Boolean operations never produce results that are out of range, both the overflow and carry flags are set to 0 after executing such instructions. The auxiliary carry flag has no utility following a Boolean instruction (its only purpose is for decimal arithmetic), so it is left undefined. The sign, zero, and parity flags are set to reflect the result of the instruction.

One Boolean instruction, NOT, is missing from the list of Boolean instructions that affect the flags. NOT does not affect the flags. This was done so that the instruction NOT AL would be compatible with its predecessor on the 8080, the CMA (Complement A) instruction.

Shift instructions are nothing more than multiplying or dividing by a power of two. The status flags reflect the status of the result with the following two exceptions: the value of the auxiliary carry flag is undefined (we are not concerned with decimal arithmetic here), and the value of the overflow flag is undefined for variable shifts (the mechanism to detect overflow in this case was too complex). The arithmetic right shift (SAR) can never generate a signed result that is out of range, and therefore the overflow flag is set to 0 after executing such an instruction.

The rotate instructions were designed to be compatible with the 8080 rotate instructions and affect the flags in exactly the same way. For this reason, they affect the carry flag and do not affect the auxiliary carry flag, sign flag, zero flag, or parity flag. For consistency, it was decided that the rotate instructions should affect the overflow flag in the same way that the shift instructions do, even though it's not clear what overflow means in this case.

The flag-restoring instructions restore the flags to some previously saved values. In particular, POPF and IRET/IRETD restore all the flags (status as well as control) to the values saved on the stack. SAHF is an odd instruction (included solely for compatibility with a similar instruction in the 8080) that restores the five 8080 status flags to values contained in AH.

All interrupts clear the the trap flag and the interrupt-enable flag. If the trap flag were not cleared, the processor would single step through the debugger when the debugger was attempting to single step through our program. Clearing the interrupt-enable flag gives the interrupt procedure the flexibility of deciding whether to allow a second interrupt to be processed by executing an STI as its first instruction.

The behavior of the carry-flag instructions, direction-flag instructions, and interrupt-flag instructions is straightforward. They set, clear, or complement the individual flag and do not affect any other flag.

The Bit Test instructions BT, BTS, BTR, and BTC return their results in the carry flag; they change no other flags. The Bit Scan instructions set the zero flag according to whether a 1-bit was found; they change no other flags. The Double Shift instructions

SHLD and SHRD act just like SHL and SHR: all the status flags are set appropriately except overflow and auxiliary carry, which are undefined.

And Now for Floating Point

In this chapter we have presented the basic instructions that the 386 is capable of executing. One thing lacking is the ability to do floating-point computations; for this the 386 relies on a 387 numeric processor. The 387 and the instructions that it executes for the 386 are presented in the next chapter.

References

The 386 instruction set is described in reference 1 and its assembly language, ASM386, in reference 2. The material in this chapter is based on the authors' presentation of similar material for the 8086 and 286 in references 3 and 4. For general information on multiple precision integer arithmetic, see reference 5.

1.   *80386 Programmer's Reference Manual*, Intel Corp., 1986.

2.   *ASM386 Assembly Language Reference Manual*, Intel Corp., 1986.

3.   S.P. Morse, *The 8086/8088 Primer*, Hayden Book Company, Rochelle Park, N.J., 1982.

4.   S.P. Morse and D.J. Albert, *The 80286 Architecture*, John Wiley and Sons, New York, 1986.

5.   D.E. Knuth, *The Art of Computer Programming, vol. 2: Seminumerical Algorithms*, Addison-Wesley, Reading, Mass., 1981.

C H A P T E R

4

FLOATING-POINT COMPUTATION

Introduction

In previous chapters we described the rich set of arithmetic instructions provided by the 386 for operating on integers. However, many problems, particularly those involving physical quantities, are phrased in terms of real numbers, that is, numbers with fractional parts. Computations involving real numbers (or their approximations) are called *numerical computations* and are the subject matter of that branch of mathematics called *numerical analysis*. Some applications of numerical computation are: scientific computation, statistics, computer graphics, simulation of continuous processes, numerical control of machine tools, process control, and navigation. All of these require that real numbers be somehow represented and manipulated by computer.

One technique for representing real numbers is to assume the existence of a *binary point* (just like a decimal point) within a 386 doubleword. For example, instead of interpreting hex 00000071 as $1110001_2 = 113_{10}$, we could assume a binary point before the third-from-the-right position and interpret the word as $1110.001_2 = 14.125_{10}$. When interpreted in this way, the 386 arithmetic instructions still do the correct things, as long as all their operands have their (assumed) binary points fixed in the same positions. Such a convention is called *fixed-point representation*.

Immediately, we see a problem: the range between the largest and the smallest nonzero numbers that can be represented is small. For example, assuming that the binary point is placed so that 20 bits are to its right (giving us less than 6 digits to the right of the decimal point), we find that the largest representable number is only $2^{12} - 1 = 4095$. If we wanted larger numbers, we would have to compromise on the the number of digits to the right of the decimal, since the position of the binary point must be fixed for all numbers.

One solution to the problem is to carefully *scale* (implicitly multiply by a scale factor) every number so that it is in range. This technique is more difficult than it may seem, since a calculation may involve intermediate results wildly different in size from the calculation's initial inputs and final outputs. One cause of this is that numerical computations may involve approximations to the notions of "infinitesimal" and "infinite" implicit within such operations as integration and differentiation. But even innocent-appearing tasks such as solving linear equations are not without difficulties.

Although manual scaling is still used today in applications where high performance is desired, the ranges of numbers are known, and programming effort is not at a premium, most programmers would rather have the computer keep track of the scaling. This is done by attaching to each number some indication of what factor it has been scaled by. If we restrict ourselves to scale factors that are powers of two, then this is the same as specifying, along with each number, a second number giving the position of the binary point in the first. The position of the binary-point may change from number to number, that is, it may "float." We have thus arrived at *floating-point representation*.

The 386 has no built-in floating-point capability. One way to obtain such capability is to write a library of subroutines implementing the various arithmetic operations. However, floating-point arithmetic can be substantially speeded by using specialized hardware. Intel manufactures the 80387 Numeric Processor Extension chip to provide just such a speedup.

The 80387 (or 387 for short) performs floating-point operations at speeds many times faster than the equivalent 386 subroutines. Programmers can include 387 instructions in their 386 programs just as if they were actual 386 instructions. When the 386 encounters a 387 instruction, it automatically passes the instruction to the 387 for execution. This creates the illusion that the 386 can execute floating-point instructions.

What happens if the 386 encounters a 387 instruction but a 387 chip is not present in the system? In this case the 386 transfers control to an exception-handler subroutine designated by the operating system. How this is done is described in Chapter 6. Intel provides an exception-handler subroutine, called E80387, which emulates in software what the 387 would do if it were present. So the E80387 software creates the illusion that a 387 is present in the system and thus maintains the illusion that the 386 can execute floating-point instructions. An ordinary (nonoperating-system) program can't tell the difference between the emulation software and the 387 hardware, except that floating-point operations run more slowly. This allows microcomputer system manufacturers to cleverly sell basic systems without 387s and then offer the 387 as a performance upgrade.

In the remainder of this chapter we first describe the floating-point formats recognized by the 387. Then we describe the architecture of the 387, including its registers and instructions. Along the way we provide examples of 387 programming and explain the reasons for the 387's more unusual features.

History of 86 Family Floating-Point Coprocessors

In order to understand some of the design decisions of the 387, we must consider the history of the 387's predecessors, the 8087 and the 287. The 8087 was developed in the late 70s, shortly after the 8086 was designed. At the same time, the industry standard for floating-point processing was being drafted. Intel was heavily involved in the development of the standard, and the 8087 closely follows what was eventually published as draft 8.0 (see reference 4).

A few years later an upgraded coprocessor, the 287, was introduced, primarily to improve the hardware interface between the 286 and its coprocessor. At that time, there were discrepancies between the current draft of the floating-point standard and the implementation of the 8087. However, the standard was not yet finalized and approved. There was still the possibility that the standard could change further, so Intel decided to hold off making changes to conform to the standard, until the standard was fixed.

Finally, by the time the 387 was developed, the standard was approved (reference 5). At this point, Intel decided that the standard took precedence over compatibility with the 387's predecessors. A couple of features present on the 8087 and 287 were actually dropped, so that the 387 would follow the standard. The features were there to provide error detection on a more refined level, and their omission does not cause compatibility problems with old software. We describe these features at appropriate points in our discussion of the 387.

Floating-Point Formats

Floating-point representation is taught in high-school science classes under the name "scientific notation." For example, the number $-1,234,000$ may be expressed in scientific notation as:

$$-1.234 \times 10^6$$

The notation contains three parts: the *sign* $-$, the *significand* 1.234, and the *exponent* 6.

Every number has many representations in scientific notation. For example, all of the following are equal:

$$13.2 \times 10^4 = 1.32 \times 10^5 = 0.132 \times 10^6 = 0.0132 \times 10^7$$

In order to avoid this multiplicity, for each number we can choose one of the many equal representations and call it *normal* or, more verbosely, *normalized*. All the rest are then "abnormal" or, more obscurely, *denormalized*. In particular, we can always choose the representation with exactly one nonzero digit to the left of the decimal point in the significand (1.32×10^5 in the above example). This is a particularly good choice, since it saves us from having to write leading zeros (for example, 0.0000132) in the significand. Thus each number will have a unique, agreed-upon normalized representation.

These concepts carry over to 387 floating-point representation. The only difference is that the significand and exponent are each represented in binary rather than decimal, and the exponent specifies a power of two rather than a power of ten. Figure 4.1 shows the three floating-point formats recognized by the 387: *single precision, double precision,* and *extended precision.* In some Intel literature, these are also called *short real, long real,* and *temporary real.* Each format is divided into the three fields previously mentioned: sign, exponent, and significand. The formats are stored in memory as a sequence of 4, 8, or 10 bytes.

Recall that for 386 integers, the least significant (rightmost) byte is stored at the lowest address, while the most significant (leftmost) byte is stored at the highest address. Thus, as you work your way to higher addresses, you encounter quantities of greater significance. The complete integer is addressed by addressing its lowest addressed (least significant) byte.

This same scheme is used by the 387 for all floating-point numbers. The lowest addressed byte of a floating-point number is the least significant byte of its significand. Working our way to higher addresses, we encounter more significant portions of the significand, then the least significant part of the exponent, then more significant portions of the exponent, and finally the highest addressed byte of the floating-point number, namely the byte containing the seven most significant bits of the exponent and the one-bit sign field.

Note that the ordering of fields in a floating-point number is consistent with the idea that more important or *significant* things should come at higher addresses. The sign field is most important in comparing the values of two floating-point numbers. Next in importance is the exponent; finally, the significand is least in importance.

Let's consider the fields of a floating-point number in detail.

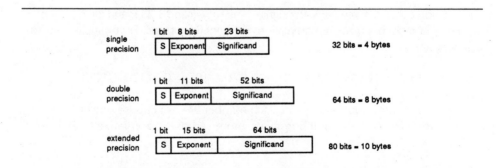

Figure 4.1 387 floating-point number formats.

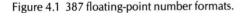

The Sign Field   The sign field is a single bit, with 0 indicating that the floating-point number is positive and 1 that it's negative. What about floating-point zero? Any floating-point number with all 0's in the exponent and significand fields is considered to be zero. Thus there are two zeros, namely $+0$ and -0. The 387 endeavors to hide this fact from the programmer. In particular, the 387's comparison instructions consider any two zeros to be equal.

The Significand Field   Significands of 387 floating-point numbers are of the form:

X . X X X X X X X . . . X
↑   X = 0 or 1
binary point

To obtain the greatest precision (that is, maximize the number of significant bits in the significand) we require that floating-point numbers be normalized, just as in our discussion of scientific notation. Floating-point exponents must be adjusted so that the leftmost (most significant) bit of the significand is not 0. Thus we need not waste precious significand bits by storing leading 0's. For example, rather than using a significand of 0.0001011 . . . 11, we must decrease the exponent by four and use a significand of 1.011 . . . 110000 instead.

We now get a payoff for working in binary. Requiring the leading binary digit of the significand to be nonzero is equivalent to requiring it to be 1 (this isn't true in bases other than two). So all significands are of the form:

1 . X X X X X X X . . . X

But if the leading bit is always 1, then there's no need to store it in every floating-point number. To get an additional bit of precision, the 387 stores single- and double-precision numbers without the leading bit. Hence it is "impossible" to have a single- or double-precision number which is not normalized. For example, if the significand field of a single- or double-precision number contains the bits 0011 . . . 101, then the significand itself is actually 10011 . . . 101. We weasel out of the word "impossible" later when we talk about error values; however, notice already that the encoding for zero (all 0 bits in the exponent and significand fields) is an exception to our rule.

For several reasons, this implicit-bit scheme is applied only to single- and double- but not to extended-precision numbers. First, it is slightly faster to operate on a number when the leading bit is explicitly present (all numbers inside the 387 are in extended format). Second, an extended-precision number already has ample bits of precision.

The Exponent Field   The exponent field specifies the power of two by which the significand must be multiplied to obtain the value of the floating-point number. Some computers, notably the IBM 360/370, use powers of sixteen instead of two. Powers of two were chosen for the 387 because of the implicit-bit trick described above, and also because they offer the greatest speed for a given amount of hardware.

In order to accommodate negative exponents, the exponent field contains the sum of the actual exponent and a positive constant called the *bias*. This guarantees that the exponent field always contains a positive integer. The bias is 127 for single precision, 1023 for double precision, and 16383 for extended precision. For example, if the exponent of a single-precision number is 5, the value stored in the exponent field is 127 + 5 = 132; if the exponent is −5, the exponent field then contains 127 − 5 = 122.

In single-precision format (see Figure 4.1) the exponent field is eight bits wide. The largest integer it can accommodate is then $2^8 - 1 = 255$. The largest possible exponent is then 255 − 127 = 128 and the smallest is 0 − 127 = −127. The 387 reserves the use of the highest and lowest exponents for handling errors (we'll get to this shortly), so the largest allowed single-precision exponent is actually 127 and the smallest is −126. Similar considerations apply to double-precision and extended-precision numbers.

Formulas for the Values of Floating-Point Numbers   We now have enough information to write down a formula for the value of a floating-point number in terms of the values stored in its various fields:

$$(-1)^{sgn}\ (1.f_1f_2\ldots f_{23})\ 2^{(E-127)} \qquad \text{(single precision)}$$
$$(-1)^{sgn}\ (1.f_1f_2\ldots f_{52})\ 2^{(E-1023)} \qquad \text{(double precision)}$$
$$(-1)^{sgn}\ (f_1.f_2\ldots f_{64})\ 2^{(E-16383)} \qquad \text{(extended precision)}$$

where:

sgn is the value stored in the sign bit
$f_1f_2\ldots$ are the bits stored in the significand field
E is the value stored in the exponent field

As an example, the single-precision number that is represented by:

1 01111110 11000000000000000000000

has s = 1, E = 126, $f_1 = 1$, and $f_2 = 1$. Thus the value is:

$$(-1)^1\ (1.11_2)\ 2^{(126-127)} = -1\ (1.75)\ 2^1 = -0.875$$

The Sizes of Floating-Point Numbers   Now that we've described the internal structure of floating-point numbers in great detail, let's step back a moment and consider why we have three different sizes of floating-point numbers at all. Table 4.1 gives the ranges and precisions of the three formats very conservatively in decimal.

The 32-bit single-precision format is quite similar to that of other computers. We note, however, that with only six digits of precision guaranteed, it is unable to represent even the reasonable number 9,999,999 completely accurately. Therefore we should take double-precision as our "default" format to avoid loss of precision and

Table 4.1 Guaranteed Decimal Range and Precision of Floating-Point Numbers

	Significant Digits	Least Power of 10	Greatest Power of 10
Single	6	−37	38
Double	15	−307	308
Extended	19	−4931	4932

use single-precision only when memory space is tight. Since the 387 internally converts all numbers to extended precision before operating upon them, arithmetic of double-precision numbers isn't much slower than arithmetic of single-precision numbers.

The 64-bit double-precision format is also not much different from that of other computers. On some computers, single- and double-precision numbers have the same size exponent fields. In our case, the exponent field increases from 8 to 11 bits. One advantage in having equal-sized exponent fields is that a double-precision number can rapidly be converted to single precision by simply dropping its four low-order bytes, and a single-precision number can be converted to double by appending four low-order zero bytes. On the other hand, increasing the exponent from 8 to 11 bits guarantees that the product of any two single-precision numbers can always be represented in double precision without any loss of precision or possibility of error. Note that we have already encountered this desirable property of multiplication in *integer* arithmetic (recall the 386 MUL instruction).

Finally, we get to 80-bit extended-precision format. This format isn't found on many other computers. Its first appearance was on the 387's original predecessor, the 8087. The purpose of extended-precision is to hold *temporary* results in order to facilitate accurate computation of double-precision *final* results. It is not intended that extended-precision be used for final results. By using this format, with its enormous range and precision (see Table 4.1), even naive numerical programmers can often match the carefully honed code of experts in precision and reliability.

To see the need for extended precision, let's consider the problem of computing the exponentiation function. The function $z = x^y$ is important because, of all the functions commonly found in programming languages, it is the most difficult to compute accurately. It would seem reasonable to expect that if x and y are accurate when represented in double-precision format, $z = x^y$ should be accurate in double-precision also. However, this is very difficult to guarantee without using an extended-precision format for storing intermediate results. To see why, let's compute z by using the standard formula:

$$z = 2^{(y\,log_2(x))}$$

Here z is the final result and y $\log_2(x)$ is an intermediate result. Decompose the intermediate result into its integer and fractional parts:

$$y \, log_2(x) \; = \; I + F$$

where I is the integer part of y $\log_2(x)$ and F is its fractional part. The floating-point number that holds this temporary result must have enough bits in its significand to represent both I and F. In order to find out how many bits are needed, let's see how many are required for I, how many for F, and then add the two numbers together. We do this by working backwards from the final result. In terms of I and F, the final result z is:

$$z \; = \; 2^{I+F} \; = \; (2^I)(2^F)$$

Since 2 to a fractional power always lies between 1 and 2, we see that 2^F is in fact the significand in the normalized floating-point representation of z, and I is its (unbiased) exponent. Since the output z spans the entire range of double-precision numbers (indeed, if y = 1 then z = x), I requires 11 bits of precision and F requires 53 (since normalized double-precision numbers have 11-bit exponent fields, 52-bit significand fields, and one implicit leading bit of 1). Thus the intermediate result I + F requires a significand of at least 11 + 53 = 64 bits. It is no accident that extended-precision provides the exact 64-bit significand that is required.

By now, you have probably asked yourself, "Why is the size of an extended-precision number ten bytes, rather than some power of two like everything else in the computer world?" In particular, subscripting through arrays of ten-byte quantities requires a (slow) multiplication by ten rather than a (fast) left-shift operation. Programmers more interested in speed than memory space might allocate sixteen (the next higher power of two) bytes to each extended-precision number and treat the extra six bytes as filler. Why then didn't the 387's designers use sixteen bytes for the total length? One reason is that more arithmetic hardware, or slower performance with the same amount of hardware, would be the result. Another reason arises from the contradiction inherent in the goals of extended precision. Extended precision has been provided in order to protect intermediate results arising from the computation of functions over double-precision numbers. But if people find extended precision *too* easy to use, they may do all computation in extended precision. But then they would need an *extended* extended precision to protect the intermediate results of these computations . . .

The Ranges of Floating-Point Numbers   The ranges of the three floating-point formats are displayed in Figure 4.2. This figure reveals some interesting facts about arithmetic on the 387. If the result of an arithmetic operation is a value less than a least negative or greater than a greatest positive value for a format, then the operation is said to have *overflowed* that format. If the result of an arithmetic operation is nonzero, yet lies between the greatest negative and least positive values for a format, then the operation is said to have *underflowed* that format.

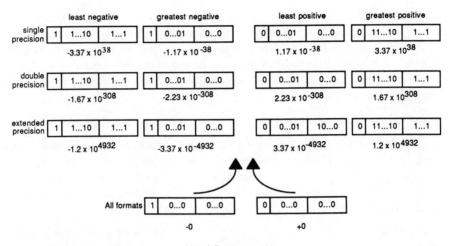

Figure 4.2 Range of numbers in normalized floating point.

Now notice that Figure 4.2 is perfectly symmetrical with regard to positive versus negative numbers. Thus, the absolute value operation can never overflow or underflow. Note that this property doesn't hold, for example, for 386 integer arithmetic.

Now focus attention on the positive numbers. If we multiply each least positive by its corresponding greatest positive, we find that in all three formats the answer is approximately 4. In other words, the greatest positive number is roughly 4 times the reciprocal of the least. Thus, the frequently occurring operations 1/x, 2/x, 3/x, and pi/x cannot produce an overflow. These operations can produce an underflow. But the 387 has the means to recover from such underflows and reduce their effects, in the case of the above operations, to the loss of at worst two bits of precision. How this feat is accomplished is our next topic for discussion.

Exception Values   Error conditions or *exceptions* sometimes arise during the execution of floating-point arithmetic operations. The most well known is division by zero, but others are possible. Here is a list of the kinds of numeric exceptions that may occur within the 387, ranked in roughly increasing order of severity:

Inexact Result—This condition arises when the result of a floating-point operation cannot be precisely represented in the desired destination format. For example, 1.0 divided by 3.0 produces in base two the nonterminating fraction 0.0101010101. . . which cannot be represented exactly in any binary floating-point format. Another example occurs if 9.87654321, represented as a double-precision number, is converted to single precision; single precision hasn't enough room for all nine significant digits.

Most users of floating-point arithmetic wouldn't consider an inexact result to be an error and would instead expect some sort of rounding or truncation to automatically take place.

Numeric Underflow—As we have already mentioned, this occurs when a nonzero result is too small in absolute value to be represented, that is, when it's too close to zero. Dividing 1.0 by the largest extended-precision number is an example. Converting the smallest positive nonzero extended-precision number to double-precision is another. Use of extended precision for all intermediate results makes this exception very unlikely.

Division by Zero—This occurs when a nonzero number is divided by zero.

Numeric Overflow—As we have already mentioned, this occurs when a result is too large in absolute value to be represented. For example, add the largest extended-precision number to itself. For another example, convert the largest extended-precision number to double-precision. Again, this exception is very unlikely if extended precision is used for all intermediate results.

Invalid Operation—This catchall category includes whatever is left over, such as division of zero by zero, square root of a negative number, and trying to use a nonexistent (empty) 387 register.

There is one more exception, called *Denormalized Operand*, which we will describe shortly.

One popular method for handling computer error conditions of all kinds is to immediately suspend the operation and transfer to an exception-handling procedure. This method is known as *trapping*. Another method is to have the obstructed operation return a special *error value* or *exception value* and allow the computation to proceed. The error-value method is rarely used in nonnumeric programming for the following reasons:

1. In order for the user to detect that an exception has occurred, the error value should be distinct from ordinary values. Error values arising from different kinds of exceptions should also be distinct. But it's often difficult to obtain the extra bits needed to mark the various error values. For example, few programmers would stand for a reduction in the range of 8-bit integers in order to accommodate a few error values.

2. Whenever a program contains a conditional jump based on a comparison, the possibility that one of the operands to the comparison is an error value must be considered. The extra cases make for a more complex program.

3. In debugging a program, a programmer works backwards in the program text from the point where the problem first appears to the instruction that is the problem's ultimate cause. The greater the distance between the mistake and its manifestation, the harder it is to find the mistake. Continuing program execution after an error makes debugging more difficult.

In floating-point computation, the situation is somewhat different.

1. The 387 allows for error values by forbidding ordinary floating-point numbers from having exponent fields of 000. . .00 binary or 111. . .11 binary (the biggest and smallest values in each format). We have already remarked about this exclusion. The reduction in floating-point range is quite small.

2. Tests of floating-point numbers are less frequent than nonnumeric tests. Furthermore, comparisons for equality and nonequality of floating-point numbers are rarely performed. The bit patterns for 387 error values are chosen so that most comparisons work out correctly, even if the programmer is ignorant of error values.

3. Even though a program produces error values for some intermediate results, it is still possible that it will produce the correct final answer. This is because floating-point computation is approximate computation. So it may pay to continue the computation for as long as possible. Error values can be used in this way to create programs which are resistant to floating-point exceptions.

From another point of view, error values simply increase the range of representation of the floating-point formats. In this view, error values aren't erroneous at all, and programmers familiar with them can use them intentionally to simplify their programs. That's why the term *exception value* is probably better than *error value*.

The 387 gives programmers the choice of trapping exceptions or allowing exception values. Exception trapping can be individually enabled or masked for each of the types of exceptions we've described. Masking one type of exception may be riskier than masking another in that a program written by a naive user may do the wrong thing if an exception value happens to turn up. Below, we describe the exception value produced for each type of exception. The descriptions are ordered in terms of increasing risk.

Inexact Result Exception   If the inexact result exception is masked, the 387 will round the result into an ordinary floating-point number rather than returning a special exception value. The 387 offers the programmer a choice of four different modes of rounding. They are all depicted in Figure 4.3. The Xs on the number lines in the figure denote infinitely precise real numbers which are the "true" results of arithmetic operations. The large dots represent the nearest 387 floating-point numbers on either side of the "true" result.

In *rounding toward zero*, also known as *chopping* or *truncating*, the "true" result is made to fit into the destination format by ignoring (zeroing) a sufficient number of low-order bits. This is equivalent to choosing the closest floating-point number that is smaller in absolute value than the "true" result (see Figure 4.3a). This type of rounding is most useful in integer arithmetic where, for example, we would like to round 3/2 into 1 and $-$ 3/2 into -1.

For applications other than simulating integer arithmetic, we would like to minimize round-off error as much as possible. For this reason, it is best to round the "true"
result to the very closest floating-point number. This method is called *rounding to
nearest* and is depicted in Figure 4.3b. If the "true" result is precisely midway between a
pair of floating-point numbers, then the 387 will break the tie by choosing the *even*
number, that is, that floating-point number of the pair with a 0 in its least significant bit.
Some computers break the tie by always rounding up; however, this introduces a
significant bias into lengthy computations. For purposes of illustration, let's use a
decimal floating-point representation with five-digit significands, assume that ties are
broken by rounding upwards, and compute the following sum:

$$a = 1.0000 \qquad b = 0.55555$$

$$
\begin{aligned}
a + b & & = 1.5556 \\
- b & & = 1.0001 \\
+ b - b & & = 1.0002 \\
+ b - b & & = 1.0003
\end{aligned}
$$

The result keeps growing, despite the fact that we are adding and subtracting the
same value. This unstable drift disappears if we compute the same sum, rounding to
nearest even:

$$
\begin{aligned}
a + b & & = 1.5556 \\
- b & & = 1.0000 \\
+ b - b & & = 1.0000 \\
+ b - b & & = 1.0000
\end{aligned}
$$

Because of these and numerous other nice properties, rounding to nearest is the
default rounding mode on the 387. The other rounding modes should be used only for
special purposes.

Figure 4.3c and 4.3d depict two more 387 rounding modes, *rounding up* (toward
$+\infty$) and and *rounding down* (toward $-\infty$). These are used to implement *interval
arithmetic*. A program using ordinary floating-point arithmetic produces a floating-
point answer which only approximates the "true" answer. It requires a difficult analysis
of the program to say in general how good an approximation the computed answer
actually is. There is an alternate approach which eliminates the need for this analysis of
round off. That is to do each arithmetic operation twice, once rounding down, the
second time rounding up. The "true" result of the arithmetic operation is then
guaranteed to lie somewhere between the two results obtained.

Unfortunately, it's usually not possible to bound the "true" result of an entire
program simply by running it first rounding down, and then again rounding up. One
problem is that multiplication by a negative number converts an upper bound to a
lower bound (and vice versa). Another is that conditional jumps based upon the results
of floating-point comparisons must be carefully analyzed. So there's no free lunch.

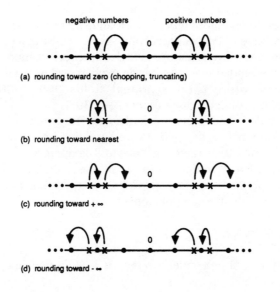

Figure 4.3 387 rounding modes.

Numeric Underflow Exception   We now encounter our first exception value. Recall that the least exponent field value 000. . .00 has not yet been used. Recall also that in single- and double-precision numbers the leading bit of the significand isn't stored but instead is always assumed to be 1. We can make the convention that whenever the exponent field is 000. . .00, we will pretend instead that it's 000. . .01 (the smallest ordinary exponent field) *and assume that the leading bit of the significand is 0, not 1.* This increases our ability to represent very small numbers. In single-precision numbers the exponent bias is 127, so an exponent field of 00000001 corresponds to an exponent of -126. We will also consider an exponent field of 00000000 to correspond to an exponent of -126, but with an implicit significand leading bit of 0. For example, consider the following single-precision numbers:

$$0 \;\; 00000001 \;\; 10000000000000000000000 \;\; \text{denotes} \;\; 1.1_2 \times 2^{-126}$$
$$0 \;\; 00000001 \;\; 00000000000000000000000 \;\; \text{denotes} \;\; 1.0_2 \times 2^{-126}$$
$$0 \;\; 00000000 \;\; 10000000000000000000000 \;\; \text{denotes} \;\; 0.1_2 \times 2^{-126}$$
$$0 \;\; 00000000 \;\; 01000000000000000000000 \;\; \text{denotes} \;\; 0.1_2 \times 2^{-127}$$

Note that the last two numbers are too small to be represented as ordinary floating-point numbers. Also observe that by permitting leading 0's in the significand, we no longer have a normalized number. In effect, we use significand leading 0's to artificially extend our exponents to more negative values, at the expense of loss of precision in the significand. This is clearly visible in the last example above. We can extend a single-precision exponent from -126 all the way down to -149 with this technique, but by then we are reduced to one bit of precision. Floating-point numbers with 000. . .00 exponent fields are called *denormals*. For the sake of consistency, we apply these conventions to extended as well as single- and double-precision numbers. We do this despite the fact that extended precision has an explicit leading significand bit. Thus, both of the extended-precision exponent fields 000000000000001 and 000000000000000 correspond to the exponent −16382.

If the numeric underflow exception is masked, the 387's response to an underflow is to generate a denormal. If the underflowed result is so small that it can't be represented as a denormal, then a zero is generated. This approach is known as *gradual underflow*. Most computers produce zero on all masked underflows; that is, they *abruptly underflow*. Gradual underflow provides a safety cushion for moderate underflow. For example, consider the computation:

$$(y - x) + x$$

where $y - x$ underflows. Abrupt underflow returns x, while gradual underflow returns the correct answer y.

In the above example, the denormal $(y - x)$ is an operand to the operation of addition. We next describe in detail what happens when denormals are used as operands. In the process, we'll introduce a new type of 386 exception, mentioned previously but not discussed.

Denormalized Operand Exception   A denormalized operand exception occurs whenever a denormal is used as an operand to an instruction. Trapping this exception is useful primarily for simulating other modes of arithmetic on the 387. Most programmers aren't interested in doing this, so if they mask the numeric underflow exception and thereby give their consent to the *production* of denormals, they will probably also mask the denormalized operand exception and consent to the *use* of denormals too. So let's see what happens if the denormalized operand exception is masked.

Operations on the 387 involving denormal operands either:

1.   Produce a zero if the result is too small to store as a denormal (for example, multiplication of two denormals) *or*

2.   Produce a denormal result if the result is small enough to store as a denormal (for example, addition of two small denormals) *or*

3.   Produce a normal result if the lack of precision in the denormal operand affects the result less than roundoff (for example, adding a denormal to a large normal) *or*

4.   Produce a normal result if the result is too big to be a denormal, even though the result lacks precision (for example, multiplication of a denormal by a big normal)

Denormals result when precision is sacrificed in order to increase range. When the 8087 was released, there was concern that the inferior precision of denormals would seriously corrupt the precision of subsequent computations in which they are used. So the 8087 and 287 don't produce a normal result in case 4 above, but instead produce an exception value called an *unnormal*. (See reference 1 for more information.) Experience has revealed that support for unnormals is not as necessary as originally feared. In typical practice, only a few bit positions are lost in case 4. This loss is more than covered by the extra bits provided by the extended-precision format. So on the 387, unnormals have been dropped: in case 4, the result is silently normalized. If it is necessary to prevent the loss of precision occurring in case 4, the user can still unmask the denormalized operand exception.

If the 387 encounters an unnormal operand, it will always cause an invalid operation exception. This is unlike the 8087 and 287, which will propagate the unnormal in the calculation. In practice, however, this will never happen, since the 387 does not produce unnormals. The only way to produce unnormals is to explicitly generate them on the 386.

Division by Zero Exception   Recall that the largest exponent field coding, 111. . .11 is still unused. A floating-point number with all 1's in the exponent field and all 0's in the significand field is called an *infinity*. Since the sign bit of an infinity may be + or −, we have two infinities: $+\infty$ and $-\infty$. Infinities are produced when (1) the division by zero exception is masked and a division by zero occurs, or (2) when the numeric overflow exception is masked and an overflow occurs. Let's treat division by zero first.

Recall that there are two zeros, namely $+0$ and -0. These give rise to signed infinities in the obvious fashion:

$$x / +0 = +\infty$$
$$-x / +0 = -\infty$$
$$x / -0 = -\infty$$
$$-x / -0 = +\infty$$

where x is greater than zero and x isn't an infinity.

What happens if infinities are used as operands? The expected things happen for multiplication and division:

$$x / +\infty = +0, \qquad -x / +\infty = -0, \qquad \text{etc.}$$
$$x * +\infty = +\infty, \qquad -x * +\infty = -\infty, \qquad \text{etc.}$$
$$+\infty / x = +\infty, \qquad -\infty / x = -\infty, \qquad \text{etc.}$$
$$+\infty * +\infty = +\infty, \qquad -\infty * +\infty = -\infty, \qquad \text{etc.}$$

where again x is greater than zero and not infinite. All multiplications and divisions involving both an infinite and a zero operand lead to an invalid operation exception, as does any infinity divided by infinity.

Difficulties can come when we consider addition, subtraction, and comparison. For these operations, much depends on whether we choose to distinguish between $+\infty$ and $-\infty$. The 387 chooses to maintain the distinction; this is called *affine* infinity

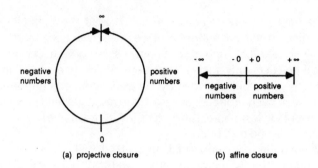

(a) projective closure   (b) affine closure

Figure 4.4 Projective and affine infinity.

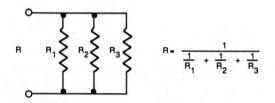

Figure 4.5 Resistors in parallel.

control (see Figure 4.4). The 8087 and 287 offer an alternative, *projective* infinity control, which is the default mode on those predecessors. Since the 287 was released, it was decided that the conservative approach offered by projective mode is not necessary. Support for projective mode was dropped from the floating-point standard, so it was dropped from the 387 also. For more information on projective mode, see reference 1.

If a finite number is added to or subtracted from an infinity, the infinity results. Addition of two infinities of the same sign and subtraction of two infinities with different signs yield the obvious things. For example, $+\infty + +\infty = +\infty$ and $-\infty - +\infty = -\infty$. Comparisons also work in the obvious manner; that is:

$$-\infty < x < +\infty$$

for every finite number x.

Figure 4.5 depicts an application involving the addition of infinities. Even if some of the resistances in the figure are zero, the 387 will deliver the correct answer, zero.

Our main concern when using infinities is that the sign of infinity might be incorrect. We next describe the primary reason for this, namely overflow.

Numeric Overflow Exception   If the numeric overflow exception is masked, then the result is set to an infinity of the same sign as the overflowed "true" result. For example, overflow when dividing a positive number by a negative number yields $-\infty$.

There is one case in which overflow does not result in infinity. If rounding is toward zero (chopping), then the result of overflow is the largest positive number (instead of $+\infty$) or the most negative number (instead of $-\infty$). This special case was added so that the 387 would conform to the standard; the 8087 and 287 return infinity in all cases.

Overflow is dangerous because (1) the sign can be unreliable, and (2) the result isn't really infinite, as in division by zero, but is simply too large to be represented. For example, consider dividing a large number by a very small one. The sign of the small number will determine the sign of the result, yet it may be only an accident of round off; that is, whether the small number is positive or negative may be determined by a round off error.

We should never mask the overflow exception unless we have carefully analyzed our program and know it can tolerate such results.

Invalid Operation Exception   We have seen that the invalid operation exception occurs when no other recovery action is possible, hence the invalid operation exception is the most serious exception.

The invalid operation exception is caused by a very heterogeneous set of conditions. For some of them (for example, runaway stack overflow) it's probably wrong to try to continue execution with an exception value, while for others (for example, division of 0 by 0) it may be possible to continue and still come up with useful results. A good strategy is to enable the invalid operation exception and let an exception handler decide. If the execution shouldn't be continued the handler can abort. If execution can be continued, the handler can return an exception value indicating the nature of the exception. Such an exception value takes the place of the numeric result and is called a *NaN*. NaN stands for "Not a Number." Any floating-point value with an exponent field of 111. . .11 (all 1's) and a significand field containing other than all 0's is considered a NaN. Hence there are many different NaNs. With this definition we have exhausted all the remaining codings possible for floating-point values.

All 387 operations that take floating-point operands and produce floating-point numbers adhere to the rule that if any of the operands are NaNs, then the largest NaN operand is the result. Thus the program continues without further exceptions, yet all descendants of NaNs are marked as suspect (that is, are NaNs). By propagating NaNs, the effect is spread like an infection, and we may find that it wasn't really serious (a common cold) or it may be an epidemic.

A problem arises in the case of operations with results which aren't floating-point numbers, and thus can't be tagged as NaNs. The main culprits are operations with integer and decimal results (no NaN encodings are defined) and comparison operations (the result is a change in program control flow). The 387 has no choice but to raise an invalid operation exception if any of these operations have NaN operands. These cases provide another reason why we recommend that the invalid operation exception not be masked.

What if the invalid operation exception is masked? Then the 387 produces a particular NaN, *indefinite*, as a result (if possible). Indefinite is coded by an exponent field of 111. . .11 and a significand *value* of 1.1. Since single- and double-precision formats have implicit significand leading bits, indefinite in these formats has a significand *field* of 1000. . .00. Since the extended-precision format has an explicit significand leading bit, indefinite in this format has a significand field of 11000. . .0.

A second use for NaNs is to represent special "numbers" whose arithmetic is defined by software. We would like these NaNs to cause an exception whenever they are used in arithmetic operations. The exception handler can compute the result and then return to the program. These are the *signaling* NaNs, as opposed to the other *quiet* NaNs, which are propagated quietly rather than signaling exceptions.

The 387 uses the first significand bit to the right of the binary point to make the distinction between signaling and quiet NaNs. If the bit is 1, the NaN is quiet; if 0, the NaN is signaling. Note that the value indefinite is a quiet NaN.

Unfortunately, on the 8087/287 all NaNs are signaling, thus making NaNs considerably less useful on these earlier machines.

Integer Formats

The 387 has instructions which convert integers to floating-point and floating-point to integers. Figure 4.6 shows the integer formats that the 387 is capable of processing. *Word integer* is simply the usual 386 16-bit integer, and *short integer* is the usual 386 doubleword (32-bit) integer. *Long integer* is the same (two's complement) format, only eight bytes long. *Packed decimal* contains 18 BCD digits, two to a byte. Packed decimal is discussed in Chapter 3. A sign bit (0 = positive, 1 = negative) is placed in an extra byte at the left (highest addressed) end of the packed decimal number. The low-order seven bits of this byte should be 0.

Attempting to convert any of the following to an integer results in an invalid operation exception: NaN, denormal, unnormal, infinity, or a number that exceeds the integer's range. What happens if the invalid operation exception is masked? The 387 will try to store an indefinite. Since there are no bits left to represent error values in word, short, and long integers, converting an indefinite to one of these formats yields

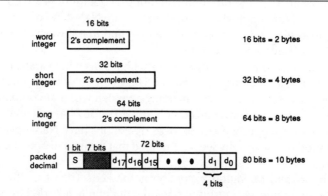

Figure 4.6 387 integer formats.

100. . .00, the most negative integer. Converting this back to floating point will produce an ordinary negative number, not an indefinite. Conversion of an indefinite to packed decimal yields:

$$1\ 1111111\ 1111\ 1111\ XXXX\ XXXX\ XXXX \ldots XXXX, X = \text{undefined}$$

that is, eight bytes of garbage (may contain any value) and two bytes of 1's. Trying to convert this back to floating point produces an undefined result.

The main use for conversions between integer and floating point is in computations where integers and floating point are mixed. Why not also do pure multiple-precision integer arithmetic by converting to floating point, doing the computation on the 387, and then converting back to integer? This is certainly possible, but it's faster to do the integer arithmetic directly on the 386, even though more than one 386 instruction per arithmetic operation might be required for multiple precision.

Registers of the 387

The 387 supplements the 386 by providing additional registers useful for floating-point computation. These registers are depicted in Figure 4.7. The floating-point operands of 387 instructions may reside either in memory or in one of the eight *numeric registers*. The numeric registers hold numbers in extended-precision format only. The 387 can access operands in the numeric registers much faster than operands in memory. The

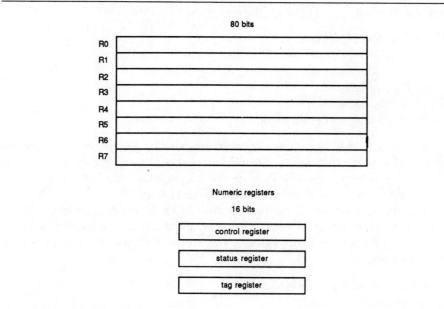

Figure 4.7 387 register set.

control register contains fields whose values modify the overall behavior of the 387; for example, exception mask bits. This register changes value only when it is explicitly loaded by the program. The *status register* contains fields which reflect conditions within the 387 but usually don't modify its behavior; for example, the condition-code bits which indicate the results of comparisons. The *tag register* is used internally by the 387 to summarize the contents of the numeric registers in order to optimize performance and detect exceptions. It is of little use to programmers. The *instruction pointer* and *operand pointer* provide the memory addresses of the most recently encountered 387 instruction and its memory operand (if any). This information is useful to exception handlers. Let's now take a detailed look at each of these registers.

The Eight Numeric Registers   We have already described the contents of the numeric registers (extended-precision floating-point numbers) in great detail, however the *addressing* of the numeric registers is somewhat unusual. A numeric register number specified in a 387 instruction is always added by the 387 to the contents of the ST field of the status register. The sum (taken modulo 8) specifies the numeric register to be used. The purpose of this is to allow the numeric registers to be used as a stack. Figure 4.8 illustrates the stack interpretation of the numeric registers, assuming that ST contains the number 5. The 387 designers felt that most programmers would want to use the numeric registers as a stack, so many 387 instructions have the side effect of modifying ST. Those programmers who wish to use the numeric registers as an ordinary register set, rather than a stack, must make sure that ST remains invariant, otherwise the numeric registers will suffer a "renumbering."

The 387 Control Register   The various fields of the 16-bit 387 control register are depicted in Figure 4.9. First there are the *exception mask* bits:

IM   Invalid Operation Mask
DM   Denormalized Operand Mask
ZM   Zero-Divide Mask
OM   Overflow Mask
UM   Underflow Mask
PM   Precision (Inexact Result) Mask.

If a mask bit is 0, then occurrence of the corresponding exception will cause the program to be suspended and a 386 interrupt to occur (see Chapter 6 for further details). If a mask bit is 1, then the corresponding exception is masked and exception values are produced, as previously described in this chapter.

The next field is the two-bit *Precision Control* (PC) field. The purpose of this field is to cause the 387 to round all numbers to something *less than* extended precision before placing them in numeric registers. The Precision Control field may have the following values:

11   round to extended precision (the default)
10   round to double precision
00   round to single precision

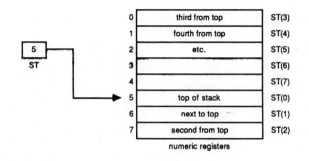

Figure 4.8 Addressing the numeric registers as a stack.

12	10-11	8-9		5	4	3	2	1	0
	IC	RC	PC		PM	UM	OM	ZM	DM	IM

Figure 4.9 387 control register.

Why would anyone want less than the maximum precision? One reason is to run older programs used on other computers. Such programs may contain tricks which depend upon the lower precision. Another reason is to accommodate those high-level languages that require a particular precision for intermediate results. For example, the C language requires that all intermediate results be kept in double precision. Reducing the precision by means of the Precision Control field has no effect on 387 instruction execution times.

The next field is the two-bit *Rounding Control* (RC) field. We have already discussed the four different rounding modes available on the 387. They are specified in the Rounding Control field as follows:

00   rounding to nearest (the default)
01   rounding down (toward $-\infty$)
10   rounding up (toward $+\infty$)
11   rounding toward zero

The next field, bit 12 of the control word, must be set to 1. This bit is the *Infinity Control* (IC) bit on the 8087 and 287. The value 1 selects affine mode (already discussed). Since the other, projective mode is not supported on the 387, its value (0) should not be specified.

The 8087 had an additional field (IEM) in its control register. This field for controlling interrupts is not needed on the 287 or 387, due to the elaborate interrupt-handling mechanism already present in the 286 and 386 (see Chapter 6).

The 387 Status Register   Figure 4.10 shows the various fields of the status register. First come the *exception flags*:

IE   Invalid Operation Exception
DE   Denormalized Operand Exception
ZE   Zero-Divide Exception
OE   Overflow Exception
UE   Underflow Exception
PE   Precision (Inexact Result) Exception

Whenever a numeric exception occurs (masked or unmasked) the 387 sets the corresponding exception flag to 1. The exception flags are "sticky," that is, the 387 will set them automatically, but it's up to the programmer to clear them by explicitly loading the status register with a new value. For example, a program may clear the exception flags, mask all exceptions, and then perform some numeric calculations. At the end of the computation the program can then check the exception flags to see if anything went wrong during the calculations. This controlled approach to exceptions is frequently easier than writing an exception handler which may be invoked at any time during the computation.

Next comes the *Stack Flag* (SF) bit, unavailable on the 8087 and 287. It identifies when an invalid operation exception is due to a 387 stack fault: either overflow (too many pushes) or underflow (too many pops). SF is set to 1 if the exception was a stack fault; 0 otherwise. Furthermore, in the stack case, the C1 bit (described shortly) is set to 1 for overflow, 0 for underflow. The exception handler can quickly distinguish the stack cases. If the 387 numeric register set is used as a stack, the handler will typically simulate a much larger stack by saving values in 386 memory on stack overflow and restoring them on subsequent stack underflow.

If the invalid operation exception is masked and stack underflow or overflow occurs during an operation, then the 387 will adjust the stack pointer ST as if nothing unusual happened, but it will return the NaN indefinite as the result of the operation.

The next field is the *Error Summary* (ES) bit. This bit is set to 1 whenever a 387 instruction produces an unmasked exception and cleared to 0 otherwise.

Bits C_0, C_1, C_2, C_3 contain the condition codes following a comparison or remainder instruction. The interpretation of the condition code bits depends on the particular instruction executed, and thus is discussed with these instructions below.

The three-bit *Stack Top* (ST) field has already been discussed; its contents are added (modulo 8) to all numeric register numbers. If the numeric registers are being used as a stack, ST contains the number of the register which is the topmost element of the stack (recall Figure 4.8).

The final field of the status register is the *Busy* (B) bit. This bit is 1 whenever the 387 is executing an instruction or signaling an interrupt. It's 0 whenever the 387 is idle. We'll see how to use this bit when we talk about 387 concurrency.

15	14	11–13	10	9	8	7	6	5	4	3	2	1	0
B	C_3	ST	C_2	C_1	C_0	ES	SF	PE	UE	OE	ZE	DE	IE

Figure 4.10 387 status register.

Tag 7	Tag 6	Tag 5	Tag 4	Tag 3	Tag 2	Tag 1	Tag 0

Figure 4.11 387 tag register.

The Tag Register   The 16-bit tag register is depicted in Figure 4.11. It contains eight fields, two bits each. Each field corresponds to one of the numeric registers, and summarizes its contents as follows:

00 Valid (that is, any finite nonzero number)
01 Zero
10 Invalid (that is, NaN or infinity)
11 Empty

Registers are tagged Empty if they are uninitialized or if they are "popped" from the numeric register stack. The 387 uses Empty tags to detect stack underflow and stack overflow.

Recall that the 8087 and 287 support unnormal numbers, but the 387 does not. To reflect this, the tag field for an unnormal number is 00 (Valid) on the 8087 and 287; it is 10 (Invalid) on the 387.

The 387 Exception Pointers   The exception pointers (instruction and operand) are provided to assist exception handlers. They come in four formats, depending on:

1.   Whether the operand size in effect for the instruction accessing the pointers is 16 bits or 32 bits. (We describe the instructions at the end of this chapter.) Recall that this is determined by the mode the 386 is in (emulation or no emulation), combined with the presence or absence of an operand size prefix.

2.   Whether the 386 is simulating the one-megabyte memory space of the 8086, or it is in one of the newer, more general addressing modes. We discuss this distinction in Chapters 5 and 6. For now, we need only know that in the 8086 case, memory pointers can be specified by a single 20-bit address; in the newer case, memory pointers consist of a 16-bit *segment selector*, combined with a 16- or 32-bit *offset*. We call the respective cases *8086 mode* and *selector mode*.

The four formats are displayed in Figure 4.12.

Operand size in effect:

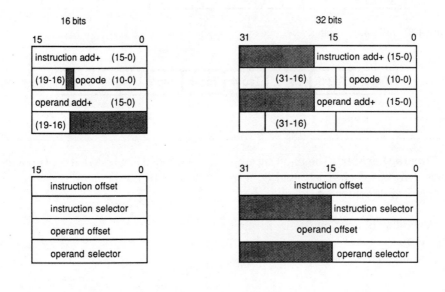

Figure 4.12 387 exception pointers.

The two 16-bit cases duplicate the functionality of the 8087 and 287, allowing emulation of 8086 or 286 systems with those coprocessors. The 32-bit cases accommodate the larger memory space of the 386, allowing 386 programs to execute floating-point instructions.

In selector mode, the pointers consist of the selectors and offsets of the offending instruction and its memory operand (if any). In 8086 mode, the 387 supplies 20-bit or 32-bit addresses for these two items and throws in the 11 low-order bits of the offending opcode as a bonus. Note that this extra information is easily obtained by following the instruction pointer.

Observe the curious bit mapping of the addresses in 8086 mode. The mapping derives from historical reasons, in connection with the method for calculating memory addresses on the 8086. We discuss that addressing method in Chapter 5.

Although one of the four formats (16 bits, 8086 mode) is the same format that is supplied by the 8087, the 287 and 387 differ from the 8087 in that the 287 or 387 instruction pointer points to the first prefix (if present) preceding the opcode, while the 8087 instruction pointer skips over all the prefixes.

Exception pointers are a part of the floating-point processor state; we can think of them as residing in the coprocessor. For 8086 and 286 systems, this is actually the case. The 386, however, maintains these pointers itself. This was done so that the 386 could work successfully with the 287, even though the 287 doesn't know about the 32-bit memory addresses supported by the 386. In 32-bit mode, the 386 ignores the outdated pointers handed to it by the 287 and substitutes its own, larger memory pointers. This gives the illusion that the 287 has been retrofitted with the ability to recognize 32-bit memory pointers.

387 Instruction Formats

The opcode formats for 387 instructions are given in Appendix B. All the opcodes begin with the same five bits (11011), which warn the 386 that it shouldn't try to execute the instruction on its own. In similar fashion, all 387 assembler opcode mnemonics (and no 386 mnemonics) begin with the letter "F", so it's easy for an assembly language programmer to spot 387 instructions in the program. An assembly language example of a 387 instruction that references memory is:

> FADD ANAME

which causes the floating-point number at ANAME in memory to be added to the numeric register indicated by ST (the register at the top of the stack). All of the usual 386 memory operand addressing modes are permitted, for example:

> FADD W[EBX]
> FADD ANAME[EBX][ESI].

Recall that the same 386 ADD assembler mnemonic was used for byte, word, and doubleword addition:

> ADD AL,BVAR   ADD AX,WVAR   ADD EAX,DVAR

The assembler figures out what instruction to generate by means of the types of the operands. The same thing holds for 387 instructions. The assembly language programmer can write:

> AVAR DD 3.7 ; single-precision 3.7
> BVAR DQ 3.7 ; double-precision 3.7
> CVAR DT 3.7 ; extended-precision 3.7

to allocate single-, double-, and extended-precision versions of the constant 3.7. The mnemonics DD, DQ, DT stand for "define doubleword," "define quad word," and (inconsistently) "define ten bytes." Then, for example:

> FADD AVAR

will correctly reference AVAR as a single-precision number while:

> FADD BVAR

will treat BVAR as double-precision. We note that the assembler permits scientific notation to be used in specifying constants. For example, 1.23e5 is 1.23×10^5.

Most 387 instructions have forms that reference a numeric register. Numeric register i is designated in assembly-language as ST(i). Since the 387 adds the contents of ST to each numeric register reference, the correct interpretation of ST(i) is "the ith register from the top of the register stack." For example:

FADD ST(3)

adds the contents of the 3rd register from the top of the register stack into the top register of the register stack. In assembly language, the top register may be designated either by ST(0) or (confusingly) by ST. Thus the assembly language statement:

FADD ST

adds the register at the top of the stack into itself (doubles it).

Some 387 instructions have no explicit references. For example, the instruction:

FABS

replaces the contents of the topmost register with its absolute value. Despite the fact that the above instruction contains no *explicit* references, it *implicitly* references the topmost register, just as all of our FADD examples implicitly reference the topmost register. We shall see that many 387 instructions implicitly reference the top few registers in this fashion.

We now describe in detail what each 387 instruction does and what each is useful for. For details of the binary formats and execution times of the various instructions, see Appendix B.

Data Transfer Instructions

The 387 data transfer instructions move data from memory to numeric registers, from numeric registers to memory, and between numeric registers. Additional data transfer instructions initialize numeric registers to various values. The data transfer instructions are listed in Table 4.2.

Load Instructions   The FLD instruction takes a single operand, which may be a numeric register or a floating-point number (of any format) in memory. This operand is *pushed* onto the top of the register stack. The effect of FLD is depicted in Figure 4.13a. In detail, first the operand of FLD is fetched and converted to extended precision (if it's

Table 4.2 Data Transfer Instructions

Push Instructions	FLD FILD FBLD	Floating Load Integer Load BCD Load
Pop Instructions	FSTP FISTP FBSTP	Floating Store and Pop Integer Store and Pop BCD Store and Pop
Copy Instructions	FST FIST	Floating Store Integer Store
Exchange Instruction	FXCH	Register Exchange
Push Constant Instructions	FLDZ FLD1 FLDPI FLDLG2 FLDLN2 FLDL2T FLDL2E	Load Zero Load One Load Pi Load $\log_{10}(2)$ Load $\log_e(2)$ Load $\log_2(10)$ Load $\log_2(e)$

not extended-precision already), next ST is decremented by 1 (modulo 8), and finally the fetched operand is placed in the (new) topmost register. For example:

        AVAR DD ?   ; a single-precision variable

        FLD AVAR

converts AVAR to extended precision and pushes it onto the register stack. The instruction:

        FLD ST(3)

will push a copy of the contents of register ST(3) onto the register stack. After execution of this instruction the old ST(3) will now be called ST(4) (remember, all numeric register references are relative to the top of the stack), and thus the contents of ST(0) will equal the contents of ST(4).

The instructions FILD and FBLD are similar to FLD, except that their operands are integers and packed decimals, respectively, in memory. All formats (16, 32, and 64 bits) of integers are allowed with FILD. The operand is converted to extended-precision floating-point before being pushed on the register stack. Thus FILD is an integer-to-floating conversion instruction in disguise, and similarly FBLD is a packed-decimal-to-

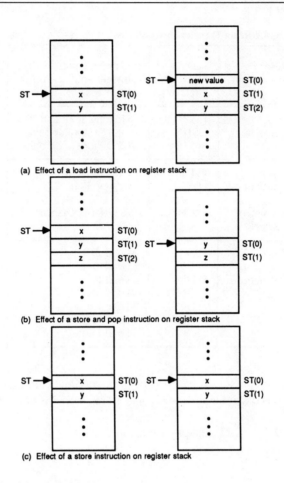

(a) Effect of a load instruction on register stack

(b) Effect of a store and pop instruction on register stack

(c) Effect of a store instruction on register stack

Figure 4.13 Effects of data transfer instructions.

floating converter. All 387 instructions that take an integer operand have assembler mnemonics beginning with "FI", and all instructions that take a packed decimal operand begin with "FB".

Store and Pop Instructions   The opposite of FLD is FSTP, which pops the top of the register stack into a specified argument. The effect of FSTP is shown in Figure 4.13b. The single operand of FSTP may be a numeric register or floating-point memory variable of any format. For example:

        AVAR DD ?   ; a single-precision variable

        FSTP AVAR

will convert the (extended-precision) contents of the topmost register to a single-precision number in AVAR, and then pop the topmost register from the stack. In general FSTP first fetches the contents of the register indicated by ST, performs any necessary conversions, stores this result in FSTP's operand, and then increments ST by 1 (modulo 8). So after executing:

    FSTP ST(3)

the register ST(3) will be renamed ST(2) and will have received the contents of the old ST(0). For another example, the instruction:

    FSTP ST(0)

pops the top of the stack, in effect throwing its value away.

The instructions FISTP and FBSTP are similar to FSTP, except they take integer memory operands (all formats) and packed-decimal memory operands, respectively. Thus, FISTP is a floating-to-integer conversion instruction in disguise, and FBSTP is a floating-to-packed-decimal converter. As part of the conversion process it is necessary to round the floating-point number into an integer. Both FISTP and FBSTP perform this rounding according to the rounding control field of the control register. On the 8087 and 287, FBSTP ignores the control register and rounds by adding 0.5 and then chopping (truncating) the result into an integer.

Store Instructions   The FST instruction copies the contents of ST(0) into a numeric register or single- or double-precision memory operand, performing any necessary conversion from extended precision. The stack pointer ST is left unaffected. The FST instruction cannot store into an extended-precision memory operand. The effect (actually, lack of effect) of FST on the register stack is depicted in Figure 4.13c. For example:

    FST ST(3)

copies the contents of ST(0) to ST(3).

The instruction FIST is similar to FST, except that it takes a 16- or 32-bit (but not 64-bit) integer memory operand. There is no FBST instruction. The reason for the dearth of formats supported by store instructions, compared to store-and-pop instructions, is that the designers of the 387's instruction set ran out of bits for encoding the 387's opcodes and had to cut somewhere. This is the place. Note however that a store can be simulated by a load (push) followed by a store-and-pop. For example:

    FLD ST(0)   ; Duplicate ST(0)
    FBSTP DECVAR ; Convert to BCD & pop

achieves the effect of the missing "FBST DECVAR".

Register Exchange Instruction   The FXCH instruction takes a single operand, namely a numeric register, and exchanges the contents of this register with the contents of ST(0). The stack pointer ST is left unchanged. For example:

FXCH ST(3)

exchanges the contents of ST(0) and ST(3).

Constant Load Instructions   The 387 has a set of instructions for pushing commonly used constants onto the register stack. For example:

FLD1

pushes 1.0 onto the register stack. The other load-constant instructions are shown in Table 4.2. Curiously, these instructions are no faster (and sometimes slower!) than loading the constants from memory.

Arithmetic Instructions

On the 387, the basic arithmetic operations add, subtract, multiply, and divide all involve two operands, the *source* and the *destination*, and produce the following effect:

$$\text{destination} \leftarrow \text{destination op source} \quad \text{where op} = +, *, -, /$$

For the noncommutative operations subtraction and division, the 387 also provides reversed versions computing:

$$\text{destination} \leftarrow \text{source op destination} \quad \text{where op} = -, /$$

In all cases one of the operands is required to be ST(0). Six variations on this basic theme are provided:

a.   Fxxx

b.   Fxxx mem

c.   Flxxx mem

d.   Fxxx ST,ST(i)

e.   Fxxx ST(i),ST

f.   FxxP ST(i),ST

where xxx = ADD, SUB, MUL, DIV, SUBR (that is, reversed subtract), or DIVR. The effects of each of these six forms are shown in pictures in Figures 4.14 (for the case of subtraction) and are described in words below.

In form a, the 387 pops both the topmost operand (the source) and the second from the top (the destination). The result of the operation is then pushed onto the stack. In form b, the given memory operand is the source and ST(0) is the destination. The stack pointer ST is left unchanged. Single- and double-precision memory operands are permitted, but not extended precision. Form c is just like form b, except the memory operand is a 16-bit or 32-bit integer rather than a floating-point number. The conversion to floating point is done automatically. Form d uses any numeric register ST(i) as the source and ST(0) as the destination. The stack pointer ST is left unchanged. Form e uses ST(0) as the source and any ST(i) as the destination. Again, the stack pointer ST isn't changed. Finally, in form f the numeric register ST(i) is the destination and ST(0) is the source. At the conclusion of the operation the source ST(0) is popped from the stack.

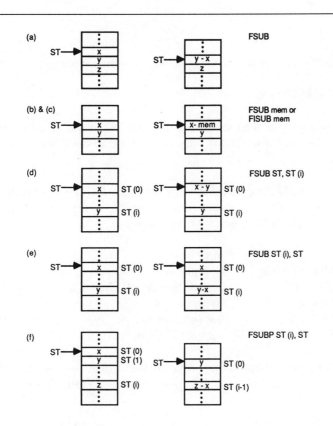

Figure 4.14 Effects of various subcontract instructions.

Table 4.3 lists the eighteen assembler mnemonics obtained by taking forms a–f of the six basic arithmetic operations.

In theory the data transfer instructions and instructions in form a alone suffice for all applications. For example, we can simulate the form b instruction:

FADD DOUBL   ; add DOUBL into ST(0)

with the two instructions:

FLD DOUBL   ; push DOUBL onto stack
FADD   ; add ST(0) and ST(1), pop

However, the single form b instruction is about 16% faster than the two-instruction simulation, for double-precision DOUBL. Form a is in fact a special case of form f which is provided by the assembler for the programmer's convenience. Writing in assembly language:

FADD

leads to exactly the same machine-language instruction as writing:

FADDP ST(1),ST.

We have now seen all the most frequently used 387 instructions. Before introducing the remaining 387 instructions, let's practice using the ones we have already discussed.

Stack-oriented 387 Programming   The use of the 387 stack-oriented instructions should be easy for all of us, especially those with stack- oriented pocket calculators. As an example, we evaluate the expression $b^2 - 4ac$:

FLD b   ; push b
FMUL ST,ST(0)   ; b^2 replaces b on top
FLD FOUR   ; assume that FOUR holds 4.0
FMUL a   ; 4a replaces 4
FMUL c   ; 4ac replaces 4a
FSUB   ; subtract ST(0) from ST(1).

Register Variables   Suppose that we want to calculate some statistics for two sets of data $(x_1, x_2, \ldots, x_n)$ and $(y_1, y_2, \ldots, y_n)$ and require the following quantities:

$$M_x = \sum_{i=1}^{n} x_i \qquad M_y = \sum_{i=1}^{n} y_i \qquad S_x = \sum_{i=1}^{n} x_i^2 \qquad S_y = \sum_{i=1}^{n} y_i^2 \qquad C_{xy} = \sum_{i=1}^{n} x_i y_i$$

Table 4.3 Basic Arithmetic Instructions

	Stack	Integer	Pop
addition	FADD	FIADD	FADDP
subtraction	FSUB	FISUB	FSUBP
reversed subtraction	FSUBR	FISUBR	FSUBRP
multiplication	FMUL	FIMUL	FMULP
division	FDIV	FIDIV	FDIVP
reversed division	FDIVR	FIDIVR	FDIVRP

We could certainly accumulate these five sums in memory variables; however, it would be faster to accumulate the sums in registers. The C programming language allows programmers to declare that certain variables are heavily used, and thus should be maintained in fast registers rather than slower memory. These are called *register variables*. Even in other high-level languages, sophisticated compilers can deduce which variables should be register variables, without the use of explicit advice from the programmer. How can we use the 387's numeric registers as register variables? This is difficult to do in a stack-oriented instruction set, but we can accomplish it on the 387 by only using instruction forms which keep the stack pointer ST invariant. If we do this then for each i, ST(i) will consistently refer to the same register. We then have the following kinds of instructions:

$$ST(i) \leftarrow ST(i) \text{ op } ST(j) \qquad (i = 0 \text{ or } j = 0)$$
$$ST(i) \leftarrow ST(j) \qquad (i = 0 \text{ or } j = 0)$$
$$ST(0) \leftarrow ST(i) \qquad (\text{exchange})$$
$$ST(0) \leftarrow \text{memory}$$
$$ST(0) \rightarrow \text{memory}$$
$$ST(0) \leftarrow ST(0) \text{ op memory}$$

where op is addition, subtraction, multiplication, division, reverse subtraction, or reverse division. Unfortunately there is no 387 instruction that loads ST(0) without pushing the stack (that is, decrementing the stack pointer ST). This means we can implement neither of the operations:

$$ST(0) \leftarrow ST(i)$$
$$ST(0) \leftarrow \text{memory}$$

as single instructions. Fortunately, it is easy to remedy this problem by preceding any FLD instructions with an FSTP ST instruction. This instruction pops the stack, "throwing away" the top register ST(0). Thus, for example, we can get the effect of:

$$ST(0) \leftarrow ST(5)$$

by writing:

```
FSTP ST          ; pop top of stack
FLD ST(4)        ; push ST(4) onto top
```

In any event, we should try to use exchange instructions (FXCH) rather than FSTP and FLD for register-to-register moves, since FXCH is faster.

Let's now write the inner loop for a program to compute the summations above; that is, we'll leave out initializations and the test for loop termination. We'll allocate registers as follows:

ESI   will hold the loop index
ST(1)   will hold M_x
ST(2)   will hold M_y
ST(3)   will hold S_x
ST(4)   will hold S_y
ST(5)   will hold C_{xy}

Here's the program:

```
FSTP ST
FLD X[ESI]        ; ST(0) ← X(i)
FADD ST(1),ST     ; M_x ← M_x + ST(0)
FST ST(6)         ; ST(6) ← ST(0)
FMUL ST(0),ST     ; ST(0) ← ST(0)*ST(0)
FADD ST(3),ST     ; S_x ← S_x + ST(0)
FSTP ST
FLD Y[ESI]        ; ST(0) ← Y(i)
FADD ST(2),ST     ; M_y ← M_y + ST(0)
FST ST(7)         ; ST(7) ← ST(0)
FMUL ST(0),ST     ; ST(0) ← ST(0)*ST(0)
FADD ST(4),ST     ; S_y ← S_y + ST(0)
FXCH ST(6)        ; ST(0) ← ST(6)
FMUL ST,ST(7)     ; ST ← ST(0) * ST(7)
FADD ST(5),ST     ; C_xy ← C_xy + ST(0)
```

Common Subexpressions   An arithmetic expression will sometimes contain a subexpression which is used in more than one place (is duplicated). Such a subexpression is called a *common subexpression*. For example, the definition of division of complex numbers:

$$\frac{a + ib}{c + id} = \frac{ac + bd}{c^2 + d^2} + i\,\frac{cb - ad}{c^2 + d^2} = e + if$$

contains the common subexpression $c^2 + d^2$. In computing the complete expression we should save the value of the common subexpression in a so-called *temporary variable* in order to avoid wasting time computing the common subexpression more than once. The temporary variable can be thrown away or re-used after we're done with it. Thus we can compute the two numbers e and f using six (not eight) multiplications, three (not four) addition/subtractions, and two divisions. If we divide numerators and denominators by c we get:

$$\frac{a + ib}{c + id} = \frac{a + b(d/c)}{c + d(d/c)} + i\frac{b - a(d/c)}{c + d(d/c)} = e + if$$

which contains the two common subexpressions d/c and c + d(d/c). We can thus compute e and f with only three multiplications, three addition/subtractions, and three divisions by the following scheme:

$$t_1 \leftarrow d/c$$
$$t_2 \leftarrow c + dt_1$$
$$e \leftarrow (a + bt_1) / t_2$$
$$f \leftarrow (b - at_1) / t_2$$

Needless to say, it's faster to keep temporary variables in registers than in memory. We can accommodate temporary register variables for common subexpressions by using the same "invariant ST" trick we used for register variables in the previous section. The following is a straightforward translation of the above scheme for complex division:

```
            FSTP ST
            FLD D            ; load d
            FDIV C
            FST ST(1)        ; ST(1) gets t₁ = d/c
            FMUL D
            FADD C
            FST ST(2)        ; ST(2) gets t₂ = c + dt₁
            FSTP ST
            FLD ST(0)        ; load t₁
            FMUL B
            FADD A
            FDIV ST,ST(2)
            FST E            ; E gets (a + bt₁) / t₂
            FXCH ST(1)       ; ST(0) gets t₁
            FMUL A
            FSUBR B
            FDIV ST,ST(2)
            FST F            ; F gets (b − at₁) / t₂
```

It is possible to speed this up by using further tricks, which we leave to the reader.

Miscellaneous Additional Arithmetic Instructions The 387 offers additional arithmetic instructions beyond the basic operations described above. These miscellaneous arithmetic instructions are listed in Table 4.4. The FABS instruction (no explicit operands) replaces the contents of ST(0) with its absolute value. Similarly, the FCHS instruction changes (that is, complements) the sign of ST(0), FRNDINT rounds ST(0) to a floating-point integer, and FSQRT replaces ST(0) with its square root. FSQRT is extremely fast: it takes only about 50% longer than division. It is particularly useful in applications where distances between points in space must be frequently computed:

$$\text{distance } (p_1 q) = \sqrt{([p_x - q_x]^2 + [p_y - q_y]^2 + [p_z - q_z]^2)}$$

and is also used in computing the elementary transcendental functions that we describe soon.

The scale instruction FSCALE adds the value (assumed to be a floating-point integer) in ST(1) to the exponent of ST(0), replacing the old value of ST(0). This is a fast way of multiplying or dividing a floating-point number by a power of two. To scale a sequence of values by the same factor, we need only load, scale, and store-with-pop each element of the sequence, with no need for intermediate stack manipulations.

The functionality of FSCALE was upgraded on the 387. If ST(1) is not an integer, its value is first chopped toward zero. The 8087 and 287 do not allow for this possibility and give undefined results if $0 < |$ ST(1) $| < 1$.

FXTRACT decomposes ST(0) into two floating-point numbers: its unbiased exponent and its signed significand. The exponent replaces the old ST(0) and the significand is pushed on top. FXTRACT is useful whenever the exponent and significand must be treated separately, such as in floating-point-to-ASCII conversions.

Note that the exponent part of the answer, which winds up in ST(1), is essentially a logarithm of the original operand. The floating-point standard specifies that FXTRACT delivers the same value for the exponent of two exceptional values as the logarithm function. So the 387 FXTRACT function was modified from the 8087 and 287 to conform to the standard. On the 387, the exponent of 0 is $-\infty$, and the zero-divide exception is raised. On the 8087, the exponent of 0 is 0, with no exception. On the 387, the exponent of $+\infty$ is $+\infty$ with no exception. The 8087 and 287 FXTRACT

Table 4.4 Miscellaneous Arithmetic Instructions

FSQRT	Square Root
FSCALE	Scale by Power of Two
FPREM	Partial Remainder (8087/287 compatible)
FPREM1	Partial Remainder (IEEE compatible)
FRNDINT	Round to Integer
FXTRACT	Extract Exponent and Significand
FABS	Absolute Value
FCHS	Change Sign

instruction raises an invalid operand exception when the operand is $+\infty$.

The partial remainder instruction FPREM computes the remainder obtained when dividing ST(0) by ST(1). The sign of the remainder is the same as the sign of ST(0). The remainder replaces the contents of ST(0). FPREM is a *partial* remainder instruction because it may give up without finishing its job. FPREM works by performing repeated scaled subtractions; in 64 subtractions it can reduce a magnitude difference of up to 2^{64}. If 64 or fewer subtractions are sufficient to reduce ST(0) to a number less than ST(1), then after executing FPREM, ST(0) will contain the correct remainder and the condition code bit C_2 in the status register is set to 0. If 64 subtractions aren't enough, then C_2 is set to 1 and ST(0) contains the reduced result obtained after the 64th subtraction. Repeatedly executing the FPREM instruction until C_2 turns 0 will produce the desired remainder exactly.

FPREM continues for only 64 subtractions in order to allow the 387 to be interrupted between successive executions of FPREM. The number 64 guarantees that FPREM will take no longer than a division instruction and thus won't increase the worst-case interrupt latency of a system using the 387.

FPREM also sets the condition code bits $C_0C_3C_1$ to the least significant three bits of the quotient. Unfortunately, this feature wasn't properly implemented on the 8087 and 287, and the condition code bits are unreliable across successive executions of FPREM on those older coprocessors. The computed partial remainder is, fortunately, unaffected by these bits. The 387 has corrected this flaw and delivers the correct result.

FPREM is provided so that we can quickly and accurately reduce the operands to transcendental instructions, and so that the operands fall within an acceptable range. On the 387, this reduction has been built into many of the transcendental instructions for all but the most extreme operand values. We give an example of an explicit argument reduction when we discuss the transcendental functions later in this chapter.

Figure 4.15a shows a graph of the FPREM function if we keep the modulus M = ST(1) fixed and vary the dividend X = ST(0). We can see from this graph that the function changes at the Y axis, assuming a different range of values. This change results from the stipulation that the sign of the answer be the same as the sign of the dividend. There are two unfortunate effects of this. First, the range of possible answers for a given modulus is doubled. This complicates algorithms which use FPREM. Second, FPREM fails to be *periodic*: we cannot depend on the value delivered for input X to remain the same if we add M to X. This could create anomalies in calculated results for periodic functions (such as trigonometric functions) that use FPREM to reduce their operands—something that the exact nature of FPREM calculation was designed to avoid.

To avoid these flaws, the floating-point standard stipulates that the remainder function should have the more regular graph shown in Figure 4.15b. This graph is achieved in the 387 with the new instruction FPREM1. The result of FPREM1 is obtained by subtracting from X the *nearest* integer multiple of M. If there are two multiples equally near (that is, X is an exact multiple of M/2), then the *even* multiple is chosen (the same policy as the round-to-nearest function). FPREM1 works exactly the same as FPREM, except that the number of subtractions performed might differ by one. We use FPREM1 when we want compatibility with the floating-point standard; we use FPREM when we want compatibility with the 8087 and 287.

Before leaving the 387 arithmetic instructions, it's worthwhile to examine Table 4.5, which gives approximate timings for various arithmetic instructions. Table 4.5 was calculated assuming that the 387 uses a clock frequency of 16 MHz. (More detailed information is in Appendix B.) Table 4.5 is useful for deciding whether the 387 is fast enough for a given application, or whether a mainframe or supercomputer is required.

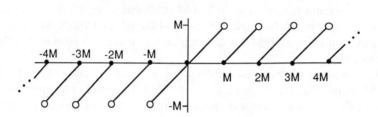

(a) Y = FPREM (X,M)

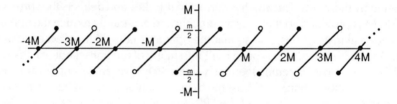

(b) Y = FPREM1 (X,M)

Figure 4.15 Graphs of FPREM and FPREM1, where x = ST(0) and M = ST(1).

Table 4.5 Approximate 387 Performance (16-MHz Clock)

Operation	Time in Microseconds	Rate in 1000 Operations/Second
ADD register to register	1.9	533
MULTIPLY register to register	3.4	296
DIVIDE register to register	5.5	182
SQUARE ROOT register to register	8.0	125
LOAD double precision	1.6	640
STORE double precision	2.8	356
LOAD 32-bit integer	4.7	308
STORE 32-bit integer	5.8	174

Comparison Instructions

The 387 comparison instructions are listed in Table 4.6. The instruction:

FCOM x

compares ST(0) to the operand x and sets the condition codes as shown in Table 4.7. The operand x may be a numeric register or a single- or double-precision operand in memory. The stack pointer ST isn't changed. The assembler allows the programmer to write:

FCOM

as an abbreviation for the instruction:

FCOM ST(1)

FICOM works just like FCOM, except that it takes a 16- or 32-bit integer memory operand. FCOMP works like FCOM, except that it pops the stack (once) after performing the comparison. FICOMP similarly works like FICOM. Finally, FCOMPP (which has no explicit operands) operates like FCOM, but it pops *both* its operands from the stack after performing the comparison.

Since the 8087 was introduced, the floating-point standard specified that comparisons involving quiet NaNs should return a result of "unordered," with no exception

Table 4.6 387 Comparison Instructions

FCOM	Compare
FUCOM	Unordered Compare
FICOM	Integer Compare
FCOMP	Compare & Pop
FUCOMP	Unordered Compare & Pop
FICOMP	Integer Compare & Pop
FCOMPP	Compare & Pop Twice
FUCOMPP	Unordered Compare & Pop Twice
FTST	Compare to Zero
FXAM	Examine

Table 4.7 Condition Codes Following a Compare

C_3	C_0	Condition
0	0	$ST(0) > x$
0	1	$ST(0) < x$
1	0	$ST(0) = x$
1	1	unordered

Table 4.8 Condition Codes Following a Test

C_3	C_0	Condition
0	0	$ST(0) > 0$
0	1	$ST(0) < 0$
1	0	$ST(0) = 0$
1	1	unordered

raised. Since the FCOM instruction raises the invalid operation exception in this case, it fails to meet the standard. So the *unordered comparison* instructions FUCOM, FUCOMP, and FUCOMPP were added with the 387. They work identically to their FCOM counterparts, except that they do not raise the invalid operand exception when one of the operands is a quiet NaN. Unfortunately, there wasn't enough room in the opcode space for memory operand forms to FUCOM—the operands for unordered comparison must be on the floating-point stack.

How do we choose whether to use the FCOM or FUCOM instructions in our programs? If we wish our program to be simple, and not consider the possibility of NaNs and the unordered condition, we use FCOM and allow the invalid operation exception handler to deal with NaN results. If we want to handle NaNs and the unordered condition ourselves, we use FUCOM.

The test instruction FTST compares ST(0) to zero and sets the condition codes as shown in Table 4.8. The examine instruction FXAM is similar to FTST, except that it computes a lot more information about ST(0) than FTST. The condition codes set after executing FXAM are shown in Figure 4.16.

So far we haven't described how to use the 387 condition codes for conditional jumps. Conditional jumping is slightly awkward because the 386 (which does the jump) and the 387 (which contains the condition codes) are on separate chips.

The instruction FSTSW AX, introduced with the 287, copies the contents of the floating-point status register (which contains the condition codes) to the 386 AX register. The condition codes can then be examined using 386 instructions. There is a fast, tricky way to do this. The 386 has an instruction SAHF (Store AH into Flags) which was originally provided on the 8086 to ensure compatibility with the Intel 8080. If we use FCOM to compare two floating-point numbers, then use FSTSW to get the 387 status into AX, then use SAHF to set the 386 flags from AH (the high-order byte of AX), we get the result shown in Figure 4.17. In particular, the 386 zero flag ZF receives the 387 C_3 bit and the carry flag CF receives C_0. The reader can now check that the 387 FCOM has led to 386 flag settings identical to what would be produced by an analogous 386 unsigned CMP (integer compare) instruction, except for the "unordered" condition which cannot arise on the 386. So, for example:

```
FCOM
FSTSW AX
SAHF
JE NOACCIDENT
```

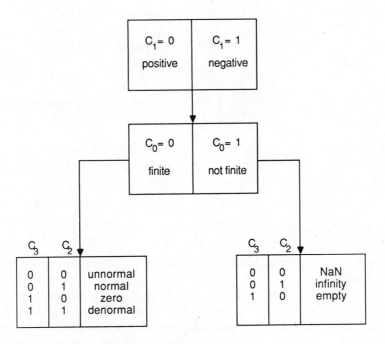

Figure 4.16 Condition codes following an examine.

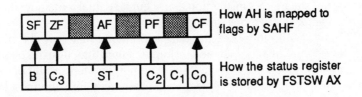

Figure 4.17 Correspondence of 387 condition codes to 386 flags.

will jump to NOACCIDENT if ST(0) and ST(1) are equal. This is no accident. The bizarre layout of the 387 condition code bits in the 387 status register and the condition code values produced by FCOM and FTST have all been designed so that the above trick will work.

If we allow the possibility that the operands are unordered, we must explicitly test for this. The following code jumps to one of four locations GREATER, EQUAL, LESS, or UNORDERED, depending on the floating-point result:

```
        FUCOM           ; unordered compare ST − ST(1)
        FSTSW AX        ; store status in AX
```

```
        SAHF              ; copy C flags to Zero and Carry flags
        JZ L1             ; jump if the Z flag is set
        JA GREATER        ; jump if ST is strictly greater than ST(1)
    LESS:

    L1:
        JC UNORDERED;  both Z and C mean ST and ST(1) are unordered
    EQUAL:
```

Take care to use the unsigned 386 conditions *Above* and *Below* for testing floating-point results, not the signed conditions *Greater* and *Less*. Thus the correct instruction above is JA (jump if above), not JG (jump if greater).

Transcendental Instructions

The *elementary transcendental* functions consist of the trigonometric functions (sine, cosine, tangent, etc.), the inverse trigonometric functions (arcsine, arccosine, arctangent, etc.), the logarithmic functions ($\log_2$, $\log_{10}$, $\log_e$), the exponential functions (x^y, 2^x, 10^x, e^x), the hyperbolic functions (sinh, cosh, tanh, etc.), and the inverse hyperbolic functions (arcsinh, arccosh, arctanh, etc.). The 387 can rapidly compute each of the elementary transcendental functions on double-precision arguments giving double-precision results accurate to within one unit in the last place. Furthermore, the computed trig functions will satisfy all of the usual trigonometric identities to within round off. The unique building blocks which make this possible are extended-precision format, the fast square root instruction, the accurate partial remainder instruction, and the transcendental instructions shown in Table 4.9.

The 8087 and 287 follow here the design principle that only the most time-consuming "inner-loops" of a computation be implemented directly in hardware. Thus, the transcendental instructions provided are extremely limited in number and also limited in the range of operands accepted. Each elementary function must be implemented as a small software subroutine, that reduces the input so that it falls into an acceptable range and uses the available building-block instructions to produce the desired result. This yields the maximum performance from a limited amount of hardware.

Table 4.9 Transcendental Instructions

FSIN	partial sine
FCOS	partial cosine
FSINCOS	sine and cosine
FPTAN	partial tangent
FPATAN	partial arctangent
FYL2X	$y \log_2(x)$
FYL2XP1	$y \log_2(x+1)$
F2XM1	$2^x - 1$

Chip fabrication technology has advanced so that the 387 has room to ease some of the operand restrictions imposed on the 8087 and 287 and to add some instructions for elementary functions. We'll start by describing the new instructions FSIN, FCOS, and FSINCOS.

Before plunging into the discussion, we should mention that the unit of measurement of angles is always the *radian*. π radians equals 180 degrees. Radian measurement is the most mathematically natural: all calculations are quickest and simplest when radians are used.

The FSIN instruction takes the sine of ST(0). Instead of simply replacing ST(0) with the answer, the 387 does a curious thing: it pushes an extra slot onto the floating-point stack, then it replaces the input operand with two numbers $Y = ST(1)$ and $X = ST(0)$, such that Y/X will give the correct answer. The reason for this is that the internal algorithm for FSIN naturally yields two such numbers. The hardware could easily have been programmed to perform the division itself before delivering the result, but the division would be wasted for many calculations involving FSIN. For example, if we follow FSIN with FDIVR instead of FDIV, we have the cosecant function instead of the sine function, at a cost of just 1 additional clock cycle. If the division were built into FSIN, we would instead have to perform another floating-point division to obtain the cosecant.

The range of allowable inputs to FSIN is generous but not unlimited: the magnitude of the input cannot exceed 2^{63}. Note that in practical applications, an angular measurement exceeding 2^{63} radians is unlikely. If we want to cover the possibility, however, we can: if the input is out of range, FSIN will leave the stack unchanged, and set the C2 bit in the status word. We need only test C2 after trying FSIN. If C2 is 0, we can return; otherwise, we exploit the trigonometric identity:

$$\sin(n\pi + x) = \sin(x) \qquad \text{for all integers n}$$

and use FPREM1, with modulus π, to reduce the input to an in-range number that will yield the same sine. Thus the following code, entered at label SINE, will compute the sine of ST(0):

```
L1:               ; jump here if ST(0) needs to be reduced
   FLDPI          ; load constant π
   FXCH           ; swap π into ST(1), input back to ST(0)
L2:               ; loop here for successive reductions
   FPREM1         ; reduce the input, modulo π
   FSTSW AX       ; fetch the 387 status word
   SAHF           ; store the C-bits to the 386 flags
   JP L2          ; C2 is now the parity flag— loop if 1
   FXCH           ; input is reduced: swap π back to ST(0)
   FSTP ST        ; discard π from the stack
SINE:             ; main entry point
   FSIN           ; try taking the sine of ST(0)
   FSTSW AX       ; fetch the 387 status word
```

```
SAHF          ; store the C-bits to the 386 flags
JP L1         ; C2 is now the parity flag—jump if 1
FDIV          ; success: compute final answer Y/X
RET           ; return to caller
```

The FCOS instruction works exactly as FSIN, except that it computes the cosine. Like FSIN, it delivers the answer as two numbers to be divided and it expects the input to be less than 2^{63} in magnitude, reporting the failure through C2 in the same way. The cosine of a number is computed by FCOS followed by FDIV; the secant of a number is computed by FCOS followed by FDIVR.

The FSINCOS instruction simultaneously computes the sine and cosine of ST(0), in a time not much longer than it takes to compute either function alone. A slot is pushed onto the stack and the two answers replace the input. ST(1) is set to the sine of the input, and ST(0) is set to the cosine. The input is restricted in magnitude to 2^{63}, just as with FSIN and FCOS.

FSINCOS is useful because many calculations involve the sine and cosine of the same quantity. For example, the following sequence of instructions takes the top two stack elements as polar coordinates (radius ST(1) and angle ST) and converts them to rectangular coordinates:

```
FSINCOS           ; stack now contains COS  SIN  r
FXCH ST(2)        ; swap: r  SIN  COS
FMUL ST(1),ST     ; multiply: r  r*SIN  COS
FMULP ST(2),ST    ; multiply and pop: r*SIN  r*COS
FXCH              ; normalize answer to ST = X, ST(1) = Y
```

FSINCOS is the last instruction we'll talk about that is new to the 387. The instructions FPTAN and FPATAN exist on the 8087 and 287 but are more severely restricted in their inputs than they are on the 387.

The FPTAN instruction works just like FSIN and FCOS, except that it produces the tangent of the input when the two answers are divided. (Note that for consistency, FSIN and FCOS should have been named FPSIN and FPCOS.) Again, inputs with magnitude greater than 2^{63} are flagged via C2. The tangent of a number is computed by FPTAN followed by FDIV; the cotangent of a number is computed by FPTAN followed by FDIVR.

On the 8087 and 287, the input to FPTAN must be checked to see that it is a valid number between 0 and $\pi/4$. If the input does not fall into that very restricted range, it must be reduced via the FPREM instruction to an in-range value. The four trigonometric identities:

$$\tan(x) = -1/\tan(x - \pi/2).$$
$$\tan(x) = 1/\tan(\pi/2 - x)$$
$$\tan(n\,\pi + x) = \tan(x) \qquad \text{for all integers n}$$
$$\tan(z) = -\tan(-z)$$

insure that we will always find an in-range value whose tangent is the same as our answer, subject to a possible negation and/or reciprocal-taking. Reference 1 gives the details on how this is done, together with the formulas for computing the sine and cosine functions from FPTAN.

The FPATAN instruction computes arctan(ST(1)/ST(0)). The top two stack elements are popped and the result is pushed onto the stack. On the 387, the operands for FPATAN are not restricted; however, the internal transformations performed by the 387 to accommodate all operands result in a strange mix of possible ranges for the answer, as shown in Table 4.10.

On the 8087 and 287, the operands for FPATAN must satisfy $0 < ST(1) < ST(0) + \infty$. It's easy to get operands into this range by using the identities:

$$arctan(x) = -arctan(-x)$$
$$arctan(x) = \pi/2 - arctan(1/x).$$

The remaining inverse trigonometric functions can be computed in similar fashion by using FPATAN, FSQRT, and the formulas in Table 4.11.

The instruction FYL2X computes $ST(1) * \log_2 ST(0)$. The two operands are popped and the result is then pushed onto the stack. FYL2X requires that $ST(0) > 0$, as would be expected for a logarithm function. The remaining logarithmic functions can be computed by using FYL2X, the formulas in Table 4.12, and the load constant instructions FLDLN2 and FLDLG2.

There is an additional logarithmic instruction, FYL2XP1 which computes:

$$ST(1) * \log_2[ST(0) + 1].$$

Here ST(0) is required to satisfy the more restrictive:

$$ST \mid (0) \mid < 1 - \frac{1}{\sqrt{2}}$$

The reason for providing this instruction is to permit high accuracy calculation of the function log(1 + x). This function is used in some computations involving interest rates and also in computing the inverse hyperbolic functions (see Table 4.13 for formulas). It would seem that log(1 + x) could be calculated by adding 1 to x and then using FYL2X,

Table 4.10 Range of Results of the FPATAN Instruction

Sign of ST(1)	Sign of ST	Lower Bound	Upper Bound	
+	+	0	$\pi/2$	
+	−	$\pi/2$	π	if $\mid ST(1) \mid < \mid ST \mid$
+	−	0	$\pi/2$	if $\mid ST(1) \mid \geq \mid ST \mid$
−	+	$-\pi/2$	0	
−	−	$-\pi$	$-\pi/2$	

Table 4.11 Formulas for Inverse Trigonometric Functions

$$\arcsin(z) = \arctan\left(\frac{z}{\sqrt{(1-z)(1+z)}}\right) = \arctan\left(\frac{y}{x}\right)$$

$$\arccos(z) = 2\arctan\left(\sqrt{\frac{1-z}{1+z}}\right) = 2\arctan\left(\frac{y}{x}\right)$$

$$\arctan(z) = \arctan\left(\frac{z}{1}\right) = \arctan\left(\frac{y}{x}\right)$$

$$\operatorname{arccot}(z) = \arctan\left(\frac{1}{z}\right) = \arctan\left(\frac{y}{x}\right)$$

$$\operatorname{arccsc}(z) = \arctan\left(\frac{\operatorname{sign}(z)}{\sqrt{(z-1)(z+1)}}\right) = \arctan\left(\frac{y}{x}\right)$$

$$\operatorname{arcsec}(z) = 2\arctan\left(\sqrt{\frac{z-1}{z+1}}\right) = 2\arctan\left(\frac{y}{x}\right)$$

z = argument of desired inverse trigonometric function f
x,y = stack-top value and next value before executing FPATAN
      so that resulting stack-top value is f(z)

Table 4.12 Formulas for Logarithmic Functions

$\log_2(x) = \mathrm{FYL2X}(x)$

$\log_e(x) = \log_e(2)\,\log_2(x) = \mathrm{FYL2X}(\log_e(2),x) = \mathrm{FYL2X}(\mathrm{FLDLN2},x)$

$\log_{10}(x) = \log_{10}(2)\,\log_2(x) = \mathrm{FYL2X}(\log_{10}(2),x) = \mathrm{FYL2X}(\mathrm{FLDLG2},x)$

but if x is very small, then the addition would cause the loss of valuable significand bits of x, resulting in an inaccurate answer. If an argument is too big for FYL2XP1, then adding 1 won't cause loss of significance and using FYL2X will produce a suitably accurate result.

The exponentiation instruction F2XM1 computes $2^{\mathrm{ST}(0)} - 1$. The result replaces ST(0). ST(0) must be in the range:

$$-1/2 \le \mathrm{ST}(0) \le 1/2$$

The 387 provides $2^x - 1$ rather than 2^x in order to avoid the loss of precision entailed when x is close to 0 (so 2^x is close to 1), and $2^x - 1$ is the actual desired function. This is

Table 4.13 Formulas for Inverse Hyperbolic Functions

$$\text{arcsinh}(x) = [\text{sign}(x)] \, [\log_e(2)] \, [\log_2(1 + z)] = \text{FYL2XP1}(\text{sign}(x) \, \text{FLDLN2}, z)$$

$$\text{where } z = |x| + \frac{|x|}{\dfrac{1}{|x|} + \sqrt{1 + \left(\dfrac{1}{|x|}\right)^2}}$$

$$\text{arccosh}(x) = [\log_e(2)] \, [\log_2(1 + z)] + \text{FYL2XP1}(\text{FLDLN2}, z)$$

$$\text{where } z = x - 1 + \sqrt{(x-1)\,(x+1)}$$

$$\text{and } x \geq 1$$

$$\text{arctanh}(x) = [\text{sign}(x)] \, [\log_e(2)] \, [\log_2(1 + z)]$$
$$= \text{FYL2XP1}(\text{FLDLN2} \, \text{sign}(x), z)$$

$$\text{where } z = \frac{2|x|}{1 - |x|}$$

$$\text{and } -1 < x < 1$$

$$\text{arccoth}(x) = \text{arctanh}(1/x)$$

$$\text{arccsch}(x) = \text{arcsinh}(1/x)$$

$$\text{arcsech}(x) = \text{arccosh}(1/x)$$

indeed the case in computing the hyperbolic functions, as shown in Table 4.14. If, on the other hand, 2^x is the desired function, then it can be obtained without loss of precision by using F2XM1 to compute $2^x - 1$ and then adding 1. All the remaining exponential functions can be obtained from F2MX1 by use of the formulas in Table 4.15.

The restricted range of F2MX1 can be handled for arbitrary x by computing $2^x - 1$ in the following fashion:

Step 1: Compute $i = \text{FRNDINT}(x)$ and $f = x - i$. This guarantees that $|f| < 1/2$ since under the default rounding mode, the FRNDINT instruction rounds to the *nearest* integer. Then:

$$2^x = (2^i)(2^f)$$

Step 2: Compute $2^f - 1$ by using F2MX1.

Table 4.14 Formulas for Hyperbolic Functions

$$\sinh(x) = \frac{\text{sign}(x)}{2} \left[(e^{|x|} - 1) + \frac{e^{|x|} - 1}{e^{|x|}} \right]$$

$$\cosh(x) = \frac{1}{2} \left[e^{|x|} + \frac{1}{e^{|x|}} \right]$$

$$\tanh(x) = \text{sign}(x) - \left[\frac{e^{2|x|} - 1}{e^{2|x|} + 1} \right]$$

$$\coth(x) = 1/\tanh(x)$$

$$\text{csch}(x) = 1/\sinh(x)$$

$$\text{sech}(x) = 1/\cosh(x)$$

Table 4.15 Formulas for Exponential Functions

$$2^x = (2^x - 1) + 1 = \text{F2XM1}(x) + 1$$

$$e^x = 1 + (2^{x \, \log_2(e)} - 1) = 1 + \text{F2XM1}(x \, \log_2(e)) = 1 + \text{F2XM1}(x \, \text{FLDL2E})$$

$$10^x = 1 + (2^{x \, \log_2(10)} - 1) = 1 + \text{F2XM1}(x \, \log_2(10)) = 1 + \text{F2XM1}(x \, \text{FLDL2T})$$

$$x^y = 1 + (2^{y \, \log_2(x)} - 1) = 1 + \text{F2XM1}(y \, \log_2(x)) = 1 + \text{F2XM1}(\text{FYL2X}(y,x))$$

Step 3:   If i = 0, then we're done.

If not, then add 1 to the number $2^f - 1$ obtained in Step 2, multiply it by 2^i by using FSCALE, and subtract 1.

On the 8087 and 287, the bottom limit for the range of F2MX1 is 0, not $-1/2$. Input values between $-1/2$ and 0 are handled by applying the formula:

$$2^f - 1 = -[2^{(-f)} - 1]/[2^{(-f)}]$$

as described in reference 1.

This completes our discussion of the 387 transcendental instructions. Before proceeding to the final group of 387 instructions, the administrative instructions, we must explore some instances when the illusion that the 386 and 387 are a single processor breaks down.

Concurrent Execution of the 386 and 387

It is possible for the 386 and 387 to both be executing instructions simultaneously. When the 386 encounters a 387 instruction, it (1) waits until the 387 becomes idle, (2) allows the 387 to begin the instruction, and then (3) immediately moves on to the next instruction. The 386 doesn't wait for the 387 to finish. If the 387 hasn't finished by the time the 386 encounters *another* 387 instruction, then the 386 will wait in step 1 as described. This strategy permits the 386 to continue running while the 387 is performing a slow instruction. For example, while the 387 is performing an FPATAN instruction, there is sufficient time for the 386 to perform approximately 200 register-to-register instructions.

Ordinarily, programmers need not think about this concurrency unless they want to fine tune their code. By waiting in step 1, the 386 guarantees that almost all programs will produce the same results as if there were only one processor instead of two. However, there are two cases in which the illusion breaks down.

Suppose that the 387 is instructed to store something in memory, which is then immediately accessed by the 386. For example:

```
FIST I
MOV EAX,I
```

Here the 386 will execute the MOV before the 387 has finished the FIST, and EAX will receive the wrong value. Note that this problem wouldn't arise if there were an intervening 387 instruction, for example:

```
FIST I
FADD ST(3)
MOV EAX,I
```

since the 386 would then wait for the FIST to end when the 386 encounters the FADD. However, intervening 386 instructions:

```
FIST I
MOV J,EBX
MOV EAX,I
```

won't help, unless they delay the 386 sufficiently for the 387 to finish the FIST. The 386 FWAIT instruction (FWAIT and WAIT are synonymous in assembly language) causes the 386 to wait for the 387 to become idle. The problem can be solved by inserting an FWAIT:

```
FIST I          ;
FWAIT           ; wait for 387 to finish FIST
MOV EAX,I   ;
```

In general, this processor synchronization problem arises whenever the 387 loads or stores at a memory location which is subsequently loaded or stored by the 386. In all cases, the problem can be solved by inserting an FWAIT somewhere between the offending 387 instruction and the offending 386 instruction.

Pandemonium would result if the 386 didn't follow the rule in step 1 above and wait for the 387. The 8086 ignores this rule, so the 8086 assembler silently and automatically inserts an FWAIT before every 8087 instruction it generates. These extra FWAIT instructions are unnecessary on the 286 and 386, and thus they need not be generated by 286 and 386 assemblers.

The second processor synchronization problem occurs in exceptions. If an unmasked exception occurs during execution of a 387 instruction, the 386 may have raced on and already executed many instructions between the time the faulty 387 instruction began and the time the exception is detected. Furthermore, the 386 ignores 387 exceptions until the 386 encounters an FWAIT or another 387 instruction, at which time the 386 interrupts itself. Thus, at the time of the interrupt, the 386's instruction pointer EIP won't point to the 387 instruction that caused the exception. However, the 387 Exception Pointers *will* correctly identify the faulty instruction. This is, in fact, the reason why the 387 has Exception Pointers at all.

There is another source of concurrency in 386 and 387 systems, this time within the 387 itself. As shown in Figure 4.18, the 387 is split into two parts—the Bus Interface Unit (BIU) and the Numeric Execution Unit (NEU). The BIU communicates with the outside world (in particular, with the 386) and contains the status and control registers. The NEU contains the numeric registers and does all the dirty work. The BIU can respond to certain instructions on its own, despite the fact that the NEU is occupied.

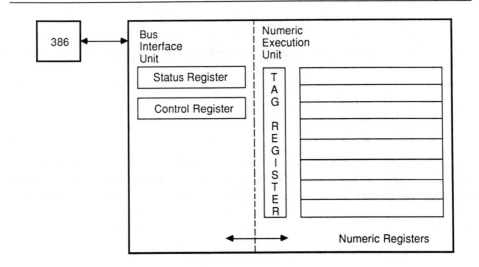

Figure 4.18 386–387 interaction.

For example, the status register contains a Busy bit which indicates whether the NEU is busy or idle. The 386 tests this bit in executing FWAIT (and in step 1 when encountering a 387 instruction) before proceeding. There is a 387 instruction, FNSTSW, which accesses the status register. FNSTSW is executed by the BIU without NEU assistance. The 386 omits the wait in step 1 when it sees FNSTSW. So FNSTSW can be used by a programmer to check the 387 Busy bit without causing the 386 to stop and wait for the 387. Thus a program can initiate a lengthy instruction on the 387 and periodically check its progress.

The "no wait" behavior of the 386 in handling FNSTSW is typical of that small group of 387 instructions that can be executed directly by the BIU. All such instructions are included in our final group, the administrative instructions.

Administrative Instructions

The 387 administrative instructions (see Table 4.16) provide access to the nonnumeric registers of the 387. Those with mnemonics that begin with FN are "no wait" instructions, that is, the 386 won't check to see if the 387's NEU is idle before giving them to the 387 for execution. Furthermore, the 386 will continue to ignore numeric exceptions when "no wait" instructions are encountered. The assembler provides a "wait" form for a "no wait" instruction if the programmer omits the N from the "no wait" instruction's FN mnemonic (see Table 4.16). The assembler generates the "wait" form instruction by generating an FWAIT instruction followed by the "no wait" instruction. This causes the 386 to respond to unmasked 387 exceptions and wait for NEU completion before executing the "no wait" instruction; in other words, causes the "no wait" instruction to act like an ordinary 387 instruction. In general, programmers should avoid the "no wait" forms unless they have carefully analyzed the effects of concurrency.

Table 4.16 Administrative Instructions

FNSTCW (FSTCW)	Store Control Word
FLDCW	Load Control Word
FNSTSW (FSTSW)	Store Status Word
FNSTSW AX (FSTSW AX)	Store Status Word into AX
FNCLEX (FCLEX)	Clear Exceptions
FNINIT (FINIT)	Initialize
FNSTENV (FSTENV)	Store Environment
FLDENV	Load Environment
FNSAVE (FSAVE)	Save State
FRSTOR	Restore State
FINCSTP	Increment Stack Pointer
FDECSTP	Decrement Stack Pointer
FFREE	Free a Register
FNOP	No Operation

The FNSTCW (FSTCW) instruction stores the 387 control register in a memory location. FLDCW loads the control register from a memory location. These two instructions are useful for changing the 387's mode of operation (rounding mode, exception mask, etc.). The 387 guarantees that these instructions will finish before the 386 can execute another instruction, so in this case, the processor synchronization problems mentioned in the previous section can't occur.

The FNSTSW (FSTSW) instruction stores the 387 status register in a memory location. FNSTSW AX (FSTSW AX) stores the status register into the 386's AX register. We have already encountered the "wait" form FSTSW AX in our discussion of conditional jumps. The AX version of FSTSW is missing from the 387's precursor, the 8087, so 8087 conditional jumping is even more awkward than on the 387. FNSTSW and FNSTSW AX are guaranteed to finish before the 386 can get to the next instruction, so again processor synchronization problems can't occur.

FNCLEX (FCLEX) clears all exception flags, the Error Summary flag, and the Busy flag in the status register. We have already mentioned that the exception flags are cumulative and must be reset explicitly by the programmer. This is the purpose of FNCLEX.

FNINIT (FINIT) initializes the control, status, and tag registers to the values shown in Table 4.17. A hardware reset signal produces the same values.

The store environment instruction FNSTENV (FSTENV) writes the control, status, tag, and exception pointer registers into the memory buffer specified by the single operand to the instruction. FNSTENV then initializes these registers as in FNINIT. The buffer occupies either 14 words or 14 doublewords, depending on the operand size in effect for the instruction. Recall that the operand size is determined by the mode the 386 is in, combined with the presence or absence of an operand size prefix. In the doubleword case, any unoccupied upper words of doublewords are undefined. The

Table 4.17 387 Initialization

Control Register	
Rounding mode	round to nearest
Precision	extended
All exceptions	masked

Status Register	
Not Busy	
Condition code is undefined	
ST = 0	
Error Summary = 0	
Exception Flags all zero	

Tag Register	
Tags all EMPTY	

offset from the start of the memory buffer of each register is shown in Table 4.18. The formats of the exception pointers are shown in Figure 4.12.

The FLDENV instruction loads an environment previously stored by FNSTENV. This pair of instructions is useful in exception handlers to gain access to the exception pointers.

FNSAVE (FSAVE) is similar to FNSTENV, except it saves all the numeric registers in addition. This causes 94 bytes (for word operand size) or 108 bytes (for doubleword operand size) of data to be dumped to memory. The offset of each component of the buffer is shown in Table 4.18.

FRSTOR restores all the 387's registers from a memory area previously stored by FNSAVE. This pair of instructions is primarily useful for task switching (see Chapter 6), since the entire state of the 387 is saved/restored.

FINCSTP and FDECSTP increment and decrement (respectively) the stack pointer ST. They don't change the tag register or any of the numeric registers; for example, FINCSTP isn't equivalent to FSTP ST.

FFREE ST(i) sets the tag of ST(i) to Empty.

FNOP has the same effect as FST ST,ST(0); that is, no operation.

There are are three instructions that existed on predecessors to the 387 that are no longer needed on the 387. If their opcodes are encountered by the 387, they are treated as FNOP. The instructions are FENI and FDISI from the 8087, and FSETPM from the 287.

This completes our tour of the 387 instruction set.

Table 4.18 Memory Buffer Offsets for FSAVE, FRSTOR, FSTENV, and FLDENV

OPERAND SIZE:	Word	Doubleword
Control Register	0	0
Status Register	2	4
Tag Register	4	8
Instruction Pointer	6	12
Data Operand Pointer	10	20
Buffer size for FLDENV and FSTENV	14 bytes	28 bytes
ST(0)	14	28
ST(1)	24	38
ST(2)	34	48
ST(3)	44	58
ST(4)	54	68
ST(5)	64	78
ST(6)	74	88
ST(7)	84	98
Buffer size for FSAVE and FRSTOR	94 bytes	108 bytes

Still to Come

Now that we have seen the instruction sets of the 386 and 387, we are ready to learn about some of the advanced features of the 386. We discuss features that form a bridge of compatibility between the 386 and its predecessors; and we discuss features that distinguish the 386 from earlier members of the 86 family, especially the original 8086. These are described in the next two chapters, along with some associated new instructions.

Later, in Chapter 7, we return to floating-point arithmetic and describe an alternative coprocessor made by Weitek Corporation. That chapter also contains some additional examples of 387 usage.

References

This chapter is closely based upon the similar chapter in reference 1. Much of the material previously appeared in reference 2. The principal reference for new 387 material is reference 3. The 8087 and 287 conform to draft 8.0 of the proposed IEEE standard *P754 Floating Point Arithmetic for Microprocessors*. This proposed standard is described and justified in reference 4. The 387 is based on the approved version of that standard, reference 5. For general information on floating-point and multiple precision integer arithmetic, see reference 6.

1.   S.P. Morse and D.J. Albert, *The 80286 Architecture*, John Wiley and Sons, New York, 1986.

2.   J. Palmer and S. Morse, *The 8087 Primer*, John Wiley and Sons, New York, 1984.

3.   *80387 Programmer's Reference Manual*, Intel Corporation, 1987.

4.   *Computer*, vol. 14, no.3, March, 1981.

5.   *IEEE Standard 754-195, IEEE Standard for Binary Floating-Point Arithmetic*, IEEE Computer Society Press, Washington, DC, 1985.

6.   D. Knuth, *The Art of Computer Programming, Vol. 2: Seminumerical Algorithms*, Addison-Wesley, Reading, Mass., 1981.

CHAPTER

5

SEGMENTATION AND COMPATIBILITY

'The time has come,' the Walrus said,
  'To talk of many things:
Of shoes—and ships—and sealing wax—
  Of cabbages—and kings—
And why the sea is boiling hot—
  And whether pigs have wings.'
(Lewis Carroll, *Through the Looking Glass*)

The time has come to talk of the far side of the 386 processor, the side of concern to the operating system. In Chapter 2 we promised that this far side would ideally be invisible to the applications programmer. Unfortunately, the world is not always ideal, especially when it comes to operating systems in computers. Let's begin by describing how and why our 386 world might be less than ideal, forcing us to think about some of the concepts in this chapter, even when we are writing applications code. The primary reason is *compatibility*.

The 386 is just one of the 86 family of microprocessors, starting with the original 8086 and running through the 386's immediate predecessor, the 286. In an ideal world, the enormous base of 8086 and 286 software would be rewritten to take advantage of the 386's capabilities. In the real world, there are problems with this:

1. Almost nobody would buy a 386 machine until the software was rewritten.

2. Almost nobody would rewrite the software until 386 machines were selling well.

The solution to the problem is to insure that the 386 is capable of emulating its predecessors. Then we would need only to write a 386 operating system capable of emulating the predecessor's operating systems to run the entire base of existing software. Thus the 386 has *emulation modes* for the 8086 and the 286 that duplicate the functionality of those processors.

We still, however, wish to encourage the rewriting of software for the 386; the revised software will motivate people to buy the newer 386 machines. To this end we strive to minimize the architectural impact of adding new 386 features. If we minimize the change to the assembly language instruction set, we make the porting of assembly language programs easier. If we minimize the change to the generated object code, we make the porting of high-level language compilers easier. Thus, an enormous number of design decisions for the 386 are biased by the design of its predecessors. We've indicated this at many points already in this book; there is a concentration of such decisions in this chapter.

Evolution of the 86 Family

Since much of this chapter is concerned with compatibility with the earlier 86 family processors, we must first learn something about the architectures of those processors. In this case, a historical approach is best since it allows us to understand the motivations behind the various engineering decisions that determined the processor architectures.

8086 Processor   The 8086 is a 16-bit machine. That means that its general registers are 16 bits in length and it performs its address calculations using 16 bits. The registers of the 8086 are shown in Figure 5.1. The general registers and the instruction pointer register should look familiar since they are simply the 8- and 16-bit subregisters of the corresponding 386 registers.

The 8086 instructions are similarly related to 386 instructions. Recall that an instruction in machine language consists of an opcode and an operand-addressing mode. The opcodes on the 8086 are a proper subset of the 386 opcodes, and the opcodes that they have in common have identical bit encodings. Operand-addressing modes on the 8086 are more restrictive than those of the 386 and are encoded differently.

Let's look at some of these restrictions. Just as on the 386, any 8086 general register may be used as an operand. Of course, the 32-bit registers (EAX, EBX, . . .) are unavailable on the 8086. Immediate operands must be less than 2^{16} in value. Just as on the 386, an 8086 memory operand address can contain a base register, an index register, and a displacement. However, on the 8086 the choices for base, index, and displacement are limited as follows:

- The base register must be one of the two registers BX or BP.

- The index register must be one of the two registers SI or DI.

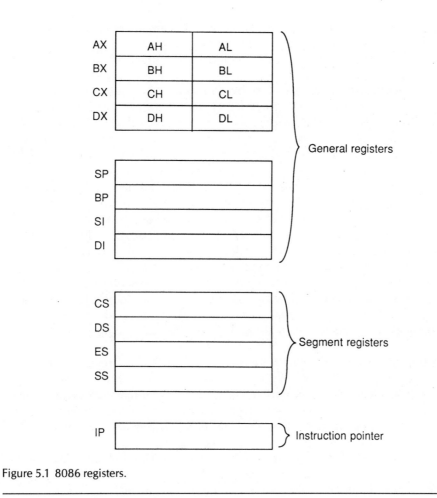

Figure 5.1 8086 registers.

- There is no scaling available for the index register (that is, the scale factor is always 1).

- The displacement value must be less than 2^{16}.

Why does the 8086 make these restrictions? The restrictions on immediates and displacements are an obvious consequence of having a 16-bit machine. The restrictions on base and index register usage serve to make the code more compact by allowing operand-addressing modes to be encoded in fewer bits. Between the time of introduction of the 8086 and the 386, the price of memory dropped by a factor of 64, and thus code compaction is far less of a concern today.

One of the design goals of the 8086 was that it have an address space at least double the 2^{16} bytes addressed by the 8080. As it turned out, the 8086 can address up to 2^{20} bytes (one megabyte) of memory (which is eight times more than the perceived need at that time). But as we have seen, on a 16-bit machine operand-address calculations are done in 16-bit arithmetic using 16-bit registers. An additional mechanism is therefore required to build addresses.

We can conceive of the one-megabyte memory as an arbitrary number of *segments*, each containing at most 2^{16} bytes. Each segment begins at a byte address that is evenly divisible by 16 (that is, the four least significant bits of the byte address are 0). At any given moment, the program can immediately access the contents of four such segments. The four segments are called the *current code segment*, the *current data segment*, the *current stack segment*, and the *current extra segment*. (The extra segment is a general-purpose area often treated as an additional data segment.) We identify each current segment by placing the 16 most significant bits of the address of its first byte into one of four dedicated registers called *segment registers*. Thus the memory location of the start of a segment is obtained by multiplying the segment register value by 16. If the segment register value is expressed in hexadecimal notation, the memory location can be expressed by appending a 0 to the existing four hex digits.

We are now in a position to create memory addresses. As we have seen, an 8086 memory operand-addressing mode yields a 16-bit address. This 16-bit address is called an *offset*. In order to create the actual memory address, the 8086 adds the offset to 16 times the contents of a segment register. The sum is a 20-bit number capable of addressing the entire one-megabyte 8086 memory space.

The segment registers of the 8086 are shown in Figure 5.1. Each register identifies a particular current segment, and they cannot be used interchangeably: CS identifies the current code segment, DS the current data segment, SS the current stack segment, and ES the current extra segment. Typically, the 8086 uses CS when fetching instructions, DS when accessing data, and SS when accessing the stack. Later in this chapter we will give more specific rules for segment register usage.

Note that if we are able to squeeze our 8086 program, data, and stack into a single segment (that is, our total memory requirements do not exceed 65536 bytes), we can ignore segmentation entirely. We do this by setting all the segment registers to the same value and then leaving them alone. Using the processor in this way is sometimes called the SMALL model of segmentation. Nowadays, of course, most major programs use more than 65536 bytes of memory. They must deal with the segmented nature of that memory. Thus, segmentation is a significant design consideration for all large programs that run on the 8086.

Let's close our survey of the 8086 architecture with a discussion of interrupts. Just like the 386, the 8086 responds to 256 different kinds of interrupts. Corresponding to each kind of interrupt is a routine (called an interrupt handler) that processes interrupts of that kind. The 8086 associates interrupts with handlers by means of a table starting at memory location zero. The table consists of 256 doubleword entries, one entry for each kind of interrupt. Each entry consists of a 16-bit IP (instruction pointer) value, followed by a 16-bit CS (code segment) value. Part of the 8086's response to an interrupt is to set CS and IP to the appropriate values as found in the table; this will cause the processor to begin executing the interrupt handler.

286 Processor   The 286 was developed in order to take advantage of improvements in processor-fabrication technology as well as to address new needs in the marketplace. These needs were:

1. *More addressable memory.* The one-megabyte address space of the 8086 was considered to be insufficient. This was a result of memory price declines that made it practical to build much larger memory subsystems. Hence a design goal of 16 megabytes was set for the 286.

2. *Protection.* The 8086's lack of a protection mechanism hampered its use in multiuser systems. Emerging microprocessors were powerful enough to support multiple users. Multiuser systems must isolate users so that a bug in one user's program won't damage other users' programs. Furthermore, such systems must protect themselves from damage by users' programs. The 286 was designed to provide protection in such multiuser environments.

3. *Virtual memory.* Virtual memory is a technique for running programs which require more memory than that physically available. (Programmers' demands for memory are insatiable.) Support for virtual memory was a requirement for the 286.

All of these needs can be met by modifying the way in which the 8086 calculates addresses. Recall that the 8086 calculates an address by deriving an offset from an operand-addressing mode and then adding that offset to the starting address of a segment. The segment start address is obtained by multiplying the contents of a segment register by 16. The 286 has a more elaborate method for obtaining segment start addresses. The segment register value is used as an index into a table in memory. This table is constructed by the operating system and has an entry, called a *descriptor*, for each segment. Each descriptor contains, among other things, a starting address for its corresponding segment. In summary, the 286 calculates an address by computing an offset from an operand-addressing mode and then adding that offset to a segment start address obtained from the descriptor indexed by the appropriate segment register. (See Figure 5.2.)

Let's now consider the three requirements mentioned above. The first is an expanded memory addressing space. On the 8086, a memory address is 20 bits long, thus limiting the size of addressable memory to 2^{20} bytes. In the table-driven scheme, the length of a memory address is limited only by the size of a descriptor. On the 286, a descriptor is eight bytes long, three bytes (24 bits) of which are used for the segment start address. Thus the 286 can address up to 2^{24} bytes (16 megabytes) of memory.

The next requirement is multiuser protection. We would like to be able to isolate one user from another. Table-driven segmentation makes this easy—simply give each user a different descriptor table! Each user can access only those segments for which there are descriptors. By placing a descriptor for a segment in one user's table but not another's, we can restrict access of that segment to the first user only. The use of individualized descriptor tables allows the 286 to give each user a different address space. In fact, the 286 can give each user the illusion of having a dedicated 286. Such

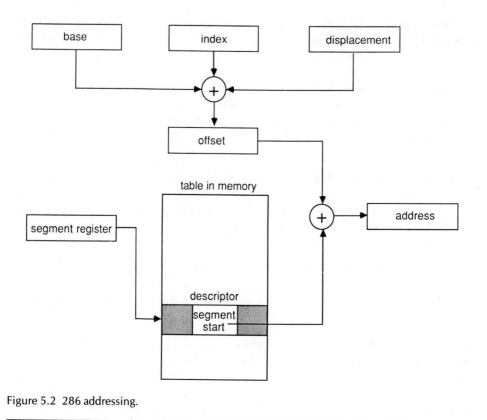

Figure 5.2 286 addressing.

imaginary 286s are called *tasks*.

Finally comes the requirement of virtual memory. The 286 implements virtual memory by keeping some of the addressable segments of a program on disk rather than in main memory. The descriptor for a segment contains a bit indicating where the segment currently resides (disk or main memory). If a program tries to access a segment that is currently on disk, the 286 will transfer control to an interrupt handler; the handler will typically move the desired segment from disk to memory, possibly by first moving some segment out of memory in order to make room. The handler will then pass control back to the interrupted program, which will continue execution as if nothing happened.

The interrupt table used by the 286 has a different format than that of the 8086. Whereas the 8086 interrupt table must start at location zero in memory, the 286 table can start anywhere. The location of the table is specified by a special 286 register.

Except for differences in address calculation, interrupt handling, and a few additional instructions, the 286 is really just a fast 8086. The same general registers, segment registers, operand-addressing modes, and instruction formats are used in both. Thus in many cases, programs can be ported from the 8086 to the 286 without change. However, there are enough differences between the two processors so that not all 8086 programs can be easily ported. For this reason, the 286 starts up in a mode called *real mode*, which emulates an 8086 exactly. If it is desired to run true 286 programs, the necessary processor tables (descriptor tables, interrupt tables, etc.) can be set up while the processor is initially in real mode. The initialization program can then accomplish the switch to 286 normal mode of operation (called *protected mode*) by changing a bit in one of the machine registers. Unfortunately, once protected mode is entered, the only way to return to real mode is to reinitialize the processor. Even though most 286-based personal computers provide some hardware and systems software support for triggering reinitialization, the switch back to real mode is still difficult.

386 Processor   The evolution of the 86 family from 16-bit processors to 32-bit processors provided many opportunities for eliminating architectural shortcomings but, at the same time, presented many challenges in the area of compatibility. The 386 expands the 16-bit general registers (AX, BX, CX, etc.) of the 8086 and 286 to 32-bit general registers (EAX, EBX, ECX, etc.) yet still retains the older registers as subregisters. Many of the operand-addressing mode restrictions of the previous processors have been dropped on the 386. Scaled indexing and 32-bit operands have been added. Address arithmetic on the 386 is done on 32 bits, rather than 16 bits as in the earlier processors.

But what about segmentation? For compatibility, the 386 also contains 286-style (16-bit) segment registers. But recall that address arithmetic is done on 32 bits, so offsets are 32 bits long. Thus segments can be up to 2^{32} (4 billion!) bytes in length. With segments that big, who needs segmentation? No application yet written uses that much main memory. Hence, it is not necessary to consider segmentation when designing programs. By setting every segment register to point to the same segment (the so-called SMALL model of segmentation), we can choose to view 386 memory as a single huge segment, and that is what we have done in all the previous chapters of this book. However, some programs (especially some operating systems) may not make that choice; they may split memory into segments, forcing the programmer to be aware of that split. There are a couple of good reasons for this. First, the program might have been originally written for a 386 predecessor, with segmentation such an integral part of the design that it was retained for the 386. Second, segmentation is good for implementing sophisticated protection policies, particularly in multiuser operating systems, as we discuss in Chapter 6.

Recall that on the 286 segments are the units of virtual memory. In other words, entire segments are swapped between disk and main memory. When the maximum size of a segment is only 64K bytes, this is a reasonable approach, but when segments can range up to 4 billion bytes, the approach becomes infeasible. For this reason, the 386 allows us to divide memory into 4096-byte *pages*. These pages can be swapped to and from disk much more effectively than segments. We talk more about this in Chapter 6.

So far we have discussed the architectural improvements to the 86 family introduced in the 386. Now we'll discuss some of the compatibility challenges faced by the 386. Just as in the 286, the 386 begins execution in a real mode that duplicates the

8086. Real mode for the 386 will be discussed in detail later in this chapter. The 386 can be switched to its normal protected mode of operation in a fashion similar to that of the 286. Furthermore, it can be switched back just as simply.

Real mode is good for running complete software systems (operating system plus application) designed for the 8086. But suppose we want to run old 8086 programs under the control of a new 386 operating system. This is difficult to do using real mode since all protection facilities disappear in real mode. The solution is provided by *virtual 8086 mode*. The 386 can apply virtual 8086 mode to an individual task, which can coexist with other 8086 tasks, and with 286 and 386 tasks. All the tasks remain under the control of a 386 operating system. We describe virtual 8086 mode in detail later in this chapter.

Let's now consider running 286 software on the 386. Since the 286 table-driven segmentation scheme is similar to that of the 386, 286 programs are much easier to accommodate on the 386 than are 8086 programs. Descriptors on the 386 are eight bytes long, just as on the 286. However, in order to support the 386's larger segments, it was necessary to change the format of the descriptors. This might have caused a problem in attempting to run 286 operating system software (which would rely on the descriptor formats) on a 386. Fortunately, this potential problem was spotted just as the 286 was being introduced. Also, fortunately, the top two bytes of every descriptor were unused by the 286 processor. Thus it was decreed that these bytes be initialized to zero and never modified by any 286 software. The 386 would then take advantage of this fact by never storing all 0's in these bytes, and hence a distinction could be made between 286 descriptors and 386 descriptors. The 286 processor doesn't check for 0's in the upper bytes, so programs that write into these bytes will still run on the 286; however, these programs will not execute correctly on a 386. More details on 286 emulation are given later in this chapter.

The most severe challenge in emulating the 8086 and 286 comes from the re-encoding of the operand-addressing modes. Recall that to get the benefits of generality, the 386 had to use operand-addressing mode encodings different from those of its predecessors, but since the 386 can emulate the 8086 and 286, the 386 must recognize the old-fashioned operand-addressing modes as well. The 386 allows the programmer to control which format operand-addressing modes are used on a per-instruction basis. Thus it is possible to insert a few 386 instructions in a 286 program or, perversely, a few 286 instructions in a 386 program.

Instruction recognition on the 386 can be controlled by prefixing the instruction with an operand-length prefix and/or an address-length prefix. We discussed operand-length prefixes in Chapter 2. Ordinary 386 instructions use either 8- or 32-bit operands. Prefixing a 386 instruction with an operand-length prefix causes it to use either 8- or 16-bit operands. Additionally, the 386 allows us to prefix 8086 and 286 instructions with an operand-length prefix. Without the prefix, such instructions use either 8- or 16-bit operands, and with the prefix, they use 8- or 32-bit operands. Thus the prefix switches the size of the largest possible operand to the value opposite from its normal value.

The address-length prefix works in a similar fashion. If the 386 is emulating the 8086 or 286, and if it encounters an instruction preceded by an address-length prefix, then the instruction's operand-addressing mode will be interpreted in 386 style rather than 8086/286 style. In other words, address arithmetic will be done in 32 bits, using 32-bit registers, with all 386 features such as scaled-indexing available. If the 386 is executing a normal 386 program, and if it encounters an instruction preceded by an address-length prefix, then the instruction's operand-addressing mode will be interpreted in 8086/286 style rather than 386 style. In other words, address arithmetic will be done in 16 bits, using 16-bit registers, with 386 features such as scaled indexing unavailable. Thus the prefix switches the address length to the value opposite its normal value.

Some 386 instructions implicitly reference register operands which aren't mentioned explicitly in the instruction. For example, the string instructions implicitly reference the ESI and EDI registers. The address-length prefix applies to these implicit registers just as it applies to registers mentioned explicitly. Table 5.1 lists the instructions with implicit registers, and indicates how these registers are affected by the address-length prefix.

The LEA instruction is noteworthy in that it is affected by both the operand-size and the address-length prefixes. The size of the registers used to compute the effective address is controlled by the address-length prefix. The size of the destination registers is controlled by the operand-size prefix. If the effective address is 16 bits and the destination is 32 bits, the address is zero extended. If the effective address is 32 bits and the destination is 16 bits, the address is truncated.

Recall that the operand-size prefix has no mnemonic in assembly language. The assembler deduces whether an operand-size prefix is required from the size of an instruction's operand. For example, the 386 instruction CALL CX requires an operand-size prefix; the 386 instruction CALL ECX does not. Similarly, the assembler deduces whether an address-length prefix is required from the nature of an instruction's operands. For example, the 386 instruction INC DWORD_VAR[BX] requires an address-length prefix, since BX isn't a 32-bit register. Table 5.2 gives examples of prefix-byte usage, both for the case of 8086/286 emulation and the case of normal 386 operation.

The Strange Saga of the LOCK Prefix Let's talk about another, more minor feature that has had its ups and downs in 86 evolution: the LOCK prefix. Recall that

Table 5.1 Implicit Registers Affected by the Address Length Prefix

Instruction	32-bit Addressing Register	16-bit Addressing Register
XLATB	EBX	BX
REP (N (Z))	ECX	CX
LOOP (N (Z))	ECX	CX
CMPS	ESI, EDI	SI, DI
INS	EDI	DI
LODS	ESI	SI
MOVS	ESI, EDI	SI, DI
OUTS	ESI	SI
SCAS	EDI	DI
STOS	EDI	DI

Table 5.2 Examples of Prefix Byte Usage

Instruction	Emulating a Predecessor?	Operand Size Prefix Needed?	Address Length Prefix Needed?
INC DWORD_VAR[EBX]	no	no	no
INC WORD_VAR[EBX]	no	yes	no
INC DWORD_VAR[BX]	no	no	yes
INC WORD_VAR[BX]	no	yes	yes
INC DWORD_VAR[EBX]	yes	yes	yes
INC WORD_VAR[EBX]	yes	no	yes
INC DWORD_VAR[BX]	yes	yes	no
INC WORD_VAR[BX]	yes	no	no

LOCK prevents other devices from accessing the processor's memory for the duration of the instruction it follows. The problem is that indiscriminate use of LOCK can result in those devices being shut out for unacceptably long periods of time. Specifically, a LOCK of a repeated string operation can last for thousands of processor clock cycles.

In the unprotected environment of the 8086, it is up to the program to take care that this does not happen: no restrictions are imposed upon LOCK usage.

When protection was introduced with the 286, some mechanism was necessary to prevent unprivileged programs from executing harmful LOCK commands. It was decided to give LOCK the same status as the input/output port instructions: if the operating system grants a program the right to execute input/output instructions, then the program can execute LOCK as well. This, however, is too restrictive. Most operating systems disallow input/output instructions in applications programs, but many allow the usage of semaphores requiring a LOCK function. So it was decided to automatically generate the functionality of LOCK whenever an XCHG instruction involving memory is executed.

The 286 solution to the LOCK situation collapsed when paging was introduced with the 386. The LOCK of a repeated string operation was deemed too difficult to support when the string operation crossed over into a nonresident page, causing the page-swapping interrupt handler to be invoked. So a completely different solution was adopted: the 386 unconditionally outlaws the LOCK of a repeated string operation. It does so by restricting the kinds of instructions that accept LOCK, as described in Chapter 3. For compatibility, however, the automatic lock action for the XCHG instruction is retained on the 386.

Writing Programs that Span Multiple Segments

As we have already mentioned, most 386 programs will be written using the so-called SMALL model of segmentation; that is, the entire program (code, data, stack) will reside in a single segment. This is done by initializing all segment registers to point to a single segment. All previous chapters assumed that this was the case; thus whenever we referred to a "memory address" we were really referring to an offset within a segment.

In this section we discuss the facilities provided by the 386 for writing programs which span several segments. Most of these facilities have been inherited from previous processors in which segmentation was much more critical. First we'll discuss how the 386 determines which segment register to use for each memory access. Next we'll describe how to move information into and out of the segment registers. Finally we'll describe how to transfer control (jump, call, etc.) from one segment to another.

Segment Register Determination Let's now consider the specific segment registers of the 386 and the segments that they address. Recall that the 8086 and 286 have four segment registers: CS, DS, SS, and ES. The 386 adds two more, namely FS and GS. The CS register points to the current code segment, where the currently executing program resides. The SS register points to the current stack segment, where the 386 stack is located. The DS register points to the current data segment, typically used for a program's main global data variables, arrays, and structures. The remaining three registers, ES, FS, and GS, point to extra data segments. Thus, at any given moment, the 386 can access up to six different segments. If there are any memory locations not accessible from any of the six segments, then a segment register must be loaded with a new value before the location can be reached.

Let's see why the 386 needs the two additional segment registers, FS and GS. Since the 386 depends less heavily on segmentation than its predecessors, it might seem strange to be adding segment registers, but there are some operating environments that rely heavily on extra segments for communication of data. One example is Intel's iRMX operating system, in which tasks pass messages to each other via special-purpose segments. Another example is the Multics operating system, in which disk files appear to programs as memory segments. In those environments, one can use FS and GS to receive data without clobbering the other four segment registers.

It's interesting to note that FS and GS are *symmetrical*; there is nothing that we can do with one of them that we cannot do with the other. This marks the first appearance of symmetrical registers on an Intel main-line microprocessor since the 8008!

How do we specify which segment register is to be used for each memory access? In three situations, the register is implicit, unchangeable, and cannot be overridden:

1. CS is always used to fetch instructions to be executed.

2. SS is always used for stack operations.

3. ES is always used when EDI is the offset in a string operation. ES is used because we would like the ability to use MOVS to copy data from one segment to another or to use CMPS to compare data in different segments.

In all other memory accesses, there is a *default segment register*, to be used in the absence of an explicit segment specification. Since most of the remaining memory accesses are to data variables and structures, the default segment register is usually DS. The exceptions are memory accesses involving EBP or ESP as the base register. Since EBP and ESP are intended to point to the stack, the default segment register for EBP- or ESP-based memory is SS.

What if we want a segment other than the default segment? In that case, we provide a *segment override prefix* before the instruction whose memory access we wish to override. There are six different prefixes, one for each segment register. The default segment register, whatever it is, can be overridden by any of the other five segments. We can now see why the use of ES as a destination in a string move can't be overridden. A segment override prefix to MOVS or CMPS applies to ESI, not EDI. It was too complicated for the 8086 to provide for two simultaneous overrides, so the destination override was simply disallowed.

Unlike prefixes such as LOCK and REP, the segment-override prefixes do not have explicit mnemonic names in assembly language. They are specified as a part of the memory operands that they refer to. For example, suppose we want to load AL with the byte at offset EBX + 10 within the segment addressed by the FS register. We can code this as:

MOV AL,FS:[EBX + 10]

Since this instruction fetches data without using EBP or ESP as the base register, the default segment register for [EBX + 10] is DS. So the "FS:" operator causes an FS-override prefix to be generated before the MOV instruction.

Let's review the mechanism for generating memory addresses from segments and offsets by considering a specific example. Suppose the just-mentioned MOV instruction is executed when EBX contains the value 0004000 hex, and FS contains a value corresponding to memory location 00023000 hex. The instruction itself is fetched by adding the offset contained in the EIP (instruction pointer) register to the memory location corresponding to the value in the CS register. To execute the instruction, the processor calculates the offset EBX + 10 = 0000400A hex and adds it to the segment location 00023000 so that the byte is fetched from location 0002700A. This is illustrated in Figure 5.3. Note that if the segment location is being calculated by multiplying by 16 (8086 style), then FS must contain the value 2300 hex. If the segment location is fetched from a table (286/386 style), then FS contains a value assigned by the operating system, whose relationship to 00023000 can only be discerned by examining the table.

There is a subtle point concerning the default segment register for memory accesses involving the EBP register. For example, suppose we wish to access memory at EBP + ESI + 10. Since there is no index scaling, we have a choice of which register to encode as the index register and which register to encode as the base register. If EBP is the base register and ESI is the index register, then the default segment register is SS. If we switch the registers, so that ESI and not EBP is the base register, then the default is DS. A clever assembler will exploit this and be capable of automatically generating code for either DS or SS, without an override prefix. A not-so-clever assembler might force the programmer to be aware of this subtlety and find, possibly by trial and error, the correct coding format for the instruction form desired.

Loading and Storing the Segment Registers   The manipulation of segment registers occurs far less frequently in a program than the manipulation of the general

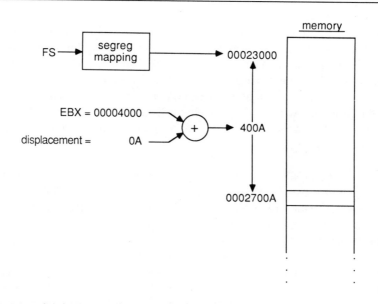

Figure 5.3 Example of memory addressing in the FS segment.

registers. Hence the instruction set for segment registers is limited. The only instructions that allow segment registers as operands are the general-purpose transfers MOV (move), PUSH, and POP. Even those instructions are more limited in the forms allowed.

The MOV instruction allows the programmer to move any segment register value to or from a word-sized general register or memory operand. The memory operand has full generality: it can include a base and/or a (scaled) index register. Table 5.3 shows examples of MOV instructions involving segment registers. The MOV forms *not* supported are:

1. MOV from one segment register to another. This can be accomplished almost as easily by pushing the source segment register and then popping the value into the destination segment register.

2. MOV of an immediate constant into a segment register. In 8086-emulation mode, there is an occasional motivation to use this form (for example, to point to the interrupt table by using a zero segment register value). In those cases, you can either move the constant into a general register and then move the general register to the segment register; or you can allocate the constant in memory and then load the segment register from the memory location. In native 386 mode, in which all segment register values are assigned by the operating system, it is hard to imagine any use whatsoever for the MOV *segreg,imm* instruction.

3. MOV of any value into the CS register. The effect of such an instruction would be to cause a new segment to become the current code segment. But the usual

incrementing of the EIP register will cause EIP to contain the offset of the next sequential instruction in the *previous* code segment. Thus the combination of CS and EIP will specify a meaningless memory address, and the processor will attempt to fetch the next instruction for execution from this meaningless address. So, unless the instruction that alters the contents of CS also puts a related value in EIP, the processor will wind up making a wild program transfer. We shall see, shortly, how to change CS and EIP with a single instruction and thus avoid this problem.

The PUSH and POP instructions allow the programmer to save and restore the values of segment registers. These instructions are listed in Table 5.4. For the same reason just described for MOV CS,*anything*, the instruction POP CS is not allowed.

Most modern high-level languages, such as Pascal and C, allow the programmer to define variables whose values are pointers to memory locations. In the 386 environment, the high-level language program can work entirely within a single segment, so that such pointers can be represented by their 32-bit offsets. In the 386's predecessors, however, programs could easily be larger than the 64K-byte capacity of a segment. Pointers for such programs had to include both the segment and the offset. The 8086 provided two instructions, LDS and LES, for loading a segment-and-offset pointer into registers for addressing; the 386 rounds out the instruction group by adding LSS, LFS, and LGS.

Each of the address transfer instructions has as its source a six-byte pointer (four-byte offset followed by two-byte segment), residing in memory. The destination consists of two registers: the segment register named by the last two letters of the instruction mnemonic, combined with a doubleword general register. The dou-

Table 5.3. Examples of MOV Instructions with Segment Registers

register to segment register	MOV ES, BX
segment register to register	MOV AX, DS
memory to segment register	MOV SS, MEMWORD
segment register to memory	MOV MEMWORD, CS

Table 5.4 PUSH and POP Instructions Involving Segment Registers

PUSH CS	
PUSH DS	POP DS
PUSH ES	POP ES
PUSH SS	POP SS
PUSH FS	POP FS
PUSH GS	POP GS

bleword destination register is given as the first operand to the instruction; the memory source is given as the second operand. Examples of these instructions are:

```
LDS EBX,MEMLOC    ; load DS and EBX with the pointer at MEMLOC
LES  EDI,MEMLOC    ; load ES and EDI with the pointer at MEMLOC
LSS  ESP,MEMLOC    ; load SS and ESP with the pointer at MEMLOC
LFS  EDX,MEMLOC    ; load FS and EDX with the pointer at MEMLOC
LGS  ESI,MEMLOC    ; load GS and ESI with the pointer at MEMLOC
```

The LSS example just listed effects a change of the 386 stack. This is a useful operation when the 386 is alternately executing more than one program, each with its own stack. LSS is not available on the 386's predecessors. It takes two MOV instructions to change stacks on a predecessor: one to load the SS segment register, and another to load the stack pointer (which is the 16-bit register SP on those predecessors). After the first MOV is executed but before the second, the combination of SS and SP does not have any significance; it certainly does not specify the top of any area reserved for a stack (except possibly by accident). This isn't a problem unless someone tries to push a value on the stack during the stack change. But that is exactly what an external interrupt or a single-step interrupt might try to do if it arrives at the wrong time. To prevent this from occurring, both the 386 and the programmer must take special action:

1. The 386 will not accept any interrupts immediately after executing a MOV or POP instruction that loads a new value into SS. (In a burst of overkill, the 8086, 8088, and 186 inhibit interrupts after a MOV or POP into *any* segment register, not just SS. This was corrected, starting with the 286.)

2. The programmer must insure that the new stack pointer is loaded immediately after any change in SS, either by using LSS, or by using two consecutive MOV instructions (one for SS and the next for ESP), taking care that the move into SS comes first.

Transferring Control Between Segments   In Chapter 3 we discussed the instructions JMP (jump to another program location), CALL (jump to a procedure, saving the return address on the stack), and RET (return from a procedure, popping the return address from the stack). What we didn't mention about those instructions is that they come in two flavors. One flavor of instruction transfers control within the current code segment. The other flavor transfers control to an arbitrary code segment (by changing the contents of CS), which then becomes the current code segment. We'll refer to these respective flavors as *near* and *far*. It is not a precise terminology, since it is possible to construct a far transfer that is nearer in physical memory than a near transfer. However, it is the terminology used by the assembly language, and it is easier to read than the more precise *intrasegment/intersegment*.

Obviously, far transfers can do everything that near transfers can do and then some. Why then do we need both? Simply because far transfers take longer to execute (they have more to do); and, with the exception of returns, they require more bytes of code (they have more to say).

The JMP instruction that we described in Chapter 3 was the near jump. Recall that the operand for the near jump is encoded as a relative offset to save code space and to provide position-independent code. Should we also encode far jumps as relative offsets? The answer is no, for these reasons:

1. The destination of a far jump is not typically to a nearby place, and thus there is no reason to expect to save any bytes by using relative offsets.

2. Far jumps specify destinations in some other code segment. If a section of code containing far jumps or calls is moved, the destination, being in some other segment, would not necessarily also be moved. Hence using relative offsets would not lead to position-independent code.

3. If segment locations are computed from descriptor tables, then there is no arithmetic relation between segment register values and physical memory locations. In that case, it is unclear how one would encode a far relative offset.

Hence, far-jump operands are encoded as absolute addresses, with both an offset and a segment register value. The 386 simultaneously loads EIP and CS with the operand value.

The 386 also provides indirect far jumps, in which the operand is a memory location containing a six-byte pointer to the jump destination. The six memory bytes consist of the four-byte offset, followed by the two-byte segment register value.

We write both far and near jumps in our program as JMP; the assembler is able to determine whether or not the destination is in the same segment as the jump instruction and generates the appropriate instruction.

The entire preceding discussion applies to the CALL instruction as well as the JMP instruction. Thus, both direct and indirect far calls are allowed, and they differ from near calls since the destination is encoded as a six-byte absolute address rather than a four-byte offset. A further difference in the far call is the return value pushed onto the stack. We must save the original CS register value as well as the 32-bit offset pointing beyond the CALL instruction. To maintain doubleword alignment of items pushed onto the stack, the CS register is padded with sixteen high 0 bits before it is pushed. The padded CS value is first first, then EIP is pushed. Because the 386 stack grows towards lower addresses, the resulting six-byte pointer pushed on the stack has the standard format (offset first, segment last).

Because eight bytes are pushed onto the stack in a far call, we must have a distinct far return instruction to pop the full six-byte address from the stack and discard the two-byte padding. This has two implications:

1. The assembler must know whether to generate a near or far return when it sees the RET mnemonic. The destination to RET is not given as an operand; it is implicitly popped from the stack. So the assembler cannot deduce the return type from an operand type.

2. The calls to a procedure must be all far or all near since the returns that are within the procedure must pop the same number of bytes that each of the calls pushed.

There is an opportunity offered by the second implication that can be used to solve the problem posed by the first. We can inform the assembler at the start of a procedure whether the procedure's calls will be far or near. The assembler can use this information to generate the correct form for any RET instructions it sees within the body of the procedure. We give the information to the assembler by defining the name of the procedure with a PROC directive and by marking the end of the procedure with an ENDP directive. The PROC directive contains the keyword NEAR or FAR, indicating the type of call that can be made to the procedure. For example:

```
UPCOUNT PROC NEAR
    INC BH
    DEC DL
    RET
UPCOUNT ENDP
```

Since UPCOUNT is declared to be a NEAR procedure, all calls to it, anywhere in the program, are assembled as near calls. The single RET instruction within the procedure body is assembled as a near return.

Note that the above PROC notation is rather verbose. Do we need to use it, even if we are not using the 386 as a segmented machine? Fortunately, the answer is no; outside of PROC..ENDP pairs, the RET instruction produces a near return. Even in a segmented environment, it is not strictly necessary to use PROC..ENDP; some assemblers accept a separate RETF mnemonic for the far return instruction. If your assembler does not have RETF, you could define a RETF macro to generate the proper code (hex CB).

What happens if we call a FAR procedure that happens to be in the same code segment as our call? In this case, the assembler must insure that the CS register is pushed onto the stack, because the far RET instruction within the procedure will expect it to be there. The straightforward way of doing this is to generate a far CALL instruction, even though the CS register will not change when the instruction is executed. There is a trickier way that consumes less code and executes more quickly: the assembler could generate a PUSH CS instruction, followed by a near CALL to the procedure. Most assemblers adopt the first, straightforward approach.

Emulating the 8086

Now that we've described the predecessors to the 386, we are ready to consider how the 386 emulates those predecessors. Let's first consider the two modes that emulate the 8086: *real mode* and *virtual 8086 mode*.

Real Mode   The 386 is in real mode whenever it is powered up or reset. The 386's paging and advanced segmentation features, described in Chapter 6, depend on tables in memory that are set up by the operating system. In real mode, those tables are not yet in place, so segment locations must be calculated by formula rather than by tables. Since the 8086's segment locations are calculated by formula, real mode simply emulates the 8086, using the multiply-by-16 formula.

What happens when an opcode is encountered in real mode that is undefined on the 8086, but has meaning on the 386? The 8086 specification makes no promises concerning action taken, so we can do anything we want. Why not perform the 386 action? This is what the 386 does; so access to the 386's 32-bit registers, general addressing modes, and new instructions is possible in real mode.

The table of interrupt-handler routines has the same location and format in 386 real mode as it does on the 8086. The table starts at location zero in the 8086's megabyte memory space and consists of 256 doubleword entries, one for each interrupt number. Each entry consists of a 16-bit instruction pointer value, followed by a 16-bit code segment register value.

The purpose of real mode is to allow the 386's start-up code to perform the initializations necessary for paging and table-driven segmentation. We describe those initializations in Chapter 6. After initialization is completed, real mode is exited by setting a bit within a special register called the *machine status word*, or *MSW*. MSW is a 16-bit register that was introduced with the 286. It is the lower half of the 386's 32-bit control register CR0. The bit mapping of these registers is shown in Figure 5.4. There are two instructions that write to MSW: the 16-bit version LMSW (Load MSW), and the 32-bit version MOV CR0,*reg*. When the bottom PE (Protection Enable) bit is set to 1, the 386 leaves real mode and enters protected mode, which encompasses all the other operating modes of the 386.

Can the PE bit be reset to return to real mode from protected mode? On the 286, it was envisioned that nobody would ever want to do this, so the LMSW instruction ignores any attempt to change the PE bit from 1 to 0. This turned out to be a mistake; most 286 machines on the market have operating systems that run only in real mode. If a program running in protected mode needs an operating system service (such as a disk file access), it must return to real mode to obtain the service. To make this possible, a circuit must be added to the computer to generate a hardware reset under program control, and the power-up code must be programmed to recognize this possibility. The 386 eliminates the need for special circuitry by allowing the MOV CR0,*reg* instruction to change PE from 1 to 0. (For 286 compatibility, the LMSW instruction still prohibits the change from protected mode to real mode.) A significant number of instructions must be executed before the MOV CR0 instruction, however, to explicitly disengage some of the features of protected mode. We discuss the necessary sequence in Chapter 6.

Real mode fails to emulate the 8086 in its actions concerning the LOCK prefix. Recall that LOCK is unrestricted on the 8086, but that LOCK is prohibited from many instructions (including string operations) on the 386. Since it was perceived that the disallowed LOCK operations were never used on the 8086 in the first place, it was decided that it was not worthwhile to allow them in any context on the 386.

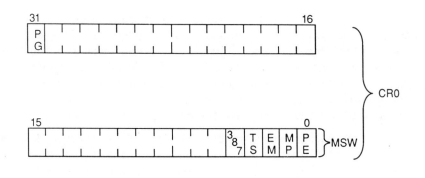

Figure 5.4 Format of the CRO register.

Virtual 8086 Mode Another weakness of the 286's design is its inability to emulate the 8086 while retaining protection and virtual memory. The only 8086 emulation mode on the 286 is real mode, and protection is completely disabled in real mode. There has been little incentive to develop protected operating systems on the 286, because it's almost impossible to run the existing 8086 software base without disabling the protection. This problem is corrected in the 386 by virtual 8086 mode, an 8086 emulation mode that runs in the 386's protected environment.

Recall that the 386 begins execution in real mode, emulating the 8086. Initialization code then switches the 386 to protected mode, its standard and most powerful mode of operation. In protected mode, the 386 supports multiple tasks. Whereas real mode applies to the *entire* 386 system, virtual 8086 mode can be applied by the operating system on a per-task basis. At any given time, some tasks may be running in virtual 8086 mode, while others are not. We describe how a task enters and leaves virtual 8086 mode in Chapter 6.

Like real mode, virtual 8086 mode calculates segment locations just as the 8086 does. Furthermore, both the default operand size and the default address length are 16 bits. This means that 8086/286 instruction formats are expected, and operand-size prefixes and address-length prefixes must be used if 386 instruction formats are to be executed. Thus virtual 8086 mode is object-code compatible with the 8086. There are, however, the following differences:

1. Memory locations are subject to mapping via the 386's paging mechanism. We can thus emulate the 8086 within a virtual memory system.

2. The 386 operating system can choose whether to grant input-output privileges to the virtual 8086 program, as we describe in Chapter 6. If privileges are not granted, then certain instructions will cause an interrupt to take place before they are executed, letting the 386 operating system regain control. The sensitive instructions are those capable of reading or writing the interrupt enable flag: STI, CLI, PUSHF(D), POPF(D), IRET(D), and INT n.

All interrupts cause the 386 to exit virtual 8086 mode and execute the interrupt handler defined by the more complicated tables we discuss in Chapter 6, not by the simple 8086-format table at location zero. Of course, the 386 operating system can choose to provide complete emulation by restarting the virtual 8086 program at the location given by the 8086-format table, with the appropriate interrupt-return information pushed onto the program's stack. Alternatively, the 386 system can handle the interrupt itself and restart the program as it sees fit.

You might think that there is a contradiction in the above two paragraphs, concerning the INT *n* instruction. If INT *n* always causes the 386 to exit virtual 8086 mode, then what difference does input/output privilege make to the INT *n* instruction? The answer is that if privilege is granted, then the *nth* entry of the 386's interrupt table is used. If privilege is not granted, then a general protection fault occurs (we discuss this in detail in Chapter 6), and the interrupt 13 handler is invoked, no matter what the value of *n* is.

Let's see why interrupt-flag instructions are sensitive and need to be trapped. Recall that a virtual 8086 mode program executes as one task among many. If it were allowed to clear the interrupt-enable flag, it could shut out timer interrupts, defeating the operating system's attempt to fairly allocate the processor amongst the various tasks. The program could then hog all computer time. The system can protect itself by trapping those instructions that change the interrupt-enable flag and then returning to the program *without changing the interrupt-enable flag*. However, the program now believes that it did indeed change the interrupt-enable flag and may later attempt to read it. To make the illusion complete, such reads must also be trapped by the operating system and fallacious information returned to the program. (Honesty and trust are not the hallmarks of a protected operating system!)

3.   The IN and OUT port instructions are subject to control by the 386 operating system. The system can set up an *I/O Permission Bitmap*, a Boolean array that tells which numbered input-output ports can be accessed by a user program. For example, if the program attempts to execute the instruction IN AL,100, the 386 will consult the 100th bit of the bitmap. If the bit is 0, the program is allowed to execute the instruction uninterrupted. If the bit is 1, an interrupt is generated before the instruction is executed, and the 386 operating system regains control. (We describe the bitmap in detail in Chapter 6.)

Why is such selective protection needed for the port instructions? The answer is that many 8086-based programs address ports directly, and many such programs must execute quickly. For example, a high-speed communications program might program a serial-port peripheral chip directly. If the 386 interrupted every time the port was accessed, the program might run too slowly to receive the serial input data. So direct, uninterrupted access to the serial port must be allowed. On the other hand, we've already seen that access to the operating system's timer chip must be disallowed. The bitmap lets the operating system grant access to the serial port while denying access to the timer chip's port.

4.   The LOCK prefix follows the 386 model of restricted usage, just as it does in real mode.

Emulating the 286

We've just seen how the 386 can emulate the 8086 on a per-task basis. Because the 286 uses a table-driven segmentation scheme similar to that of the 386, we can control 286 emulation much more precisely than 8086 emulation. In particular, we can mix 286 and 386 segments in the same program, so that 286 and 386 procedures can call each other. Let's see how the 386 can accomplish this.

Distinguishing 286 Code from 386 Code   First, the 386 must be able to tell whether it is executing 286 code or 386 code. There are only two areas of object-code incompatibility between the 286 and 386 that require special attention:

1.   Chapter 6 shows that the formats of segment descriptors are slightly different on the 386 than on the 286. Some of the differences come from expanded fields: the segment location field is expanded from 24 bits to 32 bits to accommodate the increased memory space, and the segment size limit field is expanded from 16 bits to 24 bits. Other differences derive from different interpretations of fields that exist in both 286 and 386 segment descriptors. These latter differences create incompatibility between the formats.

2.   We have already seen that the default operand size and the default address length are both 16 bits on the 286 and 32 bits on the 386.

The 386 resolves these incompatibilities by examining the code segment descriptor for the program. Descriptors are always 64 bits long on both the 286 and 386; hence we can mix 286 and 386 descriptors in the same table. The upper 16 bits of a 286 descriptor are unused. The 286 specification, foreseeing 386 expansion, insists that the unused bits be set to 0. The 386 exploits this by interpreting such a zero field as the identifier of a 286 segment. In particular, bit 54 of a 386 code segment descriptor is the *D bit*. If the D bit is 1 for the current CS segment, then the default operand size and address length is 32 bits. If the D bit is 0 (as it will be for all 286 segments), the default is 16 bits.

Now we can see how to mix 286 code and 386 code in the same program: simply put the two types of code into different segments. The 286 code can call a 386 procedure by using the far CALL instruction, and vice versa.

Distinguishing 286 Stacks from 386 Stacks   We've seen the need to distinguish 286 and 386 code segments. There is also a (less obvious) need to distinguish 286 and 386 stack segments. To understand this, we need to review how the stack operates. Recall that 86-family stacks run backwards: they start at the highest address within the stack segment and expand toward lower addresses. To accommodate this, the 286/386 protection mechanism interprets the segment limit for stack segments as a *lower* bound: if so much is pushed onto the stack that memory below the bound is accessed, an exception occurs, and the operating system can allocate more stack memory if it chooses. This condition is called *stack overflow*. The same protection mechanism is used to detect the opposite condition, *stack underflow*. If everything is popped from the stack, the stack pointer advances beyond the highest address it can represent and assumes a value of zero. An attempt to pop items from the now-empty stack will cause a read operation on location zero within the stack segment, which is below the lower bound.

Now we can see the incompatibility between 286 stacks and 386 stacks. On the 286 stack, the stack pointer is the 16-bit SP register, and the highest address in the segment is FFFF hex. When the word stored at FFFE is popped from a 286 stack, the pointer SP becomes zero, and any further attempt to pop items from the stack will cause an underflow. On the 386 stack, the stack pointer is the 32-bit ESP register, and the highest address is FFFFFFFF hex. Now if we pop a word (or doubleword) containing location FFFF, we are a long, long way from an empty stack: ESP increments to 10000 hex, not zero. Thus, the 386 must know whether it is using SP or ESP as its stack pointer. This is accomplished by examining the D bit of the stack segment descriptor: if D is 1, the segment is a 386 stack segment, and ESP is used; if D is 0, the segment is a 286 stack segment, and SP is used.

Why can't the 386 decide whether to use SP or ESP by examining the D-bit of the code segment? The answer lies in our desire to allow 286 and 386 segments to exist in the same program. If, for example, 286 code calls a 386 procedure, there is only one stack involved. The highest address of the stack (either FFFF or FFFFFFFF) was determined when the first item was pushed onto the stack; that address doesn't change simply because we have started executing 386 code. Thus, the usage of SP or ESP must be tied to the stack segment itself, not to the code segment. A hybrid 286/386 program must either use a 386 stack and sacrifice faithful emulation of 286 stack underflow, or restrict itself to a 64K-byte 286 stack and use SP instead of ESP as its stack pointer.

We conclude our discussion of 286 emulation by listing the differences that remain between the 286 and 386, even if both the code segment and the stack segment are 286 segments:

1. Instruction timing is, of course, different in many cases. For the most part, the 386 is faster than the 286.

2. There are numerous opcodes undefined on the 286 that represent new instructions and prefixes on the 386. If these opcodes are executed on the 286, an invalid opcode fault (interrupt 6) will occur. If the opcodes are executed on the 386, the 386 instruction is executed, even when the 386 is executing in a 286 code segment. It was deemed more useful to add the 386's capabilities to 286 emulation mode than it was to support 286 programs that engage in the dubious practice of using an illegal opcode to generate an INT 6 function.

3. The LOCK prefix follows the 386 model, just as we discussed in the section on 8086 emulation.

References

The 386 instruction set is described in reference 1 and its assembly language, ASM386, in reference 2. Some of the material in this chapter is based on the authors' presentation of similar material for the 8086 and 286 in references 3 and 4.

1. *80386 Programmer's Reference Manual*, Intel Corp., 1986.

2. *ASM386 Assembly Language Reference Manual*, Intel Corp., 1986.

3. S.P. Morse, *The 8086/8088 Primer*, Hayden Book Company, New York, 1982.

4. S.P. Morse and D.J. Albert, *The 80286 Architecture*, John Wiley and Sons, New York, 1986.

CHAPTER
6

THE OPERATING SYSTEM'S VIEW

Introduction

In the 1960's software and hardware mechanisms were developed for sharing a computer among a group of users. The goal was to create simultaneously for each user the illusion of having the hardware all to oneself. Each user's simulated copy of the computer is called a *task*. The creation and use of multiple tasks on a computer is called *multitasking*. One multitasking technique, called *time slicing*, is to divide each second of time into pieces and use the pieces for running different tasks. It is by means of time slicing that all users are simultaneously convinced that they each have their own, albeit slower, copy of the computer. Operating systems that use time slicing for sharing a computer among many users are called *time-sharing systems*.

Originally, the high cost of computers compared to the low cost of computer terminals provided the primary motivation for time sharing. One expensive computer could support many users, each needing only a relatively inexpensive terminal. Today, the cost of some personal computers is close to that of a terminal and thus this economic argument for time sharing is losing some of its force. But there are two additional reasons for sharing a central computer which remain valid in the era of personal computing. First, the central computer system may still include hardware that is expensive to replicate, such as high-speed/high-quality printers, large-capacity disks, magnetic tape drives, and ultra-fast central processors. Second, a shared computer can provide superior support for a group of individuals working together in a common endeavor. The central computer allows for easy and controlled sharing of programs, communication between users, updating and querying of a common database, and auditing of transactions. Thus, the ability of tasks to share information and communicate among themselves has become increasingly important.

It may someday be possible to obtain this desirable sharing of information by tying together personal computers in a high-speed network. However, such computer networks currently suffer from a need for expensive, high-speed communications links, a multiplicity of competing standards, and a number of technical problems (generally lumped under the rubric "distributed processing") which are still active research topics. So despite the existence of low-priced personal computers, shared computers are still widely used.

Multitasking isn't limited to shared computer systems. It's also used extensively in real-time systems for controlling machinery. Here, one task continuously collects information from sensors, another computes from this information how the machinery should respond, and yet another task actuates the machinery. Additional tasks accept commands from the human operator and display equipment status for the operator's benefit.

Multitasking is even showing up on personal computers. In integrated software packages, separate tasks perform word processing, spreadsheet calculations, construction of graphs, database queries, and communications. Each task is assigned its own region, or *window*, on the personal computer's screen. The user can then switch from task to task by moving from one window to another. In such integrated software packages it's vital that the user be able to transfer information between the various tasks.

A personal computer user can also use multitasking for foreground/ background computing. For example, while a user is interacting with a word processing program (the *foreground* task), his computer can simultaneously accept delivery of electronic mail, sort a file, or compile a program. These latter, *background* tasks don't require constant user attention and thus can run in parallel with the interactive foreground task. The 386 is powerful enough to handle many background tasks without degrading the response time of the foreground task.

This chapter is devoted to the features of the 386 that assist multitasking operating systems. We'll first describe the memory management features of the 386, which come under two categories:

1. Paging allows the implementation of a virtual memory system, as we mention in Chapter 5. Virtual memory allows the system to run programs larger than the available main memory by automatically moving portions of the programs between disk and memory. Hence virtual memory is useful even if multitasking isn't used. Virtual memory also allows a program to be run in different areas of memory without being reassembled or recompiled. This permits the operating system to optimize the use of memory, as tasks start and finish, by moving tasks around.

2. Segmentation allows an operating system to isolate tasks from each other. This is important so that a bug in one task won't cause the entire system to crash. Segmentation allows for the controlled sharing of information between tasks.

After discussing memory management, we describe the protection features of the 386. These features allow the operating system to protect itself and its vital information from destruction by bugs or malice on the part of the tasks under operating system control. Even in single-user systems, protection is useful for containing the effects of bugs, so that crucial subsystems (such as disk I/O) aren't damaged by programs under development.

The next subject is the set of instructions for switching the 386 from one task to another. Real-time systems, in particular, require rapid task-switching. By providing hardware support, the 386 reduces the time required to switch tasks, allowing more time to be devoted to the tasks themselves.

One possible reason for switching tasks is an exception in the task which is running. Another reason is an interrupt signal from a peripheral device connected to the 386. We'll describe how the 386 responds to exceptions and interrupts, and we'll enumerate the exceptions which are possible on the 386.

Almost all of the 386 features described in this chapter are unavailable on the 8086; they were introduced with the 286. The paging mechanism was introduced with the 386. When the 386 executes in real mode it suppresses these new features and instead mimics the behavior of the 8086. Upon reset, the 386 begins execution in real mode. It takes an initialization program to get the 386 into protected mode, where the new features are enabled. So we'll conclude the chapter by discussing system initialization.

Memory Management: Paging

Recall that in Chapters 1 through 4 we refer to 32-bit addresses within the four-gigabyte memory space of the 386. Then in Chapter 5 we revealed that we were not really talking about absolute memory addresses; we were talking about offsets within segments. A memory address is calculated by adding the offset to the segment base location. Now we have another surprise: the calculated memory address is called a *linear address*. It undergoes yet another mapping before it becomes a *physical address*, output via the 386's addressing pins. This final (no more surprises) mapping breaks memory up into *pages* that can be rearranged at the operating system's will.

Before describing the 386's paging mechanism, let's consider a couple of the overall design properties we would like the mechanism to have in order to make a 386 operating system as easy as possible to implement.

First, we would like all pages to be the same length. Not only does this simplify the hardware design of paging, but it also simplifies the operating system's algorithms for page allocation. Variable-length allocation routines are commonly plagued with fragments of unused memory that are too small to be of use. If all pages are the same length, we can divide memory into fixed page-sized slots. A chunk of unused memory can never be smaller than a page.

What fixed length do we want for our pages? If we make pages too big, it will take inordinately long to swap a page to or from the disk. If we make pages too small, our bookkeeping tables will chew up too much memory, and we'll be swapping pages too often. Also, we want to make our page size an exact multiple (one is OK) of the size of a disk sector. Otherwise, we'll waste time by being forced on every swap to read or write more than we need. On older virtual-memory computers, the page size has typically been 2048 bytes. However, some newer-generation disk systems have 4096-byte sectors, so it was decided to use 4096-byte pages. We'll see when we study the format of page tables that this turned out to be an ideal choice.

Second, we would like each task of a multitasking system to have the illusion that no other tasks are occupying any memory. We would also like to switch tasks without having to copy an entire page-table full of data. This means that we need the ability to switch page tables. Note, however, that the operating system must remain available no matter which page table is in effect.

With these requirements in mind, let's describe how the 386 allows the implementation of a paged virtual-memory system. Let's keep a specific example in mind while we discuss the features: a computer system with four megabytes of physical memory, running an operating system that makes the computer appear to have the full four gigabytes of memory.

Page Faults   Since our example computer has only four megabytes of actual memory, any memory beyond that must be stored on a disk. What happens when a program tries to access part of the additional memory? Before the memory access takes place, the 386 generates an internal interrupt of type 14, called a *page fault*. Control passes to the interrupt-14 handler, which reads the needed page into memory. This is called *swapping in*. If there isn't a free page in memory, the handler must create one by moving a page from memory to the disk. This is called *swapping out*. After the referenced page is swapped in, the interrupt handler can return to the program. The program will continue, unaware of the interruption. Thus the operating system has created the illusion we want: that all four gigabytes are in memory at the same time.

How does the page-fault handler know which page is needed by the program? The 386 stores the offending memory address in its special CR2 register. By executing a special MOV instruction of CR2 into any doubleword register, the handler identifies the page.

Let's now discuss exactly when and how page faults are detected by the 386. Whenever the 386 obtains a linear memory address, it must map it into the corresponding physical memory address.

Page Directory   The first step of the mapping is to consult Control Register CR3, which points to the *page directory*. The page directory is an array of 1024 doublewords. The purpose of the array is to split the four- gigabyte linear memory space into 1024 *page groups*, each four megabytes in length. Each doubleword in the array controls a page group.

Figure 6.1 shows the format of a doubleword page directory entry. Bits marked 0 should always be set to 0; they may have meaning on some future processor. The bit marked with a question mark is undefined and should be ignored (we'll see why in the next section). The other fields of the doubleword are defined as follows:

The P (Present) bit tells if this page group entry is really here. If P is 1, then all the other fields we will describe are valid. If P is 0, then the entire four-megabyte page group is "not present." An attempt to access any memory within the page group will

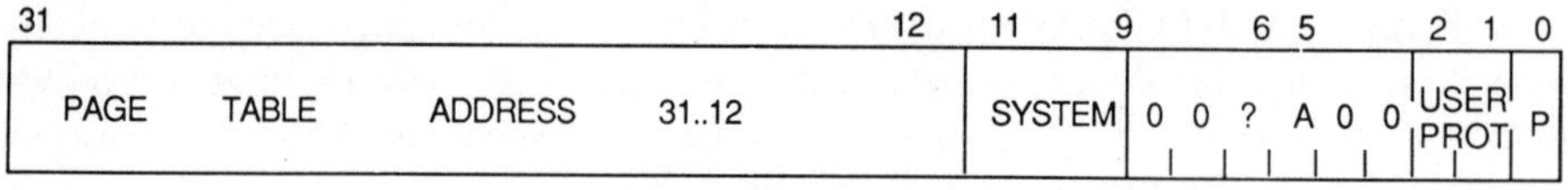

| 31 | | | | 12 | 11 | 9 | 6 | 5 | 2 | 1 | 0 |

| PAGE | TABLE | ADDRESS | 31..12 | | SYSTEM | 0 0 ? A 0 0 | USER PROT | P |

Figure 6.1 Format of a page-directory entry.

cause a page fault. Furthermore, the upper 31 bits of the page directory entry are ignored by the 386. They may be used by the operating system to store any information it chooses about the page group. We'll see shortly how a typical system will use these bits.

In our example system, a "not present" indication will always mean that the page table for this group, as well as all of its underlying pages, has been swapped out to disk. Another system might use the "not present" indicator to permanently block access to a page group, thus implementing a virtual memory system of less than four gigabytes. There is no advantage to doing so, however: memory restrictions of this type are more naturally handled by restricting the size of segments, not of linear memory.

The User Prot (User Protection) field allows more selective control over the access of a page group. The operating system can specify that some page groups can be accessed only by the operating system itself and not by a user program. If the User Prot field has a value of 0 or 1, then the page group is inaccessible to user programs. If it has a value of 2, then a user program can read from, but cannot write to, the page group. Finally, if the User Prot field is 3, there are no restrictions on user programs. If an illegal access is attempted, the 386 will generate a page fault.

The purpose of the User Prot field is to protect the operating system from being destroyed by an errant user program. We'll see later in this chapter that there are more elaborate protection mechanisms for segments. The User Prot field was added to provide simple protection for systems not using segmentation extensively. This simple mechanism does rely on the segmentation mechanism to determine whether the operating system is in control: if the 386 is running in the least privileged of four *privilege levels*, then the paging protection mechanism considers the program to be a user program. If any of the other three privilege levels is in effect, then the operating system is considered to be in control, and the User Prot field is ignored.

The A (Accessed) bit is set to 1 by the 386 whenever the page group is accessed. This can be used to compile information on page group usage. We see how this works in the next section when we discuss the corresponding bit of a page-table entry.

The System field is a three-bit field reserved for operating system use. Again, we'll describe usage when we talk about the corresponding field of the page-table entry.

Finally, we come to the most important part of the entry. The Page Table Address field gives the physical location of the *page table* for this page group. The 386 requires page tables to begin at 4K-byte boundaries in the memory space, so that the bottom 12 bits of the address of a page table are always 0. Thus, only the top 20 bits are necessary to specify a page-table location, and those 20 bits are given by the Page Table Address field.

31				12	11	9					2	1	0
PAGE	TABLE	ADDRESS	31..12		SYSTEM	0	0	D	A	0	0	USER PROT	P

Figure 6.2 Format of a page-table entry.

Page Table   The next step in mapping a 386 linear address to a physical address is to consult the page table for the appropriate page group. A page table has a format identical to the page directory: it is an array of 1024 doublewords, used to split the four-megabyte linear page group into 1024 pages, each 4096 bytes in length.

Figure 6.2 shows the format of a doubleword page-table entry. Note that the fields are almost the same as a page-directory entry. The difference is that they apply to an individual page, rather than an entire page group.

The P (Present) bit is used to indicate whether a page is in memory or on disk. The operating system will mark all pages that are present in memory by setting P to 1, and it will mark pages that aren't present in memory (are on disk) by setting P to 0. A page fault will then occur whenever a page not in memory is referenced by a program. The fault handler can read the referenced page into memory from disk, point the page to the memory (as we describe shortly), and set the P bit to 1. After the handler returns to the program, the program will continue as if nothing happened.

In contrast to the P bit, that enables the operating system to tell when to swap a page into memory, the accessed (A) bit helps the operating system choose which pages should be swapped out to disk when there isn't room for a page to be swapped in. In making this choice, the operating system will try to avoid swapping out a page which the program will want to use in the near future. Since the operating system can't precisely predict the future behavior of the program, it must make an educated guess.

It can be argued that a page that hasn't been used for a long time probably will continue being dormant. So a reasonable strategy to use, when memory space is required, is to swap out that page which hasn't been accessed for the longest period of time, that is, that page whose most recent use is furthest in the past. This is called a *least-recently-used* or LRU policy.

The A bit helps the operating system associate with each page its approximate time of last use. The A bit doesn't affect execution, but it is automatically set to 1 by the 386 whenever an access is made to a memory location within the page. The A bit becomes 0 only when it is explicitly cleared by software. Thus the A bit indicates whether a page has been accessed since software last set the A bit to 0.

All pages should initially have A set to 0. At regular intervals the operating system can scan through all page-table entries, clearing their A bits to 0. Any pages with A equal to 1 found during the scan must have been accessed after the previous scan. So the operating system should increment such pages' time-of-last-use. When it's necessary to swap out a page, the page with the lowest time-of-last-use should be chosen to be the victim.

Another bit that assists in the swapping-out process is the D (Dirty) bit. When a page is swapped into memory from disk, the operating system should set the D bit to 0. Then, whenever a program performs a memory write operation to any location within the page, the 386 will set the D bit to 1. If the page has not been written to by the time the page is swapped out again (D is still 0), the system knows that it does not need to rewrite the page to disk; the disk already holds the page, which has been unchanged.

Note that the corresponding bit within a page-directory entry (Figure 6.1) is undefined. Since page groups are not swapped out the way pages are, the D bit is of no use, so it is not supported for page groups.

The User Prot field provides protection for individual pages in exactly the same way that we described for page groups.

The System field is reserved for use by the operating system. The 386 paging mechanism ignores this field and promises to leave its settings unaltered. An operating system can do what it chooses with this field. It would typically be used to record information about the page. For example, a system adopting the least-recently-used policy for page swapping might use the System field to keep track of the status of the A (Accessed) bit. A value of 0 might mean that A was 1 the last time it was checked. If A ever becomes 0, the System field is incremented. Successive readings of A equal to 0 cause more incrementing, until the field overflows on the eighth time. At that point, the information is recorded elsewhere. If the A bit becomes 1 before the eighth consecutive 0, the System field is reset to 0, and the information is recorded elsewhere (we'll see shortly exactly where). Thus, an idle page would force the system's bookkeeping to go outside of the page-table entry only once every eight times the entry is checked.

Finally, the Page Frame Address field gives the physical location of the 4K-byte memory buffer, the *page frame*, that holds the page. Like page tables, page frames must be aligned to 4K boundaries in the memory space, so that the bottom 12 bits of the frame location are always 0. The top 20 bits are given by the Page Frame Address field.

Let's summarize what we have learned about page addressing so far by following the steps the 386 takes to map a linear address into a physical address, under the four-gigabyte virtual memory example we have been following. We'll assume that the page directory is stored at physical address 00000000, since it is the first thing that would have been allocated. Note that the size of a page frame is 1000 hexadecimal; successive frames will be allocated at 00001000, 00002000, and so on. Now suppose that a memory reference to linear address 01234567 is made. Figure 6.3 shows this address the way the 386 sees it—in binary. The top 10 bits give the page-group number, which is 4. The next 10 bits give the page number within the page group, which is hex 234. The bottom 12 bits give the location within the page frame, which is hex 567. The 386 uses these values to perform the following steps:

1. Consult the CR3 register to find the page directory. CR3 will have been loaded with the page-directory address 00000000.

2. Fetch doubleword entry number 4, at 00000010, that corresponds to page group number 4.

3. Examine the P (Present) bit and, if a user program is running, the User Prot field to verify access to the page group. Also set the A (Accessed) bit to signal that this page group has been accessed.

4. Fetch the page-table address from the top 20 bits of the entry. Let's suppose that nine page frames (including the page directory) were allocated before the first reference to this page group was made. So the page table address contains the value 00009000.

5. Fetch doubleword entry number 234 hex, at 00009000 + 4*234 = 000098D0.

6. Examine the P (Present) bit to see if the page is in physical memory. If P is 0, we generate a page fault. The fault handler will swap the page in, set the P bit to 1, and restart the instruction making the access, getting us back to this point with P equal to 1.

7. If a user program (not the operating system) is running, examine the User Prot field to verify access to the page. Set the A (Accessed) bit, and, if the memory access is a write operation, set the D (Dirty) bit.

8. Fetch the page frame address from the top 20 bits of the entry. Let's assume that 51 page frames were allocated before the first reference to this page. Since 51 is 33 hexadecimal, the frame would be located at 00033000.

9. Add the offset within the page (567) to the page frame address to get the final physical address, 00033567.

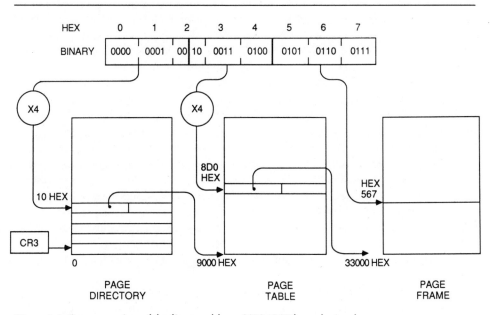

Figure 6.3 Page mapping of the linear address 01234567 hexadecimal.

Observe how perfectly the address fits together into the 32-bit word: 10 bits to specify the page group, 10 bits to specify the page, and 12 bits to specify the byte within the page. We see now why 4K bytes is the perfect choice for a page size: no other size would allow page tables to be the same size as the pages themselves.

Translation Lookaside Buffer   The steps just described make one thing obvious about the 386's paging mechanism: it introduces a lot of overhead to memory access. The 386 must fetch two doublewords from tables before it can find the memory location it wants. Is it really necessary to perform three memory fetches for every one fetch that a program requires? Fortunately, the answer is no. The 386 hardware automatically maintains an on-chip cache of thirty-two of the most recently used page table entries, called the *Translation Lookaside Buffer* (*TLB*). If a memory page is cached in the TLB, then the 386 does not bother to look in the page tables; it takes the information directly from the TLB.

Now we ask if we have traded one problem for another; must the 386 search thirty-two on-chip registers every time it makes a memory access? Again, the answer is no, because the TLB has parallel circuitry, capable of deciding very quickly if any of the thirty-two registers matches the linear address for the memory access. We discuss this mechanism in more detail later, when we discuss the support that the 386 provides for testing the TLB.

How good is the TLB at preventing extra page-table accesses? Each of the thirty-two entries covers a 4K-byte page, so that at any one moment there are 128K bytes of memory accessible without going through page tables. Obviously, one could construct a program that would make the 386's paging mechanism look bad by performing successive memory references to a number of different pages, covering more than the 128K limit. (Actually, we see in the section on testing that a well-chosen set of references from just five pages will do the trick.) However, most programs in real life access memory more sequentially. The TLB's size was decided on after performing simulations of 386 paging on real programs. The simulations show that the 32-entry TLB will catch 98% of all memory accesses. Thus, for every 100 memory accesses, there will be about two pairs of page-table lookups. The overhead is a reasonable 4%.

Note that if the page tables are changed, the TLB may no longer contain valid information about paging. For this reason, the TLB is flushed whenever the CR3 (page-directory pointer) register is loaded. Unfortunately, this is the only situation in which the 386 can easily tell that page tables have been changed. The page tables exist in the same memory space as everything else; it would require too much overhead for the 386 to distinguish page-table alterations from all the other memory write operations that programs perform. Therefore, it is up to the operating system to manually flush the TLB by reloading CR3 (even if its value doesn't change) whenever the page tables change in such a way that the TLB might be inaccurate. This will happen most often when a page is swapped out to disk and the associated P bit is changed from 1 to 0.

A Typical Paging System   Let's now consider how paging would be implemented in a typical virtual-memory operating system. We'll continue with our example of four megabytes of physical memory emulating a full four gigabytes of virtual memory.

Suppose that every 4K frame of physical memory is in use and an access is made to a page not currently in memory. The operating system must swap a page out to disk. How does the system decide which page to swap out, and how does the system find the page-table entry for that page? The answer is that the operating system maintains a data structure, the *page-frame table*, that gives information about each physical frame.

Let's now consider in detail the contents of a page-frame table entry for a simple virtual-memory system, and describe the algorithms for swapping out and swapping in pages. Each frame table entry contains the following fields:

- The *frame type* field identifies the use to which the frame is being put. There are four possibilities: empty (frame not yet allocated), directory (frame contains a page directory), table (frame contains a page table), and ordinary (frame contains ordinary, user-accessible memory).

- The *disk address* field gives the disk location of the frame's contents.

- The *time-of-last-use* field gives information about when the frame was last accessed. Recall that this information can be maintained by periodically monitoring the Accessed Bit of Page-Directory and Page-Table entries. This field is the "elsewhere" that we referred to when describing a possible usage of the System field of a Page-Table entry.

  There are two strategies that can be followed for maintaining this field: we can simply store an encoded version of the time-of-day in this field. This speeds up the field maintenance, but forces us to search the entire frame table every time we want to find the least-recently-used frame. Alternatively, we can use this field as a link in an ordered list of frames. Accessed frames are shoved to the bottom of the linked list. This requires more maintenance time but eliminates the least-recently-used search.

- The *ancestor* field gives the physical address of the paging data structure that points to this frame. If this is an empty frame then, of course, there is no ancestor. There is also no ancestor to a directory frame; however, in a multitasking system, the ancestor field might be used to identify the task associated with the directory. The ancestor to a page table frame is the directory entry that points to the table. The ancestor to an ordinary frame is the page table entry that points to it.

- The *nailed* bit is set to 1 if this frame should never be swapped out (it is "nailed" to its physical memory location). There are several reasons for nailing frames. First, the physical location of some frames must be known to the operating system—the page-frame table, for example. Second, the operating system may wish to insure that some data structures remain in memory, even if it doesn't care about their physical location. Finally, areas of physical memory accessible to Direct Memory Access (DMA) peripheral chips, and to other processors, must be nailed because those outside devices don't know about our paging.

Let's see how the above fields are used to implement swapping. To swap a page out to disk, the page handler performs the following steps:

1. Figure out which frame to swap out, using the time-of-last-use field. As we discussed, this involves either searching for the most distantly past time or fetching the top of the linked list of times. Note that an ordinary frame might have the same time-of-last-use as the page table that points to it, and a page table might have the same time-of-last-use as the directory that points to it. In these cases, the ordinary frame must be swapped out first, then the page table, and finally the directory. We must insure that whenever a page is in memory, its ancestor is also in memory; this will let us perform the steps we are about to describe.

    You might have noticed something fishy in the above paragraph—the possibility of swapping out a page directory. We discuss how this is possible when we talk about paging in a multitasking environment.

2. Consult the ancestor field of the frame-table entry to obtain the page-table or page-directory entry that points to the frame we are swapping out. If the frame is an ordinary frame, then consult the Dirty bit of the page-table entry to see if the frame has been written to. If it has (Dirty bit is 1), then write the frame to the disk. If the frame has not been written to (Dirty bit is 0), then the disk already contains a duplicate of the frame's contents, and there is no need to rewrite the frame.

    What if our frame is a page-table entry? Why isn't there a Dirty bit in its ancestor page-directory entry? To answer this, we must look closely at when a page-table entry is written to:

    *   The 386 paging hardware writes to the Accessed and the Dirty bits during the course of memory reads and writes. However, we've rigged things so that by the time we want to swap out a page-table frame, all of the underlying pages have been swapped out; there are no Accessed or Dirty bits in the entries, only (as we'll soon see) disk addresses. So the Dirty bit as set by the hardware is meaningless to us.

    *   The page-handler code writes to the page-table entry to implement the algorithms we are now describing. Note, however, that only the 386 paging hardware accesses a page-table entry as such; for a program (even an operating system program) to read or write to a page-table entry, the table must be aliased as an ordinary page. So the Dirty bit set will be that of the alias page-table entry, not the original page-directory entry. Since a page-table entry contains nothing but disk addresses at the time it is swapped out, the entry needs to be rewritten only if the disk addresses changed. If disk sectors are permanently assigned to pages, this won't happen. If they are dynamically allocated, then page-table entries might change; in that case, the system can either maintain its own Dirty bit somewhere or, simply, always rewrite page tables when swapping out. The same policy should apply to page directories if they are ever swapped out.

3. Set the Present bit of the ancestor entry to 0, leave the User Prot field unchanged, and fill the remaining 29 bits of the ancestor entry with the disk address fetched from the frame-table entry.

4. Change the frame type field to "empty." If it is possible that more than one page is swapped out before a new page is swapped in, then the rest of the frame-table entry can be used to link empty frames so they can be found quickly.

Figure 6.4 illustrates the swapping-out process for an ordinary frame. Part a shows the configuration just before the frame is swapped out. The frame-table entry points implicitly (via its position within the frame table) to a frame in physical memory. The ancestor, a page-table entry, also points to the frame. Part b shows the rearrangement of the pointers after the frame is swapped out. The page-table entry now points to the disk sector; the frame is thus free.

Let's now go through the steps for swapping in pages. Since we will usually swap in a page as a result of a page fault, we'll review all the steps performed by a page-fault handler:

1. Obtain from the CR2 register the offending memory address. Walk through the paging tables, just as the 386 hardware does, until the Not Present entry is found.

2. Fetch an empty frame. If necessary, swap a page out to disk in order to get an empty frame.

3. Set the various fields of the frame-table entry. The frame type field is determined by which page entry was marked Not Present: if it was a page-directory entry, then the frame type is "table"; if it was a page-table entry, then the frame type is "ordinary." The disk address field is taken from the top 29 bits of the page-table entry. The time-of-last-use field is set to reflect usage at the current time. The ancestor field points to the location of the page entry. The nailed bit is set to 0.

4. Read the page from the disk to the frame.

5. Set the fields of the page entry. The Present Bit is set to 1, the User Prot field was preserved from swapping out, the Address field points to the frame, and the other fields are set to 0.

6. At this point, if the page was itself a page table, we know that the underlying page will have to be swapped in before the final memory access can be made. We can save a little time by testing for that case and looping back to step 2, as applied to the underlying entry. Alternatively, we can save a little code by skipping this test and allowing the fault handler to be immediately reinvoked when we restart the program.

7. Restart the user program. The program will retry the memory access, only this time the page will have been swapped in.

We can again look at Figure 6.4 to see the swapping-in process; this time starting with part b and finishing with part a.

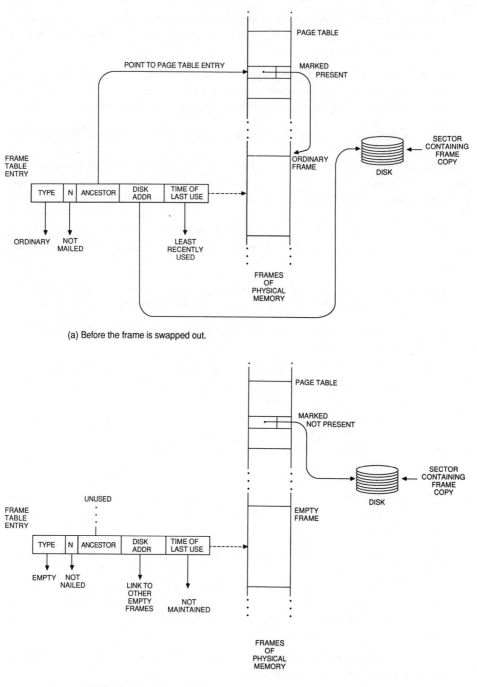

(a) Before the frame is swapped out.

(b) After the frame is swapped out.

Figure 6.4 Frame and page-table entries when a frame is swapped out to disk.

Paging Strategies   Let's now see how the paging scheme we just described can be applied to a multitasking environment. As we have already stated, we would like each task to have the illusion that it has the entire four-gigabyte memory space to itself. We can now see how the two-layered page structure of the 386 lets us do this. First, every task will have its own page directory. We'll see later in this chapter that whenever tasks are switched, the contents of the CR3 register is switched, so that the new tasks's page directory automatically takes effect. Second, the operating system can fit into just a few page groups. We replicate the corresponding page-table entries in every user's page directory.

There are just a few additional questions brought about by multitasking:

- *Is it necessary to swap out a task's pages when tasks are switched?* Absolutely not. Physical memory will typically contain a mix of pages from all currently running tasks. We rigged the swapping-out algorithm so that we could work backwards from the frame to its page entry, guaranteeing that if a frame was still in memory, its page entry would also be in memory. It's not necessary for the page entry be a part of the current task's linear space for the swapping out to be successfully completed.

- *If we replicate page-directory entries for the operating system, won't we have a problem with the ancestor field of frame table entries?* Yes, there is a problem. If we want to swap out an operating-system page table, we must find all the page-directory entries that point to it—the ancestor field of the frame-table entry would give us only one such directory entry. Then, when we swap the page table back in again, we must either update all ancestor directory entries (some of which may not be in memory), or have special page-fault code for operating-system page tables, to detect the possibility that the page is already swapped in. Note, however, that this problem applies only to page tables; each ordinary page of the operating system is pointed to by only one page-table entry. Since there are relatively few page tables, we can avoid all problems by nailing them to physical memory. For example, if the operating system occupies 16 megabytes, we need to set the Nailed bit of the frame-table entry of just four page tables.

- *Can we swap out page directories? If so, when?* Yes, we can, as long as all the underlying pages have been swapped out. Note that the paging scheme we described implicitly guarantees this. Of course, the current task's directory can never be swapped out; that would instantly destroy all memory access on the 386. But the least-recently-used policy of our paging scheme will also insure that this could never happen. The only explicit action the operating system must take is to insure that a new task's page directory is in physical memory *before* the task is started. One way of doing this would be to have the task-switching code check for this before every switch. Alternatively, many operating systems have the concept of a *suspended task* (in which the 386 is awaiting an external event, such as keyboard input), as opposed to an *active task* (in which the 386 is furiously computing something). Page directories for active tasks could be nailed to physical memory. That way, the operating system needs to check for the page directory's presence only when a task changes from suspended to active.

We now conclude our discussion of paging on the 386. The final point to make about paging is that its structure is completely independent of the structure of the programs that are running. A page is most likely just a portion of a program or data structure, cut away at an arbitrary point, possibly in the middle of an instruction or array element! Or, a page could encompass parts of segments from two completely different tasks; this could happen if a segment ended in the middle of a page, and the second segment started shortly thereafter, within the same page. Thus, paging does nothing to specify the logical structure of a 386 system. The mechanism for that is *segmentation*.

Memory Management: Segmentation

We began our description of segmentation in Chapter 5 when we discussed its evolution in the 86 family of processors. Recall that a 16-bit segment register value combines with a 16- or 32-bit offset to make a linear memory address. In real mode and in virtual 8086 mode, the 386 calculates the address of a segment by multiplying the segment register value by 16. In all other modes, the 386 obtains the segment location from memory-resident tables. We shall now describe how those tables are specified and what their format is.

Before starting the discussion, let's establish some terminology. We distinguish the table-driven segment register values by calling them *selectors*. When the 386 uses tables to locate segments, we say the 386 is in *selector mode*. When it doesn't, we say the 386 is in *8086 mode*. Thus, 8086 mode encompasses real mode and virtual 8086 mode; selector mode encompasses all the other modes of the 386.

We've stated before that a selector is mapped to a segment base address, to be added to the offset to obtain the linear memory address. Figure 6.5 shows the mapping in detail. We see that a selector contains three fields: Requestor's Privilege Level (RPL), Table Indicator (TI), and Index. The RPL field is used by operating-system software to solve the Trojan Horse problem described later. This field doesn't enter into address computation and will be discussed later in the section on rings of protection. The Table Indicator field determines which of two tables will be used to look up the base address. If TI = 0 then the Global Descriptor Table (GDT) is used. A 386 system contains a single GDT, which is shared by all tasks. If TI = 1 then the Local Descriptor Table (LDT) is used. Each task in a 386 system has its own LDT. Thus the base addresses for segments to be shared among all tasks are stored in the GDT, while those segments private to a single task have their base addresses in the task's LDT.

The Index field of the selector is used as an index into the selected table. Each entry in the table is called a *descriptor*. The table is indexed from zero, with an Index field value of i referring to the ith descriptor in the table. Descriptors are eight bytes long, and each descriptor contains a 32-bit base address for its corresponding segment. The base address occupies only four of the eight bytes constituting the descriptor. Later we will describe what the other bytes are used for.

There is an exception to the rules given above. Any selector with TI = 0 (that is, a GDT selector) and Index = 0 is considered to be a *null selector*. Null selectors don't reference the 0th GDT descriptor. It's okay to load a null selector into a segment

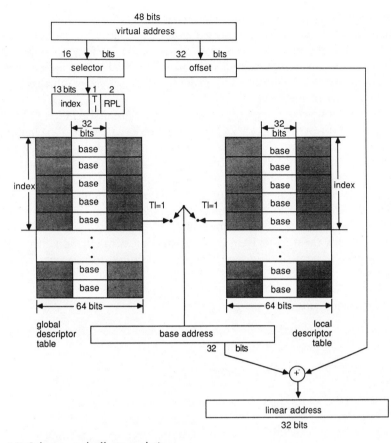

Figure 6.5 Selector-and-offset translation.

register, but any attempt to use the null selector in addressing will result in a 386 exception. So null selectors can be used as placeholders; for example, before starting a task the operating system can set DS, ES, FS, and GS to null selectors. Then an uninitialized use of any of those segment registers by the task will result in an exception.

Note that the format of a selector violates the principle that information of greater significance occurs at higher addresses. The TI and RPL field occupy the three least significant bits of the 16-bit selector, yet they are clearly more significant than the Index. They should have been assigned to the three most significant bits of the selector. The incorrect bit assignment complicates pointer arithmetic involving both selectors and offsets, since a carry out of an offset into a selector will now erroneously add to RPL, rather than to Index. This is a serious problem on the 286, in which selector-and-offset arithmetic is needed to implement arrays of more than 64K bytes. It is not so serious on the 386, since arrays up to four gigabytes can be accommodated with offset arithmetic alone.

The Segment Addressing Registers   Figure 6.6 depicts the 386 registers involved in segmented addressing. The six segment registers have already been discussed in Chapter 5. The GDT register holds the linear address of the GDT and the GDT length (in bytes) minus one. Use of a selector which indexes beyond the GDT limit produces a protection exception. Typically, the GDT register is set during system initialization and thereafter remains unchanged.

The LDT register holds a selector for a segment containing the current LDT. This selector must index a descriptor in the GDT. During a task switch, the 386 changes the entire local address space simply by reloading the LDT register. This is one reason why task switches are quite rapid on the 386. The use of a selector in the LDT register, rather than a linear address (as in the GDT register), was chosen when designing the 286, to accommodate its use of segmentation for virtual memory systems. Since LDT's are specified by a selector, they can be swapped to secondary storage by the same virtual memory mechanisms that apply to all segments.

If these were truly the only registers involved in address calculation, then address calculation would be very slow indeed. The steps required to reference a byte in memory would be:

1.   Obtain the selector from a segment register.

2.   If TI indicates the global descriptor table, then obtain the descriptor table address from the GDT register and go to step 4.

3.   If TI indicates the local descriptor table, then:

   a.   Get the selector for the LDT's segment from the LDT register.
   b.   Extract the Index field from the selector and multiply the Index by eight (shift left three bits). This is because each descriptor is eight bytes long.
   c.   Add this to the GDT address from the GDT register.
   d.   Fetch from memory the addressed descriptor.
   e.   Extract from this descriptor the base address of the segment containing the LDT.

   This base address is the descriptor table address. Proceed to step 4.

4.   Extract the Index field of the selector, multiply it by eight, and add it to the descriptor table address. Fetch from memory the descriptor at that address.

5.   Extract from the descriptor the segment base address.

6.   Add the offset to the segment base address. This is the desired linear address.

7.   Perform the desired memory access at the linear address.

We see that referencing a memory byte has also required (in the LDT case) accessing two 8-byte descriptors in memory, plus performing two 32-bit additions. (The shifting and extracting operations can be performed in zero-time by routing "wires" on the

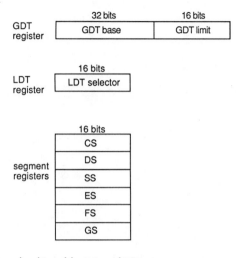

Figure 6.6 Registers involved in address translation.

chip.) Compare this to the single 20-bit addition and no additional memory accesses required in 8086 mode. Fortunately, this isn't the entire story.

We first observe that memory references generally occur more frequently than changes to segment registers and task switches. So it's worthwhile to speed up memory references at the cost of slowing down segment register loads and task switches. This trade-off is performed by associating a *shadow register* with the LDT register and with each segment register. Shadow registers are invisible to software. They are automatically updated and transparently used by the 386 hardware. Figure 6.7 shows all the address translation registers and the registers which shadow them.

Whenever a segment register is loaded with a selector, the corresponding descriptor is automatically loaded into the register, shadowing that segment register. In effect, this is done by performing steps 1–4 above. Since the descriptor is now available in the shadow register, subsequent memory references which use the segment register need only execute steps 5–7. This makes the time for a selector-mode memory reference identical to that of a memory reference in 8086 mode.

Whenever a task is switched and the LDT register is changed, the descriptor corresponding to the new LDT is automatically loaded into the LDT register's shadow register. In effect, this is done by performing steps 3a–d above. Thus steps 3a–d need not be performed whenever a segment register is subsequently loaded with a selector. So only one 32-bit addition and one memory reference to a descriptor need to be made in order to update a shadow register when a segment register is reloaded.

If a program infrequently modifies its segment registers, it will execute at approximately the same speed in selector mode as in 8086 mode. If a program frequently modifies its segment registers, it may run substantially slower in selector mode than in 8086 mode. The worst slowdown encountered in practice occurs when a program must follow a long chain of selector-and-offset pointers, since then a segment register

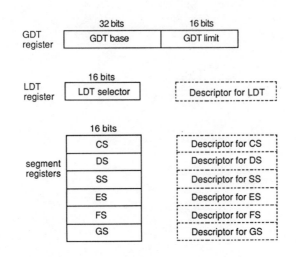

Figure 6.7 Address translation registers with their shadow registers.

must be changed for each memory reference. For example, the following program computes the length of a chain of elements, assuming that each element begins with a pointer to the next element and the last element begins with a pointer that has a zero selector.

```
        MOV ECX,0      ; ECX contains the negative chain length
        LDS EBX,chain  ; point to the first element of the chain
L1:                    ; loop here for each element of the chain
        LDS EBX,[EBX]  ; load the address of the next element
        MOV AX,DS      ; copy selector to AX, for testing
        TEST AX,AX     ; is it a null selector?
        LOOPNZ L1      ; loop if not, to fetch the next element
        NEG ECX        ; chain is terminated: negate ECX to get length
```

This program runs roughly 60% faster in 8086 mode than in selector mode. The only instruction in the above program with different execution times in 8086 and selector mode is LDS, which takes 7 processor cycles in 8086 mode and 22 in selector mode. The extra time is that required to load the shadow register of DS with a descriptor and check it for protection violations. Again, though, selector-and-offset pointers are needed much less on the 386 than on the 286, since 386 offsets are 32 bits in length. So programs such as the one just given are very rare.

To summarize, in selector mode the segment translation process transforms a selector into a segment base address by means of table lookup. One bit of the selector chooses whether a table global to the entire system or a table local to the current task should be used. The selector also contains an index, which, when applied to the appropriate table, yields a segment descriptor. This descriptor contains the address of the base of the selected segment. In order to speed memory references, whenever a

Table 6.1. Format of a Segment Descriptor

Offset byte	Description
0	Segment limit, bits 0–7
1	Segment limit, bits 8–15
2	Segment base, bits 0–7
3	Segment base, bits 8–15
4	Segment base, bits 16–23
5	Access byte
6	Bits 0–3: Segment limit, bits 16–19
	Bits 4–6: must be 0 for future compatibility
	Bit 7: G (granularity) bit
7	Segment base, bits 24–31

selector is loaded into a segment register, the corresponding descriptor is automatically loaded into a register shadowing that segment register. Thus any memory references made relative to the segment register don't require a further table lookup, since the base address of the selected segment is immediately available in the shadow register.

Anatomy of a Segment Descriptor   Table 6.1 shows the format of a segment descriptor. Descriptor tables may contain descriptors for things other than segments. These descriptors vary in format from segment descriptors and are described in later sections of this chapter. All types of descriptors, however, contain the *access byte* in the same position. The information contained in the access byte varies, depending on the type of descriptor. The access byte is coded so that it's always possible to unambiguously determine the type of a descriptor by examining its access byte.

As we mentioned in Chapter 5, the first (bottom) six bytes of a segment descriptor correspond to the nonzero six bytes of a 286 segment descriptor. The last two bytes, which are always zero in a 286 descriptor, provide the necessary extensions to accommodate the 386's 32-bit linear addresses and offsets. The *base* field is extended from 24 bits to 32 bits, and the *limit* field is extended from 16 bits to 20 bits, with an additional *granularity bit* contributing to the limit's definition. We've already described how the base field is used, so let's now consider the other fields in detail.

Figure 6.8 shows the access byte encodings for segment descriptors. The format varies, depending on whether the segment is a code segment (that is, is executable), a data segment (that is, isn't executable), or a segment containing an LDT.

Each access byte contains a 2-bit *descriptor privilege level* (DPL) field. This field enables an operating system to prevent ordinary user programs from accessing sensitive operating system segments. The DPL field is described later in the section on rings of protection.

Access bytes contain two bits, the *present* (P) bit and the *accessed* (A) bit, which enable operating systems to implement virtual memory by swapping whole segments instead of pages. They correspond to the similarly named bits in page-table entries, described earlier in this chapter. Whenever an attempt is made to load a selector into a segment register, the P bit in the corresponding descriptor is checked. If P is 0 (segment is not present in memory), a Not Present fault (INT 11) is generated by the 386, so that

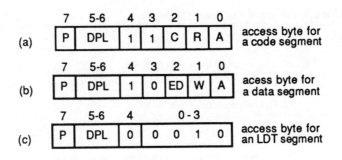

Figure 6.8 Format of segment access bytes.

the operating system can swap in the segment from disk. The A bit is set to 1 whenever the corresponding selector is loaded into a segment register. It can be monitored to determine usage just as the A bit in a page-table entry is monitored. The segment versions of the A and P bits were supplied for the 286, which does not have paging. Most 386 systems will use the paging mechanism for virtual memory; in those systems, the segment P bit is always set to 1, and the segment A bit is ignored.

Bit 1 of the access byte for a code (executable) segment is the *readable* (R) bit. If R is 1, the code segment can be read in addition to being executed. If R is 0, any attempt to read the segment will cause an exception (in particular, a *protection exception*). In either case, an attempt to write into an executable segment causes a protection exception. A protection exception is the 386's usual response to instructions which attempt to violate protection restrictions. Throughout this chapter, we will indicate those situations which lead to protection exceptions.

Bit 1 of the access byte for a data (nonexecutable) segment is the *writable* (W) bit. If W is 1, the data segment can be written in addition to being read. If W is 0, any attempt to write the segment will cause a protection exception. In either case, an attempt to execute a data segment causes a protection exception.

LDT segments can't be explicitly read, written, or executed. They can only be used implicitly within the segment address translation process. Conversely, only selectors for LDT segments may be loaded into the LDT register. So to create a local descriptor table, the operating system must first create in the GDT a descriptor for a data segment, then write descriptors into that data segment, and then change the data segment descriptor into an LDT descriptor.

The reason the 386 doesn't allow a (user) program to examine its local descriptor table is to prevent the program's behavior from depending on the particular linear addresses of its segments. That way, the operating system can freely move segments in memory by changing the base fields of their descriptors. Programs using these segments will be unaware that the segments have been moved.

Access restrictions on reading, writing, and executing are useful for maintaining system integrity, catching bugs, and preventing software piracy on multiuser systems. Also, write-access restrictions allow the dirty bit of a segment-oriented virtual-memory system to be implemented in software rather than hardware. (Recall that the dirty bit of a page-table entry is set to 1 when any byte of the page is written to.) This is done by initially marking *all* segments as nonwritable (that is, setting the W bit to 0) as they are swapped in. The first time a program tries to write a segment, a protection exception will occur. The exception handler can then determine whether writing is indeed illegal by looking in software-maintained tables. If it's legal to write the segment, the exception handler can mark the segment as writable (set W to 1 and return to the program. This will prevent further exceptions from occurring and will also warn the virtual memory software that the segment has been modified since it was swapped in.

Bit 2 of the access byte for a code segment is the *conforming* (C) bit. This bit is described later in the section on rings of protection. Bit 2 of the access byte for a data segment is the *expand down* (ED) bit. The ED bit is used to mark stack segments, which expand downward (grow toward lower addresses). The ED bit controls the interpretation of the limit value of the descriptor. During memory references the 386 will check that the segment offsets used are less than or equal to the limit; 32-bit unsigned comparisons are used for the check. The check is done in parallel with the segment-start-plus-offset calculation so it doesn't slow down the memory reference. If an offset exceeds the limit, the 386 will raise an exception.

Data segments with ED set to 1 (expand-down segments) are used to accommodate stacks. Recall that on the 386, stacks start at offset FFFFFFFF (hexadecimal) and grow downward toward lower addresses. So for stacks, the interpretation of limit stated above is inappropriate. If ED is 1, the 386 checks that offsets are strictly greater than the limit. If an offset is less than or equal to limit, (again using a 32-bit unsigned comparison) the 386 will raise an exception. Figure 6.9 compares ordinary segments to expand-down segments. In the figure, solid lines surround the legal portions of segments. Note that ED doesn't change the way in which the base field of the descriptor is used in the address calculation process. Only the check against limit is changed.

Limit checks are necessary for insuring task isolation. Without them, a task might overrun its segments and clobber another task. This might happen, for example, if a program indexes beyond the end of an array.

The limit check on expand-down (that is, stack) segments is particularly useful. An operating system can start off a task with a small stack. If the task outgrows its stack, it will produce an exception. The exception handler can then allocate more stack space to the task. Thus memory isn't wasted for pessimistically sized stacks.

The limit value of a segment is determined by combining the limit field with the *granularity* (G) bit. The G bit determines how to extend the 20-bit limit field into a 32-bit limit value. If G is 0, then the limit field defines the low 20 bits of the limit value; the high 12 bits are 0. If G is 1, then the limit field defines the high 20 bits; the low 12 bits are all 1's. Thus, we have byte-sized granularity for limit values from 0 through 1 megabyte; we have page-sized granularity for limit values greater than 1 megabyte.

A comment is in order for the case ED = 1 (stack segment) and G = 0 (byte granularity). Ideally, the 386 would define the limit value in this case by filling the high 12 bits with 1's, not 0's. This would give us byte granularity for the range of small stacks up to a megabyte in size. In reality, the 386 always fills the high 12 bits with 0's. Thus, we have byte granularity only for stacks within one megabyte of the four-gigabyte

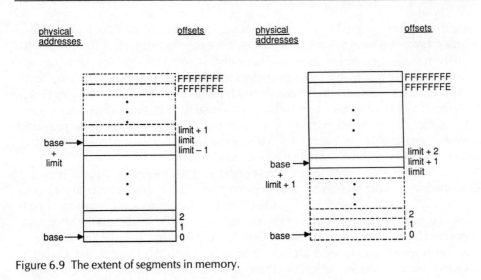

Figure 6.9   The extent of segments in memory.

maximum size. The reason for this peculiar policy is 286 compatibility. The 386 tries, whenever it can, to treat 286 (and, for that matter, 8086) emulation as a special case of the 386 environment. Thus, the 386 doesn't abandon its internal 32-bit offsets when emulating a predecessor; it merely sets the high 16 bits of all offsets to 0. And the 386 doesn't do anything different to construct the limit value for a 286 segment than it does for a 386 segment. To duplicate 286 functionality, it is necessary to provide byte granularity for small limit values, even in stack segments. It would take special-case hardware to avoid doing this for 386 segments as well; and the case-checking would slow down all segment register loads. It's more important to keep the processor fast than it is to provide byte granularity for small 386 stacks.

In summary, we have seen that a segment descriptor carries a considerable amount of information concerning its associated segment:

1. Base and limit fields define the location and size of the segment. The granularity (G) and expand-down (ED) bits tell how to interpret the limit field.

2. Present (P) and accessed (A) bits help segment-oriented virtual-memory software decide which segments to swap in and which to swap out.

3. Code, data, and LDT segments are distinguished by different access byte encodings. This enables the 386 to prohibit writing of code segments and (explicit) reading and writing of LDT segments.

4. Writable (W) and readable (R) bits can be used to impose further restrictions on the ways the segment may be accessed.

5. The descriptor privilege level (DPL) field and the conforming (C) bit are used to protect the segment from unauthorized interference. This will be described later.

Patterns of Sharing Among Tasks   The usual 386 framework for structuring address spaces is depicted in Figure 6.10a. Each task has its own local descriptor table and every task shares the common global descriptor table. So a segment is either accessible to only a single task or accessible to all tasks. Other patterns of sharing are possible.

A single-user system which doesn't require task isolation can put a null selector in the LDT register for every task. Then every task shares the same address space (see Figure 6.10b), and the operating system need not build any LDTs. This approach is attractive for small real-time systems. It is also useful for upgrading 8086 systems to 386 selector mode.

A group of related tasks can use the same LDT. All the tasks in the group will share the same address space, but the group as a whole will possess private segments isolated from the rest of the system. Such a group of tasks is sometimes called a *task force* or a *job*. Figure 6.10c depicts a system containing three task forces. This approach is probably the easiest way to implement programming languages, such as Ada, in which a single program can consist of multiple tasks. Simply implement each Ada program as a task force.

The most complex patterns of sharing and isolation can be realized by providing each task with its own LDT but allowing more than one descriptor for each segment. In order to share a segment between two tasks, each task will have in its LDT an identical descriptor for the segment. This is illustrated in Figure 6.11. The two descriptors for the same segment are called *aliases*. Of course, we need not limit ourselves to only two tasks and two aliases; any number of aliases may be used.

Aliasing provides an operating-system designer with two benefits. First, tasks can be provided only with those segment descriptors for which they have a need to know. Placing shared segment descriptors in the GDT would make them visible to all tasks, whereas aliasing can restrict segments to any desired group of tasks. Second, large messages can be efficiently passed between tasks simply by transmitting aliased segment descriptors rather than by transmitting a copy of the entire message.

Another application of aliasing is to implement a segment which is both executable and writable. Make one alias a code segment descriptor and the other a data segment descriptor. Put both aliases into the same LDT. Then the program can both execute and write the segment, simply by choosing the appropriate descriptor.

Memory-Management Instructions   The 386 has a few instructions not present on the 8086 and 186 for manipulating the address translation registers and examining the contents of descriptors. These instructions are listed in Table 6.2.

The LGDT (Load GDT register) instruction loads the GDT register from a memory operand. Six bytes are fetched from memory and loaded into the GDT register in the format shown in Figure 6.6. This instruction is used only during system initialization.

The SGDT (Store GDT register) instruction stores the contents of the GDT register into its six-byte memory operand. Such an instruction is needed by system debuggers to obtain the complete state of the processor.

The LLDT (Load LDT register) instruction loads its word operand (register or memory) into the LDT register. The operand is expected to be either a GDT selector

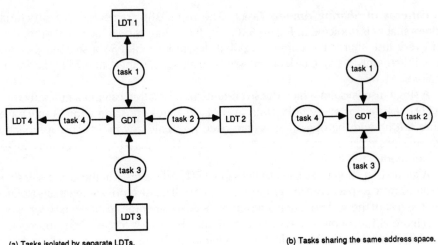

(a) Tasks isolated by separate LDTs.   (b) Tasks sharing the same address space.

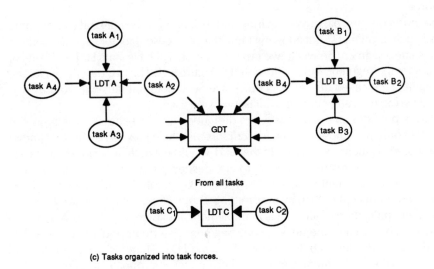

(c) Tasks organized into task forces.

Figure 6.10 Patterns of sharing and isolation among tasks.

pointing to an LDT descriptor or a null selector. Typically, the task-switch instructions described later in this chapter are used to change the LDT register rather than LLDT. The LLDT instruction is used only during initialization.

The SLDT (Store LDT register) instruction stores the contents of the LDT register into a word operand (register or memory). Unlike the previous instructions, SLDT is useful for things other than debuggers and initialization. We shall see an example of its use when we discuss time-slicing.

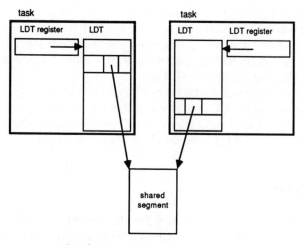

Figure 6.11 Sharing a segment by aliasing.

Table 6.2 Memory Management
Instructions

LGDT	Load GDT Register
SGDT	Store GDT Register
LLDT	Load LDT Register
SLDT	Store LDT Register
LAR	Load Access Rights
LSL	Load Segment Limit

Recall that the 386 prohibits the reading or writing of LDT segments because descriptors contain physical addresses in their base fields. Yet it might be desirable to examine information in descriptors other than the base field. The next two instructions have been provided to allow this.

The LAR (Load Access Rights) instruction has two operands. The source (second) operand is always a word (memory or general register) which is considered to be a selector. The destination (first) operand can be either a word or a doubleword. LAR copies information from the second doubleword of the descriptor selected by the source, to the destination register. Thus, the access-rights byte will be copied to the high byte of a word destination (to the high byte of the low word of a doubleword destination). A doubleword destination will receive two more meaningful bits: the D bit (bit 22), which is 1 for 386 segments and 0 for 286 segments; and the G bit (bit 23) that assists in interpreting the segment limit field. In keeping with the policy of hiding the base location, bits giving that information (0 though 7, and 24 through 31 of the doubleword destination) are masked to 0. The four bits giving limit information (bits 16 through 19) are specified as undefined in the LAR doubleword destination.

Even if the selector is invalid, LAR won't cause a protection exception. Instead, LAR will clear the zero flag. If loading is successful then LAR will set the zero flag.

The LSL (Load Segment Limit) instruction works just like LAR, except that it loads its first operand with the 32-bit limit value of the selected descriptor, rather than the access byte. Recall that the limit value is constructed from the 20-bit limit field, interpreted under the control of the granularity (G) bit. Don't forget that the interpretation of the limit value depends on the ED bit.

The LGDT instruction is permitted in real mode in order to allow system initialization software to initialize the GDT register in real mode before making the transition to protected mode. The SGDT instruction is also allowed in real mode, again for debuggers. LLDT, SLDT, LAR, and LSL are invalid opcodes in real mode.

Rings of Protection

In the previous section we described how the 386 protects one task from another. In this section we describe how the 386 enables an operating system to protect itself. We assume throughout that the 386 is in protected mode.

Protection requires enforcing three types of restrictions on ordinary (not operating-system) programs:

1. Certain instructions must not be executed by ordinary programs.

2. Certain segments, accessible to the operating system, must be made inaccessible to ordinary programs.

3. It must be impossible to gain operating-system privileges except by entering the operating system at a legal entry point.

For example, consider protecting the memory management facilities described in the previous section. Segment limits confine a task to those segments for which it has descriptors. These descriptors reside in the GDT and the task's LDT. If the descriptors in the GDT and LDT are "safe," the task must manufacture more descriptors to violate protection. One way to do this would be to use the LGDT (Load GDT register) instruction to load the GDT register and change the base of the GDT to an area of memory which is writable by the task. Thus, ordinary programs must be forbidden from using the LGDT instruction.

To see the need for the second restriction, observe that the operating system must have write-access to the GDT in order to create LDT descriptors for new tasks. But we have just seen that ordinary programs must be barred from writing in the GDT.

Task isolation can be used to enforce the second restriction. Operating-system services can be implemented as separate tasks with descriptors for any "sensitive" segments (for example, a writable segment containing the GDT) residing only in the service task's LDT. User programs can request operating-system service by means of a task switch. But this approach has some disadvantages:

1. Although a 386 task switch is relatively fast, it still takes over five times longer than a call.

2.   It's difficult to pass parameters via a task switch. In particular, virtual addresses containing LDT selectors have different mappings in tasks with different LDTs.

3.   Exception handlers often require access to the address space of a task raising an exception in order to discover the exception's cause. This access is awkward if the exception handler requires its own LDT.

For these reasons the 386 provides the following method for expanding and contracting the set of accessible segments, a method based on the procedure call rather than the task switch.

Levels of Privilege   The U.S. government uses a scheme for protecting sensitive documents that works roughly as follows. Each document is given one of the four *classifications*: top secret, secret, confidential, or unclassified. The higher the classification, the more sensitive the document. Each individual receives one of four *clearances*: top secret, secret, confidential, or not cleared. Higher clearances reflect greater trust in the individual. An individual with a particular clearance is only permitted to access documents of the corresponding or lower classification. For example, an individual with secret clearance can access secret, confidential, and unclassified documents but is denied access to top-secret documents.

The government classification scheme is depicted in Figure 6.12. Each circular band, or *ring*, in the diagram corresponds to the set of documents having the indicated classification (the top-secret disk is considered a ring, despite the fact that it surrounds nothing). So documents in inner rings are more protected than documents in outer rings, and an individual with a particular clearance can access those documents in the corresponding ring and any surrounding rings.

The 386 uses a similar scheme for protecting segments. In place of the four classifications and clearances are four *privilege levels*, numbered 0 to 3. The smaller

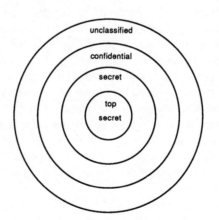

Figure 6.12 Classification of information by the U.S. government.

the level number, the more privileged the level (the opposite of what you probably expected). Privilege levels are stored in three different places:

1. Each descriptor contains a *descriptor privilege level* or DPL. For data (nonexecutable) segments, DPL is the "classification" of the segment. For segments which are executable, DPL is the "clearance" of the procedures in that segment.

2. Each selector contains a *requestor's privilege level* or RPL. We discuss this shortly.

3. A *current privilege level* or CPL is automatically maintained by the 386. The CPL is the "clearance" of the currently executing program and equals the DPL of the segment referenced by the CS register. The 386 keeps CPL in the two least significant bits of CS, wiping out the RPL field of the selector stored there.

In order to access a segment for reading or writing, a program must load a selector for that segment into a segment register. Thus it appears that a program could access any segment (even one that is more privileged than the program) simply by creating a selector for it and loading the selector into a segment register. To prevent this, the 386 will produce a protection exception if the currently executing program (CPL) is less privileged than the segment (DPL); that is, if the clearance of the program is less than the classification of the segment. In mathematical terms, the criterion for an access to be acceptable is:

$$DPL \geq CPL$$

We'll see later that a program can use RPL to temporarily reduce its privilege. So the above criterion becomes:

$$DPL \geq max(CPL, RPL) \qquad \text{(max means "the larger of. . .")}$$

Remember, the lower the number, the greater the privilege. A lower DPL means a more protected segment, and a lower CPL means a more privileged program.

It was envisioned that privilege level 1 would be used for most of the operating system, and level 0 would be used for that small portion of the operating system devoted to memory management, protection, and access control. This portion is called the *security kernel*. All security-related functions are concentrated in the security kernel, which is protected from the rest of the operating system. The security kernel should be designed so that if it is completely secure, then the operating system is also secure. Security should hold despite any mischief in parts of the operating system outside of the security kernel. Such secure systems are important in multiuser applications that manage sensitive information; some examples are government, banking, and electronic funds transfer systems.

By designing an operating system so that the security kernel is small, we derive many benefits. In particular, expensive methods which are uneconomical for large programs can be applied to a small security kernel in order to increase confidence in its correctness. These methods include exhaustive testing, examination by teams of programmers, and mathematical proofs of program correctness.

If the operating system occupies two levels, and user programs are run in another level, then we've used three levels in total. What about the fourth level? Probably the main reason for providing four levels on the 386 is that it already takes two bits to encode three levels, so the fourth level comes along free. If we assign user programs to level 3, then we are left with level 2 between the user and the operating system. Specialized programming subsystems that must be protected because they implement their own security mechanisms are good candidates for level 2. Some examples of such subsystems are: database management systems, office automation systems, and software engineering environments.

Figure 6.13 summarizes the uses for the four privilege levels. Because of this diagram (and its brother, Figure 6.12), privilege levels are sometimes called *rings of protection*. Just because the 386 provides four rings of protection, systems designers don't have to use all four. A simple, unprotected system can be built solely in ring 0. A traditional "user/supervisor" system can be constructed in two rings by assigning the supervisor (that is, the operating system) entirely to ring 0 and the user entirely to ring 3.

We have already remarked that it's necessary to restrict the use of certain 386 instructions. Table 6.3 lists these privileged instructions, some of which are introduced later in the chapter. The first part of Table 6.3 lists instructions that may only be executed in ring 0. Executing them in any other ring causes a protection exception. I/O instructions aren't included in this category, since we may or may not wish to limit their use to the security kernel. The 386 flags (described in Chapter 2) contain an I/O privilege-level (IOPL) field which specifies the least privileged ring in which I/O instructions are permitted. If any of the instructions in the second part of Table 6.3 are executed in a ring less privileged than IOPL, then a protection exception results. If any of the instructions in the third part of Table 6.3 are executed in a ring less privileged than IOPL, then the I/O Permission Bitmap (described in Chapter 5) is checked to verify legal access.

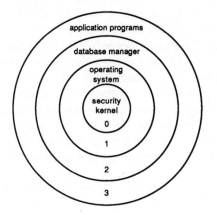

Figure 6.13 Use of 286 privilege levels.

Table 6.3. Privileged Instructions

Instructions illegal above level 0	LIDT,LLDT,LGDT,LTR LMSW,SMSW,CLTS,HLT MOV involving CRx, DRx, TRx
Instructions illegal above I/O level	STI,CLI
Instructions subject to I/O permission bitmap	IN, OUT, INS, OUTS
Instructions modified according to level	IRET,POPF

We have just seen an example of some sensitive information, namely IOPL, contained in the flags. The only other sensitive item in the flags is the Interrupt-enable Flag (IF). Although ordinary user programs shouldn't be allowed to change these fields, instructions which load the flags register have legitimate uses and shouldn't be banned from less privileged rings. So if an instruction which loads the flags register (namely IRET or POPF) is executed in a ring other than 0, the IOPL field will remain unchanged; if such an instruction is executed in a ring less privileged than IOPL, IF also will remain unchanged. In either case, no exception will result.

You might think that the above-mentioned restrictions on IF and IOPL should be the other way around: that IOPL-access should be tied to the IOPL-level, and that IF-access should be restricted to level 0. This is not the case. It is sometimes necessary to shut off interrupts when programming some peripheral chips, so if a program has IOPL privileges, it has a legitimate access to the IF flag. On the other hand, the value of IOPL should be set once at system initialization and never changed. This is properly the function of the security kernel only.

Calling Across Rings   Recall that protection requires that it be impossible to gain operating-system privileges except by entering the operating system at a legal entry point. On many computers, a special "supervisor call" instruction is used as the standard way to request operating-system services. On the 386 this is accomplished with an ordinary far call to a procedure in a more protected ring. One of the design goals of the 386 was that all far calls appear to caller and callee to work the same, whether or not the calls cross from one ring to another. That way, a (separately compiled) subprogram need not be changed if it is moved from one ring to another. Furthermore, compilers don't have to handle cross-ring calls as a special case. So programs in higher-level languages can call the operating system directly. This goal was almost, but not entirely, met on the 386, as we shall see.

At first it might appear that to maintain protection, the 386 must prohibit less privileged procedures from calling more privileged procedures. That way, the 386 would prevent the user's program from performing operations that should only be done by the operating system. But it would also prevent the user's program from obtaining the legitimate services that it needs from the operating system. Thus the 386 does permit a less privileged procedure to call a more privileged one, but it limits the access

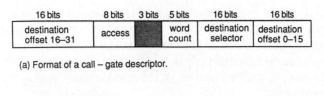

(a) Format of a call – gate descriptor.

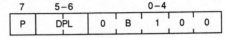

(b) Access byte in a call – gate descriptor.

Figure 6.14 Format of a call gate.

to certain legal entry points. This way the 386 allows a user's program to obtain from the operating system only those services that the operating system is willing to make available to the user's program.

Legal entry points are identified on the 386 by special descriptors called *call gates*. The calling program performs an indirect transfer through the call gate; the CALL instruction in the calling program references the call gate and the call gate specifies the entry point in the called program. Now all that's needed to give a user program access to a particular operating-system procedure is to provide a call gate having a low enough privilege that it can be accessed by the user's program and have that call gate reference an entry point into the highly protected operating system. In particular, a call-gate descriptor contains selector and offset of the desired entry point in the more privileged segment. The call instruction is a far call with the selector referencing the call gate; the offset here is ignored.

One benefit from storing the entry-point address in the call gate, rather than in the call, is that a procedure can be modified and recompiled without requiring the recompilation of any programs that call it through the gate. Only the far address in the gate needs to be changed to match any changes in the procedure's entry point. Thus, old programs can be run on a new version of an operating system, as long as the positions in the GDT of all the gates for old operating-system services are unchanged.

Figure 6.14 shows the format of a call-gate descriptor. The present (P) bit has the same effect here as in a segment descriptor. The DPL field specifies how much privilege is needed to access the gate; that is, the gate can only be used if CPL $\leq$ DPL. The destination selector and offset specify the desired entry point. The destination must be a code segment; gates-to-gates are forbidden. The RPL field of the destination selector is ignored. The five-bit *word count* field specifies the number of parameter (double)words passed in the call. Why this field is necessary and what to do if there are more than $2^5 - 1 = 31$ (double)words of parameters will be explained later. The B bit distinguishes between a 286 call gate and a 386 call gate. If B is 0, it is a 286 gate: the word cound refers to 16-bit words, and the upper 16 bits of the destination offset are ignored. If B is 1, it is a 386 gate: the word count refers to 32-bit doublewords, and all 32 bits of the destination offset are used.

Figure 6.15 illustrates the use of a call gate. Here, the call gate has a DPL of 2 and references a code segment with a DPL of 0. So the call gate may be used as a target for calls originating in rings 0, 1, and 2. The gate cannot be used from ring 3. In addition, the code segment can be called directly by any program in ring 0.

In order to analyze the mechanism of calls and returns in selector mode, let's consider the three cases:

1. The caller and callee are equally privileged.

2. The caller is less privileged than the callee.

3. The caller is more privileged than the callee.

If the calling segment and the called segment are equally privileged, then calls and returns work just as described in Chapter 3. This is true even if the call goes through a gate. The gate simply redirects the destination of the call. Figure 6.16a shows the stack contents after a call. This is just as in Chapter 3.

If the calling segment is less privileged then the called segment, then the call must go through a gate. In addition, the called procedure must use a different, more-privileged stack segment than the calling procedure. There are two reasons for this. First, the called procedure must guard against a possible stack overflow, which will occur if the calling procedure allocates insufficient stack space. It is for this reason that most operating systems on almost all computers switch to their own stacks when called. The 386 switches stacks automatically in cross-ring calls.

The second reason for switching stacks is more subtle. The 386 allows tasks to share segments. It is possible that the less-privileged stack segment of the less-privileged caller is shared with another task. A malevolent less-privileged program executing in this other task might possibly clobber the stack segment while it is being used by the more-privileged called procedure in the first task. In general, privileged procedures should consider less-privileged writable segments to be volatile.

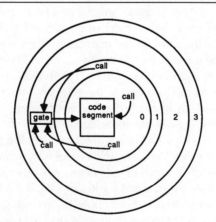

Figure 6.15 Example of the use of a call gate.

The 386 obtains the new values of the SS and ESP registers for the new stack from a special segment called the *task state segment* (TSS), associated with the task. Each task has its own task state segment. We will have a lot more to say about task state segments in the next section. For the moment, all we need to know is that each task state segment contains three potential pairs of new values for SS,ESP: one for each of the rings 0, 1, and 2. A task state segment doesn't need a pair for ring 3, since it's impossible to have a call where the caller is less privileged than a ring 3 callee.

After loading SS and ESP to point to the new stack, the 386 pushes the old values in SS and ESP (that is, the ones which point to the top of the old stack) onto the new stack. The 386 then copies all the parameters from the old stack to the new. The word-count field from the gate determines how many words to copy. Finally, the 386 pushes the old values of CS and EIP (the return address) onto the new stack. The stack contents after the call are shown in Figure 6.16b.

The 386 didn't have to copy the parameters onto the new stack; the called procedure could have accessed them from the caller's stack. However, this would again present a volatility problem. Furthermore it would require the called procedure to be aware that a stack switch had occurred. By having the 386 automatically copy the parameters, the called procedure can work the same, whether it's called from its own or from a different ring.

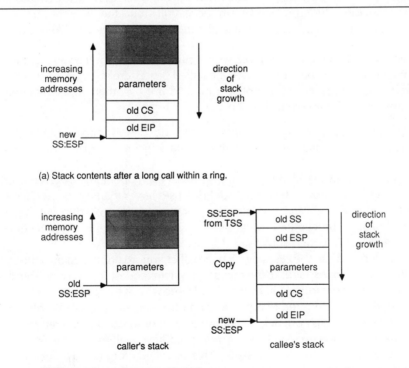

(a) Stack contents after a long call within a ring.

(b) Stack contents after a cross-ring call.

Figure 6.16 Stack contents after long calls.

Comparing Figure 6.16a to 6.16b, we see that the top portion of the stack, as seen by the called procedure, is indeed the same in both cases. The return instruction can tell that it's returning from a cross-ring call by comparing the current value of CPL to the CPL of the calling program. (Recall that CPL is stored in the RPL field of the CS register, so the 386 can determine the CPL of the calling program by examining the value of CS that was pushed on the stack as part of the return address.) In returning from a cross-ring call, the return instruction will:

1.   Pop the return address into the CS and EIP registers

2.   Pop the parameters from the callee's stack

3.   Switch back to the caller's stack by popping the old values of SS and ESP into the SS and ESP registers

4.   Pop the parameters from the caller's stack

5.   Continue execution in the caller

In addition, the return instruction will zero any other segment register (DS, ES, FS, or GS) that points to a segment more privileged than the caller. This prevents the caller from illegally accessing privileged segments accidentally left over by the callee.

In general, this call/return mechanism successfully blurs the difference between a cross-ring and intraring call. This is true in all but the following two unlikely cases:

1.   If more than 31 parameter (double)words must be passed, or if a variable number of parameters must be passed, then the called procedure must detect whether or not it has been called from another ring, and if it has, then explicitly copy the parameters from the old stack to the new.

2.   If the called procedure builds a *display* (see the discussion of ENTER and LEAVE in Chapter 3), the display must refer to the old stack in the case of a cross-ring call.

The first case is easily avoided by making sure that each operating-system procedure which may be called from a less-privileged ring uses fewer than 32 (double)words of parameters. The second can be avoided by placing all such procedures at the outermost level of static procedure nesting or by writing operating-system procedures in languages (such as C) which don't use a display.

Finally, let's analyze the case in which the caller is more privileged than the callee. This unlikely case corresponds to the operating system requesting a service from a user program and, in fact, is forbidden by the 386. To see why, we must focus on the return rather than the call. Here the return instruction transfers control from a ring of low privilege to a ring of high privilege. Suppose that, prior to executing a return instruction, a malicious program fabricates a return address (values for the CS and EIP registers) and pushes it onto the stack. This is called "forging" a return address. Furthermore, suppose that this forged return address corresponds to a protected entry point in the operating system. When the return instruction is executed, the user program will enter the operating system at the illegal entry point. So if calls to, and thus returns from, less-privileged rings were permitted, a malicious user could break into the operating system. For this reason, such calls and returns produce a protection exception.

In order to insure security when returning from a less-privileged procedure to a more-privileged one, the 386 could have included a more complicated call/return mechanism. Rather than providing such a mechanism (the current mechanism is complicated enough!), it was decided instead to produce an exception. If it's absolutely necessary to make such a call, then a special procedure in ring 0 can be written to accomplish the call by software simulation.

We have seen how a call gate is used in calling a protected procedure. The 386 also allows a program to jump to a call gate under certain circumstances. To see the danger in such a jump, suppose a program pushes a forged return address onto the stack. The program could then do a cross-ring jump through a call gate to a more-privileged procedure which expects to be called, not jumped to. The jump would masquerade as a call. When the privileged procedure eventually executes its return instruction, execution will continue at the location specified by the forged return address, which might be an illegal entry point in the more-privileged ring—so protection would fail. For this reason, far jumps are only allowed within a ring. Jumps to destinations in another ring lead to a protection exception. A jump to a call gate is permitted only if the destination of the call gate is in the same ring as the jump instruction.

We've just described two ways in which security might have been breached if the 386 hadn't prohibited certain kinds of instructions. Catching such potential loopholes in a processor design isn't an easy job. In fact, cross-ring jumps were initially designed into the 286, until it was realized how dangerous they are.

In summary, it is forbidden for a procedure to call a less-privileged procedure. A procedure can call a more-privileged procedure, but the call must go through a gate. If a procedure calls a procedure of equal privilege, a gate is optional. Jumps are only allowed between segments of equal privilege, and a gate is optional here too.

The Trojan Horse Attack   Consider an operating-system procedure in ring 1 which writes the current date and time into a string at a location specified by the procedure's single parameter: a selector-and-offset address. A malicious program in ring 3 calls this procedure, passing as a parameter an address containing a selector for a segment in ring 2. The ring 1 procedure then writes the date and time at the indicated location, clobbering the ring 2 segment. The malicious program has used the parameter as a "Trojan Horse," which causes the destruction of the ring 2 segment after the parameter is brought into ring 1 by the naive date-and-time procedure.

The RPL field in selectors and the ARPL (Adjust RPL) instruction have been provided to foil such an attack. The RPL field, in effect, artificially increases the current ring number (decreases the privilege) that applies when its selector is used. In particular, the increased ring number is max(CPL, RPL). Hence we can use RPL to tag a selector with the degree of trust we have in it. The called procedure should contain

ARPL instructions that set the RPL's of all selector parameters to the privilege level of the calling program. By doing so, the called procedure can guard against the type of Trojan Horse attack described above. This is illustrated in Figure 6.17.

A slightly better approach is to set RPL to the maximum (lower privilege) of the old RPL and the caller's privilege level. That way, a selector's RPL won't decrease (become more privileged) if it's passed along a chain of increasingly privileged, cautious procedures, each of which sets RPL and then calls the next.

The ARPL instruction has two operands: the first is a word operand (memory or register) and the second is a register word operand. Both are assumed to be selectors. The RPL field of the first is set to the maximum of both RPL's. If ARPL increases the RPL of the first operand, then it sets the zero flag; otherwise, it clears the zero flag. A cautious procedure can thus load the selector from its return address into a register and then apply ARPL to each parameter selector in order to guard against attack.

Those programmers unconcerned about Trojan Horses may find the following two observations reassuring:

1.   If a program uses an RPL of 0 in all of its selectors, it can be used in any ring without danger of spurious protection exceptions. This is because the criterion for a legal access is:

$$DPL \geq max(CPL,RPL) = max(CPL,0) = CPL$$

2.   A program running just in ring 3 (the user ring) produces the same results, no matter what RPL values it uses. This is because the criterion for a legal access is:

$$DPL \geq max(CPL,RPL) = max(3,RPL) = 3$$

Finally, while we're on the subject of cautious programs, there are two instructions that check whether or not a segment is accessible without risking a protection excep-

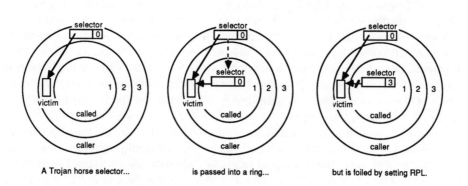

A Trojan horse selector...   is passed into a ring...   but is foiled by setting RPL.

Figure 6.17 Foiling a Trojan horse attack.

tion. VERR (Verify for Reading) takes a word operand (memory or register) which is considered to be a selector. If it's okay to use the selector for reading, then VERR sets the zero flag. If not, then VERR clears the zero flag. The instruction VERW (Verify for Writing) is similar to VERR, except it checks to see if writing is permitted.

Conforming Segments A disadvantage in using ARPL is that it must be explicitly applied by software. If a procedure never needs more privilege than the program that calls it, then the 386 provides an automatic technique for adjusting its privilege.

For example, a system might contain a procedure for converting binary integers to ASCII which is used in every ring. Since calls to less-privileged procedures are forbidden, this conversion procedure must reside in ring 0 in order to be callable from ring 0. In general, however, the conversion procedure requires only enough privilege to access its arguments and return its result, that is, only as much privilege as the program which calls it. The 386 has an elegant mechanism for handling this.

Recall that executable (and only executable) segments have a *conforming* (C) bit in their descriptors. If the conforming bit is set, then the usual rules regarding CPL and DPL don't apply. The rules described below apply instead.

Procedures in a conforming segment may be called or *jumped to* directly from any program no more privileged than the conforming segment: the caller's CPL must be greater than or equal to the conforming segment's DPL. No call gate is needed, and no stacks are switched. When the transfer to the conforming segment is made, CPL isn't changed; it remains at the level of the calling program. Thus a conforming segment automatically "moves outward" or "conforms" to the ring of its caller. This rule holds true even if the conforming segment is called through a gate.

Code segments sometimes contain constant values that are used by the program and hence are read when the program is executed. Ordinarily, if a code segment is readable, then it's readable only from the ring that contains it and any lower-numbered (more-privileged) rings. In order for a readable conforming segment to be able to access its own embedded constants, readable conforming segments may be read from *any* ring.

Multitasking

The 386 supports multiple tasks by switching from one task to another. To accomplish this, the 386 associates with each task a memory segment containing all the information needed to start and stop the task. This special segment is called a *task state segment* (TSS). The 386 has a 16-bit register, called the *task register*, which contains a GDT selector for the task state segment of the currently running task. In order to speed access to the selected task state segment, the task register is shadowed by a register containing the selected descriptor. Although the task register may be loaded and stored using the LTR (Load Task Register) and STR (Store Task Register) instructions, the task register is typically manipulated automatically by the 386 as part of a task switch.

The main use for a task state segment is to hold the contents of a task's registers when the 386 isn't executing that task. In particular, the 386 performs (approximately) the following steps when it switches to another task:

1. The 386 saves all its program-visible registers (except for the GDT register) in the task state segment referenced by the task register.

2. The 386 then loads the task register with a selector for the new task state segment.

3. Finally, the 386 reloads its registers from the new task state segment and continues execution in the new task.

Task state segments (like LDT's) have their own special descriptors. Only selectors for task state segment descriptors may be loaded into the task register. The format of a task state segment descriptor is shown in Figure 6.18. All of the fields should be familiar by now, except for the *busy* (B) bit. The 386 sets the busy bit in the task state segment descriptor for the currently running task. It clears the busy bit when it abandons the task for another. This bit is used in systems with multiple 386's for preventing two 386's from executing the same task at the same time. Switching to a busy task causes a protection exception.

The format of a 386 task state segment is shown in Figure 6.19. There is always a fixed, 104-byte buffer at the beginning of the segment. Following that is a variable-length *system status* buffer that can be defined by the operating system. This buffer is used to store extra information useful to operating system software (the task's owner, accounting information, etc.). At the end of a 386 task state segment is another variable-length buffer, identifying which input/output ports are accessible to the task.

The first field of a task state segment is the *back link* field. We will discuss this field later. Next come the selector-and-offset addresses for three stacks, one for each of the rings of protection 0–2. Each address specifies the bottom (highest address) of a stack. We described how these stacks are used in cross-ring calls in the previous section.

The next 18 doublewords of a task state segment are used for saving registers. Any registers not appearing in Figure 6.19 (the GDT register, the task register, shadow

(a) Task state segment descriptor.

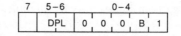

(b) Access byte for TSS descriptor.

Figure 6.18 Task segment descriptor format.

registers, etc.) aren't saved during a task switch. Such registers either remain unchanged or are recomputed during the task switch. One of the reasons for the fast task-switch time on the 386 (17 microseconds, using a 16-MHz 386) is that the amount of information that must be saved or recomputed is comparatively small.

The final doubleword of the 104-byte buffer contains two fields: the *bitmap offset* field and the *debug trap* bit. We'll discuss the debug trap bit later, in the section on debugging in protected mode. The bitmap offset field gives the offset (from the start of the segment) of the I/O permission bitmap, which follows the system status buffer. Thus, the length of the system status buffer is always the bitmap offset minus 104.

We already mentioned the I/O permission bitmap in Chapter 5, when we talked about virtual 8086 mode. Recall that the bitmap grants selective access to input/output

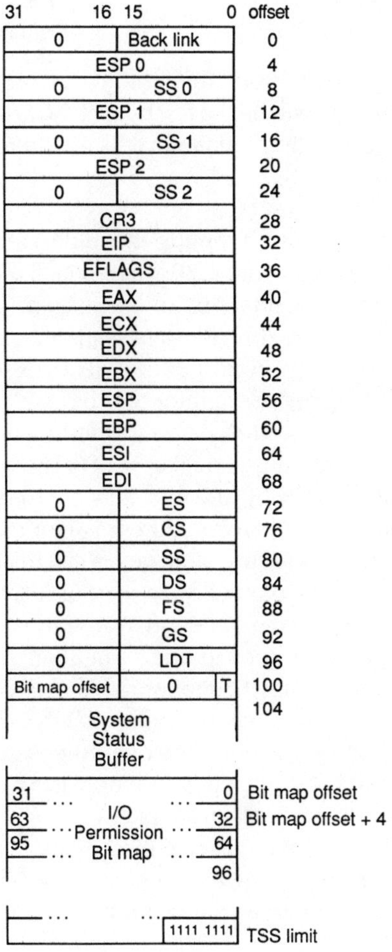

Figure 6.19 386 task state segment.

ports on the 386. If the *n*th bit in the bitmap is 0, the task can access port *n*. If the *n*th bit is 1, then any attempt by the task to access port *n* will cause a general protection fault. There are several things to note about the bitmap:

1. Since word-wide I/O is viewed by the 386 as an access to two consecutive ports, both of the corresponding bits in the bitmap must be set to 0 for the word-wide access to be allowed. Similarly, all four corresponding bits must be set to 0 for a doubleword-wide I/O operation to be allowed.

2. In the completely general case, the bitmap must be 8K bytes long to specify access for each of the 64K ports. However, the bitmap can be truncated by limiting the length of the task state segment containing the bitmap. Any truncated bytes are interpreted as containing all 1's (no permission granted). In particular, the system can completely deny access to ports by truncating the entire bitmap: that is, by setting the bitmap offset to a value greater than the limit of the task state segment.

3. For obscure implementation reasons, the system *must* provide an all-1's byte at the end of the bitmap. This byte will be the last byte of the task state segment (its offset is one less than the segment limit). If the byte is not there, then the bitmap is not guaranteed to function correctly.

For compatibility, the 386 also supports the older 286 format for task state segments. That format is shown in Figure 6.20. The initial fixed buffer is only 44 bytes long. There is no I/O permission bitmap, so the system status buffer's length is determined by the segment limit. A 286 task state segment is distinguished by a value of 0 instead of 1 in bit 3 of the access byte in the segment's descriptor.

A selector for a task state segment descriptor can't be used for reading or writing the task state segment; it can only be used for performing task switches. There is no special task-switch instruction on the 386. Instead, a far JMP (Jump) instruction that targets a task state segment causes not a jump, but a task switch to the corresponding task. In this case, the offset portion of the JMP's target address is ignored. This is similar to the situation described in the previous section, in which a call instruction acted differently depending upon whether it targeted a code segment or a gate. But great pains were taken by the 386's designers so that the same call instruction in a program would work correctly, regardless of whether it goes to code segments or through gates. A task switch is so different from a jump that it's unreasonable to expect to substitute a jump-to-task-state-segment for a jump-to-code-segment (or vice versa) and still have the program do anything meaningful. The functions of a jump instruction and a task switch instruction were combined into a single opcode simply to save opcodes.

The usual protection rules for segments apply to task state segments. A task state segment can only be used within the ring specified by its DPL or a lower-numbered (more privileged) ring. A *task gate*, however, enables a program to switch to a task corresponding to a task state segment in a lower-numbered ring. The format of a task gate is shown in Figure 6.21.

Task gates, as opposed to call gates, provide no entry-point restrictions; however, they can still be used to provide protection. For example, suppose that a particular task

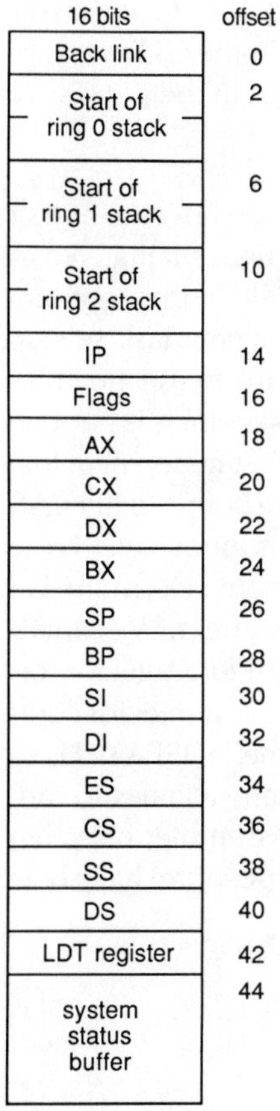

16 bits
offset
Back link
0
Start of ring 0 stack
2
Start of ring 1 stack
6
Start of ring 2 stack
10
IP
14
Flags
16
AX
18
CX
20
DX
22
BX
24
SP
26
BP
28
SI
30
DI
32
ES
34
CS
36
SS
38
DS
40
LDT register
42
44
system status buffer

Figure 6.20 286 task state segment.

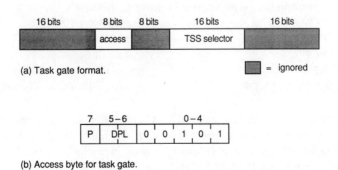

16 bits
8 bits
8 bits
16 bits
16 bits
access
TSS selector
= ignored
(a) Task gate format.
7
5–6
0–4
P
DPL
0
0
1
0
1
(b) Access byte for task gate.

Figure 6.21 Format of a task gate.

performs a service that we wish to limit to selected user tasks. We can place the task state segment for the service task in the GDT at ring 0. Those tasks entitled to use the service can be given task gates for it in their LDTs. Tasks without the gate can't get the service.

Example: Time Slicing   Let's see how the 386's task switch instruction enables us to implement a simple version of time slicing. We assume that all task state segments contain a two-byte software *link* field in their optional portions. This enables us to link task state segments into lists by placing task selectors in the link fields. Figure 6.22 depicts a waiting list for tasks wishing to use the 386 processor. The task register points to the task state segment of the task which is currently running. The link field of each task state segment points to the task state segment for the next task in line. The link field of the last task state segment in line points to the first.

Since task state segment descriptors can't be used for read or write access, we assume that each task state segment descriptor is immediately followed by a data segment descriptor for the same segment. We can obtain a selector for the aliased data segment descriptor by adding eight to a selector for the task state segment descriptor (recall that the three low-order bits of a selector contain the RPL and TI fields).

The following procedure, named DISPATCH, moves the currently running task to the end of the waiting list and then switches to the next task in line. This is called a *round-robin* scheduling policy. Assembler directives for defining the fields in a task state segment (called TSS in the procedure) have been omitted, but all other assembler directives are included.

```
DISPATCH PROC FAR            ; tell assembler this is a procedure
    PUSHF                    ; save flags on stack
    PUSH DS                  ; save DS on stack
    PUSH AX                  ; save AX on stack
    STR AX                   ; move task register to AX
    ADD AX,8                 ; bump selector to get TSS alias
    MOV DS,AX                ; can now read the TSS
    JMP DS:PWORD PTR link-4  ; switch to next task

; resume here when control returns to this task
    POP AX                   ; restore AX
    POP DS                   ; restore DS
    POPF                     ; restore flags
    RET                      ; return to caller, within this task
DISPATCH ENDP                ; tell assembler that proc ends
```

What happens if a program calls DISPATCH? After saving some registers and obtaining read access to the current task state segment, DISPATCH executes an indirect JMP to the address whose selector is stored in the link field of the current task state segment. (The phrase PWORD PTR causes the assembler to generate an indirect far jump; the -4 causes the four bytes before the link field to be interpreted as the offset

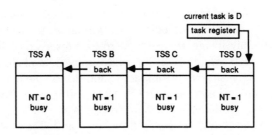

Figure 6.22 A chain formed by three task calls.

of the far address, which is in this case ignored.) Since this selector points to a task state segment, the JMP instruction produces a task switch rather than a jump. This causes the current task to be suspended and the next task in line to be resumed. The instruction pointer (EIP) of the suspended task, saved in its task state segment, will point to the POP instruction following the JMP. If each of the other tasks in line also calls DISPATCH sometime during its execution, then eventually the suspended task will reach the front of the list again and will be resumed. Execution will continue at the POP, and DISPATCH will return. So calling DISPATCH has no net effect on the task that calls it, but gives the other tasks a chance to run.

Unfortunately, we can't rely on tasks to be considerate enough to call DISPATCH at regular intervals. Instead, we can use an interval timer (such as Intel's 8254 programmable timer chip) to send an interrupt signal to the 386, say, every thousandth of a second. If we convert DISPATCH to an interrupt procedure (delete PUSHF and POPF, and replace RET with IRETD) and associate it with the timer interrupt, then DISPATCH will be called automatically every thousandth of a second. Thus each task will receive a time slice of (just under) a thousandth of a second—we have implemented time slicing.

Switching Numeric Tasks   One reason task switching on the 386 is so rapid is that only 72 bytes' worth of registers must be saved and restored. But the 386 task switch instruction doesn't take into account the 387. The complete register state for a 387 takes up another 108 bytes. Saving and restoring this extra information can substantially slow task switching.

The easiest way to accommodate a 387 is to allocate 108 bytes in the system status buffer of every task state segment and to modify the DISPATCH procedure by adding an FSAVE instruction before, and an FRSTOR after, the task switch instruction. But this wastes time by unnecessarily saving and restoring the 387's registers in tasks which don't use the 387. Most of the tasks in a system will probably be such nonnumeric tasks.

It would be nice if the operating system could avoid saving and restoring the 387's registers unless doing so is strictly necessary. The trick is to remember the last task that executed a 387 instruction and to delay saving the 387's registers for that task until a different task executes a 387 instruction. To accomplish this, the 386 maintains several floating-point status bits in the machine status word (MSW).

Recall that we mentioned MSW in Chapter 5 in connection with the PE bit. MSW is the lower half of the 386's 32-bit CR0 register. The format of the machine status word is shown in Figure 5.4. Only six bits are used; the rest are reserved for future expansion. The designers of the 286 forgot about the philosophy behind 86 family assembly language and named the instructions for loading and storing the machine status word LMSW rm16 (it should have been named MOV MSW,rm16) and SMSW rm16 (it should have been named MOV rm16,MSW), where "rm16" is any 16-bit general register or memory operand. When the 32-bit instructions were added for the 386, they were named correctly: MOV CR0,rm32 and MOV rm32,CR0.

If there is a floating-point chip (either a 287 or a 387) connected to the 386, then the operating system should set the *emulation mode* (EM) bit of the machine status word to 0 during system initialization. If the EM bit is 1, then the 386 will cause a No Math Unit Available exception whenever it encounters a floating-point instruction. So if EM is 1, the No Math Unit Available exception handler can emulate 387 instructions in software. Furthermore, if the 387 is emulated in software, its *simulated registers* are stored in memory as part of the task's local address space. This makes it unnecessary to save and restore the simulated registers during task switches.

The *task switched* (TS) bit of the machine status word is automatically set to 1 each time the 386 performs a task switch. This bit remains set until it's cleared by the CLTS (Clear Task Switched) instruction (no operands). If the 386 encounters a floating-point instruction and finds that TS is 1, then a No Math Unit Available exception results (regardless of the state of EM). So an exception handler for No Math Unit Available should first check the EM bit: if it's 1, then emulate the instruction; if it's 0, then:

1. Clear the TS bit.

2. Check to see if the current task is the same as the last task which triggered this exception. If so, return to the program. If not, save the 387's registers in the task state segment of the last task to trigger the exception.

3. Restore the 387's registers from the current task state segment.

4. Make note of the fact that the current task is now the last task to trigger this exception.

5. Return to the program.

Upon returning to the program in step 2 or 5 above, the 386 (and 387) will continue execution with the floating-point instruction that caused the exception. Since TS is now cleared, the instruction will continue without causing another No Math Unit Available exception.

If a 387 is connected to the 386, then the operating system should set the *math present* (MP) bit of the machine status word to 1 during system initialization. Then when TS is 1, the 386 will catch WAIT instructions as well as floating-point instructions.

The 8086 doesn't have a No Math Unit Available exception or task switching, so to achieve 8086 compatibility in real mode, the bits TS, MP, and EM should all be set to 0. Since task switches can't happen in real mode, TS will remain 0, and the No Math Unit Available exception will never occur. Table 6.4 summarizes the usage of the MP and EM bits.

The remaining bits of CR0 are the *protection enabled* (PE) bit, the *paging enabled* (PG) bit, and the 387 bit. We discuss these bits later, in the section on system initialization.

Debugging in Protected Mode   It's time to re-examine the debugging support facilities we described in Chapter 3, taking into consideration what we now know about paging, segmentation, and multitasking. Recall that the 386 provides breakpoint registers, into which the debugger can plug the 32-bit addresses of breakpoints in our program or data areas. We've found that addresses are a lot more complicated than they appeared to us in Chapter 3. Just what kind of addresses does the debugger use for breakpoint registers, anyway? The answer brings both good news and bad news: breakpoints are linear addresses. That's good news, because the debugger doesn't have to walk through page table entries in order to calculate what to plug into a breakpoint register. That's bad news, because the debugger *does* have to walk through segment descriptors in order to calculate what to plug into a breakpoint register.

We must also consider debugging in a multitasking environment. The existence of a single set of breakpoint registers for the entire machine creates two problems:

1.   We've discussed paging strategies in which the page tables are switched when tasks are switched. Under those strategies, the linear address space can be redefined on a task switch. If the old task is running the debugger and has breakpoints set, the breakpoints could take effect in the new task, where they would apply to arbitrary and different memory pages.

2.   Sooner or later, two users will want to be debugging at the same time. They each need their own set of breakpoint registers.

Table 6.4. EM and MP Bit Settings

EM	MP	
0	1	387 is present
1	0	387 is absent
0	0	8086 compatible
1	1	forbidden

The problems could be averted by including the debug registers among those automatically saved and restored on a task switch. But this would add 6 doublewords to the 18 already saved, slowing down all task switches by about 30%. That's too big a penalty to pay, considering that the vast majority of tasks won't be using the debug registers. If this argument sounds familiar to you, it's because we just applied it to the floating-point registers, and the solution we adopt is the same: we concoct ways to insure that the debug registers are swapped only when needed.

First, we must insure that the old task's breakpoints are disabled on a task switch. This is accomplished by clearing, on every task switch, the local breakpoint-enable bits L1 through L4 in the DR7 register. The bits can be cleared in parallel with the rest of the task-switching activities, so it consumes no time; thus we can clear the bits whether they need it or not.

Second, we must insure that the new task's debugger settings, if there are any, are restored on a task switch. This is done by having the debugger manipulate the task state segment for the task: it can set the debug trap bit to 1, and it can maintain an image of the task's debugger registers in the system status buffer. The debugger must update the image whenever it writes to the registers. If the debug trap bit is 1 when a task is entered, then the 386 generates a debugger interrupt (type 1), to give the debugger the chance to load that task's debug register settings, using the image it has maintained.

Recall that there is also an LE bit in the DR7 register that slows down the bus operations of the 386, so that breakpoints can work properly. LE is also disabled on every task switch, so that the entire 386 system isn't slowed down just because one user is running a debugger.

Of course, we must accommodate the poor soul who must debug the operating system itself. That person must be able to set breakpoints that remain in effect across task switches. For this reason, the bits L1–L4 and LE have global versions: G1–G4 and GE. The G bits are not cleared on task switches. To avoid the pitfalls we've mentioned, the person who is debugging the operating system must take care that global breakpoints are set only in global memory pages, and that no individual tasks are running a debugger while global debugging is taking place.

Note that the debugger must have access to segment descriptor tables and task state segments in order to do its job in a protected environment. This means that parts of the debugger must execute at level 0, the highest privilege level. But it would be unacceptable for the debugger to be part of the operating system; there should be a wide variety of debuggers available to 386 users, each tied to a particular programming environment and/or hardware configuration. The solution is for the operating system to provide a set of debugger-oriented services. Debuggers would run as user programs, typically with the minimum privilege level. Instead of accessing the debug registers directly, the debuggers would rely on the system services to interface with the 386's debugging facilities. Note that specification of breakpoints to the operating system would be by selector-and-offset combination: the debugger service routines would calculate the resulting linear address. That way the operating system can maintain its policy of keeping segment locations secret from user programs.

Calling a Task   Many operating systems support a style of interaction typified by the following example. Suppose we are debugging our program with an interactive debugger. We discover that we must modify an input file, so we give a command to the debugger which suspends the debugger and initiates a new task containing an interactive text editor. While using the text editor, we decide to delete a file. We give a command to the text editor to initiate the file-deletion program. The text editor initiates a new task containing the file-deletion program and suspends itself. When the file-deletion program is done, the text editor is resumed at the point where we requested the file deletion. When we are finally done editing file, we terminate the text editor, which places us back in the debugger at the point where we left it. We then continue debugging.

Note that at any time only one task is running, and task switching follows a stacklike discipline. The 386 supports this arrangement directly in hardware. Just as it allows a JMP instruction to reference a task state segment or task gate, the 386 also allows a CALL instruction to reference a task state segment or task gate. A CALL that targets a task state segment or task gate causes a task switch to the selected task, just as in a JMP. But in addition, the 386 puts a selector for the outgoing task (that is, the old contents of the task register) into the *back link* field of the incoming task's task state segment. It also sets the *nested task* (NT) flag in the incoming task. Figure 6.22 shows what happens if task A (which was initiated by a JMP) calls task B, which calls task C, which calls task D.

A JMP to a task sets NT to 0, so NT tells whether a task has been initiated by JMP or by CALL. Another difference between JMP and CALL is the treatment of the busy (B) bit in the TSS descriptor. Recall that the running task has B set to 1, so an attempt by a second 386 processor to execute the task at the same time will cause an exception. JMP clears B in the outgoing task and sets B in the incoming task. CALL, on the other hand, doesn't touch B in the outgoing task but still sets B in the incoming task. Thus every task in a chain of calls will have B set (see Figure 6.22). This has the effect of prohibiting re-entrant or recursive task calls.

An IRETD (or IRET—the distinction is ignored in this case) instruction in a task with NT set to 1 causes a task switch back to the task referenced in the back link field of the current task state segment. If NT is 0, then IRETD works as described in Chapter 3.

One reason that IRETD, rather than RET, is used to return from a called task is to allow ordinary procedures to be used within the called task. The 386 automatically clears NT for the duration of any interrupt procedures so they also work correctly.

A second reason for using IRETD for task return is that the most important use for task calls is in interrupt handling. We obtain many advantages by responding to an interrupt with a task call rather than with a procedure call. Such called tasks are called *interrupt tasks,* and we have much more to say about them in the next section.

If we call a procedure, allow it to return, and then call it once more, we will (obviously) enter the procedure at the same place in both calls. If we call a task, allow it to return, and then call it once more, we will re-enter the task at the instruction following the IRETD which returned to us. For this reason, tasks which are designed to be called usually have the following form:

        start:

                .

                .

                .

            perform a service

                .

                .

                .

            IRETD

            JMP start

Entering and Leaving Virtual 8086 Mode   Let's see how virtual 8086 mode fits into the multitasking environment we've been discussing. The 386 knows that it is in virtual 8086 mode when the VM bit (bit 17) of the EFLAGS register is 1. Figure 3.4 shows the position of VM within the EFLAGS register. To enter or leave virtual 8086 mode, the EFLAGS register must be changed. Note, however, that segment registers are interpreted differently in virtual 8086 mode than in selector mode. In particular, the value in the CS register will be reinterpreted from a table selector to a multiply-by-16 value when the switch is made. So any instruction that changes the VM bit must simultaneously change CS (and hence EIP) to specify where the next instruction in the new environment can be found. The only instructions that change both the flags and the instruction pointer are IRET(D), and task-switching CALLs and JMPs.

Let's think about entering virtual 8086 mode via the IRET(D) instruction. Virtual 8086 mode grants a program access to the entire first megabyte of the linear address space. If such access was not planned by the operating system, then the megabyte might contain code from other tasks or from the operating system itself. An errant program could trash that code with an ill-advised IRET(D). A malicious program, if it has access to any part of the first megabyte, could place code in that part, and jump there via a virtual-8086-activating IRET(D), thus gaining access to the whole megabyte. Hence, the act of entering virtual 8086 mode via IRET(D) must be restricted to privilege level 0 (highest privilege). It's not necessary to be at level 0 to enter virtual 8086 mode via a task switch: if the EFLAGS image within a task state segment has a VM bit set to 1, that setting must have been made by the operating system.

We must also make a decision about the privilege level of virtual 8086 mode itself. In selector mode, the privilege level is decided by the bottom two bits of the CS selector. This mechanism cannot be used in virtual 8086 mode, because all 16 bits of segment register values are used for address calculation. Since the sole purpose of virtual 8086 mode is to run existing 8086 applications, it is not envisioned that any 386 operating-system code will run in virtual 8086 mode. So instead of adding a mechanism to decide privilege level in a virtual 8086 task, we simply decree that the privilege level is always 3 (least privilege).

Because virtual 8086 mode was introduced with the 386, we do not need to support it in 286 tasks; in fact, it is simpler to prohibit virtual 8086 mode in 286 tasks. We have already done so implicitly by placing the VM bit in the upper 16 bits of the EFLAGS register. Those bits do not exist in a 286 task statement segment, so it is impossible to specify a 286 task as a virtual 8086 task.

Let's now think about exiting virtual 8086 mode. We've already mentioned in Chapter 5 that virtual 8086 mode can be exited by exceptions and interrupts. This can hardly be avoided if the 386 operating system is to retain control. Should we provide any other means for exiting virtual 8086 mode? The answer is no. The interrupt mechanism is sufficient, and if we add other means (such as exiting on far jumps or calls), we simply degrade the faithful emulation of 8086 functionality.

So far in our discussion of virtual 8086 mode, we have gathered a sizeable collection of constraints surrounding virtual 8086 mode. Let's see what these constraints add up to. Virtual 8086 mode is limited to 386 tasks, so we can forget about the 286 IRET instruction; IRETD will always be the form used if we do not enter virtual 8086 mode via a task switch. Virtual 8086 mode is exited via interrupts or exceptions. Since the interrupt handler will return to virtual 8086 mode via IRETD, the handler must be in privilege level 0. Since the virtual 8086 code itself is at privilege level 3, the 386 must switch stacks when invoking the handler, as we've seen in the section on calling across rings. We saw in Figure 6.16b how this is done. However, there is one last constraint that adds one more complication to the interrupt process. The 386 must flush all the segment registers before leaving virtual 8086 mode. Those registers may contain multiply-by-16 values that have never been interpreted or checked as selectors. Since the whole 386 protection mechanism hinges on checking selector values *before* they are loaded into segment registers, it would defeat protection if the existing segment register values were allowed to slip through unchecked. Before the segment registers are flushed, they are saved on the stack, so they can be restored on return. Figure 6.23 shows the format of the stack after virtual 8086 mode is exited. When the 386 executes the returning IRETD instruction, it must consult the VM bit of the EFLAGS image on the stack to see if the extra segment registers are there to be popped and to see whether the return CS is a selector or a multiply-by-16 segment register value.

Interrupts and Exceptions

A 386 program may be interrupted for one of three reasons:

1. A peripheral device connected to the 386 sends the 386 an interrupt signal.

2. A 386 (or 387) instruction causes an exception.

3. The program executes an INT (Interrupt) instruction.

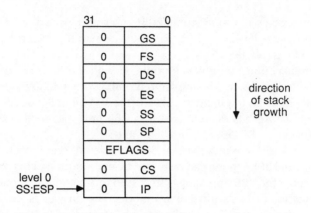

Figure 6.23 Format of the stack after virtual 8086 mode is exited.

Each specific cause of an interrupt is assigned a number between 0 and 255. Some interrupt numbers are already assigned by the 386 (such as all the 386 exceptions), some are assigned by the hardware system in which the 386 is embedded (such as disk drive interrupts), some are reserved for future expansion, and all the rest are free to be used by software.

When an interrupt occurs, the 386 uses the interrupt number as an index into a table. It extracts from the table the address of an *interrupt handler*, which is then called to perform the specific processing required by the interrupt. The effect is almost (but not quite) as if a call instruction were inserted into the program at the point of interruption.

We've just described, in outline, interrupt processing on the 386 in both real and protected modes. The two modes differ considerably, however, in their details.

Interrupts and Exceptions in Real Mode   We have already discussed real mode interrupts in Chapters 3 and 5, so we'll just summarize here. The interrupt number is used to index a table of four-byte entries. This table is stored beginning at physical address zero, and continuing for $256 \times 4 = 1024$ bytes. Each entry in the table is the real address of the start of an *interrupt procedure*. Interrupt procedures are similar to ordinary procedures (with no parameters) except that:

1. When an interrupt procedure is invoked, the 386 pushes the flags onto the stack before pushing the return address.

2. The trap flag (TF) and the interrupt-enable flag (IF) are cleared before entering the interrupt procedure.

3. The interrupt procedure must return using IRET, rather than RET, in order to automatically restore the flags.

Table 6.5 Real Mode Reserved Interrupts

0	Divide Error Exception
1	Debugger Trap Interrupt
2	Non-maskable Interrupt
3	Breakpoint
4	Overflow Exception
5	Range Exceeded Exception
6	Invalid Opcode Exception
7	No Math Unit Available Exception
8	IDT Too Small Exception
9	Math Unit Segment Overrun Exception
10	Reserved
11	Reserved
12	Stack Segment Overrun Exception
13	Segment Overrun Exception
14	Reserved
15	Reserved
16	Math Unit Exception
17	
•	
•	Reserved
•	
31	

Table 6.5 lists the reserved interrupt numbers for 386 real mode. Most of these have already been discussed in this chapter or in Chapters 3 or 5. The ones remaining are:

Divide Error Exception—This occurs if the quotient is too large or the divisor is zero. On the 8086, the return address provided to the interrupt procedure for this exception is the address of the next instruction after the divide. On the 286 and 386, exception return addresses consistently point to the first byte of the guilty instruction. Any prefixes are considered part of the instruction. We'll see the benefits of this convention when we discuss "restartability" later in this section.

Invalid Opcode Exception—This occurs if an invalid opcode or an instruction of length greater than ten bytes is encountered. The only way to build a "legal" instruction of such a length is to duplicate some of the instruction's prefixes. This exception was introduced with the 286: the 8086 has no instruction-length restrictions; furthermore, the behavior of the 8086 is unpredictable when an invalid opcode is encountered.

IDT Too Small Exception—See the section on protected mode, to follow.

Stack Segment Overrun Exception—This occurs when a stack reference (push or pop) beyond an offset of FFFF hexadecimal is attempted. On the 8086, such an operation would wraparound the stack pointer to offset 0.

Segment Overrun Exception—This occurs if a memory operand to a 386 instruction doesn't fit in a segment other than SS, for example, a word operand is stored at offset FFFF hexadecimal. On the 8086, such an operand would wrap around the segment to offset 0.

Math Unit Segment Overrun Exception—The same, except that a 387 instruction is the culprit.

Math Unit Exception—This is what happens on the 386 if any unmasked 387 exceptions occur.

Interrupt Priorities   Some peripheral-device interrupts are more urgent than others. If we wait one millisecond before responding to an interrupt from a keyboard, the typist can't tell the difference. If we wait one millisecond before responding to an interrupt from a disk drive, the disk will have rotated to a new position by the time we respond. We may have to wait for the disk to rotate back to its original position and try again. If we wait one millisecond before responding to an interrupt from a precision machine tool, the tool may damage the part it's machining.

What is needed is some way to prioritize the device interrupts in a system, so that more urgent interrupts will have priority over less urgent ones. The 386 doesn't contain the hardware to do this, so all interrupting devices are connected to an interrupt controller chip, such as Intel's 8259A, which in turn is connected to the 386.

The 8259A interrupt controller has many modes of operation. In its most commonly used mode, each device is assigned a unique priority ranking. If two devices interrupt simultaneously, the interrupt controller sends the higher priority interrupt to the 386 and remembers the lower priority interrupt. As soon as the 386 is finished processing the higher priority interrupt, the interrupt controller sends it the lower priority interrupt.

How does the interrupt controller know when the 386 is through processing an interrupt? This is accomplished by having the programmer insert special instructions at the end of each external device's interrupt procedure. These instructions output a special *end-of-interrupt* code to a port connected to the interrupt controller. The instructions are:

```
MOV DX,INT_PORT_NUM
MOV AL,EOI_CODE
OUT DX,AL
```

The port number INT_PORT_NUM and the end-of-interrupt code EOI_CODE depend on the particular hardware system and the mode of operation of the interrupt controller.

What happens if an interrupt from a device occurs while the 386 is in the midst of an interrupt procedure? If the new interrupt has a priority less than or equal to the interrupt being serviced, the interrupt controller will delay the new interrupt until the interrupt procedure is done. If the new interrupt has higher priority than the one being serviced, there are two cases:

1. If interrupts are enabled (IF is 1), the interrupt procedure will itself be interrupted and the higher priority interrupt procedure will be invoked. This is called *interrupt nesting* and is correctly handled by both the 386 and the interrupt controller.

2. If interrupts are disabled (IF is 0), the new interrupt will be delayed until the interrupt procedure returns, despite the fact that the new interrupt has higher priority.

By default, the 386 (in real mode) disables interrupts upon entering an interrupt procedure. This is okay if the interrupt procedure is only a few instructions long, but if the interrupt procedure is lengthy, then it should re-enable interrupts in order to avoid delaying higher priority interrupts. Executing the STI (Set Interrupt Enable Flag) instruction accomplishes this.

Interrupts in Protected Mode In protected mode, the interrupt table contains descriptors for the various interrupt handlers and is called the *interrupt descriptor table* (IDT). The linear base address and limit of the IDT are held in the *IDT register*. The IDT and IDT register are depicted in Figure 6.24.

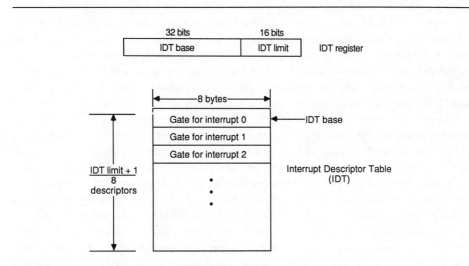

Figure 6.24 Interrupt descriptor table and IDT register.

The IDT register may be loaded and stored by using the LIDT and SIDT instructions, which work just like the LGDT and SGDT instructions described earlier in the chapter. Another thing the IDT has in common with the GDT is that there's only one IDT. The IDT register isn't changed when tasks are switched. If we want to support task-specific interrupt tables, we can do so by exploiting the fact that the IDT register holds a linear address, not a physical address: we can change the paging tables for the IDT-pointed page.

The IDT register is typically loaded during system initialization and then is left alone. Since some system initialization is done while the 386 is in real mode, the LIDT instruction is permitted in real mode. In fact, the LIDT instruction provides the system programmer with the ability to move the interrupt table or change its limit and yet execute entirely in real mode. Furthermore, the "IDT Too Small" exception (impossible when the limit allows for all 256 interrupt handlers) can now occur in real mode. Since these features destroy compatibility with the 8086, it's unlikely that many system programmers will choose to use the LIDT instruction except in preparation for switching to protected mode. Including this ability in real mode, however, simplifies the 386 chip by making real and protected mode more alike. A similar rationale applies to the real mode Segment Overrun exception.

To maintain 8086 compatibility, the IDT register is initialized with a base address of zero and a limit of $256 \times 4 - 1 = 1023$. (Each entry in the 8086 interrupt table is four bytes long, and there are up to 256 different interrupt types.)

But enough of real mode, let's get back to protected mode.

Gates in the IDT   As shown in Figure 6.24, IDT entries in protected mode are gate descriptors. Using eight-byte descriptors rather than four-byte addresses (as is done in real mode) provides more flexibility in invoking interrupt handlers. Three types of gates are allowed in the IDT: trap gates, task gates, and interrupt gates. Trap and interrupt gates are new types of gates which are only allowed in the IDT. Their formats are shown in Figure 6.25. Which type of gate to use depends on the cause of the interrupt.

Trap gates are the standard kind of gate to use for *exceptions*. Exception-handling procedures referenced by trap gates are invoked in a manner identical to real mode, except that the interrupt-enable flag IF is left unchanged upon entry. This is exactly what we want in an exception handler, since we don't want exceptions within a task to turn off the operating system's time-slicing mechanism by ignoring timer interrupts.

Task gates are the standard kind of gate to use for *external interrupts*. Interrupt handlers referenced by task gates are invoked by a task call operation, as described in the section on multitasking. This is exactly what we want in dealing with interrupt signals from external devices, since typically, such signals aren't directed to the currently running task but to the 386 operating system as a whole. It's irrelevant which user's task happens to have the processor at the time the interrupt signal is received, so there's no point in running the interrupt handler as a procedure in some user's task.

If an interrupt-handling task runs with interrupts enabled, it may itself be interrupted by a device with a higher interrupt priority. The 386 task call mechanism ensures that this situation (nested task calls) is handled correctly. In fact, the main

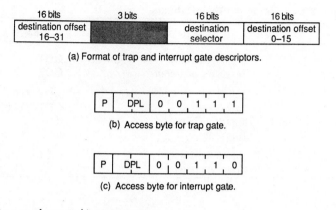

(a) Format of trap and interrupt gate descriptors.

(b) Access byte for trap gate.

(c) Access byte for interrupt gate.

Figure 6.25 Format of trap and interrupt gates.

reason the 386 provides task calling at all is to allow correct and efficient implementation of interrupt-handling tasks.

Task gates should also be used to handle exceptions that are so severe that the affected task can't support a procedure call (the Invalid TSS exception is an example). In this case, running the interrupt handler as a separate task provides the isolation needed to take effective action.

There are occasions when task gates shouldn't be used for external interrupts. If the interrupt handler consists of only a few instructions, then faster response can be obtained by using a trap gate or interrupt gate (defined shortly), which causes a fast procedure call rather than a task switch. The dispatch procedure described earlier in the chapter is an example. But if the interrupt handler is more than a few instructions, the difference in time between a procedure call and a task switch becomes negligible compared to the time spent in the body of the interrupt handler.

The final type of gate allowed in the IDT is an interrupt gate. Interrupt gates work the same as trap gates, except that they disable interrupts (clear IF) before calling the referenced interrupt procedure. So going through an interrupt gate in protected mode produces an effect similar to an interrupt in real mode. Thus interrupt gates may be used to provide compatibility with real mode. They can also be used in those cases where a task gate is undesirable, as previously indicated.

We have now discussed all the various types of descriptors and all the tables in which descriptors may appear. Table 6.6 lists the types of descriptors, shows where they are permitted, and indicates how the access byte identifies each type.

Protection Rules for Interrupts   How protection rules are applied to an interrupt depends on the source of the interrupt. The reason the source is considered is to prevent a malicious user's program from executing an INT instruction with a peripheral device's interrupt number, thus tricking the operating system into believing that the device has signaled an interrupt.

Table 6.6 Types of Descriptors and Their Habitats

Access Byte	Type of Descriptor	Where Found
***00010	Local Descriptor Table Segment	GDT
***000*1	Task State Segment	GDT
***0*100	Call Gate	GDT,LDT
***00101	Task Gate	GDT,LDT,IDT
***0*110	Interrupt Gate	IDT
***0*111	Trap Gate	IDT
10	Data Segment	GDT,LDT
11	Code Segment	GDT,LDT

* = 0 or 1

If the source of an interrupt is an INT instruction, then the usual rules of privilege apply: the gate may only be used if the INT instruction is executed from the ring containing the gate or from a lower numbered (more privileged) ring. So the operating system can protect IDT gates from being entered by unauthorized INT's. If the source of the interrupt isn't an INT instruction, then the gate may be entered from any ring. Thus exceptions and device interrupts, which may occur at any time and in any ring, are always correctly serviced.

There are some protection rules that apply no matter what the interrupt source is. In the case of a trap gate or interrupt gate, the interrupt procedure (as opposed to the gate) must be at least as privileged as the interrupted program, otherwise a protection exception occurs. This is the same restriction against upward calls that we saw when discussing call gates. No such restriction applies to task gates.

Since device interrupts can occur at any time, these rules imply that all device interrupt *procedures* must be in ring 0. This is another good reason for using task gates, rather than trap or interrupt gates, to handle device interrupts.

Error Codes   In protected mode, many of the 386 exceptions provide additional information (other than just the return address) to the exception handler. This information identifies the nature of the error. For these exceptions, the 386 pushes the return address followed by a 16-bit *error code* onto the stack just before entering the exception handler. In the case of a task gate, there's no return address, and only the error code is pushed.

There are two classes of error codes: *page-fault* error codes, pushed before page faults, and *segmentation* error codes, pushed before segmentation exceptions.

The format of a page-fault error code is shown in Figure 6.26a. If the page fault was caused by a violation of page protection, the *protection bit* (P) is set to 1; if the fault was caused by a not-present page, the protection bit is set to 0. The other two bits assist in the identification of a protection violation (but they are valid in the other case as well). The *user bit* (U) is set to 1 if the access causing the fault originated when the 386 was executing in user mode (privilege level 3); it is set to 0 otherwise. The *write bit* (W) is set to 1 if the access was a write operation; it is set to 0 if the access was a read operation.

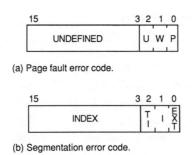

(a) Page fault error code.

(b) Segmentation error code.

Figure 6.26 Format of error codes.

The format of a segmentation error code is shown in Figure 6.26b. The error code indicates which segment or gate is the cause of the error. The error code looks like a selector, but the three bits that would be the RPL have a different interpretation.

If the *IDT bit* (I) of the error code is 1, the index refers to the IDT, rather than the GDT or LDT as in a normal selector. For example, if an interrupt indexes beyond the limit of the IDT, the error code produced will have I set to 1 and will contain the illegal index. If I is 0, then the descriptor table is determined by TI, as in a normal selector.

If the *external bit* (EXT) of the error code is 1, the interrupted instruction isn't responsible for generating the exception. For example, if a device interrupt causes a reference to a not-present segment, the error code will have EXT set to 1 and will select the segment descriptor that's marked not present. If EXT is 0, the fault lies with the interrupted instruction.

Protected Mode Reserved Interrupts   Table 6.7 lists all the reserved interrupts for 386 protected mode. The return address column tells where an exception handler's return address will point, relative to the faulty instruction. The error code column tells whether the interrupt produces an error code.

An exception is *restartable* if, after removing the cause of the exception, we can continue the program by re-executing the interrupted instruction. For example, a Divide Error is restartable because we can always increase the divisor and rerun the division instruction. On the other hand, if ADC (Add With Carry) writes into a read-only data segment, the resulting protection exception isn't restartable. ADC will obliterate the carry flag before it detects the exception. So if we make the segment writable and rerun the ADC, we'll get the wrong answer. Table 6.7 indicates which exceptions are restartable.

Restartability is most important in exceptions arising from not-present pages or segments. In a virtual memory system, such an exception is not an error, but rather the mechanism which triggers swapping; it causes the operating system to read the not-present page or segment into memory and continue the program. It's exceedingly difficult, if not impossible, to produce a reliable implementation of virtual memory on a computer where not-present exceptions aren't restartable.

Table 6.7 Protected Mode Reserved Interrupts

	Interrupt	Return Address	Restartable?	Error Code?
0	Divide Error	First byte of instr	Yes	No
1	Debug Exception	Depends on cause	Yes	No
2	Non-Maskable Interrupt	Not Applicable	Yes	No
3	Breakpoint	Next instr	Yes	No
4	Overflow	Next instr	Yes	No
5	Range Exceeded	First byte of instr	Yes	No
6	Invalid Opcode	First byte of instr	Yes	No
7	No Math Unit Available	First byte of instr	Yes	No
8	Double Fault	First byte of instr	No	Yes
9	Reserved	—	—	—
10	Invalid TSS	First byte of instr	Yes	Yes
11	Not Present	First byte of instr	Yes	Yes
12	Stack Exception	First byte of instr	No	Yes
13	Protection Exception	First byte of instr	No	Yes
14	Page Fault	First byte of instr	Yes	Yes
15	Reserved	—	—	—
16	Math Unit Exception	Next Floating-Point Instruction	No	No
17				
•				
•				
•	Reserved	—	—	—
31				

On the 386, not-present pages will always cause a Page Fault; not-present segments either cause a Not-Present Exception or a Stack Exception. Both the Page Fault and the Not-Present Exception are fully restartable, and the Stack Exception is restartable if it's caused by a not-present segment (there are other causes that aren't restartable). So the Stack Exception handler in a segment-oriented virtual-memory system must check the present (P) bit of the faulty stack segment's descriptor and transfer to the virtual memory manager if the stack segment isn't present (P = 0). If the stack segment is present, the Stack Exception handler can handle the exception on its own.

The only interrupts in Table 6.7 which haven't been discussed are the following:

Double Fault—This happens if an abnormal exception occurs while trying to invoke the handler for a previous exception. The possible previous exceptions are the segmentation exceptions (10, 11, 12, or 13) and the page-fault exception (14). It is normal for a page fault to occur within a segmentation exception handler, so that will not cause a double fault. It is *not* normal for a page fault to occur within the page-fault handler; the page-fault handler must never be swapped out. All other faults are considered abnormal when they occur in any of the above-listed handlers.

The double fault is a very serious exception. If a *third* exception occurs while trying to invoke the Double-Fault exception handler, the 386 enters *shutdown*. During shutdown, the 386 ceases activity and can only be awakened by a reset or a nonmaskable interrupt.

The purpose of this exception is to eliminate the possibility of infinite loops of interrupts. First, software is given a chance to break the loop (Double Fault). If software fails, then hardware takes over (shutdown). As bad as shutdown is, at least a shut-down 386 can respond to an emergency signaled by a nonmaskable interrupt. This might not be true in an infinite interrupt loop.

Stack Exception—This has two possible causes. One is a not-present stack segment (already discussed); the other is a stack overflow or underflow. This exception is restartable, except for some overflows caused by PUSHA and underflows caused by POPA. The problem is that these instructions push or pop multiple bytes of data, and some of these bytes may be successfully transferred before the overflow or underflow occurs. So if the instruction is re-executed, too much data may be pushed or popped in total.

System Initialization

If this were a book on the 8086, there would be no need for this section. For an 8086, it's only necessary to initialize the registers to execute a program. But we have seen that we must provide special tables in memory in order to execute programs in 386 protected mode, and we also must initialize many more registers. So in this section we describe some of the peculiarities and pitfalls of 386 initialization. The references at the end of this chapter contain sample initialization programs.

386 Reset   The 386 has an input pin called RESET that forces the 386 to its *reset* state, in which the 386 assumes that it has just been powered on. All circuits containing a 386 will assert RESET for a substantial fraction of a second when power is applied, to allow the power supply to stabilize to acceptable levels. Unlike its predecessors, the 386 recognizes this fact of life and does not automatically enter its reset state when powered on. In addition to the power-on circuitry, many 386 computers will have a (not too accessible!) button that allows the operator to reset the machine without powering down.

After reset, the 386 begins execution in real mode rather than protected mode for the following reason. Real mode is almost identical to the 8086, and like the 8086, it requires no prerequisites for executing a program. So we can set up all the tables and registers required for protected mode while we're still in real mode and then make the transition to protected mode. Thus, by having the 386 start up in real mode, we not only achieve compatibility with the 8086, but we also solve the architectural problem of how to initialize protected mode.

386 Component Testing   Most initialization code performs some amount of system testing, to verify the correct operation of system components such as memory and peripheral chips. The 386 augments this effort with an extensive series of component testing capabilities. Most of these capabilities are encompassed by the 386 *self-test*. Here's how it works:

1.   The system designer decides that self-test is a desirable feature and arranges the circuitry so that it takes place whenever a hardware reset is performed on the 386. This is accomplished by seeing to it that the BUSY input pin is active whenever the 386 RESET pin goes from inactive to active.

2.   Once it is wired that way, the 386 will flex its little electronic muscles for about a half-million clock cycles (1/32 of a second on a 16MHz machine) every time it is reset.

3.   The results of the self-test are left in the EAX register before the first instruction is executed. If EAX is zero, the test was a success. If EAX is nonzero, the test failed. All the initialization code needs to do is test EAX before its initial value is clobbered and report the failure if EAX is nonzero.

Another aid to component testing is the *test register* set, which allows access to the 386 paging mechanism's translation lookaside buffer (TLB). In the normal course of events, the buffer is invisible to the programmer; it is used by the paging mechanism to store recently used page-table entries. The test registers TR6 and TR7 provide a control mechanism for reading and writing to the translation lookaside buffer to see if it is working correctly.

To understand how the TR6 and TR7 registers work, we must know something about the internal workings of the TLB. The TLB is *four-way set associative*. When a linear page address is presented to the 386 paging mechanism, it has a function applied to it that has eight possible values (this kind of function is called a *hash* function). The function tells which four of the thirty-two TLB registers could possibly hold the matching page address. Then parallel circuitry determines, in one operation, if any of the four candidate registers has the matching address.

The format of TR6 and TR7 is shown in Figure 6.27. The 386 provides a special form of the MOV instruction to transfer values to or from any doubleword general register (for example, MOV EAX,TR6; MOV TR7,EDX). Using these special MOV instructions, we can either write an entry to the TLB buffer or look up an entry in the TLB buffer.

To write to the TLB buffer:

1.   Construct a value to move to TR7. The physical address we want stored goes into the top 20 bits. We set PL to 0 if we want the 386 to choose which of the four possible registers it will use; we set PL to 1 and REP to our choice if we want to choose which register to use.

2.   MOV the constructed value to TR7.

3. Construct a value to move to TR6. The C bit is 0, to signal that we are writing an entry. We set the V bit to 1 unless we wish to erase this TLB; in that case, we set V to 0 and don't bother with the remaining fields. The D, U, and W bits contain the values we desire for the Dirty bit and the high and low User Prot field bits, respectively. The D#, U#, and W# bits should be set to the opposite value as their non-# counterparts. The linear address field contains the linear address that we wish to look up. We must take care not to write the same linear address to two different registers, or else the lookup mechanism will become very confused.

4. MOV the constructed value to TR6.

   To look up a TLB entry:

1. Construct a value to move to TR6. The C bit is 1, to signal that we are reading an entry. The V bit must be 1, unless we are sure that there is only one empty register in the group, and we want to find that register. The D, U, and W bits are set to the values we require for the lookup to succeed, and the D#, U#, and W# bits are set to the opposite values. If any bit is a "don't-care" bit, we can signal that by setting both the # and non-# versions of the bit to 1. The linear address field contains the address we want to find.

2. MOV the constructed value to TR6.

3. MOV TR7 into a register to read the results. If the PL bit (mask 10 hexadecimal) is 1, the entry was found and the other bits contain the results. If PL is 0, the entry was not found and the other bits are undefined.

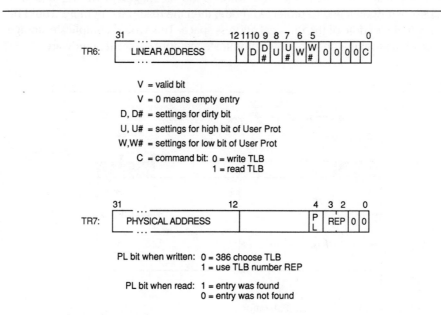

Figure 6.27 TR6 and TR7 registers.

The Initial Address Space   Figure 6.28 shows the initial values of the 386 SS, DS, ES, CS, and EIP registers. These define the initial real mode address space and the address of the first instruction to be executed. It's interesting to note that the initial values of SS, DS, and ES are zero in the 386 as in the 8086; they're zero in the 8086 for reasons of 8086 compatibility with the earlier 8080 processor.

A close look at Figure 6.28 should provoke you to ask the following questions:

The maximum physical address space in real mode is one megabyte, yet CS points to a segment occupying the top 64 kilobytes in a four-gigabyte address space. How can this be?

After reset, the 386 artificially appends 12 high-order 1-bits to every 20-bit address produced using CS. This produces the 32-bit address shown. This convention applies only to CS and not to the other segment registers. The 386 continues to do this until it executes an instruction that changes CS (for example, a far jump). Once CS is changed, high-order 1-bits are no longer appended, and the address space shrinks to the usual single megabyte.

That's bizarre! Why doesn't the 386 just use the 20-bit address and locate the code segment at the top 64 kilobytes of the usual real mode one-megabyte address space?

The CS register points to a segment containing the initialization program. The initialization program can't be stored in ordinary random-access memory because we want it to remain when the power is shut off. Memories allowing this are typically read-only. So if the 386 were to do as suggested above, and if it subsequently switched to protected mode, then the read-only memory would be stuck in the middle of the physical address space. This would complicate storage allocation programs and possibly complicate memory controller hardware.

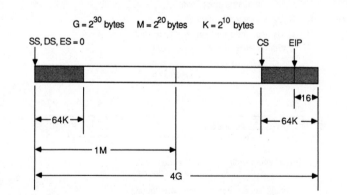

Figure 6.28 386 address space at initialization.

Well then, how about setting CS to zero and storing the initialization program at the low end of memory?

That's where the real mode interrupt table must be stored.

Okay. I'm convinced.

Detecting the Presence of a 287 or 387   In Chapter 4 we saw that the 386 provides a fair amount of flexibility for its floating-point coprocessor: it will accept either a 287 or a 387, or it can emulate the floating-point instruction set in software. It is necessary, however, for certain bits of the CR0 register to be set to appropriate values for correct floating-point operation to take place. If the coprocessor configuration is known at the time the initialization program is coded, then, of course, the appropriate values can simply be given as an immediate constant within the program. Most often, however, this is not the case. Most systems contain a socket for the coprocessor, which may or may not be filled. Some systems may have sockets for *both* the 287 and 387, for flexibility. (Two sockets are necessary because the 287 and 387 have a different number of pins, arranged differently. It would be disastrous, though, to fill both sockets at once!) So the most general initialization code must be able to tell if a coprocessor is present, and if it is, whether it is a 287 or 387.

The 387 was cleverly designed to assert the opposite signal (0) than the 287 does on the ERROR output pin when it is reset. The 386 checks its ERROR input when it is reset and automatically programs the *387 bit* of the CR0 register to reflect the result: 1 for the 387, 0 for the 287. What happens when there are no coprocessors installed? The system can, and should, be designed so that an unconnected input pin appears as a 1. Thus, the 387 bit will be set to 0. If there is no 287 socket in the system, then our initialization code needs to make no more tests; it knows that there is no coprocessor present.

If there is a 287 socket in the system, then we need a way to distinguish a 287 from an empty socket. We do this by trying some floating-point instructions. In particular, we execute an FNINIT instruction (with EM set to 0, of course) and then an FSTSW AX instruction. If a 287 is connected, then FNINIT will initialize the lower eight bits of the 287 Status register (the Exception Flags) to all 0's and FSTSW AX will set AX to the contents of the Status register. If the 287 socket connections are designed to Intel's specifications (see reference 9), then it's guaranteed that at least one of the lower eight bits of AX will be 1 after executing the above two instructions if the socket is empty.

In any case, it is up to our initialization software to set or clear the emulation mode (EM) and math present (MP) bits, according to the presence of a coprocessor. The 387 bit is the only bit set automatically for us.

Making the Transition to Protected Mode   The 386 is switched from real mode to protected mode by using either the LMSW (Load Machine Status Word) instruction or the MOV CR0,xxx instruction to load the machine status word with a word in which the protection enable (PE) bit is 1. Following are some peculiarities of this transition.

It's obvious that the transition should only be made after the appropriate registers (GDT register, IDT register, etc.) and tables (GDT, IDT, etc.) are initialized. What's not so obvious is that the initial GDT and task state segment shouldn't reside in read-only memory. This is because the 386 will try to set the accessed (A) bit in any segment descriptors it accesses and change the busy (B) bit in any task state segment descriptors it uses. So the initialization program should move these items from the initialization read-only memory into ordinary memory before using them in protected mode.

Before getting to the next peculiarity, we must make a digression. Recall from Chapter 4 that the 387 is divided into two portions (the Bus Interface Unit and the Numeric Execution Unit) that can operate independently of each other. The 386 is similarly divided into six units that operate concurrently. (See Figure 6.29.) The *Code Prefetch Unit* fetches instruction bytes in sequence and puts them on a waiting list, or *queue*. The *Instruction Decode Unit* takes instruction bytes from this queue, decodes them into an internal form, and puts these internal instructions into another queue. The *Execution Unit* executes these internal instructions. The *Segmentation Unit* converts selector-and-offset addresses into linear addresses. The *Paging Unit* converts linear addresses into physical addresses. The *Bus Interface Unit* fields bus access requests (memory and I/O ports) from the other units, prioritizes them, and turns them into sequences of signals on the 386's output pins.

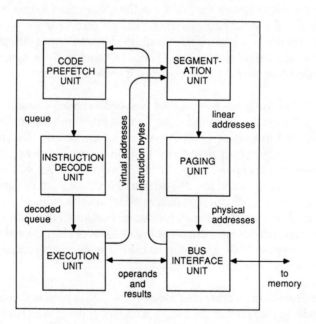

Figure 6.29 Functional units of the 386.

Dividing the 386 into units that operate concurrently greatly speeds 386 execution. Jump (or call) instructions are the hardest to handle. When the Execution Unit executes a jump to another location, it must tell the Code Prefetch and Instruction Decode Units to throw away all the instruction bytes they have queued, since these are the bytes following the jump instruction in memory. The Execution Unit then must wait until the first instruction at the jump's target address passes through each of the other five units before it can begin again. This is why a conditional jump on the 386 takes longer if the jump actually occurs.

Suppose we execute an LMSW instruction that switches the 386 to protected mode. After the Execution unit has finished executing the LMSW instruction, the queue of internal instructions will still contain internal instructions produced by the Instruction Decode Unit under the assumption that the 386 is in real mode. If these are used by the Execution Unit in protected mode, then incorrect results may be produced.

The solution is to follow the LMSW instruction with a near JMP instruction. This instruction will work correctly, despite the fact that it's decoded in real mode and executed in protected mode. It's not necessary to reinitialize CS; even an apparently useless JMP to the next instruction will do. The JMP will cause all the queues to be flushed and all subsequent instructions to be correctly decoded into protected mode internal instructions.

Making the Transition to Paged Mode   When the 386 is powered up, the paging mechanism is disabled; all linear addresses are passed directly to the output pins as physical addresses. Paging remains disabled as long as the *PG bit* of the CR0 register remains 0. If we do not want paging, we simply refrain from setting the PG bit. If we do want paging, we perform the following steps:

1.   We set up page tables and point CR3 to the page directory for those tables. The instructions that make the transition to paged mode must be within a page whose linear address maps to its physical address, or else a wild jump will occur when paged mode takes effect.

2.   We must insure that protected mode is entered either before or at the same time as paged mode. Paging is not available in real mode.

3.   We execute a MOV CR0,xxx instruction, where xxx has its PG bit (the top bit) set to 1.

4.   We flush the instruction prefetch queue with a seemingly spurious JMP instruction, just as we did when entering protected mode.

Making the Transition from Protected Mode Back to Real Mode   As we mentioned in Chapter 5, some systems might want to switch from protected mode back to real mode. We must be aware, however, that many of the features of protected mode are not disabled in real mode; they are instead configured to comply with real mode.

This eliminates the need, in many cases, for the 386 to check to see whether it is in real or protected mode. If we want to return to real mode, we must explicitly reset various tables and registers to values compatible with real mode. This is done as follows:

1. We insure that the code for the following steps has the following two properties:

    a. The code exists in a segment whose limit is exactly FFFF hexadecimal. This loads the CS register with the limit it needs to have in real mode.

    b. The code exists in a page whose linear address is identical to its physical address. This prevents a wild jump from occurring in the next step.

2. We disable paging by clearing the PG bit in CR0.

3. We set CR3 to zero to empty out the Translation Lookaside Buffer.

4. We load all segment registers except CS with a selector that points to a descriptor that specifies a byte granular, expand-up, writable, present segment, with a limit of FFFF hexadecimal. The selector's base value can be anything—the base is ignored in real mode.

5. We disable interrupts using the CLI instruction. If there is a possibility that a nonmaskable (NMI) interrupt could occur during this sequence, we must provide external circuitry to disable NMI under software control and engage that circuitry at this time.

6. We shift to real mode by clearing the PE bit of the CR0 register.

7. We insure that the code for the following steps is in the real mode memory space, and we use a far JMP to jump to that code. This flushes the instruction queue and puts appropriate values in the access rights of the CS register.

8. We use the LIDT instruction to load the base and limit of the real-mode interrupt vector table.

9. We re-enable interrupts by reversing the actions of step 5.

10. We load the segment registers as needed by the real-mode code.

End of the Intel Architecture

This finishes our discussion of the 386 and 387 architectures. We now move on to the next chapter and a discussion of an alternate numeric coprocessor offered by Weitek Corporation.

References

Except for the new features of paging and virtual 8086 mode, the 386's protection mechanism is nearly identical to the 286, so the more widely available base of 286 literature will suffice to supplement this chapter. This chapter is based on the equivalent chapter in reference 1. The main Intel-published reference is reference 2. The 286 protection mechanism was inspired by protection in the MULTICS operating system, as described in references 3 and 4. Reference 5 is devoted to security kernels. The article by Roger Schell is most relevant. For a general introduction to operating systems, see reference 6. For details on the wiring of 386 systems, see reference 7.

1. S.P. Morse and D.J. Albert, *The 80286 Architecture*, John Wiley and Sons, New York, 1986.

2. *iAPX 386 Programmer's Reference Manual*, Intel Corp., 1986.

3. R. M. Graham, "Protection in an Information Processing Utility," *Communications of the ACM*, vol. 11, no. 5, May, 1968, 365–369.

4. M. D. Schroeder and J. H. Saltzer, "A Hardware Architecture for Implementing Protection Rings," *Communications of the ACM*, vol. 15, no. 3, March, 1972, 157–170.

5. *Computer*, vol. 16, no. 7, July, 1983.

6. A. M. Lister, *Fundamentals of Operating Systems*, Springer-Verlag, New York, 1984.

7. *80386 Hardware Reference Manual*, Intel Corporation, 1986.

CHAPTER

7

HIGH-SPEED FLOATING-POINT COMPUTATION

Some applications require so much floating-point arithmetic that the 387, even though fast, becomes the "bottleneck" of the system. To solve this problem, some companies provide special circuits for floating-point processing that are faster than the 387 can provide. One such circuit, the WTL 1167 floating-point coprocessor board by Weitek (pronounced "Way-tek") Corporation, is designed specifically for the 386. The Weitek board has fewer instructions than the 387, but it is several times as fast. Even the functions not provided by the Weitek instruction set can be executed more quickly as skillfully coded Weitek subroutines than as individual 387 instructions! The 387 and the Weitek board have different programmatic interfaces, so that we can construct a system containing both coprocessors. This chapter presents a programmatic description of the Weitek coprocessor. We first describe the Weitek registers and instruction set, and then we describe the somewhat convoluted way the 386 accesses those resources. Finally, we program an example on both the 387 and the Weitek board and compare performance.

Weitek Registers

Data Registers The Weitek coprocessor has a whopping 31 data registers, each 32 bits in length. The registers are numbered 1 through 31. You might ask why there isn't a register number 0. The answer is that 0 is used to specify an operand residing outside the Weitek coprocessor; that is, in memory or in the 386. We show how this works when we talk about the 386 interface later on.

We can calculate and store numbers in these registers in any of three formats:

1. A single-precision floating-point number can occupy any one register. The format is exactly the same as the 387's single-precision number described in Chapter 4.

2. A double-precision floating-point number can occupy any two consecutive registers as long as the register number of the first register is even. Again, the format is the same as the corresponding 387 number, except that two doublewords are switched from the 387 storage convention; the most significant doubleword occupies the first (even-numbered) register, and the least significant doubleword occupies the next (odd-numbered) register. For example, we can store a double-precision number in registers 4 and 5 and specify that register pair as an operand to a Weitek arithmetic instruction. We could not use registers 5 and 6 as a double-precision operand, because the first register number (5) is odd. (If we tried, we would get erroneous results with no error reported.)

3. There are instructions for converting floating-point numbers to or from a 32-bit integer format. There is nothing to prevent us from storing these integer forms in Weitek registers. Unlike the 387, however, the Weitek coprocessor cannot use such forms directly in floating-point arithmetic.

Note that the 80-bit extended-precision format used by the 387 is not available on the Weitek coprocessor. Remember that extended precision was provided to protect intermediate results arising from the computation of functions over double-precision numbers. Since speed is the most important consideration for Weitek users, Weitek does not indulge in the luxury of extended precision. Weitek users must be more careful about loss of precision in floating-point calculations than their pampered 387 brethren.

The Process Context Register In addition to the data registers there is a single 32-bit *process context register* (CTX). CTX can be written to set the various control flags of the Weitek coprocessor; it can also be read to save or examine the control settings and also to read various status flags. Figure 7.1 shows the format of CTX.

The uppermost byte of CTX is the *mode field*. Five of the bits in the mode field are fixed, as shown in the figure (except during initialization, as we describe later). The other three bits control rounding. The two-bit RND field offers the same rounding options that the 387 offers. The IRND flag offers an option not available on the 387: by setting it we can specify that floating-to-integer conversions round towards zero (chop), no matter what the RND field specifies.

The next-highest byte of CTX is the *exception mask field*. The bits of this field work the same as the exception mask bits of the 387 control word: setting a mask bit to 0 will cause the Weitek to generate a 386 interrupt when the corresponding exception occurs. Setting a mask bit to 1 inhibits the interrupt and causes the coprocessor to return an exception value, allowing the program to continue its calculations. Most of the exceptions have the same names and work the same way as 387 exceptions. There are a few differences in the list of exceptions:

1. The 387 has a denormalized operand exception, and the Weitek coprocessor does not. In the Weitek, denormalized inputs to all arithmetic operations are quietly assumed to be zero. Denormalized outputs are also quietly converted to zero.

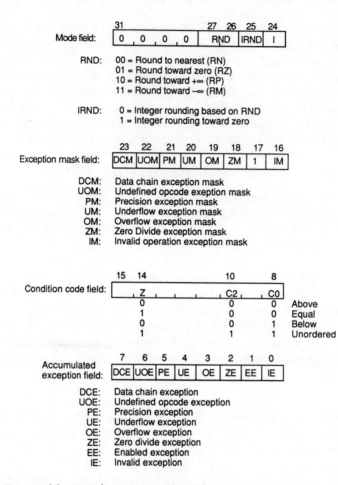

Figure 7.1 Format of the Weitek process context register.

(This is the "fast" mode of the floating-point standard; it also duplicates the way things are done on recent minicomputers and mainframes such as the DEC and Cray-1 computers.)

2. The Weitek has an *undefined opcode exception*, invoked when the 386 program attempts to execute a nonexistent instruction in the Weitek space. We'll see how that can happen when we discuss the 386 interface.

3. The Weitek has a *data chain exception*. Like the undefined opcode exception, this exception can occur only in a misprogrammed instruction sequence. In this case, the exception sometimes arises when the program attempts to interpret the data in its registers incorrectly—either taking a single-precision number as half of a double-precision number, or vice versa. We say "sometimes" because this error is detected only in special circumstances. The Weitek does not, in general, keep

track of which types of numbers are in which of its registers. It could not do so because the loading of a double-precision number from the 386 is indistinguishable from the loading of two single-precision numbers. But the Weitek *does* keep track of number types in its internal data bus. Furthermore, the Weitek has a feature called *data chaining* that optimizes the transfer of data within its internal bus. We'll say more about data chaining later. For now, we'll just say that if a data-chained operand is interpreted incorrectly (single for double, or double for single), the Weitek processor raises the data chain exception.

The third-highest byte of CTX is the *condition code field*, set by the Weitek during its compare and test instructions. These bits are arranged in the same way as the corresponding bits of the 387, so that we can load the condition codes into the 386 flags register in the same way. We show an example later.

The lowest byte of CTX is the *accumulated exception field* that works similarly to the exception bits of the 387's status register. The field contains one bit for each of the seven Weitek exception types. If any exception, masked or unmasked, occurs, the corresponding bit is set to 1. The bit remains 1 until it is explicitly cleared. Just as with the 387, a program can mask a given exception, and then wait until the end of a long computational sequence to check for the occurrence of that exception. Or the exception can be unmasked, and the bit can be used by the exception handler to identify the type of exception that occurred. In the unmasked case, the handler *must* clear the exception bit, because the bit actually controls the generation of interrupts to the 386. If the bit is not cleared, another exception will occur immediately after the Weitek interrupt is re-enabled.

There is one bit in the accumulated exception field, the *exception enabled bit* (EE), that does not reflect the status of an individual exception. It is analogous to the 387's error summary (ES) bit and is set to 1 whenever *any* unmasked exception occurs. Like the other bits, it must be cleared explicitly by the exception handler to avoid an immediate second interrupt.

The Weitek Instruction Set

Table 7.1 shows the instruction set of the Weitek coprocessor. You can see from the table that we are providing a new syntax for the operands to the instructions. Almost every instruction has exactly two operands (even if one of them is the constant zero), the operands are enclosed in brackets, and they are separated by a backslash instead of a comma. We shall explain our curious behavior when we describe the 386 interface.

Note also that we are providing our own mnemonics for these instructions. The table shows Weitek's mnemonics, so that you can follow reference 1 along with this chapter. Weitek's mnemonics have a syntax that would be difficult for most 386 assemblers to digest. We have selected our mnemonics for clarity and for conformity with 387 mnemonics. We have also reversed the order of operands from that given in Weitek literature to conform to Intel's standard (destination first, source last).

Table 7.1 The Weitek Instruction Set

Instruction	Description	Weitek Mnemonic
Data Movement Instructions		
W_LOAD[L \R]	L = R	LOAD
W2_LOAD[L \R]	L = R	LOAD
W_STOR[L \0]	386 data = L	STOR
W2_STOR[L \0]	386 data = L	STOR
W_LOADCTX	Process Context Register = 386 data	LDCTX
W_STORCTX	386 data = Process Context Register	STCTX
Data Conversion Instructions		
WS_FLOAT[L \R]	L = integer R	FLOAT.S
WD_FLOAT[L \R]	L,L + 1 = integer R	FLOAT.D
WS_FIX[L \R]	integer L = R	FIX.S
WD_FIX[L \R]	integer L = R,R + 1	FIX.D
W_SINGLE[L \R]	L = R,R + 1	CVTS.D
W_DOUBLE[L \R]	L,L + 1 = R	CVTD.S
Dyadic Arithmetic and Comparison Instructions		
WS_ADD[L \R]	L = R + L	ADD.S
WD_ADD[L \R]	L,L + 1 = R,R + 1 + L,L + 1	ADD.D
WS_SUBR[L \R]	L = R − L	SUB.S
WD_SUBR[L \R]	L,L + 1 = R,R + 1 − L,L + 1	SUB.D
WS_MUL[L \R]	L = R * L	MUL.S
WD_MUL[L \R]	L,L + 1 = R,R + 1 * L,L + 1	MUL.D
WS_MULN[L \R]	L = − (R * L)	MULN.S
WD_MULN[L \R]	L,L + 1 = − (R,R + 1 * L,L + 1)	MULN.D
WS_AMUL[L \R]	L = |R| * |L|	AMUL.S
WD_AMUL[L \R]	L,L + 1 = |R,R + 1| * |L,L + 1|	AMUL.D
WS_DIVR[L \R]	L = R / L	DIV.S
WD_DIVR[L \R]	L,L + 1 = R,R + 1 / L,L + 1	DIV.D
WS_COMR[L \R]	compare R − L	CMPT.S
WD_COMR[L \R]	compare R,R + 1 − L,L + 1	CMPT.D
WS_UCOMR[L \R]	unordered compare R − L	CMP.S
WD_UCOMR[L \R]	unordered compare R,R + 1 − L,L + 1	CMP.D
Monadic Arithmetic and Comparison Instructions		
WS_NEG[L \R]	L = − R	NEG.S
WD_NEG[L \R]	L,L + 1 = − R,R + 1	NEG.D
WS_ABS[L \R]	L = |R|	ABS.S
WD_ABS[L \R]	L,L + 1 = |R,R + 1|	ABS.D
WS_TESTR[1 \R]	compare R − 0	TSTT.S
WD_TESTR[1 \R]	compare R,R + 1 − 0	TSTT.D
WS_UTESTR[1 \R]	unordered compare R − 0	TST.S
WD_UTESTR[1 \R]	unordered compare R,R + 1 − 0	TST.D
Triadic Arithmetic Instructions		
WS_MULADD[L \R]	add R * L into register 2	MAC.S
WD_MULADD[L \R]	add R * L into registers 2,3	MACD.S

Most of the operations supported by Weitek come in two flavors: one for single-precision operands and one for double-precision operands. In such cases, we distinguish the flavors by starting the single-precision mnemonic with WS_ and the double-precision mnemonic with WD_. Also, we emphasize the double-precision operands in the description column of the table by giving register pairs: L,L+1 for a left-hand double-precision operand; R,R+1 for a right-hand double-precision operand. For example, WD_ADD[4 \6] adds the register pair 6,7 into the register pair 4,5.

Data Movement Instructions   These instructions move doublewords between the 386 and the Weitek and also between single registers of the Weitek. All the instructions in this group work on 32 bits at a time—there are no instructions for moving 64-bit double precision numbers.

W_LOAD[L \R] is the workhorse of the group, allowing movement from any Weitek register to any other Weitek register. By selecting R = 0, we can move data from the 386 to any Weitek register. You might also think that by selecting L = 0, we could move data from a Weitek register to the 386. Unfortunately, there is an addressing problem that prevents this from working correctly. Instead, there is the W_STOR[L \0] instruction, which moves data from Weitek register L to the 386. Later, in the 386 interface section, we'll describe why W_LOAD[L \0] misbehaves, and we'll see that the W_STOR form allows us to store a whole block of Weitek registers into 386 memory with a single block-move instruction.

We hope that by now you're intensely curious about the 386 interface section! Let us pique your curiosity further by stating that W2_LOAD and W2_STOR are functionally identical to W_LOAD and W_STOR. They are provided for speed optimization, as we describe in (you guessed it!) the 386 interface section.

Finally, W_LOADCTX and W_STORCTX are provided to move data to and from the Process Context Register.

Data Conversion Instructions   Weitek provides instructions for converting data from any one of the three data types supported (single, double, and 32-bit integer) to any other type. There are six instructions, one for each combination:

WS_FLOAT	for integer → single
WD_FLOAT	for integer → double
WS_FIX	for single → integer
W_DOUBLE	for single → double
WD_FIX	for double → integer
W_SINGLE	for double → single

Dyadic Arithmetic and Comparison Instructions   Each of the four simple arithmetic functions is available. To save hardware in the Weitek controller chip, the subtraction and division instructions had to come in reversed form; WS_SUBR and WD_SUBR subtract the destination operand from the source, just as FSUBR does on the 387. Similarly, WS_DIVR and WD_DIVR divide the source operand by the destination, just as FDIVR does on the 387. To atone for the inconvenience this might cause, Weitek provides extra multiplication functions: WS_AMUL and WD_AMUL give the absolute value of a product, and WS_MULN and WD_MULN give the negative of a product. The MULN function is particularly effective in alleviating the inconvenience of reversed subtraction. For example, the determinant of a matrix is a sequence of sums and differences of matrix-entry products. If we use MULN to calculate those products that are subtracted, then we can simply add all the terms and not worry about the order of operands.

There are also operations for comparing two floating-point numbers to tell whether the first is greater, the numbers are equal, the second is greater, or the numbers are unordered (one or both is a NaN). The condition code field is set as in Figure 7.1. Again to save hardware, the Weitek uses a reversed subtraction to make the comparison. This means that the comparison result applies to the *right* operand, not the left operand. Just as with the 387, we can choose our instruction according to whether we wish an exception to be generated in the unordered case. WS_UCOMR and WD_UCOMR produce no exception if the result is "unordered"; WS_COMR and WD_COMR produce an invalid operation exception if the result is "unordered."

Monadic Arithmetic and Comparison Instructions   There are two functions provided, negation and absolute value, that need just one input operand. On the 387, these functions always place the answer in the same location as the input. Since the Weitek instruction form always has two operands, there is no extra cost in allowing the output to be different than the input. So WS_NEG and WD_NEG set the left operand to the negative of the right operand, and WS_ABS and WD_ABS set the left operand to the absolute value of the right operand. Of course, we can make the left and right operands the same, yielding the same functionality as the corresponding 387 instructions.

The test instructions WS_TESTR, WD_TESTR, WS_UTESTR, and WD_UTESTR are identical to the comparison instructions, except that the right operand is compared to the constant zero, not to the left operand. In these instructions, the left operand field is ignored.

Triadic Arithmetic Instructions   There are two special-purpose instructions that act on three operands. These are the multiply-and-accumulate instructions WS_MULADD and WD_MULADD. The two source operands are given explicitly; the instruction multiplies the operands together and adds the result into the implicitly fixed destination: register 2 for WS_MULADD, registers 2 and 3 for WD_MULADD.

Notice that WD_MULADD's inputs are single-precision numbers. The product is computed as a double-precision number and added into registers 2 and 3. This is the only arithmetic instruction that retains the extra digits produced when numbers are multiplied. All the other WD_ instructions take double-precision inputs to produce their double-precision result.

The 386 Interface

Now comes the moment we've been waiting for—when we see how the Weitek coprocessor interfaces with the 386. To understand why the interface was designed that way it is, we must consider the problem Weitek has as an outside manufacturer wishing to make a coprocessor. Where do the Weitek opcodes fit in the 386 opcode space? The vastly different register structure of the Weitek precludes using the 387 opcode space for Weitek instructions. The few unused slots are reserved by Intel. If Weitek somehow used those slots, Weitek software would almost certainly be incompatible with future 86-family processors.

The solution is to make the Weitek board a *memory-mapped* device. This means that the system designer must set aside a chunk of the 386's memory space to be occupied by the device. Memory-mapped devices look like memory to the 386 but actually aren't. Any memory access by the 386 to the device's memory chunk is a signal to the device to take some sort of action. In this case, the size of the reserved memory chunk is 65536 bytes, and the action to be taken depends on which of the 65536 possible addresses is given. The designer will typically locate the Weitek board's memory chunk near the top of the 386's four-gigabyte memory space just below the initialization read-only memory. Let's play designer and assume that we have set aside a megabyte, FFF0 0000 through FFFF FFFF hexadecimal, for read-only memory. We can wire the Weitek board to occupy the 64K bytes just below ROM: from FFEF 0000 through FFEF FFFF.

Now that we have wired our Weitek board, let's consider how the 386 views that board. Suppose that the 386 tries to write a doubleword to the Weitek memory area. This means that the 386 will supply the Weitek board with an address (in the Weitek area) and 32 bits of data to write. If the Weitek board were a memory board, it would use the address to determine *where to put* the data. But instead, the Weitek board interprets the address as an instruction telling it *what to do with* the data (load it into some register, add it to a register, ignore it, etc.).

Similarly, suppose that the 386 tries to read a doubleword from the Weitek memory area. The 386 will supply an address within the Weitek area and will expect the Weitek board to respond with 32 bits of data. Again, the Weitek board will interpret the address not as an ordinary memory address, but as an instruction telling how to get the data (for example, by storing one of the Weitek registers).

Figure 7.2 shows how the Weitek board views a 32-bit address. The top 16 bits identify the address as falling within the Weitek's memory area. If the top bits don't match the value we assigned (FFEF), the memory access is not a Weitek command, so it is ignored by the Weitek board. The next 6 bits identify which Weitek command is to

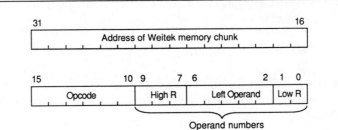

Figure 7.2 Format of a Weitek memory address.

be executed. The bottom 10 bits identify the operands to the command—5 bits for the 32 possible values of the left operand, and 5 bits for the same number of values for the right operand. We'll see shortly why the right-operand field is split up the way it is. If an operand refers to the nonexistent register 0, the 32 bits of data supplied by the 386 (when writing) or expected by the 386 (when reading) are used as the operand.

Describing a Weitek Instruction in 386 Assembly Language   Table 7.2 shows the various six-bit opcode combinations for the Weitek instructions. Also shown is the hexadecimal value that the opcodes produce when they are placed into the six-bit field of the memory address. If we provide a memory address whose opcode field does not match one of the values in the table, we'll get an undefined opcode exception, as mentioned earlier.

Let's now see how we can execute the instruction WS_MUL[3 \0] in our sample system. This instruction multiplies a 386-supplied operand into register 3. To perform the multiplication, we need to do two things:

1.   We need to provide the Weitek board with the address within Weitek's 64K-byte memory chunk corresponding to WS_MUL[3 \0]. The base of the memory chunk is FFEF0000. To this we add 0800, shown in Table 7.2 for the WS_MUL instruction. Finally, we place the values 3 and 0 into the operand fields, which adds another 000C to the total. The address we want is FFEF800C.

2.   We need to supply the single-precision value that the Weitek board will multiply into its register 3. Since data is transmitted by the 386 during memory write operations, we need to make a memory write to the Weitek location FFEF800C. So we load any 386 doubleword register with the floating-point number to be multiplied and MOV that register into the Weitek memory location. Since a MOV from EAX to memory results in the shortest 386 opcode, let's use EAX. The WS_MUL[3 \0] instruction is thus:

        MOV [0FFEF800CH], EAX

The above instruction form is not very desirable for real program code, as it completely disguises the fact that a floating-point multiplication is taking place, as well as disguising the destination operand to the multiplication. We can improve things quite a bit by providing a list of Weitek EQUate directives at the top of our program. We define the location of the Weitek chunk within our system:

        WEITEK EQU 0FFEF0000H

Then we provide a list of EQU directives, one for each Weitek mnemonic. Each directive would use the hexadecimal value found in Table 7.2. Thus the directive for WS_MUL would be:

        WS_MUL EQU WEITEK + 0800

Table 7.2 Opcodes for Weitek Instructions

Mnemonic	Binary Opcode	Hex Offset	Mnemonic	Binary Opcode	Hex Offset
WS_ADD	000000	0000	WD_ADD	100000	8000
W_LOAD	000001	0400	W2_LOAD	100001	8400
WS_MUL	000010	0800	WD_MUL	100010	8800
W_STOR	000011	0C00	W2_STOR	100011	8C00
WS_SUBR	000100	1000	WD_SUBR	100100	9000
WS_DIVR	000101	1400	WD_DIVR	100101	9400
WS_MULN	000110	1800	WD_MULN	100110	9800
WS_FLOAT	000111	1C00	WD_FLOAT	100111	9C00
WS_COMR	001000	2000	WD_COMR	101000	A000
WS_TESTR	001001	2400	WD_TESTR	101001	A400
WS_NEG	001010	2800	WD_NEG	101010	A800
WS_ABS	001011	2C00	WD_ABS	101011	AC00
WS_UCOMR	001100	3000	WD_UCOMR	101100	B000
WS_UTESTR	001101	3400	WD_UTESTR	101101	B400
WS_AMUL	001110	3800	WD_AMUL	101110	B800
WS_FIX	001111	3C00	WD_FIX	101111	BC00
W_SINGLE	010000	4000	W_LOADCTX	110000	C000
W_DOUBLE	010001	4400	W_STORCTX	110001	C400
WS_MULADD	010010	4800	WD_MULADD	110010	C800

In a relocatable assembler, such as Intel's 386 assembler, we might wish to define WEITEK as a relocatable segment and the individual mnemonics, such as WS_MUL, as variables having the indicated hexadecimal offsets within the segment. This allows the location of the Weitek memory chunk to be determined when the program is fed to the linker, allowing the same source code to work for differently configured systems.

Having defined the Weitek mnemonics, we can now transform our instruction into the more readable:

          MOV WS_MUL[000C],EAX

which unfortunately still disguises the values of the Weitek operands. Here we need a little help from our assembler. If a 386 assembler wants to optimally support Weitek code, it should provide an expression arithmetic operator, which we'll call \ , that combines numbers to its left and right by placing them into the Weitek operand fields shown in Figure 7.2. If we have such an operator, we can write:

          MOV WS_MUL[3 \0],EAX

which reveals (at last!) why we have been using our strange notation for Weitek operands.

If our assembler does not provide the \ operator, it might instead provide a macro facility powerful enough to let us define an in-line macro that duplicates the functionality.

For example, in Intel's assembler, the macro definition would be:

```
%*DEFINE(WT(L,R))(
      [(L * 4) + (R MOD 4) + SHL(R/4,7)]
)
```

and our WS_MUL instruction would be the slightly more cumbersome:

```
MOV WS_MUL @WT(3,0),EAX
```

Specifying Register-to-Register Instructions   Now that we have worked out a good 386 assembly language notation for Weitek instructions, let's try some other instruction forms. How, for example, do we code a Weitek instruction that does not involve a 386 operand? An example of such an instruction would be WD_SUBR[4\18], which subtracts the double-precision register pair 4,5 from pair 18,19 and leaves the result in 4,5. Here we want to code a memory access to the appropriate location in the Weitek space, knowing that the Weitek will neither receive nor send any data to the 386. We could specify a memory read, but if we did, the 386 destination register for our read would be filled with garbage, because the Weitek board won't respond with any data. To avoid this, we specify another memory write operation. The 386 will transmit an operand, which the Weitek board will cheerfully ignore. Since no data is actually being transferred to or from the 386, we can make the operation a byte transfer from any register we wish. Thus we can code:

```
MOV WD_SUBR[4\18],AL
```

At this point a warning is in order. We have coded the above instruction as a byte transfer not only for efficiency but also out of necessity. To understand this, let's consider what would happen if we instead coded a doubleword form MOV WD_SUBR[4\18],EAX. In our sample system, the WD_SUBR would correspond to memory location FFEF9000. The \ function splits the binary encoding of 18 (10010) into 100 and 10, and inserts the code for 4. We get 100 00100 10, which is hexadecimal 112. Thus our instruction appears to the 386 as a doubleword write to memory location FFEF9112; but FFEF9112 is not aligned on a doubleword boundary. When doubleword operands aren't aligned, the 386 makes two memory write operations, as shown in Figure 7.3. First it will write the bottom half of EAX to the top half of FFEF9110; then it will write the top half of EAX to the bottom half of FFEF9114. The Weitek board will misinterpret this as two consecutive floating-point instructions, instead of the one WD_SUBR that was intended. So we must always be very careful to code *byte*, not doubleword, transfers for our register-to-register instructions.

Specifying the 386 as the Destination   We can now start to appreciate why the operand fields are laid out as they are within a memory address and also to appreciate why the W_STOR instruction is necessary. When a 386 operand (register number 0) is specified as the source (right-hand) operand to a Weitek instruction, the associated

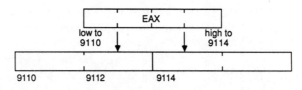

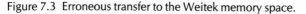

Figure 7.3 Erroneous transfer to the Weitek memory space.

memory address will always be a multiple of four, since the right-operand field is zero. This means that we can get away with specifying a doubleword memory transfer, without having to be afraid that the transfer will be split into two memory accesses. We cannot, however, specify a 386 operand as the left-hand operand to an instruction, because if the right-hand register number were not a multiple of four, we would have our double-access problem. For example, MOV EAX,W_LOAD[0 \1] doesn't work. We must instead code:

MOV EAX,W_STOR[1 \0]

For the same reason, we cannot specify a 386 operand as the destination to any of the Weitek arithmetic functions; WS_ADD[0 \3], for example, would not work. You might think you could get around the problem by cleverly specifying a register number that is a multiple of four; for example, WS_ADD[0 \8]. But even this won't work: the execution of the addition requires the Weitek to first input the value from the 386, add its register 8 into it, and then output the result back to the 386. From the 386's point of view, this looks like a "write then read" operation, something that the 386 is not prepared to handle in just one memory access. An extremely canny assembler will issue an error message if a \ operator has a left operand of zero.

Block Moves of Weitek Numbers   We still haven't indicated why the right-hand operand's field is split up in the Weitek memory address. After all, we could have satisfied the multiple-of-four requirement simply by having the right-hand operand occupy the lower five bits of the address. The reason it's not done that way involves the 386 block-move instruction. Suppose we have an array of numbers that we would like to load into consecutive Weitek registers. This will happen, for example, if we are restoring the Weitek machine state for an individual task within a multitasking operating system. The numbers are located in the array WEITEK_VALUES, which contains 31 doublewords. We can code the following:

```
MOV ECX,31                    ; load the number of registers in the array
MOV ESI,WEITEK_ARRAY          ; source points to the array in memory
MOV EDI,OFFSET W_LOAD[1 \0]   ; destination points to Weitek space
REP MOVSD                     ; values are copied to the Weitek space
```

Each repetition of MOVSD adds four to the destination pointer EDI. The left-operand field is cleverly located so that adding four to EDI adds one to the left-operand register number. So successive MOVSDs cause successive Weitek registers to be loaded. We can similarly copy data from the Weitek registers to 386 memory by using W_STOR:

```
MOV ECX,31                        ; load the number of registers in the array
MOV ESI,OFFSET W_STOR[1 \0]       ; source points to Weitek space
MOV EDI,WEITEK_ARRAY              ; destination points to the array in memory
REP MOVSD                         ; registers are copied to 386 memory
```

Interaction between the 387 and the Weitek Board   Some interesting possibilities arise in systems containing both a 387 and a Weitek board. Recall from Chapter 4 that many 387 instructions apply directly to 386 memory. If we apply such instructions to the Weitek part of the 386 space, we can obtain some direct interactions between the 387 and the Weitek board. For example, the following instructions transfer single-precision numbers directly between the 387's ST(0) register and Weitek registers:

```
FST W_LOAD[3 \0]      ; move ST(0) to Weitek register 3
FSTP W_LOAD[10 \0]    ; move ST(0) to Weitek register 10, and pop 387 stack
FLD W_STOR[19 \0]     ; push Weitek register 19 onto the 387 stack
```

We can even perform arithmetic on one coprocessor, using operands directly from the other coprocessor's register set. Examples:

```
FADD W_STOR[6 \0]     ; add Weitek register 6 into ST(0)
FCOM W_STOR[15 \0]    ; compare ST(0) to Weitek register 15 (flags in 387)
FDIV W_STOR[1 \0]     ; divide ST(0) by Weitek register 1
FST WS_ADD[4 \0]      ; add ST(0) into Weitek register 4
FST WS_MUL[9 \0]      ; multiply ST(0) into Weitek register 9
FST WS_COMR[15 \0]    ; compare ST(0) to Weitek register 15 (flags in Weitek)
```

Unfortunately, these direct transfers work only for single-precision operands. Because Weitek stores the high doubleword of a double-precision number first, the two doublewords must be switched when they go from one coprocessor to the other. So although we can code and execute the double-precision forms of the examples we just gave, the results will be wrong because the instructions won't switch the doublewords.

Memory Pages in the Weitek Space   There is one last mystery we promised to solve in this section—why there are instructions W2_LOAD and W2_STOR identical to W_LOAD and W_STOR. This is a performance embellishment having to do with the 386's paging mechanism. Recall from Chapter 6 that the 386 maintains a Translation Lookaside Buffer (TLB) to keep track of recently accessed memory pages, so that the 386 doesn't need to walk through its page directories every time it makes a memory access. The assumption in the TLB's design is that consecutive memory fetches will be limited to just a few memory pages. This assumption breaks down a bit in the Weitek space. What appears to the 386 as a 4096-byte memory page is in reality just four different Weitek instructions with all the various operand combinations. If there is too great a mix of different Weitek instructions in a code sequence, the capacity of the TLB is strained, degrading performance. Weitek tries to alleviate this potential problem by lumping the four most common functions, LOAD, STOR, ADD, and MUL, into the same memory page. However, ADD and MUL come in two flavors: WS_ADD and WS_MUL for single-precision numbers, and WD_ADD and WD_MUL for double-precision numbers. So two sets of LOAD and STOR instructions are provided: one to share a memory page with WS_ADD and WS_MUL, and the other to share a page with WD_ADD and WD_MUL. If your program concentrates on single-precision arithmetic, use W_LOAD and W_STOR; if it concentrates on double, use W2_LOAD and W2_STOR. By doing this, you might save some clock cycles in the 386's paging overhead.

Double Precision and 386 Operands   You might wonder what happens when a double-precision instruction is attempted that specifies a 386 source operand. Since the 386 can transfer only 32 bits at a time, it cannot yield the entire operand. The answer is that the Weitek board simplistically assumes that the operand is the register pair 0,1. Thus, the upper half of the operand is taken from the 386, and the lower half is taken from Weitek's register number 1. For example, we can execute the following code to multiply the number given in variables UPPER and LOWER in 386 memory into register pair 30,31 of the Weitek:

```
MOV EAX,LOWER                ; fetch the lower half
MOV W2_LOAD[1 \0],EAX        ; move the lower half into register 1
MOV EAX,UPPER                ; fetch the upper half
MOV WD_ADD[30 \0],EAX        ; add the (UPPER,LOWER) pair into 30,31
```

By cleverly providing the special 0,1 register pair, Weitek allows us to achieve the optimal performance from the 386's 32-bit data path, even when the data doesn't fit into 32 bits.

Note that we took our own advice given in the last section and used W2_LOAD, to keep both Weitek memory references within the same 386 page.

Loading Comparison Results into 386 Flags   Recall from Chapter 4 the problem we face with conditional jumping based on floating-point comparisons: the 386 is doing the jumping, but the coprocessor contains the condition codes. We solve this problem in the same tricky way with the Weitek that we do with the 387: we copy the condition codes to the AH register, then use the obscure SAHF instruction to move the codes into the 386 flags. The condition codes have been cleverly positioned within Weitek's CTX register so that they fill AH when we move CTX into EAX. For example, suppose we wish to compare register pair 20,21 to register pair 8,9. We execute the following instruction sequence:

```
MOV WD_UCOMR[8 \ 20],AL    ; perform comparison 20,21 − 8,9
MOV EAX,W_STORCTX[0]       ; copy Weitek's CTX to the 386's EAX
SAHF                       ; copy condition codes to the 386's flags
```

We follow the sequence just given with one or more conditional jump instructions that act on the flag settings just loaded. If the 386's parity flag (P) is set, the result of the comparison was "unordered." If not, we can treat the Carry and Zero flags as if an unsigned integer comparison was just made. Remember that the comparison was R − L, so the mnemonics Above and Below refer to 20,21 in relation to 8,9. Thus a JB instruction will take the jump if 20,21 is below 8,9.

Initializing the Weitek Board

The various component chips of the Weitek board require some initialization in order to perform correctly. The initialization is accomplished by a sequence of LOADCTX operations, using mysterious values. It's not necessary to understand those values to program the Weitek, so Weitek doesn't explain them (and neither shall we). Since the LOADCTX instruction ignores the operand fields in its memory address, we can use the 386's block-move instruction to perform the LOADCTX sequence. The following code does the job, assuming that we have already defined the constants WEITEK_ROUNDING and WEITEK_MASK, which define the initial rounding modes and exception mask that we want. The values given are for a 16-MHz system; they may change when faster systems are introduced:

```
WEITEK_INITS DD 016000000H              ; WTL 1164/1165 Flowthrough Timer
           _ DD 064000000H              ; WTL 1164 Accumulate Timer
           _ DD 0A0000000H              ; WTL 1165 Accumulate Timer
           _ DD 030000000H              ; Reserved Mode Bits (set to 0)
           _ DD (WEITEK_ROUNDING * 256 + WEITEK_MASK) * 010000H
N_WEITEK_INITS EQU 5

MOV ESI,OFFSET WEITEK_INITS             ; point to array of values
MOV ECX,N_WEITEK_INITS                  ; load the number of values
MOV EDI,OFFSET W_LOADCTX                ; destination is the Weitek space
REP MOVSD                               ; load the values from the memory
                                          array
```

Evaluating Weitek Performance

Let's now see how we can count clock cycles in Weitek code to estimate the execution speed of our programs. Like the 386, the Weitek board derives much of its speed through parallel processing. While a previous result is being calculated, the next instruction is being decoded. Also like the 386, this results in some uncertainty when it comes to adding up precise clock counts for sequences of instructions.

Table 7.3 lists the clock counts of the Weitek instruction set. Whenever consecutive Weitek instructions come quickly enough, the instructions overlap. The number of clock cycles saved in the overlap depends on the relationship between the result (left operand) of the previous instruction and the sources of the new instruction. Any match of the previous result register and a new source register is called data chaining, as we mentioned earlier. The Weitek controller is carefully designed to optimize data chaining. It waits for the previous result only if it is needed for the next instruction. It also seizes any opportunities it might find to simultaneously transmit the previous result to both the destination register and the new instruction's arithmetic chip. The number of clock cycles saved for each form of data chaining is listed in Table 7.4.

Let's use the values listed in Tables 7.3 and 7.4 to calculate the clock counts for the following instruction sequence:

```
MOV WS_MUL[1 \2],AL      ; no previous instructions available for overlap
MOV WS_ADD[3 \4],AL      ; previous destination (1) chained to neither operand
MOV WS_ADD[1 \3],AL      ; previous destination (3) chained to right operand
MOV WS_SUBR[1 \5],AL     ; previous destination (1) chained to left operand
MOV WS_ADD[1 \1],AL      ; previous destination (1) chained to both operands
```

Table 7.3 Instruction Types and Clock Counts

Instruction Type	Nonoverlapped clock count
W_LOAD,W2_LOAD,W_LOADCTX	4 + 4
W_STOR,W2_STOR,W_STORCTX	4 + 4
WS_MUL, WS_AMUL, WS_MULN	7 + 4
WD_MUL, WD_AMUL, WD_MULN	13 + 4
WS_DIV	32 + 4
WD_DIV	65 + 4
Other Dyadic WS_	7 + 4
Other Dyadic WD_	11 + 4
Monadic WS_	6 + 4
Monadic WD_	9 + 4
WS_MULADD	13 + 4
WD_MULADD	18 + 4

Table 7.4 Overlap Savings for Each Type of Data Chaining

Previous Destination (Left Operand) is Chained To	Number of Cycles Saved
neither operand	4
left operand only	5
right operand only	4
both operands	3

Each of the instructions given has a basic clock count of $7 + 4 = 11$ cycles. The first instruction does not benefit from any overlapping, so it takes the full count of 11 cycles to execute. The second and third instructions each overlap by 4 cycles, so they take 7 cycles to execute. The fourth instruction illustrates the most efficient form of data chaining, saving 5 cycles. Thus the instruction executes in only 6 cycles. The last instruction shows the slowest form of data chaining, saving only 3 cycles, causing the instruction to execute in 8 cycles.

Instruction overlap is subject to the condition that the next instruction is fed to the Weitek board before the previous instruction has completed. So if the 386 is not fast enough (there are too many intervening non-Weitek instructions in the program, or an external interrupt has occurred between instructions), the Weitek cannot overlap anything, and the full clock counts must apply.

We can now see the complexities involved in estimating execution times and in tuning our code for optimum performance. In principle, we can exploit the fact that the Weitek is a coprocessor and execute 386 code while the Weitek is working. For most calculations, however, the Weitek is so fast that we won't have time to do much before the Weitek is ready again. And if we insert too many 386 instructions, we'll lose the advantages of instruction overlapping. In general, then, it is best to provide Weitek instructions as quickly as possible. If we attempt another Weitek instruction before the previous one is complete, the Weitek board holds the 386 in waiting, just as the 387 does, until it is ready.

The one Weitek operation that does allow enough time for 386 processing is division. For example, the double-precision division instruction takes a relatively hefty 65 clock cycles. The Weitek board will even cooperate by accepting LOAD and STOR instructions before the division is complete, as long as neither of the operands to the division are involved in the LOAD/STOR.

Let's evaluate Weitek performance by programming a benchmark task, first using the Weitek, then the 387. We'll select a task that shows the Weitek to its best advantage, using single-precision numbers in arrays small enough to fit into the Weitek register set. The benchmark task is to perform a vector multiplication of the array pointed to by EDX into the array pointed to by EBX. Each element of the result is the product of the corresponding elements of the inputs. Each array contains $N = ECX$ doublewords in the single-precision format. N is guaranteed not to exceed 31.

On the Weitek, our strategy is to copy one entire array into the Weitek register set, multiply the other array into the registers, and finally copy the registers back out to the destination. Each of the three stages (even the multiplication!) can be accomplished by a single 386 block-move operation. The code is as follows:

```
MOV EBP,ECX                    ; save the count
MOV ESI,EBX                    ; source is the first array
MOV EDI,OFFSET W_LOAD[1 \0]    ; destination is Weitek register 1
REP MOVSD                      ; move first array to the Weitek registers
MOV ECX,EBP                    ; restore the count
MOV ESI,EDX                    ; source is the second array
MOV EDI,OFFSET WS_MUL[1 \0]    ; destination multiplies into register 1
```

```
REP MOVSD                           ; multiply second array into the registers
MOV ECX,EBP                         ; restore the count
MOV ESI,OFFSET W_STOR[1 \0]         ; source is Weitek register 1
MOV EDI,EBX                         ; destination is the original first array
REP MOVSD                           ; copy the result array back to memory
```

Each of the MOV instructions takes 2 clock cycles to execute. Each REP MOVSD instruction takes $(5 + 4N)$ cycles for the 386 to execute. For the Weitek board, the first (LOAD) move will take an extra 4 cycles for the nonoverlapped first number, plus 4 cycles for each number: a total of $(4 + 4N)$. There might be some overlap between the 5-cycle 386 overhead and the 4-cycle Weitek overhead, but we'll assume not and take the total time for the first REP MOVSD to be $(9 + 4N)$ cycles. Following that, the 386 takes 6 cycles to execute the following three MOV instructions plus some overhead time for the next REP MOVSD. This is probably too long for the Weitek to overlap the last LOAD of the previous REP MOVSD with the first MUL of the new REP MOVSD. So we'll count another 4 cycles of nonoverlap overhead, plus 7 cycles for each multiply, and assign $(9 + 7N)$ cycles to the second REP MOVSD. Similarly, we'll assign $(9 + 4N)$ cycles to the third REP MOVSD. Adding in the 18 cycles for the nine MOV instructions, we have a grand total of $45 + 15N$ cycles.

Now let's program the same benchmark using the 387. Here we have a simple loop that does the complete processing of each element before moving on to the next. The code is as follows:

```
D EQU DS:DWORD PTR 0        ; type declaration shortens the following source

L1:                         ; loop here for each element of the array
    FLD D[EBX]              ; push the element from the first array
    FMUL D[EDX]             ; multiply-in the second array element
    FSTP D[EBX]            ; pop the answer into the first array
    ADD EBX,4              ; advance the first array pointer to the next element
    ADD EDX,4              ; advance the second array pointer to the next element
    LOOP L1                ; loop to process another element
```

The floating-point instructions in the loop take about 20, 31, and 44 cycles, respectively. The 386 instructions execute concurrently with the FSTP instruction, so they add no clock cycles to the total. So the total is $95N$. If N is 13 or more, the Weitek loop is more than six times as fast! As we stated, this benchmark shows the Weitek to its best advantage. Weitek claims an overall performance improvement of about three or four times over the 387.

Summary

This finishes our presentation of the 386, 387, and Weitek processors. We have seen how these three processors are organized and have studied their instruction sets in detail. Furthermore, we have examined the ability of the 386 and 387 to emulate previous processors in the 86 family. And finally, we have learned about the advanced features of the 386, such as memory management, protection, and multitasking. Using the 386, we can build a system as powerful as the most powerful contemporary minicomputers and more powerful than the mainframe computers of only a few short years ago.

The 386 represents a milestone in microprocessor evolution. Only a small gap now remains between microcomputer functionality and that of mainframe computers. As the evolution continues, we will surely see the microprocessor overtake the mainframe.

References

Most of the material in this chapter is based on reference 1, which describes the controller chip that defines the programmatic interface to the Weitek board. For a detailed look at the individual arithmetic chips of the Weitek board, see reference 2.

1. *WTL 1163 Floating Point Controller*, Weitek Corporation, Sunnyvale, CA, 1986.

2. *WTL 1164/WTL1165 64-Bit IEEE Floating-Point Multiplier/Divider and ALU*, Weitek Corporation, Sunnyvale, CA, 1986.

APPENDIX
A

386 INSTRUCTION SET SUMMARY

We present here the complete 386 instruction set, together with the opcode encoding for each instruction form and the number of clock cycles each instruction takes to execute. We'll begin by describing the implicit prefix bytes that may come before the explicit opcodes given for an instruction. Then we'll explain the contents of each column of the instruction-set chart. After that, we'll give some examples showing how to steer through the complications. Finally, we present the instruction chart itself.

Implicit Prefix Bytes

Table A.1 lists the implicit prefix bytes of the 386. The operand-length prefix was described in Chapter 2; the others were described in Chapter 5.

Table A.1. Opcodes for Implicit Prefix Bytes

Opcode	Implicit Prefix
67	Address length prefix
2E	CS segment override prefix
3E	DS segment override prefix
26	ES segment override prefix
64	FS segment override prefix
65	GS segment override prefix
66	Operand length prefix
36	SS segment override prefix

The Opcode Column

Each 386 instruction is encoded as a sequence of one or more bytes. Part of the encoding identifies the instruction being used; this is called the *opcode* of the instruction. Other parts of the encoding may identify the operands to the instruction. The opcode column entry describes the complete encoding, including the opcode and operand fields, for each instruction. Specific numeric values are presented in hexadecimal, with hex digits A through F presented as capital letters. Other symbols that appear in the opcode column are defined as follows:

/ *followed by a digit 0 through 7*—Recall from Chapter 2 that most 386 memory references are specified by an effective address containing a base register, and/or a (scaled) index register, and/or a fixed displacement value. All 386 instructions that accept effective address memory operands contain an encoded field that specifies the components of the effective address: the base register if any, the index register and scale factor if any, and the displacement value, if any. For historical reasons, the field is called the *ModRM field;* it always begins with a *ModRM byte.* Table A.2 charts the meanings of the ModRM byte when 16-byte addressing is in effect; Table A.3 does the same when 32-bit addressing is in effect.

Let's now disect the /n found in the opcode column for any instruction. The digit n tells the column (0 through 7) in Table A.2 or A.3 from which a ModRM value for this instruction will be taken. The row is determined by the memory addressing form that was selected by the operand. The last 8 rows give register values: one of these rows is used if a register is selected for a register-or-memory operand. Values from rows marked s-i-b signal that another byte, the *sign-index-base* byte, follows the ModRM byte. Table A.4 charts the meanings of the sign-index-base byte. The row across the top identifies the base register used for each column in the table. The column to the right identifies the index register and scale factor used for each row of the table.

Immediately following the ModRM byte and the possible sign-index-base byte is a 1-, 2-, or 4-byte displacement if d8, d16, or d32 was specified in the ModRM or sign-index-base tables. The word and doubleword forms d16 and d32 are given "backwords": the least significant bytes always come first.

/r—Two-operand instructions having one register operand and one register-or-memory operand will have /r in the opcode field, which also represents a ModRM field. The r identifies the register operand, according to one of the top rows of Table A.2 or A.3. The register-or-memory operand is encoded just as with the /n form just described.

+r—Some instructions containing a register operand have the corresponding register number encoded into the first opcode byte. Those instructions have +r appended to that opcode byte value. The encoded register numbers are the same as those given across the top rows of Tables A.2 or A.3.

Table A.2. ModRM Byte Values with 16-bit Addressing in Effect

segreg =	ES	CS	SS	DS	FS	GS			
rb =	AL	CL	DL	BL	AH	CH	DH	BH	
rw =	AX	CX	DX	BX	SP	BP	SI	DI	
rd =	EAX	ECX	EDX	EBX	ESP	EBP	ESI	EDI	
digit =	0	1	2	3	4	5	6	7	
									Reg-or-memory operand:
Mod RM byte:	00	08	10	18	20	28	30	38	[BX + SI]
	01	09	11	19	21	29	31	39	[BX + DI]
	02	0A	12	1A	22	2A	32	3A	[BP + SI]
	03	0B	13	1B	23	2B	33	3B	[BP + DI]
	04	0C	14	1C	24	2C	34	3C	[SI]
	05	0D	15	1D	25	2D	35	3D	[DI]
	06	0E	16	1E	26	2E	36	3E	d16 (simple var)
	07	0F	17	1F	27	2F	37	3F	[BX]
	40	48	50	58	60	68	70	78	[BX + SI] + d8
	41	49	51	59	61	69	71	79	[BX + DI] + d8
	42	4A	52	5A	62	6A	72	7A	[BP + SI] + d8
	43	4B	53	5B	63	6B	73	7B	[BP + DI] + d8
	44	4C	54	5C	64	6C	74	7C	[SI] + d8
	45	4D	55	5D	65	6D	75	7D	[DI] + d8
	46	4E	56	5E	66	6E	76	7E	[BP] + d8
	47	4F	57	5F	67	6F	77	7F	[BX] + d8
	80	88	90	98	A0	A8	B0	B8	[BX + SI] + d16
	81	89	91	99	A1	A9	B1	B9	[BX + DI] + d16
	82	8A	92	9A	A2	AA	B2	BA	[BP + SI] + d16
	83	8B	93	9B	A3	AB	B3	BB	[BP + DI] + d16
	84	8C	94	9C	A4	AC	B4	BC	[SI] + d16
	85	8D	95	9D	A5	AD	B5	BD	[DI] + d16
	86	8E	96	9E	A6	AE	B6	BE	[BP] + d16
	87	8F	97	9F	A7	AF	B7	BF	[BX] + d16
	C0	C8	D0	D8	E0	E8	F0	F8	rmv = eAX rmb = AL
	C1	C9	D1	D9	E1	E9	F1	F9	rmv = eCX rmb = CL
	C2	CA	D2	DA	E2	EA	F2	FA	rmv = eDX rmb = DL
	C3	CB	D3	DB	E3	EB	F3	FB	rmv = eBX rmb = BL
	C4	CC	D4	DC	E4	EC	F4	FC	rmv = eSP rmb = AH
	C5	CD	D5	DD	E5	ED	F5	FD	rmv = eBP rmb = CH
	C6	CE	D6	DE	E6	EE	F6	FE	rmv = eSI rmb = DH
	C7	CF	D7	DF	E7	EF	F7	FF	rmv = eDI rmb = BH

Default segment register is SS for memory addresses containing a BP base; DS for other memory effective addresses.

ib, iw, or iv—Instruction forms containing an immediate (constant) operand have the same operand in their encoded form where the ib, iw, or iv is seen: ib is always a single byte, and iw is always a two-byte word. The v of iv stands for "variable-length": it is either a word or doubleword, depending on the operand length in effect for the instruction.

Table A.3. ModRM Byte Values with 32-bit Addressing in Effect

segreg =	ES	CS	SS	DS	FS	GS			
rb =	AL	CL	DL	BL	AH	CH	DH	BH	
rw =	AX	CX	DX	BX	SP	BP	SI	DI	
rd =	EAX	ECX	EDX	EBX	ESP	EBP	ESI	EDI	
digit =	0	1	2	3	4	5	6	7	
									Reg-or-memory operand:
ModRM byte:	00	08	10	18	20	28	30	38	[EAX]
	01	09	11	19	21	29	31	39	[ECX]
	02	0A	12	1A	22	2A	32	3A	[EDX]
	03	0B	13	1B	23	2B	33	3B	[EBX]
	04	0C	14	1C	24	2C	34	3C	s-i-b, baserow #1
	05	0D	15	1D	25	2D	35	3D	d32 (simple var)
	06	0E	16	1E	26	2E	36	3E	[ESI]
	07	0F	17	1F	27	2F	37	3F	[EDI]
	40	48	50	58	60	68	70	78	[EAX] + d8
	41	49	51	59	61	69	71	79	[ECX] + d8
	42	4A	52	5A	62	6A	72	7A	[EDX] + d8
	43	4B	53	5B	63	6B	73	7B	[EBX] + d8
	44	4C	54	5C	64	6C	74	7C	s-i-b, baserow #2
	45	4D	55	5D	65	6D	75	7D	[EBP] + d8
	46	4E	56	5E	66	6E	76	7E	[ESI] + d8
	47	4F	57	5F	67	6F	77	7F	[EDI] + d8
	80	88	90	98	A0	A8	B0	B8	[EAX] + d32
	81	89	91	99	A1	A9	B1	B9	[ECX] + d32
	82	8A	92	9A	A2	AA	B2	BA	[EDX] + d32
	83	8B	93	9B	A3	AB	B3	BB	[EBX] + d32
	84	8C	94	9C	A4	AC	B4	BC	s-i-b, baserow #3
	85	8D	95	9D	A5	AD	B5	BD	[EBP] + d32
	86	8E	96	9E	A6	AE	B6	BE	[ESI] + d32
	87	8F	97	9F	A7	AF	B7	BF	[EDI] + d32
	C0	C8	D0	D8	E0	E8	F0	F8	rmv = eAX rmb = AL
	C1	C9	D1	D9	E1	E9	F1	F9	rmv = eCX rmb = CL
	C2	CA	D2	DA	E2	EA	F2	FA	rmv = eDX rmb = DL
	C3	CB	D3	DB	E3	EB	F3	FB	rmv = eBX rmb = BL
	C4	CC	D4	DC	E4	EC	F4	FC	rmv = eSP rmv = AH
	C5	CD	D5	DD	E5	ED	F5	FD	rmv = eBP rmb = CH
	C6	CE	D6	DE	E6	EE	F6	FE	rmv = eSI rmb = DH
	C7	CF	D7	DF	E7	EF	F7	FF	rmv = eDI rmb = BH

Default segment register is SS for memory addresses containing an EBP base; DS for other memory effective addresses.

cb, cv—CALLs and JMPs to locations within the same code segment are encoded via an offset relative to the instruction following the CALL or JMP. Destinations of short jumps (within 128 bytes in either direction from the next instruction) are encoded by the one-byte signed quantity cb. Destinations of near jumps are encoded by cv, which is a signed word if we are emulating a 16-bit predecessor and a signed doubleword if we are in native 386 mode. Again, these quantities are "backwards," with the least significant bytes given first.

Table A.4. Values for the s-i-b Byte

Base:									
row #1	[EAX]	[ECX]	[EDX]	[EBX]	[ESP]	d32	[ESI]	[EDI]	
row #2	[EAX]+d8	[ECX]+d8	[EDX]+d8	[EBX]+d8	[ESP]+d8	[EBP]+d8	[ESI]+d8	[EDI]+d8	
row #3	[EAX]+d32	[ECX]+d32	[EDX]+d32	[EBX]+d32	[ESP]+d32	[EBP]+d32	[ESI]+d32	[EDI]+d32	

									Index:
s-i-b byte:	00	01	02	03	04	05	06	07	[EAX]
	08	09	0A	0B	0C	0D	0E	0F	[ECX]
	10	11	12	13	14	15	16	17	[EDX]
	18	19	1A	1B	1C	1D	1E	1F	[EBX]
					24				none
	28	29	2A	2B	2C	2D	2E	2F	[EBP]
	30	31	32	33	34	35	36	37	[ESI]
	38	39	3A	3B	3C	3D	3E	3F	[EDI]
	40	41	42	43	44	45	46	47	[EAX*2]
	48	49	4A	4B	4C	4D	4E	4F	[ECX*2]
	50	51	52	53	54	55	56	57	[EDX*2]
	58	59	5A	5B	5C	5D	5E	5F	[EBX*2]
									undefined
	68	69	6A	6B	6C	6D	6E	6F	[EBP*2]
	70	71	72	73	74	75	76	77	[ESI*2]
	78	79	7A	7B	7C	7D	7E	7F	[EDI*2]
	80	81	82	83	84	85	86	87	[EAX*4]
	88	89	8A	8B	8C	8D	8E	8F	[ECX*4]
	90	91	92	93	94	95	96	97	[EDX*4]
	98	99	9A	9B	9C	9D	9E	9F	[EBX*4]
									undefined
	A8	A9	AA	AB	AC	AD	AE	AF	[EBP*4]
	B0	B1	B2	B3	B4	B5	B6	B7	[ESI*4]
	B8	B9	BA	BB	BC	BD	BE	BF	[EDI*4]
	C0	C1	C2	C3	C4	C5	C6	C7	[EAX*8]
	C8	C9	CA	CB	CC	CD	CE	CF	[ECX*8]
	D0	D1	D2	D3	D4	D5	D6	D7	[EDX*8]
	D8	D9	DA	DB	DC	DD	DE	DF	[EBX*8]
									undefined
	E8	E9	EA	EB	EC	ED	EE	EF	[EBP*8]
	F0	F1	F2	F3	F4	F5	F6	F7	[ESI*8]
	F8	F9	FA	FB	FC	FD	FE	FF	[EDI*8]

cp—Far CALLs and JMPs have destinations consisting of a segment register value together with an absolute offset within the segment indicated. The segment register values are always 16 bits (2 bytes); the offsets are either 16 or 32 bits. Thus the encoded destination cp is either 32 or 48 bits. The offset comes first, then the segment register value.

The Instruction Column

Following the opcode field is the instruction itself, as it is written in 386 assembly language. Capital letters are given to the assembler as they are shown. Most of the operands containing lower-case letters appear as they do in the opcode column, as we just described.

eAX—This is either AX or EAX, depending on the operand size (16 or 32 bits) in effect for the instruction.

rmb, rmw, rmd, rmv—These operands can be either a general register or a memory quantity of the size indicated (byte, word, doubleword, or variable word-or-doubleword).

rb, rw, rd, rv—An operand with one of these specifications must be a general register of the size indicated.

mb, mw, md, mv—An operand with one of these specification must be a memory quantity of the size indicated.

m—This specification indicates a memory operand of indeterminate size.

m2v—This operand to the BOUND instruction specifies a memory operand of either two words or two doublewords (depending on operand size), that specify the bounds to be used.

rv/m—This operand to the Bit Test Instruction specifies either a register whose size matches the operand size in effect (16 or 32 bits), or a memory array of indeterminate length.

segreg—This operand must be a segment register.

The Clock Cycles Column

Following the instruction field is a field telling the number of clock cycles the instruction takes to execute. You can translate this into a time: for a 16-MHz 386, you can divide the number of clock cycles by 16 to obtain the number of microseconds the instruction takes to execute.

There are a couple of circumstances that may increase the cycle counts shown. First, you must add one clock cycle count whenever both a base and an index register are used in a memory address. Second, the counts shown assume that the instruction has already been prefetched and decoded. If it hasn't, then extra cycles will apply. In the case of jumps to new program code, the extra cycles are explicitly shown by +m (described shortly). The extra cycles could occur in other cases, however: if there is a string of extremely fast instructions, the 386's execution unit could race ahead of the instruction prefetch and decode units.

Many of the instructions list two clock cycle counts. In most cases the first (smaller) count applies when a register is selected for the register-or-memory operand; the second (larger) count applies when a memory operand is selected. Here is a list of instruction categories having multiple clock counts that do *not* depend on register versus memory:

1. For conditional jump instructions, the first (smaller) count applies if the jump is not taken; the second (larger) count applies if the jump is taken.

2. For instructions that load values into segment registers, the first (smaller) count applies if the 386 is in 8086 mode; that is, if the value loaded will be multiplied by 16 to get the segment's memory location. The second (larger) count applies if the 386 is in selector mode; that is, the value loaded is an index into a descriptor table. The instructions involved are LDS, LES, LFS, LGS, LSS, MOV segreg,rw; and POP segreg.

3. The MOV CRn,rd instruction form lists three clock counts, one for each value of n (0, 2, or 3).

Some of the clock cycle counts have variable amounts added to them. Here are the explanations for those amounts:

+*m*—All instructions that change the instruction pointer cause the 386's internal queue of instruction bytes to be flushed. For all such instructions, you add m to the clock cycle count, where m is the number of *units* in the next instruction (at the jump destination) to be executed. A unit is a single byte of the encoded instruction, except that an immediate constant is one unit, and a displacement component of a memory address is one unit.

+*nc*—String instructions preceded by a repeat prefix have execution times that depend on the repeat count (initial value of CX or ECX). This count c is multiplied by the value *n* indicated for each instruction, and added to the overhead amount indicated.

+*3n*—The Bit Scan instructions BSF and BSR add three cycles for each zero bit scanned before the one bit is found. If n is the number of zero bits, the total clock cycle count is 10 + 3n.

+*4ib*—An ENTER instruction whose second (level) operand is greater than 1 has a cycle count that depends on the level operand ib, as given.

Finally, there are some instruction groups, marked with an asterisk (*) in the clock cycle column, that have timing specifications too complicated to squeeze into the space given. These specifications are presented in their full glory in Table A.5. The instruction times given for task switches are listed by Intel as "approximate."

The Description Column

Following the cycle count is a concise description, for reference purposes, of the instruction. The only explanation we might need to provide here is that the term "vword" stands for either word or doubleword, depending on the operand size in effect for the instruction.

Table A.5. Instructions with Complicated Clock Counts

Opcode	Clock Cycles	Description
9A cv	17 + m	CALL far direct, 8086 mode
9A cv	34 + m	CALL far direct, selector mode
9A cv	52 + m	CALL gate, same privilege
9A cv	86 + m	CALL gate, more privilege, no parameters
9A cv	94 + 4x + m	CALL gate, more privilege, x parameters
9A cv	300 − C_OLD − NEW + GATE	CALL to task
FF /3	22 + m	CALL far indirect, 8086 mode
FF /3	38 + m	CALL far indirect, selector mode
FF /3	56 + m	CALL gate, same privilege
FF /3	90 + m	CALL gate, more privilege, no parameters
FF /3	98 + 4x + m	CALL gate, more privilege, x parameters
FF /3	305 − C_OLD − NEW + GATE	CALL to task
	6 + 3*MEM + NDIGITS	IMUL, all forms
E4 ib	6 + IO_PROT	IN AL,ib
E5 ib	6 + IO_PROT	IN eAX,ib
EC	7 + IO_PROT	IN AL,DX
ED	7 + IO_PROT	IN eAX,DX
6C	9 + IO_PROT	INSB
6D	9 + IO_PROT	INSW or INSD
CC	33	INT 3 in real mode
CD ib	37	INT ib in real mode
CE	3,35	INTO in real mode
	59	INT any, protected mode, same privilege
	99	INT any, protected mode, more privilege
	119	INT any from virtual 8086 mode
	309 + I_OLD − NEW	INT any via task gate
CF	22	IRET in real mode
CF	38	IRET in selector mode, same privilege
CF	82	IRET to lesser privilege
CF	275 − IR_OLD	IRET to different native 386 task
CF	224 − IR_OLD	IRET to different virtual 8086 task
CF	271	IRET from 386 to 286 task
CF	232	IRET from 286 task to another 286 task
EA cv	12 + m	JMP far direct, 8086 mode
EA cv	27 + m	JMP far direct, selector mode
EA cv	45 + m	JMP to call gate, same privilege
EA cv	303 − J_OLD − NEW + GATE	JMP to task
FF /5	31 + m	JMP far indirect, 8086 mode
FF /5	43 + m	JMP far indirect, selector mode
FF /5	49 + m	JMP to call gate, same privilege
FF /5	308 − J_OLD − NEW + GATE	JMP to task
	6 + 3*MEM + NDIGITS	MUL, all forms
E6 ib	4 + IO_PROT	OUT ib,AL
E7 ib	4 + IO_PROT	OUT ib,eAX
EE	5 + IO_PROT	OUT DX,AL
EF	5 + IO_PROT	OUT DX,eAX
6E	8 + IO_PROT	OUTSB
6F	8 + IO_PROT	OUTSW or OUTSD
F3 6C	7 + 6c + IO_PROT	REP INSB
F3 6D	7 + 6c + IO_PROT	REP INSW or REP INSD
F3 6E	6 + 5c + IO_PROT	REP OUTSB

Table A.5. Instructions with Complicated Clock Counts

Opcode	Instruction	Cycles	Description
F3 6F	6 + 5c + IO_PROT		REP OUTSW or REP OUTSD
	18 + m		RET far, 8086 mode (with or without operand)
	32 + m		RET far, selector mode, same privilege
	68		RET far, lesser privilege, switch stacks
C_OLD	= 2 if CALLing a 386 task from a 286 task; 0 otherwise.		
GATE	= 9 if the CALL or JMP is to a task gate; 0 if an ordinary task.		
IO_PROT	= 6 if real mode, 0 if protected mode and the current privilege level is at least as privileged as IOPL, 20 if CPL is not as privileged (>) IOPL.		
J_OLD	= 0 if the old task in a JMP is a 386 task, 2 if it is a 286 task.		
MEM	= 1 if a memory operand is involved, 0 if only registers are involved.		
N_DIGITS	= 3 if the multiplier (last operand) is 7 or less. Otherwise, NDIGITS is the number of binary digits in the multiplier, when leading zeroes are stripped.		
NEW	= 0 if the new task is a 386 task, 83 if it is a virtual 8086 task, and 27 if it is a 286 task.		
I_OLD	= 0 if the old task (before the INT) is a 386 task, +5 if it is a virtual 8086 task, and −2 if it is a 286 task.		
IR_OLD	= 0 if the old task (before the IRET) is a 386 task, 10 if the old task is a 286 task.		

Examples of Specific Instructions

Let's work through a few specific instructions, picking our way through the charts to determine the opcode encoding and the cycle count for each instruction. We'll assume that the instructions are to be executed when the 386 is in its native mode, not emulating one of its predecessors.

We'll start with the instruction, MOV DX,SS:W[BP + DI], which moves the memory word whose segment is SS and whose offset is BP + DI into the DX register. Since we're using the 16-bit registers BP and DI to address the memory, we'll need an address-length prefix (67 hex) to override the default 32-bit address length of 386 native mode. Since the operands are words and not doublewords, we'll also need an operand-length prefix (hex 66) to override the default doubleword operand size. Since SS is the default segment for indexing involving the BP register, we do not need a segment override prefix byte for this instruction. Now we find the general form for our instruction in the main chart:

8B/r   MOV rv,rmv   2,4   Move RM vword into vword register

The 8B indicates that the first opcode byte beyond the prefix bytes is hex 8B. The /r indicates that a ModRM field follows the 8B byte. We consult Table A.2 to find the ModRM byte. The rv part of the instruction form is DX; so we find DX the top of the table: it heads the third column. The rmv part of the instruction form is [BP + DI]; so we find [BP + DI] along the right-hand column of the table: it marks the fourth row. The third column and fourth row intersect at the value 13 hex; so 13 hex is the ModRM byte. There is no displacement value in our memory address; so the ModRM byte is the entire ModRM field. The complete encoding for the instruction is 67 66 8B 13. (The 67 and 66 prefix bytes could be switched with no effect). We can also examine the clock cycles field of the MOV rv,rmv entry: we find the two counts 2 and 4. Since the rmv for our instruction is a memory operand and not a register operand, the instruction takes the larger count, 4 cycles (plus 1 cycle for using both a base and an index), to execute.

Next, let's do the instruction SUB ESI,EDI. There is no memory addressing here, so neither an address-length nor a segment-override prefix is necessary. The operands are doublewords, so an operand-length prefix isn't needed either. Looking in the chart, we find something curious: our instruction fits either of the two forms:

| 29 /r | SUB rmv,rv | 2,6 | Subtract vword register from RM vword |
| 2B /r | SUB rv,rmv | 2,7 | Subtract RM vword from vword register |

If we use the first form, ESI is the rmv operand, and we are led to the second-to-last row of Table A.3. EDI is the rv operand, and we are led to the last column of the table. The ModRM byte is therefore FE hex, and the full instruction is encoded 29 FE. On the other hand, if we use the second form, ESI is the rv operand, and we are led to the second-to-last *column* of the table. EDI is the rmw operand, and we are led to the last *row* of the table. In this case the ModRM byte is FF hex, and the full instruction is encoded 2B FF. Thus SUB ESI,EDI has two valid encodings: 29 FE and 2B FF, and an assembler may choose either one. In both cases, the rmv operand is a register, to the smaller clock count of 2 cycles applies.

Now let's try ADD FS:W[ECX + 14],7. Since EBP is not involved in the memory addressing, DS is the default segment register. We'll need an FS-override prefix (64 hex). Since our destination operand is a word, we'll need an operand-length prefix (66 hex) to override the default doublword operand length. We won't need an address-length prefix, since the addressing being used is found in the default Table A.3. We find the following form in the main chart:

| 83 /0 ib | ADD rmv,ib | 2,7 | Add immediate byte into RM vword |

The first byte following the prefixes is therefore 83 hex. The /0 tells us to consult column 0 (the first column) of Table A.3. The value 14 in the memory address is a byte-sized displacement value, so we find the entry [ECX] + d8 along the right side of the table. Taking the intersection of that row with the first column, we find the ModRM byte value 41 hex. The ModRM field is completed by the displacement byte 14 decimal, which is 0E hex. Following the ModRM field is the second, immediate operand ib, which for our instruction is 7. The complete encoding is thus 64 66 83 41 0E 07. The higher cycle count of 7 applies, since a memory operand was used.

Let's try a scaled index: XOR DS:[EBX*4 + EDX + 1000H],ECX. Here we have doubleword indexing, doubleword operands, and the default DS segment, so no prefixes are necessary. The instruction form from the chart is:

| 31/r | XOR rmv,rv | 2,6 | Exclusive-OR vword register into RM vword |

The presence of the index register forces us to Table A.4. We have a displacement 01000, which doesn't fit in a byte. So we select the entry [EDX] + d32 from baserow #3 across the top of Table A.4. We intersect this column with the row marked [EBX*4] to obtain a sign-index-base byte of 9A hex. Now we go back to Table A.3 for the ModRM byte: we pick the column headed by ECX and the row labeled s-i-b, baserow #3. These intersect at 8C hex. The ModRM field thus consists of the ModRM byte 8C, the s-i-b byte 9A, and the "backwords" displacement 00 10 00 00. The complete instruction encoding is thus 31 8C 9A 00 10 00 00. The clock count, 6, is augmented by a penalty of 1 cycle for having both a base and an index in the memory address; therefore, the instruction takes 7 cycles to execute.

Finally, let's try a direct near JMP instruction. We'll assemble the instruction at offset 10000 hex within a segment, and assume that the destination is at 800 hex within the same code segment. The instruction form for this is:

E9 cv   JMP cv   7 + m   Jump near (vword offs relative to next instr)

No prefixes are necessary for this instruction, since we will be using the default doubleword relative offset. The instruction will occupy five bytes, so the address of the following instruction is 10005. The relative offset is thus 800 − 10005 = FFFF07FB. Encoding the operand "backwords," we obtain the full instruction encoding E9 FB 07 FF FF. The number of clock cycles for the jump depends on the size of the instruction at the destination 800. For example, if the two-byte instruction SUB EDI,ESI is at 800, then the jump takes 7 + 2 = 9 cycles. If the XOR instruction we just examined is at 800, then the jump takes 7 + 4 = 11 cycles because the instruction has 4 units: 3 individual encoded bytes plus the 1 displacement address.

Opcode	Instruction	Clock Cycles	Description
37	AAA	4	ASCII adjust AL (carry into AH) after add
D5 0A	AAD	19	ASCII adjust before div (AX = 10*AH + AL)
D4 0A	AAM	17	ASCII adjust after mul (AL/10: AH = Quo AL = Rem)
3F	AAS	4	ASCII adjust AL (borrow from AH) after sub
14 ib	ADC AL, ib	2	Add with carry immediate byte into AL
15 iv	ADC eAX, iv	2	Add with carry immediate vword into eAX
12 /r	ADC rb,rmb	2, 6	Add with carry RM byte into byte register
80 /2 ib	ADC rmb,ib	2, 7	Add with carry immediate byte into RM byte
10 /r	ADC rmb,rb	2, 7	Add with carry byte register into RM byte
83 /2 ib	ADC rmv,ib	2, 7	Add with carry immediate byte into RM vword
81 /2 iv	ADC rmv,iv	2, 7	Add with carry immediate vword into RM vword
11 /r	ADC rmv,rv	2, 7	Add with carry vword register into RM vword
13 /r	ADC rv,rmv	2, 6	Add with carry RM vword into vword register
04 ib	ADD AL,ib	2	Add immediate byte into AL
05 iv	ADD eAX, iv	2	Add immediate vword into eAX
02 /r	ADD rb,rmb	2, 6	Add RM byte into byte register
80 /0 ib	ADD rmb,ib	2, 7	Add immediate byte into RM byte
00 /r	ADD rmb,rb	2, 7	Add byte register into RM byte

(continued)

Opcode	Instruction	Clock Cycles	Description
83 /0 ib	ADD rmv,ib	2, 7	Add immediate byte into RM vword
81 /0 iv	ADD rmv,iv	2, 7	Add immediate vword into RM vword
01 /r	ADD rmv,rv	2, 7	Add vword register into RM vword
03 /r	ADD rv,rmv	2, 6	Add RM vword into vword register
24 ib	AND AL,ib	2	Logical-AND immediate byte into AL
25 iv	AND eAX,iv	2	Logical-AND immediate vword into eAX
22 /r	AND rb,rmb	2, 6	Logical-AND RM byte into byte register
80 /4 ib	AND rmb,ib	2, 7	Logical-AND immediate byte into RM byte
20 /r	AND rmb,rb	2, 7	Logical-AND byte register into RM byte
81 /4 iv	AND rmv,iv	2, 7	Logical-AND immediate vword into RM vword
21 /r	AND rmv,rv	2, 7	Logical-AND vword register into RM vword
23 /r	AND rv,rmv	2, 6	Logical-AND RM vword into vword register
63 /r	ARPL rmw,rw	20, 21	Adjust RPL of rmw to ≥ RPL of rw
62 /r	BOUND rv,m2v	10	INT 5 unless [m] ≤ rv ≤ [m+size v]
0F BC	BSF rv,rmv	10+3n	Set rv to lowest position of NZ bit in rmv
0F BD	BSR rv,rmv	10+3n	Set rv to highest position of NZ bit in rmv
0F BA /4 ib	BT rv/m,ib	3, 6	Set Carry flag to bit # ib of array at rv/m
0F A3 /r	BT rv/m,rv	3, 12	Set Carry flag to bit # rv of array at rv/m
0F BA /7 ib	BTC rv/m,ib	6, 8	Set CF to, then compl bit ib of array at rv/m
0F BB /r	BTC rv/m, rv	6, 13	Set CF to, then compl bit rv of array at rv/m
0F BA /6 ib	BTR rv/m, ib	6, 8	Set CF to, then reset bit ib of array at rv/m
0F B3 /r	BTR rv/m, rv	6, 13	Set CF to, then reset bit rv of array at rv/m
0F BA /5 ib	BTS rv/m, ib	6, 8	Set CF to, then set bit ib of array at rv/m
0F AB /r	BTS rv/m, rv	6, 13	Set CF to, then set bit rv of array at rv/m
9A cp	CALL cp	*	Call far segment, immediate seg-and-offset cp
E8 cv	CALL cv	7+m	Call near, offset relative to next instr
FF /3	CALL mp	*	Call far segment, seg-and-offset in memory
FF /2	CALL rmv	7+m, 10+m	Call near, offset absolute at RM vword
98	CBW	3	Convert byte into word (AH = top bit of AL)
99	CDQ	2	Convert dword to qword (EDX = top bit of EAX)
F8	CLC	2	Clear carry flag
FC	CLD	2	Clear direction flag so eSI and eDI will incr
FA	CLI	3	Clear interrupt enable flag; interrupts disabled
0F 06	CLTS	5	Clear task-switched flag in CR0
F5	CMC	2	Complement carry flag
3C ib	CMP AL,ib	2	Subtract imm byte from AL for flags only
3D iv	CMP eAX,iv	2	Subtract imm vword from eAX for flags only
3A /r	CMP rb,rmb	2, 6	Subtract RM byte from byte reg for flags only
80 /7 ib	CMP rmb,ib	2, 5	Subtract imm byte from RM byte for flags only
38 /r	CMP rmb,rb	2, 5	Subtract byte reg from RM byte for flags only
83 /7 ib	CMP rmv,ib	2, 5	Subtract imm byte from RM vword for flags only
81 /7 iv	CMP rmv,iv	2, 5	Subtract imm vword from RM vword for flags only
39 /r	CMP rmv,rv	2, 5	Subtract vword reg from RM vword for flags only
3B /r	CMP rv,rmv	2, 6	Subtract RM vword from vword reg for flags only
A6	CMPS mb,mb	10	Compare bytes ES:[eDI] from [eSI], adv eSI,eDI
A7	CMPS mv,mv	10	Comp vwords ES:[eDI] from [eSI], adv eSI,eDI
A6	CMPSB	10	Comp bytes ES:[eDI] from DS:[eSI], adv eSI,eDI
A7	CMPSD	10	Comp dwords ES:[eDI] from DS:[eSI], adv eSI,eDI
A7	CMPSW	10	Comp words ES:[eDI] from DS:[eSI], adv eSI,eDI
99	CWD	2	Convert word to dword (DX = top bit of AX)

Opcode	Instruction	Clock Cycles	Description
98	CWDE	3	Sign-extend word AX to doubleword EAX
27	DAA	4	Decimal adjust AL after addition
2F	DAS	4	Decimal adjust AL after subtraction
FE /1	DEC rmb	2, 6	Decrement RM byte by 1
FF /1	DEC rmv	2, 6	Decrement RM vword by 1
48 + r	DEC rv	2	Decrement vword register by 1
F6 /6	DIV rmb	14, 17	Unsigned divide AX by RM byte (AL = Quo AH = Rem)
F7 /6	DIV rmd	38, 41	Unsigned divide EDXEAX by RM vword (EAX = QuoEDX = Rem)
F7 /6	DIV rmw	22, 25	Unsigned divide DXAX by RM vword (AX = Quo DX = Rem)
C8 iw 00	ENTER iw,0	10	Make stack frame, iw bytes loc stor, 0 levels
C8 iw 01	ENTER iw,1	12	Make stack frame, iw bytes loc stor, 1 level
C8 iw ib	ENTER iw,ib	11 + 4ib	Make stack frame, iw bytes loc stor, ib lvls.
F4	HLT	5	Halt
F6 /7	IDIV rmb	19	Signed divide AX by RM byte (AL = QuoAH = Rem)
F7 /7	IDIV rmd	43	Signed divide EDXEAX by RM vword (EAX = Quo EDX = Rem)
F7 /7	IDIV rmw	27	Signed divide DXAX by RM vword(AX = Quo DX = Rem)
F6 /5	IMUL rmb	*	Signed multiply (AX = AL * RM byte)
F7 /5	IMUL rmv	*	Signed mul (eDXeAX = eAX * RMv word)
6B /r ib	IMUL rv,ib	*	Signed mul immediate byte into vword register
69 /r iv	IMUL rv,iv	*	Signed mul immediate vword into vword register
0F AF /r	IMUL rv, rmv	*	Signed mul rmv into rv
6B /r ib	IMUL rv,rmv,ib	*	Signed mul (rv = RM vword * immediate byte)
69 /r iv	IMUL rv,rmv,iv	*	Signed mul (rv = RM vword * immediate vword)
EC	IN AL,DX	*	Input byte from port DX into AL
E4 ib	IN AL,ib	*	Input byte from immediate port into AL
ED	IN eAX,DX	*	Input vword from port DX into eAX
E5 ib	IN eAX,ib	*	Input vword from immediate port into eAX
FE /0	INC rmb	2, 6	Increment RM byte by 1
FF /0	INC rmv	2, 6	Increment RM vword by 1
40 + r	INC rv	2	Increment vword register by 1
6C	INS rmb,DX	*	Input byte from port DX into ES: [eDI]
6D	INS rmv,DX	*	Input vword from port DX into ES: [eDI]
6C	INSB	*	Input byte from port DX into ES:[eDI]
6D	INSD	*	Input dword from port DX into ES:[eDI]
6D	INSW	*	Input word from port DX into ES:[eDI]
CC	INT 3	*	Interrupt 3 (debug trap) ⎫ far call,
CD ib	INT ib	*	Ipt numbered by imm byte ⎬ flags pushed
CE	INTO	*	Ipt 4 if overflow flag is 1 ⎭ first
CF	IRET	*	Ipt return (far return and pop flags)
CF	IRETD	*	Ipt return (far return and pop flags)
77 cb	JA cb	3, 7 + m	Jump short if above (CF = 0 and ZF = 0)
0F 87 cv	JA cv	3, 7 + m	Jump near if above UNSIGNED
73 cb	JAE cb	3, 7 + m	Jump s if above or equal (CF = 0)
0F 83 cv	JAE cv	3, 7 + m	Jump n if above or equal

(continued)

Opcode	Instruction	Clock Cycles	Description
72 cb	JB cb	3, 7 + m	Jump s if below (CF = 1) UNSIGNED
0F 82 cv	JB cv	3, 7 + m	Jump n if below
76 cb	JBE cb	3, 7 + m	Jump s if below or equal
0F 86 cv	JBE cv	3, 7 + m	Jump n if below or equal (CF = 1 or ZF = 1)
72 cb	JC cb	3, 7 + m	Jump s if carry (CF = 1)
0F 82 cv	JC cv	3, 7 + m	Jump n if carry
E3 cb	JCXZ cb	5, 9 + m	Jump s if CX register is zero
74 cb	JE cb	3, 7 + m	Jump s if equal (ZF = 1)
0F 84 cv	JE cv	3, 7 + m	Jump n if equal
E3 cb	JECXZ cb	5, 9 + m	Jump s if ECX register is zero
7F cb	JG cb	3, 7 + m	Jump s if greater (ZF = 0 and SF = OF)
0F 8F cv	JG cv	3, 7 + m	Jump n if greater SIGNED
7D cb	JGE cb	3, 7 + m	Jump s if greater or equal (SF = OF)
0F 8D cv	JGE cv	3, 7 + m	Jump n if greater or equal
7C cb	JL cb	3, 7 + m	Jump s if less (SF ≠ OF) SIGNED
0F 8C cv	JL cv	3, 7 + m	Jump n if less
7E cb	JLE cb	3, 7 + m	Jump s if less or equal
0F 8E cv	JLE cv	3, 7 + m	Jump n if less or equal (ZF = 1 or SF ≠ OF)
EB cb	JMP cb	7 + m	Jump s (signed byte relative to next instruction)
EA cp	JMP cp	*	Jump far (immediate segment-and-offset)
E9 cv	JMP cv	7 + m	Jump near (vword offs relative to next instruction)
FF /5	JMP mp	*	Jump far, seg-and-offset in memory
FF /4	JMP rmv	7 + m, 10 + m	Jump near to RM vword (absolute offset)
76 cb	JNA cb	3, 7 + m	Jump short if not above (CF = 1 or ZF = 1)
0F 86 cv	JNA cv	3, 7 + m	Jump near if not above
72 cb	JNAE cb	3, 7 + m	Jump s if not above or equal (CF = 1)
0F 82 cv	JNAE cv	3, 7 + m	Jump n if not above or equal
73 cb	JNB cb	3, 7 + m	Jump s if not below (CF = 0)
0F 83 cv	JNB cv	3, 7 + m	Jump n if not below
77 cb	JNBE cb	3, 7 + m	Jump s if not below or equal (CF = 0 or ZF = 0)
0F 87 cv	JNBE cv	3, 7 + m	Jump n if not below or equal
73 cb	JNC cb	3, 7 + m	Jump s if not carry (CF = 0)
0F 83 cv	JNC cv	3, 7 + m	Jump n if not carry
75 cb	JNE cb	3, 7 + m	Jump s if not equal (ZF = 0)
0F 85 cv	JNE cv	3, 7 + m	Jump n if not equal
7E cb	JNG cb	3, 7 + m	Jump s if not greater (ZF = 1 or SF ≠ OF)
0F 8E cv	JNG cv	3, 7 + m	Jump n if not greater
7C cb	JNGE cb	3, 7 + m	Jump s if not greater or equal (SF ≠ OF)
0F 8C cv	JNGE cv	3, 7 + m	Jump n if not greater or equal
7D cb	JNL cb	3, 7 + m	Jump s if not less (SF = OF)
0F 8D cv	JNL cv	3, 7 + m	Jump n if not less
7F cb	JNLE cb	3, 7 + m	Jump s if not less or equal (ZF = 0 and SF = OF)
0F 8F cv	JNLE cv	3, 7 + m	Jump n if not less or equal
71 cb	JNO cb	3, 7 + m	Jump s if not overflow (OF = 0)
0F 81 cv	JNO cv	3, 7 + m	Jump n if not overflow
7B cb	JNP cb	3, 7 + m	Jump s if not parity (PF = 0)
0F 8B cv	JNP cv	3, 7 + m	Jump n if not parity
79 cb	JNS cb	3, 7 + m	Jump s if not sign (SF = 0)
0F 89 cv	JNS cv	3, 7 + m	Jump n if not sign
75 cb	JNZ cb	3, 7 + m	Jump s if not zero (ZF = 0)

Opcode	Instruction	Clock Cycles	Description
0F 85 cv	JNZ cv	3, 7 + m	Jump n if not zero
70 cb	JO cb	3, 7 + m	Jump s if overflow (OF = 1)
0F 80 cv	JO cv	3, 7 + m	Jump n if overflow
7A cb	JP cb	3, 7 + m	Jump s if parity (PF = 1)
0F 8A cv	JP cv	3, 7 + m	Jump n if parity
7A cb	JPE cb	3, 7 + m	Jump s if parity even (PF = 1)
0F 8A cv	JPE cv	3, 7 + m	Jump n if parity even
7B cb	JPO cb	3, 7 + m	Jump s if parity odd (PF = 0)
0F 8B cv	JPO cv	3, 7 + m	Jump n if parity odd
78 cb	JS cb	3, 7 + m	Jump s if sign (SF = 1)
0F 88 cv	JS cv	3, 7 + m	Jump n if sign
74 cb	JZ cb	3, 7 + m	Jump s if zero (ZF = 1)
0F 84 cv	JZ cv	3, 7 + m	Jump n if zero
9F	LAHF	2	Load: AH = flags SF ZF xx AF xx PF xx CF
0F 02 /r	LAR rv,rmw	15, 16	Load: high(rv) = access rights, selector rmw
C5 /r	LDS rv,rmp	7, 22	Load RM pointer into DS and vword register
8D /r	LEA rv,m	2	Calculate offset given by m, place in rv
C9	LEAVE	4	Set eSP to eBP, then POP eBP; undo prev ENTER
C4 /r	LES rv,rmp	7, 22	Load RM pointer into ES and vword register
0F B4 /r	LFS rv,rmp	7, 25	Load RM pointer into FS and vword register
0F 01 /2	LGDT m	11	Load 6 bytes at m into GlobalDT register
0F B5 /r	LGS rv,rmp	7,25	Load RM pointer into GS and vword register
0F 01 /3	LIDT m	11	Load 6 bytes at m into InterruptDT register
0F 00/2	LLDT rmw	20	Load LocalDT register with GDT-entry rmw
0F 01 /6	LMSW rmw	10, 13	Load 16-bit RM word into Mach Stat Word reg
F0	LOCK (prefix)	0	Assert BUSLOCK signal for the next instruction
AC	LODS mb	5	Load byte [eSI] into AL, advance eSI
AD	LODS mv	5	Load vword [eSI] into eAX, advance eSI
AC	LODSB	5	Load byte [eSI] into AL, advance eSI
AD	LODSD	5	Load dword [eSI] into EAX, advance eSI
AD	LODSW	5	Load word [eSI] into AX, advance eSI
E2 cb	LOOP cb	11 + m	noflags DEC eCX; jump short if eCX ≠ 0
E1 cb	LOOPE cb	11 + m	nf DEC eCX; jump s if eCX ≠ 0 and equal
E0 cb	LOOPNE cb	11 + m	nf DEC eCX; jump s if eCX ≠ 0 and not equal
E0 cb	LOOPNZ cb	11 + m	nf DEC eCX; jump s if eCX ≠ 0 and not zero
E1 cb	LOOPZ cb	11 + m	nf DEC eCX; jump s if eCX ≠ 0 and zero (ZF = 1)
0F 03 /r	LSL rv,rmw	20, 21	Load: rv = byte granular seg limit, selector rmw
0F 03 /r	LSL rv,rmw	25, 26	Load: rv = page granular seg limit, selector rmw
0F B2 /r	LSS rv,rmp	7,22	Load RM pointer into SS and vword register
0F 00 /3	LTR rmw	23, 27	Load task register with rmw
A0 iv	MOV AL, xb	4	Move simple byte variable (offset iv) into AL
0F 22 /n	MOV CRn,rd	10, 4, 5	Move rd into control register n (= 0, 2, or 3)
0F 23 /n	MOV DRn,rd	16	Move rd into debug register n (= 6, 7)
0F 23 /n	MOV DRn,rd	22	Move rd into debug register n (= 0, 1, 2, 3)
A1 iv	MOV eAX,xv	4	Move simple word variable (offset iv) into eAX
B0 + r ib	MOV rb,ib	2	Move immediate byte into byte register
8A /r	MOV rb,rmb	2, 4	Move RM byte into byte register
0F 20 /n	MOV rd,CRn	6	Move control register n (= 0, 2, or 3) into rd
0F 21 /n	MOV rd,DRn	14	Move debug register n (= 6, 7) into rd

(continued)

Opcode	Instruction	Clock Cycles	Description
0F 21 /n	MOV rd,DRn	22	Move debug register n (=0, 1, 2, 3) into rd
0F 24 /n	MOV rd,TRn	12	Move test register TRn (=6, 7) into rd
C6 /0 ib	MOV rmb,ib	2	Move immediate byte into RM byte
88 /r	MOV rmb,rb	2	Move byte register into RM byte
C7 /0 iv	MOV rmv,iv	2	Move immediate vword into RM vword
89 /r	MOV rmv,rv	2	Move vword register into RM vword
8C /r	MOV rmw,segreg	2	Move segreg into RM word
B8 + r iv	MOV rv,iv	2	Move immediate vword into vword register
8B /r	MOV rv,rmv	2, 4	Move RM vword into vword register
8E /r	MOV segreg, mw	5, 19	Move memory word into any segreg except CS
8E /r	MOV segreg,rw	2, 18	Move word register into any segreg except CS
0F 26 /n	MOV TRn,rd	12	Move rd into test register TRn (=6, 7)
A2 iv	MOV xb,AL	2	Move AL into simple byte variable (offset iv)
A3 iv	MOV xv,eAX	2	Move eAX into simple vword variable (offset iv)
A4	MOVS mb,mb	7	Move byte [eSI] to ES: [eDI], advance eSI, eDI
A5	MOVS mv,mv	7	Move vword [eSI] to ES: [eDI], advance eSI, eDI
A4	MOVSB	7	Move byte DS:[eSI] to ES: [eDI], adv eSI, eDI
A5	MOVSD	7	Move dword DS:[eSI] to ES:[eDI], adv eSI, eDI
A5	MOVSW	7	Move word DS:[eSI] to ES:[eDI], adv eSI, eDI
0F BF /r	MOVSX rd, rmw	3, 6	Move word to dword, with sign-extend
0F BE /r	MOVSX rv,rmb	3, 6	Move byte to vword, with sign-extend
0F B7 /r	MOVZX rd,rmw	3, 6	Move word to dword, with zero-extend
0F B6 /r	MOVZX rv, rmb	3, 6	Move byte to vword, with zero-extend
F6 /4	MUL rmb	*	Unsigned multiply (AX = AL * RM byte)
F7 /4	MUL rmv	*	Unsigned multiply (eDXeAX = eAX * RM vword)
F6 /3	NEG rmb	2, 6	Two's complement negate RM byte
F7 /3	NEG rmv	2, 6	Two's complement negate RM vword
90	NOP	3	No Operation
F6 /2	NOT rmb	2, 6	Reverse each bit of RM byte
F7 /2	NOT rmv	2, 6	Reverse each bit of RM vword
0C ib	OR AL, ib	2	Logical-OR immediate byte into AL
0D iv	OR eAX, iv	2	Logical-OR immediate vword into eAX
0A /r	OR rb,rmb	2, 7	Logical-OR RM byte into byte register
80 /1 ib	OR rmb,ib	2, 7	Logical-OR immediate byte into RM byte
08 /r	OR rmb,rb	2, 6	Logical-OR byte register into RM byte
81 /1 iv	OR rmv,iv	2, 7	Logical-OR immediate vword into RM vword
09 /r	OR rmv, rv	2, 6	Logical-OR vword register into RM vword
0B /r	OR rv,rmv	2, 7	Logical-OR RM vword register
EE	OUT DX,AL	*	Output byte AL to port number DX
EF	OUT DX,eAX	*	Output vword eAX to port number DX
E6 ib	OUT ib,AL	*	Output byte AL to immediate port number ib
E7 ib	OUT ib,eAX	*	Out vword eAX to immediate port number ib
6E	OUTS DX,rmb	*	Out byte [eSI] to port number DX, adv eSI
6F	OUTS DX,rmv	*	Out vword [eSI] to port number DX, adv eSI
6E	OUTSB	*	Out byte DS:[eSI] to port number DX, adv eSI
6F	OUTSD	*	Out dword DS:[eSI] to port number DX, adv eSI
6F	OUTSW	*	Out word DS: [eSI] to port number DX, adv eSI
1F	POP DS	7, 21	Set DS to top of stack, increment eSP by 2
07	POP ES	7, 21	Set ES to top of stack, increment eSP by 2
0F A1	POP FS	7, 21	Set FS to top of stack, increment eSP by 2
0F A9	POP GS	7, 21	Set GS to top of stack, increment eSP by 2

Opcode	Instruction	Clock Cycles	Description
8F /0	POP mv	5	Set memory vword to top of stack, incr eSP by 2 or 4
58+r	POP rv	4	Set vword reg to top of stack, incr eSP by 2 or 4
17	POP SS	7, 21	Set SS to top of stack, increment eSP by 2
61	POPA	24	Pop DI, SI, BP, x, BX, DX, CX, AX (SP ignored)
61	POPAD	24	Pop EDI, ESI, EBP, x, EBX, EDX, ECX, EAX (ESP ign.)
9D	POPF	5	Set flags reg to top of stack, incr eSP by 2
9D	POPFD	5	Set eflags reg to top of stack, incr eSP by 2
0E	PUSH CS	2	Set [eSP-2] to CS, then decrement eSP by 2
1E	PUSH DS	2	Set [eSP-2] to DS, then decrement eSP by 2
06	PUSH ES	2	Set [eSP-2] to ES, then decrement eSP by 2
0F A0	PUSH FS	2	Set [eSP-2] to FS, then decrement eSP by 2
0F A8	PUSH GS	2	Set [eSP-2] to GS, then decrement eSP by 2
6A ib	PUSH ib	2	Push sign-extended immediate byte
68 iv	PUSH iv	2	Set [eSP-v] to imm vword, decr eSP by v = 2 or 4
FF /6	PUSH mv	5	Set [eSP-v] to memory vword, then decr eSP by v
50+r	PUSH rv	2	Set [eSP-v] to vword reg, then decr eSP by v
16	PUSH SS	2	Set [eSP-2] to SS, then decrement eSP by 2
60	PUSHA	18	Push AX, CX, DX, BX, original SP, BP, SI, DI
60	PUSHAD	18	Push EAX, ECX, EDX, EBX, original ESP, EBP, ESI, EDI
9C	PUSHF	18	Set [eSP-2] to flags reg, then decr eSP by 2
9C	PUSHFD	18	Set [eSP-4] to eflags reg, then decr eSP by 4
D0 /2	RCL rmb,1	9, 10	Rotate 9-bit quan (CF, RM byte) left once
D2 /2	RCL rmb,CL	9, 10	Rotate 9-bit quan (CF, RM byte) left CL times
C0 /2 ib	RCL rmb,ib	9, 10	Rotate 9-bit quan (CF, RM byte) left ib times
D1 /2	RCL rmv,1	9, 10	Rotate v + 1-bit quan (CF, RM vword) left once
D3 /2	RCL rmv,CL	9, 10	Rotate v + 1-bit quan (CF, RM vword) left CL times
C1 /2 ib	RCL rmv,ib	9, 10	Rotate v + 1-bit quan (CF, RM vword) left ib times
D0 /3	RCR rmb,1	9, 10	Rotate 9-bit quan (CF, RM byte) right once
D2 /3	RCR rmb,CL	9, 10	Rotate 9-bit quan (CF, RM byte) right CL times
C0 /3 ib	RCR rmb,ib	9, 10	Rotate 9-bit quan (CF, RM byte) right ib times
D1 /3	RCR rmv,1	9, 10	Rotate v + 1-bit quan (CF, RM vword) right once
D3 /3	RCR rmv,CL	9, 10	Rotate v + 1-bit quan (CF, RM vword) right CL times
C1 /3 ib	RCR rmv,ib	9, 10	Rotate v + 1-bit quan (CF, RM vword) right ib times
F3 6C	REP INSB	*	Input eCX bytes from port DX to ES:eDI
F3 6D	REP INSD	*	Input eCX dwords from port DX to ES:eDI
F3 6D	REP INSW	*	Input eCX words from port DX to ES:eDI
F3 A4	REP MOVSB	5+4c	Move eCX bytes from eSI to ES:eDI
F3 A5	REP MOVSD	5+4c	Move eCX words from eSI to ES:eDI
F3 A5	REP MOVSW	5+4c	Move eCX words from eSI to ES:eDI
F3 6E	REP OUTSB	*	Output eCX bytes from eSI to port DX
F3 6F	REP OUTSD	*	Output eCX dwords from eSI to port DX
F3 6F	REP OUTSW	*	Output eCX words from eSI to port DX
F3 AA	REP STOSB	5+5c	Fill eCX bytes at ES:eDI with AL
F3 AB	REP STOSD	5+5c	Fill eCX dwords at ES:eDI with EAX
F3 AB	REP STOSW	5+5c	Fill eCX words at ES:eDI with AX
F3 A6	REPE CMPSB	5+9c	Find nonmatch in eCX bytes at ES:eDI and eSI
F3 A7	REPE CMPSD	5+9c	Find nonmatch in eCX dwords at ES:eDI and eSI

(continued)

Opcode	Instruction	Clock Cycles	Description
F3 A7	REPE CMPSW	5 + 9c	Find nonmatch in eCX words at ES:eDI and eSI
F3 AE	REPE SCASB	5 + 8c	Find non-AL in eCX bytes at ES:eDI and eSI
F3 AF	REPE SCASD	5 + 8c	Find non-EAX in eCX dwords at ES:eDI and eSI
F3 AF	REPE SCASW	5 + 8c	Find non-AX in eCX words at ES:eDI and eSI
F2 A6	REPNE CMPSB	5 + 9c	Find match in eCX bytes at ES:eDI and eSI
F2 A7	REPNE CMPSD	5 + 9c	Find match in eCX dwords at ES:eDI and eSI
F2 A7	REPNE CMPSW	5 + 9c	Find match in eCX words at ES:eDI and eSI
F2 AE	REPNE SCASB	5 + 8c	Find AL in eCX bytes at ES:eDI and eSI
F2 AF	REPNE SCASD	5 + 8c	Find EAX in eCX dwords at ES:eDI and eSI
F2 AF	REPNE SCASW	5 + 8c	Find AX in eCX words at ES:eDI and eSI
CB	RET	*	Return to far caller
C3	RET	10 + m	Return to near caller
CA iw	RET iw	*	RET (far), pop iw bytes
C2 iw	RET iw	10 + m	RET (near), pop iw bytes pushed before Call
D0 /0	ROL rmb,1	3, 7	Rotate 8-bit RM byte left once
D2 /0	ROL rmb,CL	3, 7	Rotate 8-bit RM byte left CL times
C0 /0 ib	ROL rmb,ib	3, 7	Rotate 8-bit RM byte left ib times
D1 /0	ROL rmv,1	3, 7	Rotate v-bit RM vword left once
D3 /0	ROL rmv,CL	3, 7	Rotate v-bit RM vword left CL times
C1 /0 ib	ROL rmv,ib	3, 7	Rotate v-bit RM vword left ib times
D0 /1	ROR rmb,1	3, 7	Rotate 8-bit RM byte right once
D2 /1	ROR rmb,CL	3, 7	Rotate 8-bit RM byte right CL times
C0 /1 ib	ROR rmb,ib	3, 7	Rotate 8-bit RM byte right ib times
D1 /1	ROR rmv, 1	3, 7	Rotate v-bit RM vword right once
D3 /1	ROR rmv,CL	3, 7	Rotate v-bit RM vword right CL times
C1 /1 ib	ROR rmv,ib	3, 7	Rotate v-bit RM vword right ib times
9E	SAHF	3	Store AH into flags SF ZF xx AF xx PF xx CF
D0 /4	SAL rmb,1	3, 7	Multiply RM byte by 2, once
D2 /4	SAL rmb,CL	3, 7	Multiply RM byte by 2, CL times
C0 /4 ib	SAL rmb,ib	3, 7	Multiply RM byte by 2, ib times
D1 /4	SAL rmv,1	3, 7	Multiply RM vword by 2, once
D3 /4	SAL rmv,CL	3, 7	Multiply RM vword by 2, CL times
C1 /4 ib	SAL rmv,ib	3, 7	Multiply RM vword by 2, ib times
D0 /7	SAR rmb,1	3, 7	Signed divide RM byte by 2, once
D2 /7	SAR rmb, CL	3, 7	Signed divide RM byte by 2, CL times
C0 /7 ib	SAR rmb,ib	3, 7	Signed divide RM byte by 2, ib times
D1 /7	SAR rmv, 1	3, 7	Signed divide RM vword by 2, once
D3 /7	SAR rmv,CL	3, 7	Signed divide RM vword by 2, CL times
C1 /7 ib	SAR rmv,ib	3, 7	Signed divide RM vword by 2, ib times
1C ib	SBB AL,ib	2	Subtract with borrow imm byte from AL
1D iv	SBB eAX,iv	2	Subtract with borrow imm vword from eAX
1A /r	SBB rb,rmb	2, 7	Subtract with borrow RM byte from byte reg
80 /3 ib	SBB rmb,ib	2, 7	Subtract with borrow imm byte from RM byte
18 /r	SBB rmb,rb	2, 6	Subtract with borrow byte reg from RM byte
83 /3 ib	SBB rmv,ib	2, 7	Subtract with borrow imm byte from RM vword
81 /3 iv	SBB rmv,iv	2, 7	Subtract with borrow imm vword from RM vword
19 /r	SBB rmv,rv	2, 6	Subtract with borrow vword reg from RM vword
1B /r	SBB rv,rmv	2, 7	Subtract with borrow RM vword from vword reg
AE	SCAS mb	7	Compare bytes AL-[eDI], advance eDI
AF	SCAS mv	7	Compare vwords eAX-[eDI], advance eDI
AE	SCASB	7	Compare bytes AL-ES:[eDI], advance eDI

Opcode	Instruction	Clock Cycles	Description	
AF	SCASD	7	Compare dwords EAX–ES:[eDI], advance eDI	
AF	SCASW	7	Compare words AX–ES:[eDI], advance eDI	
0F 97	SETA rmb	4, 5	Set byte to 1 if above else 0	UNSIGNED
0F 93	SETAE rmb	4, 5	Set byte to 1 if above or equal else 0	
0F 92	SETB rmb	4, 5	Set byte to 1 if below else 0	UNSIGNED
0F 96	SETBE rmb	4, 5	Set byte to 1 if below or equal else 0	
0F 92	SETC rmb	4, 5	Set byte to 1 if carry else 0	
0F 94	SETE rmb	4, 5	Set byte to 1 if equal else 0	
0F 9F	SETG rmb	4, 5	Set byte to 1 if greater else 0	SIGNED
0F 9D	SETGE rmb	4, 5	Set byte to 1 if greater or equal else 0	
0F 9C	SETL rmb	4, 5	Set byte to 1 if less else 0	SIGNED
0F 9E	SETLE rmb	4, 5	Set byte to 1 if less or equal else 0	
0F 96	SETNA rmb	4, 5	Set byte to 1 if not above else 0	
0F 92	SETNAE rmb	4, 5	Set byte to 1 if not above or equal else 0	
0F 93	SETNB rmb	4, 5	Set byte to 1 if not below else 0	
0F 97	SETNBE rmb	4, 5	Set byte to 1 if not below or equal else 0	
0F 93	SETNC rmb	4, 5	Set byte to 1 if not carry else 0	
0F 95	SETNE rmb	4, 5	Set byte to 1 if not equal else 0	
0F 9E	SETNG rmb	4, 5	Set byte to 1 if not greater else 0	
0F 9C	SETNGE rmb	4, 5	Set byte to 1 if not greater or equal else 0	
0F 9D	SETNL rmb	4, 5	Set byte to 1 if not less else 0	
0F 9F	SETNLE rmb	4, 5	Set byte to 1 if not less or equal else 0	
0F 91	SETNO rmb	4, 5	Set byte to 1 if not overflow else 0	
0F 9B	SETNP rmb	4, 5	Set byte to 1 if not parity set else 0	
0F 99	SETNS rmb	4, 5	Set byte to 1 if not sign else 0	
0F 95	SETNZ rmb	4, 5	Set byte to 1 if not zero else 0	
0F 90	SETO rmb	4, 5	Set byte to 1 if overflow else 0	
0F 9A	SETP rmb	4, 5	Set byte to 1 if parity set else 0	
0F 9A	SETPE rmb	4, 5	Set byte to 1 if parity even else 0	
0F 9B	SETPO rmb	4, 5	Set byte to 1 if parity odd else 0	
0F 98	SETS rmb	4, 5	Set byte to 1 if sign else 0	
0F 94	SETZ rmb	4, 5	Set byte to 1 if zero else 0	
0F 01 /0	SGDT m	9	Store Global Descriptor Table reg to m	
D0 /4	SHL rmb,1	3, 7	Multiply RM byte by 2, once	
D2 /4	SHL rmb,CL	3, 7	Multiply RM byte by 2, CL times	
C0 /4 ib	SHL rmb,ib	3, 7	Multiply RM byte by 2, ib times	
D1 /4	SHL rmv,1	3, 7	Multiply RM vword by 2, once	
D3 /4	SHL rmv,CL	3, 7	Multiply RM vword by 2, CL times	
C1 /4 ib	SHL rmv,ib	3, 7	Multiply RM vword by 2, ib times	
0F A5	SHLD rmv,rv,CL	3, 7	Set rmv to high of ((rmv,rv) SHL CL)	
0F AD	SHLD rmv,rv,CL	3, 7	Set rmv to low of ((rv,rmv) SHR CL)	
0F A4 ib	SHLD rmv,rv,ib	3, 7	Set rmv to high of ((rmv,rv) SHL ib)	
0F AC ib	SHLD rmv,rv,ib	3, 7	Set rmv to low of ((rv,rmv) SHR ib)	
D0 /5	SHR rmb,1	3, 7	Unsigned divide RM byte by 2, once	
D2 /5	SHR rmb,CL	3, 7	Unsigned divide RM byte by 2, CL times	
C0 /5 ib	SHR rmb,ib	3, 7	Unsigned divide RM byte by 2, ib times	
D1 /5	SHR rmv,1	3, 7	Unsigned divide RM vword by 2, once	
D3 /5	SHR rmv,CL	3, 7	Unsigned divide RM vword by 2, CL times	
C1 /5 ib	SHR rmv,ib	3, 7	Unsigned divide RM vword by 2, ib times	

(continued)

Opcode	Instruction	Clock Cycles	Description
0F 01 /1	SIDT m	9	Store Interrupt Descriptor Table reg to m
0F 00/0	SLDT rmw	2	Store Local Descriptor Table reg to RM word
0F 01 /4	SMSW rmw	2, 3	Store Machine Status Word to RM word
F9	STC	2	Set carry flag
FD	STD	2	Set direction flag so eSI and eDI will decrement
FB	STI	3	Set interrupt enable flag, interrupts enabled
AA	STOS mb	4	Store AL to byte [eDI], advance eDI
AB	STOS mv	4	Store eAX to vword [eDI], advance eDI
AA	STOSB	4	Store AL to byte ES:[eDI], advance eDI
AB	STOSD	4	Store EAX to dword ES:[eDI], advance eDI
AB	STOSW	4	Store AX to word ES:[eDI], advance eDI
0F 00/1	STR rmw	23, 27	Store task register to RM word
2C ib	SUB AL,ib	2	Subtract immediate byte from AL
2D iv	SUB eAX,iv	2	Subtract immediate vword from eAX
2A /r	SUB rb,rmb	2, 7	Subtract RM byte from byte register
80 /5 ib	SUB rmb,ib	2, 7	Subtract immediate byte from RM byte
28 /r	SUB rmb,rb	2, 6	Subtract byte register from RM byte
83 /5 ib	SUB rmv,ib	2, 7	Subtract immediate byte from RM vword
81 /5 iv	SUB rmv,iv	2, 7	Subtract immediate vword from RM vword
29 /r	SUB rmv,rv	2, 6	Subtract vword register from RM vword
2B /r	SUB rv,rmv	2, 7	Subtract RM vword from vword register
A8 ib	TEST AL,ib	2	AND imm byte into AL for flags only
A9 iv	TEST eAX,iv	2	AND imm vword into eAX for flags only
84 /r	TEST rb,rmb	2, 5	AND RM byte into byte reg for flags only
F6 /0 ib	TEST rmb,ib	2, 5	AND imm byte into RM byte for flags only
84 /r	TEST rmb,rb	2, 5	AND byte reg into RM byte for flags only
F7 /0 iv	TEST rmv,iv	2, 5	AND imm vword into RM vword for flags only
85 /r	TEST rmv,rv	2, 5	AND vword reg into RM vword for flags only
85 /r	TEST rv,rmv	2, 5	AND RM vword into vword reg for flags only
0F 00 /4	VERR rmw	10, 11	Set ZF if segment can be read, selector rmw
0F 00 /5	VERW rmw	15, 16	Set ZF if segment can be written, selector rmw
9B	WAIT	6	Wait until BUSY pin is inactive (HIGH)
90 + r	XCHG eAX,rv	3	Exchange vword register with AX
86 /r	XCHG rb,rmb	3, 5	Exchange RM byte with byte register
86 /r	XCHG rmb,rb	3, 5	Exchange byte register with RM byte
87 /r	XCHG rmv,rv	3, 5	Exchange vword register with RM vword
90 + r	XCHG rv,eAX	3	Exchange AX with vword register
87 /r	XCHG rv,rmv	3, 5	Exchange RM vword with vword register
D7	XLAT mb	5	Set AL to memory byte [eBX + unsigned AL]
D7	XLATB	5	Set AL to memory byte DS:[eBX + unsigned AL]
34 ib	XOR AL,ib	2	Exclusive-OR immediate byte into AL
35 iv	XOR eAX,iv	2	Exclusive-OR immediate vword into AX
32 /r	XOR rv,rmb	2, 7	Exclusive-OR RM byte into byte register
80 /6 ib	XOR rmb,ib	2, 7	Exclusive-OR immediate byte into RM byte
30 /r	XOR rmb,rb	2, 6	Exclusive-OR byte register into RM byte
81 /6 ir	XOR rmv,iv	2, 7	Exclusive-OR immediate vword into RM vword
31 /r	XOR rmv,rv	2, 6	Exclusive-OR vword register into RM vword
33 /r	XOR rv,rmv	2, 7	Exclusive-OR RM vword into vword register

APPENDIX
B

387 INSTRUCTION SET SUMMARY

This appendix presents the complete instruction set of the 387 floating-point coprocessor, along with the opcode bytes generated and the number of clock cycles each instruction takes to execute. Let's first describe each of the columns of the table.

The Opcode Column

The opcodes are given using the same format as the 386 opcodes in Appendix A. When a specific opcode can be presented, it is given in hexadecimal. The / notation for the ModRM byte is the same as Appendix A, and tables A.2 through A.4 apply. The operands associated with / are always memory operands, never register operands. Thus, by looking at Table A.2 or Table A.3, you can see that the hex values C0 through FF for the ModRM byte are unused by the / instruction forms. They are instead interpreted as completely different instructions, shown in our instruction chart with explicit second-opcode byte values in the C0–FF range. Many of those instructions have +i in the second byte, indicating a floating-point stack register number to be added to the C0–FF value shown.

Some 387 instructions have two forms, one whose mnemonic starts with FN, the other with F. The FN form does not wait for the 387 to have completed its previous instructions; the F form does. The opcodes for these forms differ by the absence or presence of an FWAIT instruction byte, hex 9B, before the 387 instruction.

Recall that since most 387 instructions have FWAIT functionality built into them, a preceding 9B byte is not necessary. This is also true of the 287, but the 8087 needs an explicit 9B FWAIT before almost every instruction.

The Instruction Column

Following the opcode field is the 387 instruction, as written in assembly language. As with the 386 instruction set, all capital-letter mnemonics are given just as shown. Operands containing lower-case letters are as follows:

ST—the top element of the floating-point stack.

ST(i)—element number i of the floating-point stack. The range of i is from 0 through 7.

mem10r—a 10-byte memory quantity containing an extended-precision floating-point number.

mem8r—an 8-byte memory quantity containing a double-precision floating-point number.

mem4r—a 4-byte memory quantity containing a single-precision floating-point number.

mem10d—a 10-byte quantity containing the special Binary Coded Decimal format recognized by the FBLD and FBSTP instructions.

mem4i—a 4-byte quantity representing a signed integer in two's-complement notation.

mem2i—a 2-byte quantity representing a signed integer in two's-complement notation.

The Clock Cycles Column

Following the instruction field is a field telling the number of clock cycles the instruction takes to execute. Any instructions give a range of clock cycles that depend on the values of the operands. As with the 386, you can translate the cycle count into an execution time: if the 387 is also running at 16 MHz, you divide the cycle count by 16 to obtain the number of microseconds.

The Description Column

Following the cycle count is a concise description, for reference purposes, of the instruction. The byte counts given in the descriptions of FLDENV, FNSAVE, FNSTENV, FRSTOR, FSAVE, and FSTENV refer to the size of the memory operand. The first count applies if a word operand size is in effect for the instruction; the second count applies if a doubleword operand size is in effect.

Opcode	Instruction	Clock Cycles	Description
D9 F0	F2XM1	211–476	$ST \leftarrow 2^{ST}) - 1$
D9 E1	FABS	22	$ST \leftarrow \mid ST \mid$
DE C1	FADD	26–34	$ST1 \leftarrow ST(1) + ST$, pop
D8 /0	FADD mem4r	24–32	$ST \leftarrow ST + mem4r$
DC /0	FADD mem8r	29–37	$ST \leftarrow ST + mem8r$
DC C0+i	FADD ST(i),ST	26–34	$ST(i) \leftarrow ST(i) + ST$
D8 C0+i	FADD ST,ST(i)	23–31	$ST \leftarrow ST(i) + ST$
DE C0+i	FADDP ST(i),ST	26–34	$ST(i) \leftarrow ST(i) + ST$, pop
DF /4	FBLD mem10d	266–275	push, $ST \leftarrow mem10d$
DF /6	FBSTP mem10d	512–534	$mem10d \leftarrow ST$, pop
D9 E0	FCHS	24–25	$ST \leftarrow -ST$
9B DB E2	FCLEX	17	clear exceptions
D8 D1	FCOM	24	compare $ST - ST(1)$
D8 /2	FCOM mem4r	26	compare $ST - mem4r$
DC /2	FCOM mem8r	31	compare $ST - mem8r$
D8 D0+i	FCOM ST(i)	24	compare $ST - ST(i)$
D8 D9	FCOMP	26	compare $ST - ST(1)$, pop
D8 /3	FCOMP mem4r	26	compare $ST - mem4r$, pop
D8 /3	FCOMP mem8r	31	compare $ST - mem8r$, pop
D8 D8+i	FCOMP ST(i)	26	compare $ST - ST(i)$, pop
DE D9	FCOMPP	26	compare $ST - ST(1)$, pop both
D9 FF	FCOS	123–848	push, $(ST(1)/ST) \leftarrow$ cosine (old ST)
D9 F6	FDECSTP	22	decrement stack pointer
DE F9	FDIV	91	$ST(1) \leftarrow ST(1) / ST$, pop
D8 /6	FDIV mem4r	89	$ST \leftarrow ST / mem4r$
DC /6	FDIV mem8r	94	$ST \leftarrow ST / mem8r$
DC F8+i	FDIV ST(i),ST	91	$ST(i) \leftarrow ST(i) / ST$
D8 F0+i	FDIV ST,ST(i)	88	$ST \leftarrow ST / ST(i)$
DE F8+i	FDIVP ST(i),ST	91	$ST(i) \leftarrow ST(i) / ST$, pop
DE F1	FDIVR	91	$ST(1) \leftarrow ST / ST(1)$, pop
D8 /7	FDIVR mem4r	89	$ST \leftarrow mem4r / ST$
DC /7	FDIVR mem8r	94	$ST \leftarrow mem8r / ST$
DC F0+i	FDIVR ST(i),ST	91	$ST(i) \leftarrow ST / ST(i)$
D8 F8+i	FDIVR ST,ST(i)	88	$ST \leftarrow ST(i) / ST$
DE F0+i	FDIVRP ST(i),ST	91	$ST(i) \leftarrow ST / ST(i)$, pop
DD C0+i	FFREE ST(i)	18	empty $ST(i)$
DE /0	FIADD mem2i	71–85	$ST \leftarrow ST + mem4i$
DA /0	FIADD mem4i	57–72	$ST \leftarrow ST + mem2i$
DE /2	FICOM mem2i	71–75	compare $ST - mem2i$
DA /2	FICOM mem4i	56–63	compare $ST - mem4i$
DE /3	FICOMP mem2i	71–75	compare $ST - mem2i$, pop
DA /3	FICOMP mem4i	56–63	compare $ST - mem4i$, pop
DE /6	FIDIV mem2i	136–140	$ST \leftarrow ST / mem2i$
DA /6	FIDIV mem4i	120–127	$ST \leftarrow ST / mem4i$
DE /7	FIDIVR mem2i	135–141	$ST \leftarrow mem2i / ST$
DA /7	FIDIVR mem4i	121–128	$ST \leftarrow mem4i / ST$
DF /0	FILD mem2i	61–65	push, $ST \leftarrow mem2i$
DB /0	FILD mem4i	45–52	push, $ST \leftarrow mem4i$
DF /5	FILD mem8i	56–67	push, $ST \leftarrow mem8i$

(continued)

Opcode	Instruction	Clock Cycles	Description
DE /1	FIMUL mem2i	76–87	ST ← ST * mem2i
DA /1	FIMUL mem4i	61–82	ST ← ST * mem4i
D9 F7	FINCSTP	21	increment stack pointer
9B DB E3	FINIT	39	initialize 80387
DF /2	FIST mem2i	82–95	mem2i ← ST
DB /2	FIST mem4i	79–93	mem4i ← ST
DF /3	FISTP mem2i	85–95	mem2i ← ST, pop
DB /3	FISTP mem4i	79–93	mem4i ← ST, pop
DF /7	FISTP mem8i	80–97	mem8i ← ST, pop
DE /4	FISUB mem2i	71–83	ST ← ST − mem2i
DA /4	FISUB mem4i	57–82	ST ← ST − mem4i
DE /5	FISUBR mem2i	72–84	ST ← mem2i − ST
DA /5	FISUBR mem4i	58–83	ST ← mem4i − ST
DB /5	FLD mem10r	44–44	push, ST ← mem10r
D9 /0	FLD mem4r	20	push, ST ← mem4r (+5 clocks if 0.0)
DD /0	FLD mem8r	25	push, ST ← mem8r (+5 clocks if 0.0)
D9 C0+i	FLD ST(i)	14	push, ST ← old ST(i)
D9 E8	FLD1	24	push, ST ← 1
D9 /5	FLDCW mem2i	19	control word ← mem2i
D9 /4	FLDENV mem	71	environment ← mem (14 or 28 bytes)
D9 EA	FLDL2E	40	push, ST ← $\log_2 e$
D9 E9	FLDL2T	40	push, ST ← $\log_2 10$
D9 EC	FLDLG2	41	push, ST ← $\log_{10} 2$
D9 ED	FLDLN2	41	push, ST ← $\log_e 2$
D9 EB	FLDPI	40	push, ST ← π
D9 EE	FLDZ	20	push, ST ← +0.0
DE C9	FMUL	29–57	ST(1) ← ST(1) * ST, pop
D8 /1	FMUL mem4r	27–35	ST ← ST * mem4r
DC /1	FMUL mem8r	32–57	ST ← ST * mem8r
DC C8+i	FMUL ST(i),ST	29–57	ST(i) ← ST(i) * ST
D8 C8+i	FMUL ST,ST(i)	46–54	ST ← ST * ST(i)
DE C8+i	FMULP ST(i),ST	29–57	ST(i) ← ST(i) * ST, pop
DB E2	FNCLEX	11	nowait clear exceptions
DB E3	FNINIT	33	nowait initialize 80387
D9 D0	FNOP	12	no operation
DD /6	FNSAVE mem	375–376	mem ← 80387 state (94 or 108 bytes)
D9 /7	FNSTCW mem2i	15	mem2i ← control word
D9 /6	FNSTENV mem	103–104	mem ← environment (14 or 28 bytes)
DF E0	FNSTSW AX	13	AX ← status word
DD /7	FNSTSW mem2i	15	mem2i ← status word
D9 F3	FPATAN	314–487	ST ← arctan(ST(1)/ST), pop
D9 F8	FPREM	74–155	ST ← REPEAT(ST − ST(1)) 287 compat.
D9 F5	FPREM1	95–185	ST ← REPEAT(ST − ST(1)) IEEE compat.
D9 F2	FPTAN	191–573	push, ST(1)/ST ← tan (old ST)
D9 FC	FRNDINT	66–80	ST ← round(ST)
DD /4	FRSTOR mem	308	80387 state ← mem (94 bytes or 108 bytes)
DD /3	FSAVE mem	375–376	mem ← 80387 state (94 or 108 bytes)
D9 FD	FSCALE	67–86	ST ← ST * $2^{ST(1)}$

Opcode	Instruction	Clock Cycles	Description
D9 FE	FSIN	122–847	push, (ST(1)/ST) ← sine(old ST)
D9 FB	FSINCOS	194–885	push, ST(1) ← sine, ST ← cos (old ST)
D9 FA	FSQRT	122–129	ST ← $\sqrt{ST}$
D9 /2	FST mem4r	44	mem4r ← ST
DD /2	FST mem8r	45	mem8r ← ST
DD D0 + i	FST ST(i)	11	ST(i) ← ST
D9 /7	FSTCW mem2i	15	mem2i ← control word
D9 /6	FSTENV mem	103–104	mem ← environment (14 or 28 bytes)
DB /7	FSTP mem10r	53	mem10r ← ST, pop
D9 /3	FSTP mem4r	44	mem4r ← ST, pop
DD /3	FSTP mem8r	45	mem8r ← ST, pop
DD D8 + i	FSTP ST(i)	12	ST(i) ← ST, pop
DF E0	FSTSW AX	13	AX ← status word
DD /7	FSTSW mem2i	15	mem2i ← status word
DE E9	FSUB	26–34	ST(1) ← ST(1) − ST, pop
D8 /4	FSUB mem4r	24–32	ST ← ST − mem4r
DC /4	FSUB mem8r	28–36	ST ← ST − mem8r
DC E8 + i	FSUB ST(i),ST	26–34	ST(i) ← ST(i) − ST
D8 E0 + i	FSUB ST,ST(i)	29–37	ST ← ST − ST(i)
DE E8 + i	FSUBP ST(i),ST	26–34	ST(i) ← ST(i) − ST
DE E1	FSUBR	26–34	ST(1) ← ST − ST(1), pop
D8 /5	FSUBR mem4r	25–33	ST ← mem4r − ST
DC /5	FSUBR mem8r	29–37	ST ← mem8r − ST
DC E0 + i	FSUBR ST(i),ST	26–34	ST(i) ← ST − ST(i)
D8 E8 + i	FSUBR ST,ST(i)	29–37	ST ← ST(i) − ST
DE E0 + i	FSUBRP ST(i),ST	26–34	ST(i) ← ST − ST(i), pop
D9 E4	FTST	28	compare ST − 0.0
DD E1	FUCOM	24	unordered compare ST − ST(1)
DD E0 + i	FUCOM ST(i)	24	unordered compare ST − ST(i)
DD E9	FUCOMP	26	unordered compare ST − ST(1), pop
DD E8 + i	FUCOMP ST(i)	26	unordered compare ST − ST(i), pop
DA E9	FUCOMPP	26	unordered compare ST − ST(1), pop both
9B	FWAIT	6	wait for 80387 ready
D9 E5	FXAM	30–38	C3—C0 ← type of ST
D9 C9	FXCH	18	exchange ST and ST(1)
D9 C8 + i	FXCH ST(i)	18	exchange ST and ST(i)
D9 F4	FXTRACT	70–76	push, ST(1) ← expo, ST ← significand
D9 F1	FYL2X	120–538	ST ← ST(1) * $\log_2$ST, pop
D9 F9	FYL2XP1	257–547	ST ← ST(1) * $\log_2$(ST + 1), pop

APPENDIX
C

386 OPCODE SPACE

This appendix charts the mapping of opcode values into 386 instructions. The first chart has a box for each of the 256 possible first-opcode bytes. Some of those values do not completely determine the instruction mnemonic used; we must go to all or part of a second opcode byte to determine the mnemonic. Those instructions are labeled 2byte, Immed, Shift, Unary, INC/DEC, and Indirect. They are broken down by the supplementary charts that follow the main chart.

The notation for operands is described in Appendix A. If you are using the charts in this appendix to disassemble a 386 instruction, you will also want to consult Tables A.2 through A.4 to disassemble the ModRM field if it exists in the instruction.

Let's go through a sample disassembly to see how it is done. Suppose we want to disassemble the sequence of hex bytes:

F6   84   5D   34   12   00   00   08

as executed in native 386 mode. We look in the last row F of the main chart, in the column headed 6. We find the box labeled Unary rmb. We go to the Unary row of the supplementary chart and see that we'll have to extract the digit number from the ModRM byte to find out which entry is being used. We look for the ModRM byte, 84, in the body of Table A.3. We find it in the column headed "digit = 0," and the row labeled s-i-b, baserow #3. Since the digit is 0, the box to use in the Unary row is the one underneath /0; namely, TEST rm,i. Since the F6 box from the main chart said Unary rmb, our instruction form is TEST rmb,ib. Our ModRM entry indicated an s-i-b byte, so we go to Table A.4 and find the next instruction byte, 5D. It is in the column whose baserow #3 is labeled [EBP] + d32. It is also in the row labeled [EBX ∗2]. The next four instruction bytes, 34 12 00 00, give the displacement d32 in reverse order. After that comes the immediate value ib, which is 08. The instruction is therefore TEST B[EBP + EBX∗2 + 01234H],8. Aren't you glad there are disassembling debuggers that will do this job for us?

	0	1	2	3	4	5	6	7	8	9	A	B	C	D	E	F
0	ADD rmb,rb	ADD rmv,rv	ADD rb,rmb	ADD rv,rmv	ADD AL,ib	ADD eAX,iv	PUSH ES	POP ES	OR rmb,rb	OR rmv,rv	OR rmb,rb	OR rmv,rv	OR AL,ib	OR eAX,iv	PUSH CS	2 byte
1	ADC rmb,rb	ADC rmv,rv	ADC rb,rmb	ADC rv,rmv	ADC AL,ib	ADC eAX,iv	PUSH SS	POP SS	SBB rmb,rb	SBB rmv,rv	SBB rmb,rb	SBB rmv,rv	SBB AL,ib	SBB eAX,ib	PUSH DS	POP DS
2	AND rmb,rb	AND rmv,rv	AND rb,rmb	AND rv,rmv	AND AL,ib	AND eAX,iv	Ovride ES:	DAA	SUB rmb,rb	SUB rmv,rv	SUB rmb,rb	SUB rmv,rv	SUB AL,ib	SUB eAX,iv	Ovride CS:	DAS
3	XOR rmb,rb	XOR rmv,rv	XOR rb,rmb	XOR rv,rmv	XOR AL,ib	XOR eAX,iv	Ovride SS:	AAA	CMP rmb,rb	CMP rmv,rv	CMP rmb,rb	CMP rmv,rv	CMP AL,ib	CMP eAX,iv	Ovride DS:	AAS
4	INC eAX	INC eCX	INC eDX	INC eBX	INC eSP	INC eBP	INC eSI	INC eDI	DEC eAX	DEC eCX	DEC eDX	DEC eBX	DEC eSP	DEC eBP	DEC eSI	DEC eDI
5	PUSH eAX	PUSH eCX	PUSH eDX	PUSH eBX	PUSH eSP	PUSH eBP	PUSH eSI	PUSH eDI	POP eAX	POP eCX	POP eDX	POP eBX	POP eSP	POP eBP	POP eSI	POP eDI
6	PUSHA PUSHAD	POPA POPAD	BOUND rv,m2v	ARPL rmw,rw	Ovride FS:	Ovride GS:	Operand Length	Address Length	PUSH iv	IMUL rv,rmv,iv	PUSH ib	IMUL rv,rmv,ib	INSB	INSW INSD	OUTSB	OUTSW OUTSD
7	JO short	JNO short	JB short	JAE short	JE short	JNE short	JBE short	JA short	JS short	JNS short	JPE short	JPD short	JL short	JGE short	JLE short	JG short
8	Immend rmb, ib	Immend rmv, iv	XCHG eAX, eDX	Immend rmv, ib	TEST rmb, rb	TEST rmv, rv	XCHG rmb, rb	XCHG rmv, rv	MOV rmb, rb	MOV rmv, rv	MOV rb, rmb	MOV rmv, rv	MOV rmw, segr	LEA rv, m	MOV segr, rmw	POP rmv
9	NOP	XCHG eAX, eCX	XCHG eAX, eDX	XCHG eAX, eBX	XCHG eAX, eSP	XCHG eAX, eBP	XCHG eAX, eSI	XCHG eAX, eDI	CBW CWDE	CWD CDQ	CALL far	FWAIT	PUSHF PUSHFD	POPF POPFD	SAHF	LAHF
A	MOV AL, xb	MOV eAX, xv	MOV xb, AL	MOV xv, eAX	MOVSB	MOVSW MOVSD	CMPSB	CMPSW CMPSD	TEST AL, rb	TEST eAX, iv	STOSB	STOSW STOSD	LODSB	LODSW LODSD	SCASB	SCASW SCASD
B	MOV AL, ib	MOV CL, ib	MOV DL, ib	MOV BL, ib	MOV AH, ib	MOV CH, ib	MOV DH, ib	MOV BH, ib	MOV eAX, iv	MOV eCX, iv	MOV eDX, iv	MOV eBX, iv	MOV eSP, iv	MOV eBP, iv	MOV eSI, iv	MOV eDI, iv
C	Shift rmb, ib	Shift rmv, ib	RET iw (near)	RET (near)	LES rv, rmp	LDS rv, rmp	MOV rmb, ib	MOV rmv, iv	ENTER iw, ib	LEAVE	RET iw (far)	RET (far)	INT 3	INT ib	INTO	IRET IRETD
D	Shift rmb, 1	Shift rmv, 1	Shift rmb, CL	Shift rmv, CL	AAM (0A)	AAD (0A)		XLATB	387 space	387 space	387 space	387 space	387 space	387 space	387 space	387 space
E	LOOPNE short	LOOPE short	LOOP short	JeCXZ short	IN AL, ib	IN eAX, ib	OUT ib, AL	OUT ib, eAX	CALL near	JMP near	JMP far	JMP short	IN AL, DX	IN eAX, DX	OUT DX, AL	OUT DX, eAX
F	LOCK		REPNE	REP REPE	ALT	CMC	Unary rmb	Unary rmv	CLC	STC	CLI	STI	CLD	STD	INC/DEC rmb	Indirect

■ = unused opcode

(continued)

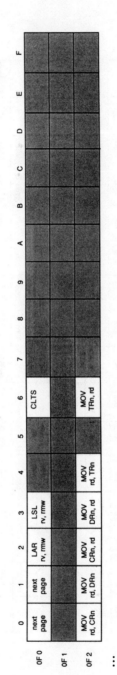

	/0	/1	/2	/3	/4	/5	/6	/7
0F 00	SLDT rmw	STR rmw	LLDT rmw	LTR rmw	VERR rmw	VERW rmw		
0F 01	SGDT m	SIDT m	LGDT m	LIDT m	SMSW rmw		LMSW rmw	
BTx 0F BA					BT rv/m, ib	BTS rv/m. ib	BTR rv/m, ib	BTC rv/m, ib

 = unused opcode

APPENDIX

D

387 OPCODE SPACE

The 387 opcodes are buried in the 386 opcode space on the second half of row D (see Appendix C). Thus all instructions having a first opcode byte of D8 through DF are 387 instructions. Furthermore, all such instructions have a ModRM byte following. If the ModRM value is 00 through BF, the instruction performs a memory reference. If the ModRM value is C0 through FF, the instruction is a nonmemory instruction, and is decoded differently. The first chart applies to the instructions that access memory; the second chart applies to the ones that do not.

Let's disassemble some sample instructions to see how the charts work. First, let's do DC 1D 00 05 01 00. The ModRM byte 1D is less than C0, so we'll use the first (memory operand) chart in this appendix. Before looking there, through, we consult Table A.3 to determine that the value 1D is in the column headed digit = 3 and in the row labeled d32 (simple var). Now we go to the first chart in this appendix, to the DC row and the column headed /3. We find the form FCOMP mem8r. The simple memory variable containing the eight-byte real operand is at the address given by the last four bytes of the instruction: 00 05 01 00. Thus the instruction is FCOMP Q[010500H].

Second, let's disassemble D9 EA. The ModRM byte EA is greater than C0, so the second chart is used. In the D9 row, in the column headed E8 + i, we find FLDcon. We go to the FLDcon row in the supplementary chart; since EA is E8 + 2, we consult the + 2 column in that chart. Our instruction is FLDL2E.

Finally, let's disassemble D8 CC. The ModRM byte CC is greater than C0, so we look in the second chart, in the D8 row under the C8 + i column. The instruction form given is FMUL ST,ST(i). Since CC is C8 + 4, we have i = 4, so our instruction is FMUL ST,ST(4).

MEMORY-OPERAND INSTRUCTIONS (ModRM from 00 through BF)

ModRM: First:	/0	/1	/2	/3	/4	/5	/6	/7
D8	FADD mem4r	FMUL mem4r	FCOM mem4r	FCOMP mem4r	FSUB mem4r	FSUBR mem4r	FDIV mem4r	FDIVR mem4r
D9	FLD mem4r		FST mem4r	FSTP mem4r	FLDENV mem	FLDCW mem2i	FSTENV mem	FSTCW mem2i
DA	FIADD mem4i	FIMUL mem4i	FICOM mem4i	FICOMP mem4i	FISUB mem4i	FISUBR mem4i	FIDIV mem4i	FIDIVR mem4i
DB	FILD mem4i		FIST mem4i	FISTP mem4i		FLD mem10r		FSTP mem10r
DC	FADD mem8r	FMUL mem8r	FCOM mem8r	FCOMP mem8r	FSUB mem8r	FSUBR mem8r	FDIV mem8r	FDIVR mem8r
DD	FLD mem8r		FST mem8r	FSTP mem8r	FRSTOR mem		FSAVE mem	FSTSW mem2i
DE	FIADD mem2i	FIMUL mem2i	FICOM mem2i	FICOMP mem2i	FISUB mem2i	FISUBR mem2i	FIDIV mem2i	FIDIVR mem2i
DF	FILD mem2i		FIST mem2i	FISTP mem2i	FBLD mem10d	FILD mem8i	FBSTP mem10d	FISTP mem8i

▨ = unused opcode

NON-MEMORY INSTRUCTIONS (ModRM byte from C0 through FF)

ModRM: first:	C0+i	C8+i	D0+i	D8+i	E0+i	E8+i	F0+i	F8+i
D8	FADD ST,ST (i)	FMUL ST,ST (i)	FCOM ST (i)	FCOMP ST (i)	FSUB ST, ST (i)	FSUBR ST, ST (i)	FDIV ST, ST (i)	FDIVR ST, ST (i)
D9	FLD ST (i)	FXCH ST (i)	FNOP (D0)		Unary	FLDcon	GRP F0	GRP F8
DA						FUCOMPP (E9)		
DB					Control			
DC	FADD ST (i), ST	FMUL ST (i), ST			FSUBR ST (i), ST	FSUB ST (i), ST	FDIVR ST (i), ST	FDIV ST (i), ST
DD	FFREE ST (i)		FST ST (i)	FSTP ST (i)	FUCOM ST (i)	FUCOMP ST (i)		
DE	FADDP ST (i), ST	FMULP ST (i), ST		FCOMPP (D9)	FSUBRP ST (i), ST	FSUBP ST (i), ST	FDIVRP ST (i), ST	FDIVP ST (i), ST
DF					FSTSW AX (E0)			

	+0	+1	+2	+3	+4	+5	+6	+7
Unary	FCHS	FABS			FTST	FXAM		
FLDcon	FLD1	FLDL2T	FLDL2E	FLDPI	FLDLG2	FLDLN2	FLDZ	
Grp F0	F2XM1	FYL2X	FPTAN	FPATAN	FXTRACT	FPREM1	FDECSTP	FINCSTP
Grp F8	FPREM	FYL2XP1	FSQRT	FSINCOS	FRNDINT	FSCALE	FSIN	FCOS
Control	FENI 8087 only	FDISI 8087 only	FCLEX	FINIT	FSETPM 287only			

▨ = unused opcode

APPENDIX
E

DICTIONARY OF 386/387 TERMINOLOGY

8086 mode—a 386 execution mode in which segment register values are multiplied by 16 to obtain the associated memory address. This mode encomapasses both real mode and virtual 8086 mode.

above—a possible result of *unsigned* comparison of two 386 integer operands.

access byte—a field in a descriptor containing protection information and identifying the descriptor's type.

accumulator—another name for the AL, AX, EAX, or ST(0) registers. More functions can be performed using the accumulator than other registers or memory, though on the 386 most functions can be performed on any general register or memory location.

address space—all the bytes of memory accessible to a program.

address translation—converting a segment register value and offset to a linear address.

addressing mode—the specification of an operand in an instruction.

affine infinity control—a liberal mode of operation, used by the 387, in which infinities may be used in all operations where they make sense. Positive and negative infinities are considered distinct.

aliases—two or more descriptors referring to the same segment.

architecture—the interface between the hardware and the program. The architecture is the minimum knowledge of the machine that the assembly-language programmer must possess.

argument reduction—massaging numbers into ranges acceptable to the 387's transcendental instructions.

ASCII—American Standard Code for Information Interchange. ASCII defines a binary encoding for all the letters A–Z, a–z, numbers 0–9, various punctuation marks, and assorted special symbols.

assembler—a program that translates from human-readable assembly language to binary machine language.

assembler directive—a construct in assembly language which generates no instructions but provides bookkeeping information to the assembler.

assembly language—a symbolic notation for writing machine instructions. Assembly language provides a more convenient means of generating instructions than writing strings of 1's and 0's.

backwords—a tongue-in-cheek description of the 386's method of storing words and doublewords with the least significant bytes at the lowest memory addresses.

base address—the linear address of the start of a segment.

BCD—see binary-coded decimal.

below—a possible result of *unsigned* comparison of two 386 operands.

bias—a constant added to the value of the exponent of a floating-point number before storing the exponent. A bias is used to avoid storing negative numbers in the exponent field of a floating-point number.

binary-coded decimal—a representation for numbers in which each decimal digit is represented by four bits.

binary point—in binary, the concept analogous to *decimal point* in decimal. For example, in the binary number 101.11 the binary point separates the integer part 101 = 5 from the fraction part .11 = 1/2 + 1/4 = 3/4.

bit—binary digit. A bit can take on the value 0 or 1.

breakpoint—a location of memory that is marked so that a program will exit to a debugger if it accesses the location. Most computers support breakpoints only in program code; the 386 also allows breakpoints in data areas.

bug—an error in the coding of a program, causing the program to malfunction.

bus—a set of lines running throughout a computer system to which the processor and every coprocessor, memory device, and peripheral device connects.

byte—a unit of storage consisting of 8 bits.

central processing unit—that component of a computer system which carries out the instructions specified by software. The 386 is a central processing unit.

chip—an integrated circuit, together with the plastic or ceramic piece that houses the circuit.

compiler—a program that translates from a high-level language into machine language.

conforming—a property of a segment indicating that each procedure in that segment will, when called, move outward to the ring of its caller.

CPL—see current privilege level.

CPU—see central processing unit.

current privilege level—the privilege level of the program that is currently executing. The current privilege level is stored in the least significant two bits of the CS register.

data chaining—the coordination that takes place when the output register of an instruction is also the input register of the next instruction.

debugger—a tool for examining the behavior of a running program. Debuggers are used to locate bugs, so that they can be eliminated.

denormal—a nonzero floating-point number with a 00. . . 0 exponent field. Denormals are the exception values produced by the 387 if the Numeric Underflow exception is masked.

descriptor—an 8-byte quantity specifying an independently protected object. The descriptor for an object specifies the object's base address or the address of its entry point, in addition to protection information.

descriptor cache—see shadow register.

descriptor privilege level—a field in a descriptor indicating how protected the descriptor's object is. If a descriptor specifies an executable segment, then the descriptor privilege level indicates how privileged the procedures in that segment are.

descriptor register—see shadow register.

direct addressing—specifying a memory location by an address embedded in an instruction.

displacement—an 8-, 16-, or 32-bit value specified in an instruction and used for computing the address of a memory operand.

display—a list of pointers to the stack frames of the procedures in which the currently executing procedure is enclosed. A display provides the currently executing procedure easy access to the variables in the procedures that enclose it.

double precision—a floating-point format in which each number takes 8 bytes.

doubleword—a 4-byte unit of data storage.

DPL—see descriptor privilege level.

EIP—see instruction pointer.

elementary transcendental functions—the trigonometric, exponential, logarithmic, hyperbolic, inverse trigonometric, and inverse hyperbolic functions.

error value—see exception value.

exception—a condition occurring when a 386 or 387 instruction violates the rules of normal operation. On the 386, an exception causes an interrupt. On the 387, an exception may cause an interrupt or may be masked and yield a special value instead.

exception value—a special value that is produced by a 387 instruction if it causes a masked exception.

expand-down—a property of a segment that causes the 386 to check that, in all accesses to that segment, offsets are greater than the segment's limit. This property is used for stack segments.

expand-up—a property of a segment that causes the 386 to check that, in all accesses to that segment, offsets are no greater than the segment's limit. Typically, all segments other than stack segments have this property.

explicit cache—see shadow register.

exponent—that part of a floating-point number that specifies a scale factor. For example, in the decimal floating-point number 3.7×10^5, the exponent is 5.

extended precision—a floating-point format in which each number takes 10 bytes. Extended precision should only be used for intermediate results.

far—in a different segment.

field—one or more contiguous bits that represent a piece of some larger item of data.

flag—a field in the flags register. A flag indicates the status of a previously executed instruction or controls the operation of the processor.

floating-point—a way to approximately represent real numbers on a computer.

frame—a page-sized block of physical memory that is allocated by the operating system's virtual-memory manager.

gate—either a call gate, trap gate, interrupt gate, or task gate. The first three kinds of gates are descriptors that specify procedure entry points. A task gate is a descriptor that specifies a task.

GDT—see Global Descriptor Table.

general register—one of the 8-bit registers AL, BL, CL, DL, AH, BH, CH, DH; or the 16-bit registers AX, BX, CX, DX, SI, DI, BP, SP; or the 32-bit registers EAX, EBX, ECX, EDX, ESI, EDI, EBP, ESP.

giga—(1) prefix meaning one billion (10^9). (2) the power of two closest to one billion, namely $2^{30} = 1,073,741,824$. This second definition is used when referring to computer memory (gigabyte, gigabit, etc.).

Global Descriptor Table—a table in memory containing descriptors for segments that are shared by all tasks.

gradual underflow—a technique for handling moderate cases of numeric underflow by resorting to numbers that aren't normalized.

greater—a possible result of *signed* comparison of two 386 integer operands.

hardware—a physical part of a computer: either a chip, a circuit board, or a complete box.

hertz—cycles per second.

hexadecimal—base 16. The hexadecimal digits are 0, 1, 2, 3, 4, 5, 6, 7, 8, 9, A(=10), B(=11), C(=12), D(=13), E(=14), F(=15).

high-level language—a programming language further removed from the machine than assembly language. Examples are C, BASIC, Pascal, and FORTRAN.

Hz—see hertz.

IDT—see Interrupt Descriptor Table.

immediate operand—a constant contained in an instruction and used as an operand.

implicit bit—the leading bit of a normalized floating-point number which, since it's always 1, is omitted.

indefinite—a NaN produced by the 387 in response to a masked Invalid Operation exception where none of the operands involved are themselves NaNs.

index register—a register that is being used as a component in the calculation of a 386 memory address, with a scale factor of 1, 2, 4, or 8. Any 32-bit general register except ESP can be an index register. In 16-bit addressing mode, SI and DI are the only index registers, and there is no scaling.

indirect addressing—accessing a memory location by first fetching the desired address from some other memory location or register.

infinity—a floating-point number with an exponent field of 11. . .1 and a significand field of 00. . .0. An infinity is produced as an exception value in response to a masked Division by Zero or Overflow exception on the 387.

instruction—a single step in a program.

instruction pointer—a register containing the offset of the instruction currently being executed. The segment containing this instruction is always pointed to by the CS register.

integrated circuit—an electronic circuit fabricated on a single piece of silicon.

interrupt—a forced call, not appearing explicitly in a program, that is triggered as the result of an exception, or a signal from a device external to the 386, or a special interrupt instruction.

interrupt controller—a component that prioritizes multiple interrupt requests.

Interrupt Descriptor Table—a table in memory, indexed by interrupt number, containing gates to the corresponding interrupt handlers.

interrupt handler—a procedure or task that is called in response to an interrupt.

interrupt procedure—a procedure that is invoked in response to an interrupt.

interrupt task—a task that is activated in response to an interrupt.

IP—see instruction pointer.

K—see kilo-.

kilo—(1) a prefix meaning one thousand (10^3). (2) the power of two closest to one thousand, namely $2^{10} = 1024$. This second definition is used when referring to computer memory (kilobytes, kilobits, etc.).

LDT—see Local Descriptor Table.

less—a possible result of *signed* comparison of two 386 integer operands.

linear address—a 386 memory address as it exists after a segment register value has been combined with an offset, but before it has been remapped by the paging mechanism into a physical address.

linear memory—the 386 memory space defined by linear addresses.

local address space—the collection of segments accessible through a task's LDT.

Local Descriptor Table—a table in memory containing descriptors for segments that are private to a task.

lock—in a multiple processor system, a signal from one processor preventing the others from accessing memory. The processor will have exclusive use of the memory untill it stops sending the signal.

long integer—387 terminology for a 64-bit integer.

LRU—least recently used.

M—see mega-.

machine status word—a 386 register containing a bit for controlling the 386 mode (real versus protected) and bits which control 386 execution of floating-point instructions.

masked exception—on the 387, an exception which produces an exception value rather than an interrupt. Exceptions may be masked and unmasked by setting bits in the 387's control register.

masking—a means of examining only certain bits in a word. This is usually done by *and*ing the word with a mask containing 1's in the desired bit positions.

mega—(1) a prefix meaning one million (10^6). (2) the power of two closest to one million, namely $2^{20} = 1,048,576$. This second definition is used when referring to computer memories (megabyte, megabit, etc.).

memory—a medium for storing programs and data.

memory management—386 facilities for mapping the address space of a task into the available memory.

memory-mapped device—a peripheral device that masquerades as a sequence of memory locations. Memory-writes to one of the locations by the 386 output to the device, and memory-reads input from the device.

microcomputer—a computer based on a microprocessor.

microprocessor—a central processing unit implemented on a single chip.

mnemonic—a symbolic name, particularly for opcodes. It's easier to remember a mnemonic than a binary opcode.

MSW—see machine status word.

multiple-precision arithmetic—arithmetic on integers larger than a doubleword.

multitasking—the creation and use of multiple tasks on a computer.

NaN—see Not-a-Number.

nano-—a prefix meaning one billionth (10^{-9}).

near—within the same segment.

NMI—see nonmaskable interrupt.

nonmaskable interrupt—a signal to the 386 from an external device indicating that a catastrophe has occurred or is imminent.

normalized—a binary floating-point number is normalized if the most significant bit of its significand is 1.

not present—in a virtual memory system, this describes a page that is on disk but not in main memory.

Not-a-Number—an exception value produced by the 387 in response to a masked Invalid Operation exception, or produced by a program in response to an unusual condition.

null selector—a selector in which all bits are 0's except possibly for RPL.

offset—a 32-bit quantity specifying the position of a byte within a segment.

opcode—that part of an instruction which specifies the operation to be performed, as opposed to the items upon which the operation is performed.

operand—an item used as an input or output by an instruction.

operand-addressing mode—see addressing mode.

overflow—(1) an exception that occurs when a number is too large in absolute value to be represented. (2) stack overflow is an exception that occurs when too much data is pushed onto a stack.

packed BCD—see packed decimal.

packed decimal—a representation for integers in which each decimal digit is represented by four bits, and each byte is used to represent two decimal digits.

page—a 4096-byte block of 386 memory. On the 386, a page of physical memory can be assigned to any linear address, allowing the 386 to implement a virtual-memory system.

page frame—see frame.

page group—a 1024-page (four-megabyte) block of 386 linear memory. Each 386 page table defines the pages of a single page group.

parameter—an item transmitted to a procedure by its caller.

parity—an indication of whether a number is even or odd. The 386 parity flag indicates whether the number of 1's in a byte is even or odd.

peripheral device—an electronic device connected to the 386. Peripheral devices communicate with the 386 by means of input and output instructions, memory-mapped I/O, and interrupts.

physical address—a number transmitted to the memory hardware in order to specify the location of a memory access.

pointee—an item in memory referenced by a pointer.

pointer—an item of data that specifies a memory location. On the 386, a pointer can be either a 32-bit offset or a 48-bit segment-and-offset combination.

pop—to remove an item of data from a stack.

port—a connection to an I/O device which may be used by input and output instructions.

position-independent code—code that will execute properly regardless of where it is placed in memory.

prefix—a byte preceding the opcode of an instruction, specifying that the instruction should be repeated, or locked, or that an alternate segment should be used, or that the operands or address registers should be other than the default size.

privilege level—a number in the range 0–3 indicating degree of protection, degree of privilege, or degree of trust; 0 is the most trusted level, 3 the least.

procedure—a portion of a program performing a particular function that may be used at several points in the program.

process—see task.

processor—see central processing unit.

processor clock—see processor cycle.

processor cycle—a unit for measuring instruction execution time.

programmable read-only memory—a computer memory device that can be read normally, but requires a special electronic device to write its data. The device retains its memory even when power is lost, so it can be used to store the program that is executed when a computer is first powered on.

projective mode—a conservative mode of operation, available on the 287 but not on the 387, in which infinities may only be used in operations that are safe. Positive and negative infinities are considered to be equal.

PROM—see programmable read-only memory.

Protected Mode—a mode of operation in which the 386 offers multitasking, virtual memory, and advanced protection facilities.

push—to add an item of data to a stack.

quadword—an 8-byte unit of data storage.

quiet NaN—a 387 register value that is Not-a-Number, but will not cause an exception if used in certain 387 operations. See also Signaling NaN.

radian—the unit of angular measurement assumed by all 387 trigonometric functions: π radians $= 180°$.

ready-list—a list of tasks waiting to use the processor.

Real Address Mode—a limited mode of operation adopted by the 386 when reset, in which the 386 closely mimics the behavior of the 8086.

real mode—see Read Address Mode.

real-time system—a computer system which must react rapidly to external stimuli. Computer systems for controlling vehicles, scientific instruments, or other forms of machinery are real-time systems.

re-entrant procedure—a procedure that can be invoked while it is already in execution from some previous invocation.

register—memory contained within a particular device. A device can access its registers faster than it can access external memory.

requestor's privilege level—a field in a selector indicating the degree of trust a program has in the contents of the selector's segment.

reset—a signal that causes computer hardware to reinitialize itself. Hardware reset is part of system initialization.

restartable—an instruction is restartable after suffering a particular exception if, after removing the cause of the exception, the program may be correctly continued by re-executing the instruction.

ring—see privilege level.

rounding—a method for reducing the precision of a number in order to fit the number into a format that provides insufficient precision. The 387 offers a choice of four rounding techniques.

RPL—see requestor's privilege level.

scale factor—a number (1, 2, 4, or 8) that is multiplied by an index register value in order to calculate a memory address. The scale factor determines whether the register indexes bytes, words, doublewords, or quadwords.

security kernel—that part of an operating system devoted to protection and security.

segment—a block of memory of any size up to four gigabytes, addressed by a segment register. Segments are assigned by the operating system to individual tasks, and they are used by the operating system to protect tasks from one another.

segment register—one of the registers CS,DS, ES, FS, GS, or SS. Each segment register can address a different segment.

selector—a 16-bit segment register value that is interpreted as an index into a descriptor table.

selector mode—a mode of 386 operation in which segment register values are selectors. Selector mode encompasses all of protected mode, except for virtual 8086 mode.

semaphore—a variable shared between tasks or processors that is used for synchronization. A value of zero means proceed; a nonzero value means wait.

shadow register—a hidden register associated with a visible register. A shadow register holds the descriptor corresponding to the selector in the associated visible register.

short integer—387 terminology for a 32-bit integer.

shutdown—a quiescent state from which the 386 may be awakened only by a reset or nonmaskable interrupt.

sign—plus or minus.

sign extending—the means by which a two's-complement number is extended to another two's-complement number that contains more bits. This is done by appending bits on the left equal to the sign bit of the original two's-complement number.

signed—accommodating both positive and negative numbers.

sign-magnitude—a representation for integers in which one bit represents the sign and the remaining bits represent the absolute value of the integer.

signaling NaN—a 387 register value that will cause an exception to be generated if it is used in any 387 calculations. See also Quiet NaN.

significand—in a floating-point number, that quantity which is scaled by the exponent. For example, in the decimal floating-point number 3.7×10^5, the significand is 3.7.

single precision—the smallest floating-point format on the 387. Each single-precision number takes four bytes.

single stepping—executing a program one instruction at a time and pausing after each instruction. The pause allows a programmer to examine the effect of the instruction.

software—the programs that run on a computer. See also hardware.

stack—a data storage area from which items are retrieved in the reverse of the order in which they are stored. Items are both added and removed at the top of the stack.

stack frame—storage for the values of a procedure's local variables corresponding to a particular invocation of the procedure. These values are stored on a stack so that they can be conveniently allocated and deallocated upon procedure entry and exit.

sticky bit—a bit that is automatically set to 1 by hardware, but must be cleared to 0 explicitly by software. The value of the bit thus *sticks* at 1.

subroutine—see procedure.

swapping—moving a segment from disk to memory (swapping in) or memory to disk (swapping out) as performed by a virtual memory system.

system initialization—a series of operations performed by hardware and software when power is first applied to a computer system. Some computers have a separate switch, rather than the power switch, for triggering system initialization.

task—a simulated copy of a computer. A single 386 can support many tasks, all appearing to run concurrently.

task dispatching—selecting a task that isn't running and then running it.

task force—a group of related tasks that share the same LDT.

task state segment—a segment that holds the contents of a task's registers when the 386 is executing another task.

task switch—changing from one task to another. The current task is suspended, and an incoming task is resumed.

time slicing—a technique for allowing several tasks to share a single computer. The computer rapidly switches from one task to another, never staying with a single task for longer than a small, fixed amount of time.

TLB—see Translation Lookaside Buffer.

transfer of control—instead of executing the instruction stored after the current instruction in memory, begin executing instructions in sequence starting at some new location. Jump, conditional jump, call, and return instructions, and interrupts, cause a transfer of control.

Translation Lookaside Buffer—An area of the 386's internal storage that contains the linear and physical addresses of the most recently accessed memory pages.

trichotomy—the law of arithmetic that says that for any two numbers x and y, $x < y$, $x = y$, or $x > y$.

Trojan horse—a seemingly innocent object which, when brought into a privileged environment by a trusted but naive program, causes a security violation.

TSS—see task state segment.

two's complement—a binary representation for integers in which a number is negated by complementing each bit and adding one to the final result.

unbiased exponent—the value of the exponent of a floating-point number, as opposed to what's stored in the exponent field. The exponent field contains the unbiased exponent plus a constant bias.

underflow—(1) numeric underflow is an exception that occurs when a number is too small in absolute value to be represented as a normalized floating-point number. (2) stack overflow is an exception that occurs when an instruction attempts to pop more data off the stack than currently is on the stack.

unnormal—an extended-precision floating-point number with an ordinary exponent but a leading bit of zero in its significand. Unnormals are produced by the 8087/287 but are never produced by the 387.

unordered—a possible result of the comparison of two floating-point values that occurs when one or both of the values is a NaN.

unpacked BCD—a representation for integers in which each decimal digit is represented by four bits, and each byte contains only a single decimal digit.

unsigned—accommodating only positive numbers and zero, not negative numbers.

virtual address—see linear address.

virtual memory—a technique for running programs that are larger than the available memory. Pieces of the program are stored on disk and are moved to memory only when necessary. This movement is automatically performed by the operating system and is invisible to the program.

word—a two-byte unit of data. Many people consider the definition of "word" to be machine-dependent, indicating the largest unit of data commonly accessible to a machine. On the 386, that unit is four bytes, but we call it a doubleword.

word integer—387 terminology for a 16-bit integer.

INDEX

The abbreviation def. stands for definition. The terms are defined in Appendix E, Dictionary of 386/387 Terminology, page 296.